DE PAUL UNIVERSITY
BOOK
DE PAUL U.
BOOK STORE
NEW
USED
7.20
CASH
S
25 EAST JACKSON

ADMINISTRATIVE ORGANIZATION

PRENTICE-HALL INTERNATIONAL SERIES IN MANAGEMENT

BAUMOL *Economic Theory and Operations Analysis*

CHURCHMAN *Prediction and Optimal Decision*

HOLT, MUTH, MODIGLIANI, AND SIMON *Planning Production, Inventories and Work Force*

MILLER AND STARR *Executive Decisions and Operations Research*

PFIFFNER AND SHERWOOD *Administrative Organization*

PRENTICE-HALL, INC.

PRENTICE-HALL INTERNATIONAL, INC., UNITED KINGDOM AND EIRE

PRENTICE-HALL OF CANADA, LTD., CANADA

J. H. DE BUSSY, LTD., HOLLAND AND FLEMISH-SPEAKING BELGIUM

DUNOD PRESS, FRANCE

MARUZEN COMPANY, LTD., FAR EAST

C. BERTELSMANN VERLAG, WEST GERMANY AND AUSTRIA

John M. Pfiffner

Professor of Public Administration
University of Southern California

Frank P. Sherwood

Professor of Public Administration
University of Southern California

ADMINISTRATIVE ORGANIZATION

PRENTICE-HALL, INC.

Englewood Cliffs, N.J.

Library of Congress Catalog Card No.: 60-10778

First printing . . . . April, 1960
Second printing . . . . January, 1961
Third printing . . . . January, 1962
Fourth printing . . . . . October, 1963
Fifth printing . . . . June, 1964
Sixth printing . . . . March, 1965

Printed in the United States of America

00861-C

Preface

Studies of administrative organization tend to cluster at one or the other of two poles. At one end is the traditional framework of job content, job structure, and job relationships—the mechanistic, engineering approach to the problem. At the other end is the human behavioral orientation, in which the sociologists, psychologists, and anthropologists have been most prominent. As a result there has been a need for introductory materials which seek a middle ground between these two contrasting extremes. To provide such materials is the essential purpose of this book.

However, it is not an easy task, partly because the study of organization is still in its infancy, partly, too, because of a second contrast between the two extremes. This contrast involves the values systems of each position. Those who are involved in the disciplines of industrial management, with its concern for formal structural concepts, place considerable store by the values of productivity, individual competition, and the efficiency of the individual plant or enterprise. Social scientists, at the opposite pole, take a more humanistic attitude toward the actors in organizations, regarding authority, for example, as coming from within the group rather than from the top down.

These contrasts are here set down in their most extreme forms, if only for lack of time to delineate their subtler features. If the value systems of the authors had to be epitomized in the same brevity, they would state that the traditional organization management concepts have an enduring content that is universal, but that these should be modified by the more humane values of an age in which the dignity of man is receiving greater emphasis.

A final unavoidable contrast is the asserted difference between public and private administration. Obviously, the fact that this book has been written indicates the authors' belief that the poles are really poles and that there is a large common ground in between. Furthermore, the environmental factors which cause private cooperative endeavors to differ from public ones can themselves be identified as common facts of the organizing process, though their impact may differ from situation to situation. It is our general position, too, that the playback between private and public administration has been much greater than is commonly realized. Public administration has always drawn heavily upon industrial environment and theory. Conversely, the human and political elements in the organizational environment represent areas where governmental administrators have particularly contributed in rationalizing the managerial role.

Our chief acknowledgment goes to the officials of the University of Southern California, particularly Dean Henry Reining, Jr., for making available the facilities and time necessary to produce this book. If it possesses some interest or value for others, this is largely due to the dynamic, progressive, and scholarly environment in which we live and function.

A book is inevitably the product of many people besides the authors. This book is no exception; and special appreciation is due the following for their helpful suggestions and criticisms: Professor Albert H. Rubenstein, Department of Industrial Engineering, the Technological Institute, Northwestern University; Professor Chris Argyris, Department of Industrial Administration, Yale University; and Professor William B. Storm, School of Public Administration, University of Southern California. David Vanderburgh provided invaluable editorial assistance; and Susie Sherwood, a dutiful wife, and Yoshiyuki Arikawa, soon to be a fine engineer, saw that the typing and many other details were superbly handled.

John M. Pfiffner
Frank P. Sherwood

Table of Contents

PART TWO • ORGANIZATION STRUCTURE

Part One

ORGANIZATION IN THE SOCIETY

ONE

The Molding of Organization in the Modern Society

What to Look for in This Chapter . . .

How organizations have grown in size

How organizations have grown in complexity

How new ideas of cooperation have changed theories of organization

How all organizations have begun to acquire new and various goals

Among the myriad patterns of human life, the characteristic of group behavior has always predominated. Whether the way of life is simple or complex, primitive or sophisticated, its human qualities always involve to a marked degree the interaction of two or more persons. The effective group may be just the minimum of two, or it may, perhaps more typically, be larger.

The overwhelming facts of group life in recent years, however, center on the growing dominance of very large groups, or organizations, in our patterns of living. Keeping pace with the advent and development of the Industrial Revolution, the organizational way of life is most vividly exemplified in the most industrialized countries. If, as seems likely, these countries have taken a path that all must follow, more and more of the world's billions of people will live a way of life whose outstanding feature is participation in large organized groups.

Change in this direction has already been incredibly rapid. One indication of this is the tendency of people to live in cities, where they become involved in highly complex organizations for attaining social, political, and economic goals. At the dawn of the twentieth century only 16 million of the world's people dwelt in the larger cities—those over a hundred thousand in population. By the middle of the century the number had increased 20 times, to 314 million.

Where economic organizations are concerned, the trend toward more and bigger ones seems inevitable to many scholars; the goals of such organizations, involving the production of goods to satisfy man's needs, seem to require size and complexity for the sake of efficiency. One of the first to point out the economic advantages of the *organization of scale* was the German sociologist Max Weber, who coined the term *bureaucracy* to characterize this type of organization. He believed that it was man's supreme expression of efficiency, achieved by de-personalizing the individual, and emphasizing the significance of rules and standard norms of conduct. The bureaucratic organization was, to Weber, man at his most rational, and he buttressed his thesis with a systematic study of the major societies in world history. Without accepting either his data or his conclusions entirely, we may note the wide acceptance of Weber's basic assumption, that rational and efficient economic behavior is found most often in large-scale organizations.

Why Have Organizations Grown in Size?

It seems inevitable, too, that peoples not yet industrialized will seek a more highly organized economic way of life as rapidly as their circumstances will permit. The material benefits to be reaped from such organization have been very heavily impressed upon these peoples by the tremendous strides in living standards among industrialized populations. Nor is the desire for materialistic betterment a mark of any one philosophy or political system, but rather cuts across curtains of iron, bamboo, and currency, to make itself felt in governmental decisions everywhere, at all levels.

The nation whose economy has been based on the small family-size farm unit will therefore have little chance to improve without industrializing, urbanizing, and, in short, organizing in ways radically different from those hallowed by custom and authority. In the wake of economic changes, social and political adjustments involving organizations of scale will follow, and probably require a more painful transition than the economic.

Nor has the highly industrialized nation, such as our own, seen the end of the changes brought by organization, since the pressures we generate as consumers are as strong as ever. We expect our real income to continue at least a 2 per cent annual rise, so that by 1985 it will buy half again as much as it will today. In the realization of this expectation the man-hour will become more valuable through technological improvement of machines and methods. To the adjustment in work habits attendant on this must be added the extension of already marked maladjustments brought about by the move to the cities. In the powerful society as in the weak, then, the trend toward organizations works like a tidal force.

Technological advances. It is not hopes and desires alone that have created a world of large-scale organizations, however. Radical improvement in man's control over his environment, while constituting the goals at a given level of economic organization, have at the same time laid the foundations of new types of organization to come. The development in the eighteenth century of efficient and controllable sources of energy, particularly of steam, made the factory system of production a possibility. The subsequent history of the utilization of these sources has been one of refinements so productive as to be almost revolutionary in themselves. In the relationship of workers to machinery the work of Eli Whitney, Henry Ford, and Frederick Taylor has been crucial. Whitney was probably the first to adapt successfully the principle of interchangeable parts to large-scale manufacture—muskets were the first product made in this way. Ford became famous, not only for his Model T, but for organizing its assembly—from interchangeable parts—around a continuous production line, enabling workers to specialize more and more narrowly in particular tasks. Taylor, known as the father of scientific management, provided the rationale for organizing workers according to the specialized requirements of the assembly line.

Communication and control. Given the economic needs and the systems of machinery and workers to satisfy them, we have not yet mentioned another factor in the development of economic organizations. The processes that come to a climax in the busy assembly lines have their beginnings and endings elsewhere. They must begin in the extraction and transportation of raw materials, continue through countless processes of refinement, finishing, shaping, and sub-assembly merely to place the necessary parts on the line for final assembly. Then the finished products that come off the line in such stunning quantity must flow steadily into healthy markets to earn wages and profits for their producers. These beginnings and endings are crucial phases in the economic organization; on the scale required for steady mass production, they can take place only because of revolutionary growth in the communication sciences.

In the early years of the American presidency the Chief Executive and his Cabinet stayed in touch by the simple expedient of living within walking distance of one another. When President John Adams was in his summer residence in Massachusetts, however, he was almost completely out of touch with the capitol. If somehow steel mills and automobile factories could be made to exist in 1800, imagine coordinating their operations under conditions like these:

> From Boston to New York the mail took five days in 1790. . . . By 1802 an unbroken line of stagecoaches was opened from Boston to Savannah, requiring twenty-two and one half days for the journey. . . . To send a notice from Philadelphia to Georgia in 1794 required thirteen days; it was as distant in point of time as Pittsburgh.[1]

The electronic age that has come into its own since World War II has brought new highs of effectiveness to systems of organizational control. Although the basic means of electronic communication are well known to all, new applications have enabled industries to set up fantastic interlinkages of far-flung inventories that would have been unheard-of even ten years ago. As will be

---

[1] Leonard D. White, *The Federalists* (New York: Macmillan, 1948), pp. 480-481.

seen several times in our discussion, the emergence of these new technologies in communication is working a noteworthy revolution in much of our thinking about organization.

Increased ability to move goods has been paralleled by the growing ability to advertise them through new and newly expanded media. To pick just one example, since Repeal the growth of national advertising has enabled the brewing industry to concentrate in a few large companies where before were many smaller ones. Then, most towns of 200 thousand had several breweries; today, not all of them have even one. Curiously, the nationally-advertised brands rarely distribute from one central point—savings in transportation more than offset possible savings to be effected through scale operations at one central plant. The real scale effect apparently is in the national sales and advertising organization.

The large organization, in summary, has not grown up because of a series of favorable choices rationally made between alternatives. It is rather a consequence of such factors as demand for higher living standards, technological changes, and the laws of economics. Large-scale organizations are an inseparable feature of our social landscape.

Simple Organization Patterns in the Historical Past

As far back as recorded history instances can be found in other civilizations of the amassing of large organizations of people to achieve some particular purpose. Perhaps the Egyptian pyramids and other monumental construction achievements are the first such examples to come to mind.

What is common to all these pre-industrial scale organizations, however, is that they were massively simple groups put together to perform a tremendous job that was simply the endless repetition of a simple one. Obedient to the principle that the organization is conditioned by the circumstances that give it rise, these groups were structurally nothing but the innumerable repetition of but one human relationship—the one-way authoritarian relation which in its "pure" form is that between master and slave.

Another common feature of these organizations, tied in with their authoritarian character, is that *levels* of authority, from the highest to the lowest, were relatively few compared to those of post-industrial organizations of scale. Simple, undifferentiated functions to be performed make it possible for one person to supervise effectively the performance of many, and without obscuring in any way the clean-cut lines of authority. Such a pattern is still to be found in many of the lesser developed countries of the world today. One chief clerk, for example, might have 80 clerical employees reporting *directly and exclusively* to him.

Today's Complexity of Factors

If the organizational proliferation in today's world is causing much concerned study, then, it is evidently not just because of the size of the groups involved. The kinds of structure that have developed in response to the complex forces at work in our society are obviously a far cry from those that were based on the master-slave relationship. There is much more to be learned and said about the new groups.

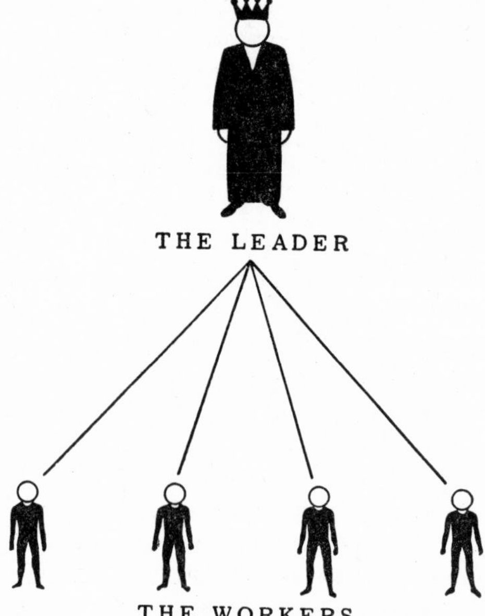

CHART 1-1. *The organization of the past—simple direct lines of authority—no specialists, few levels.*

What is the social milieu in which today's organizations thrive? In the first place, there is in many of our modern societies a recognition of individual human dignity that has taken centuries to develop to the present point, where it is now implicit to a large degree in organizations of all kinds. Much of mankind's concern with his social arrangements in the Western world for the past 2,000 years has centered on the question of the individual's relationship to the political organization. Man has immemorially been forced to attach himself to one group or another for protection against other groups, and for economic benefits. But perhaps not before the last two centuries has the idea taken hold that he has certain rights *as an individual* in the group. The roots of this Western democracy in the cultural and technological movements of post-Renaissance Europe can be, and have been, endlessly traced; suffice it to say that democratic ideals are a distinct though integral part of the total environment, including businesses, voluntary associations, and even the administrative apparatus of the government, as well as the purely political systems at all levels.

More education. Growing education levels are another sign of the change in individual circumstances. At the turn of the century in the United States, less than five per cent of college-age population was actually in college. By 1975 it has been estimated that fifty per cent of this age group will be in college. In one Middle Eastern country, which provides a rather typical picture of trends in the lesser developed nations, many cities report a more than one hundred per cent increase in school enrollment in the decade of the 'fifties alone. As people secure more education, it is inevitable that their expectation levels will also rise. They will expect greater recognition of their capacities and competencies. In the United States, where nearly everyone is already a high school graduate, the problem is perhaps to be seen in its most extreme form. The authoritarian "master-slave" pattern simply does not fit.

Full employment. Finally, increasing standards of living have worked a subtle but important change in authority relationships in the American society particularly. With full employment, which is certainly a part of the economically healthy society, the worker has considerable opportunity to move from job to job. Unlike the peasant of old, he is not tied to any overlord. The American em-

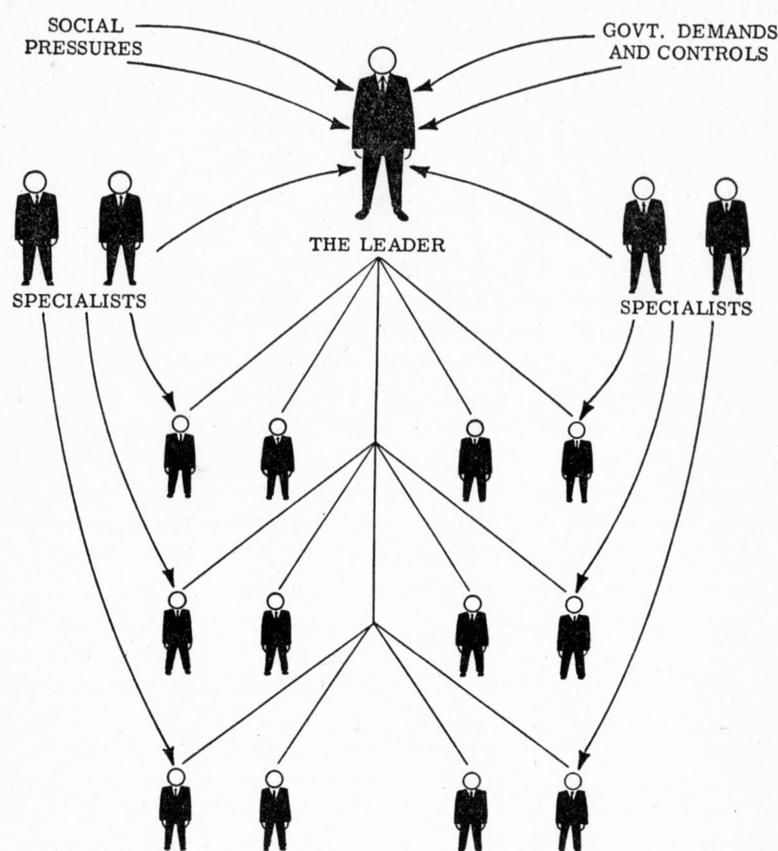

CHART 1-2. *Today's complexity in organizations. A complicated society produces complicated organizations—many specialists, many levels.*

ployee, for a variety of reasons ranging from the strength of his trade union to his own opportunity to save substantial amounts of money, has obtained an economic independence which must be recognized in thinking about present day organization.

The *individual* thus occupies a substantially *different* role in modern American organizations from the one he held in other times and places. While he may not choose to take advantage of all his privileges, there can be no doubt that even the lowliest employee in the United States today lives in a human enterprise system which bears no relationship at all to that of the pyramid builders.

New Understandings of Human Cooperation

Not only is the role of the individual in society changing, but the basis of human cooperation is also being amended as a consequence of research in social psychology during the last quarter century. Pragmatic considerations are causing administrators to become much more concerned about new and different patterns of organizational leadership behavior. Research results strongly indicate that legalism as the basis for order-giving in the old straight line authority sense is one of the *least successful* long term ways of getting maximum effort from people. Thus the organization environment must be such as to foster positive support for stated objectives; it calls for relationships that are *coordinative* in nature.

Additional Goals for Organization

Another significant factor in the organizational environment is that cultural values are constantly changing. While trends are not easily measurable, it does seem quite apparent that contemporary organizations more than ever must be concerned with *multiple goals.* For the great military commanders of the past, the purpose was clear and unmistakable: conquer. In the construction of the pyramids, the goal was a single one: completion. Everything else was subordinated to these ends. However, for most organizations, the goal orientation is no longer so simple and straightforward. Industrialized societies have over the last century developed the rather sophisticated and intangible value of efficiency.

More recently employee satisfaction and welfare have become important values. Increasingly, too, it is being recognized that organizations, private or public, are part of a larger social system and cannot operate in continued conflict with the goals of that larger system. Philip Selznick, in *Leadership in Administration,* points out that organizations are social institutions and that administrators must develop a greater awareness of this broadened responsibility.[2] It is therefore not a question of organizing to get the pyramids built as rapidly as possible; in modern-day civilizations the question of maximum use of resources, of employee welfare, and of impact on the total economy also affect the nature of coordinative relationships.

Task Specialization

Finally, it must be recognized that task specialization, as developed by both Taylor and Ford, has taken root deeply in the organization culture. What this has essentially meant is that much of the coordination which once was handled by the individual in his performance of the complex job now involves a great many persons each performing a simpler job and hence involves a plenitude of relationships. To illustrate the point, a shoe factory in Iran visited by one of the authors employed only two kinds of specialists, those who made men's shoes and those who made women's shoes. Within these two categories the workers undertook the full task of fashioning a pair of shoes from cutting the leather to the final stitching and trimming. The factory itself was small, employing about 15 people, and the problem of organization was virtually nonexistent. The owner directly supervised all employees. There was no need to coordinate the work between individuals. This is in contrast to the situation in a large shoe factory in the United States, where specialization was introduced more than half a century ago. Today no one individual plays a major part in the production of any shoe; and much of the organizational energy must be directed toward integrating the efforts of these many individuals who are combining to produce that single shoe.

In the United States the classic study bearing on this momentous change is the "Yankee City" series by W. Lloyd Warner and Paul Lunt. In analyzing the factors causing industrial strife in a small, homogeneous New England community of 17,000, Warner and Lunt concluded that the principal difficulty arose from the

[2] "The argument of this essay is quite simply stated: The executive becomes a statesman as he makes the transition from administrative management to institutional leadership." Philip Selznick, *Leadership in Administration* (Evanston, Ill.: Row, Peterson, 1957), p. 4.

breakdown of the skill hierarchy in the industry.[3] As one author has explained the implications of the study,

> . . . When shoemaking was in the handicraft stage there was a definite hierarchy of jobs based on skill, and the worker progressed from apprentice to journeyman to master craftsman. In the modern shoe factory, however, "no longer is it possible for him to start in low-skilled jobs and progressively prepare himself for higher-skilled jobs." Mechanization and minute division of labor have reduced nearly all jobs to the same relatively low skilled level. There is therefore no hierarchy of graded jobs in which to ascend. . . .[4]

The Organization as a Social Entity

From our discussion so far it should be clear that there is no easy way to understand organization behavior. Selznick has suggested that organizations should be regarded as "natural communities."[5] As such, they are subject to the same kinds of influences, pressures, prejudices, and biases as any of the social organisms. A structuring of legitimate authority relationships is not enough.

The modern administrator's task of creating an effective coordinating mechanism is infinitely more complicated than the administrative problem of an Egyptian Pharaoh leading an undifferentiated mass of peasants and captives who had no rights as individuals and whose interests therefore played no important part in organizational objectives. The important thing to note is that the significant differences in the situation do not appear to stem primarily from differences of size but from the change in the total fabric of the society. The organization as a democratic social entity, and therefore containing all the conflicts and opportunities for cooperation to be expected of any group of self-aware individuals, will be a recurring point of emphasis in this book. As James D. Mooney has written,

---

[3] W. Lloyd Warner and Paul Lunt, *The Social Life of a Modern Community* (New Haven: Yale University Press, 1941). This is the first of five volumes published from the study of "Yankee City."

[4] Ruth Rosner Kornhauser, "The Warner Approach to Social Stratification," in Reinhard Bendix and Seymour Martin Lipset, *Class Status and Power* (Glencoe, Ill.: Free Press, 1953), p. 235.

[5] Selznick, *op. cit.*, p. 13.

> Organization, therefore, refers to more than the frame of the edifice. It refers to the complete body, with all its correlated functions. It refers to those functions as they appear in action, the very pulse and heartbeats, the circulation, and respiration, the vital movement, so to speak of the organized unit. It refers to the coordination of all these factors as they cooperate for the common purpose.[6]

SUMMARY

Modern technology has made it possible for people to gather and sustain themselves in larger human units than were ever before possible. As more and more people have become involved in these organizations, our interest in their effective functioning as a distinct problem of the society has also increased.

The movement toward large-scale organization would appear to be closely related to industrialization. Peoples throughout the world have sought to industrialize as a means of improving their standards of living.

The technological changes most significant in bringing about organizations of scale lie in the field of communications. Through communications, controls have been expanded far beyond face-to-face relationships; they are reaching new highs of effectiveness in the electronic age. Mass media of communication have changed the whole concept of marketing and advertising, and thus have had their effect on organization size.

But the dimensions of the problem of organization in the modern society cannot be seen by looking at numerical size alone. What is more significant is the tremendous increase in the complexity of these organizations. They have moved far from the classically simple "master-slave" relationship where the distinction between worker and leader was clear-cut and the levels in the organization few.

The many factors that have operated to make modern organizations complex are just those which have served to complicate the entire fabric of society. They include: (1) the liberation of the individual in our social philosophy and policies; (2) the development of new understandings of the nature of human cooperation;

---

[6] James D. Mooney, *The Principles of Organization*, revised edition, (New York: Harper and Brothers, 1947), p. 3.

(3) the broadening range of organization goals; and (4) the movement toward task specialization.

It is important to recognize that organizations, as social entities, are typically susceptible to all the conflicts and opportunities for cooperation that exist in the society as a whole. Because organizations are complicated social organisms, they must be viewed in their total, multi-dimensional context, rather than from a narrow, mechanical point of view.

TWO

Complexity of Organization: The Concept of Overlays

What to Look for in This Chapter . . .

How we simplify the complex factors working on the formal organization setup by thinking of them as overlays—

- Sociometric network of private likes and dislikes for others
- Functional network dependent on special skills and knowledge
- Grid of centers where decisions are really made
- Pattern of power—politics at work
- Channels of communication

Definition of organization, involving—

- Patterned ways of relating people
- Groups so large that their members do not meet face-to-face with each other
- Complexity of tasks
- Conscious and systematic patterns aimed at accomplishing mutually agreed purposes

We have considered matters at enough length to get a general idea of the place of organizations in our modern social structure, and the way that they have grown up in response to, and in pace with, other features of society. It should be clear, however, that understanding organizations and their functioning is going to be a book-length project.

This chapter and the next will include two ways of looking closer at our subject before we attempt to study an over-all theory of organization. Our two ways will suggest to us in greater detail some of the factors that make present-day organizations so complex. It should not be assumed that actual organizations will exhibit two distinct categories of features, following the outlines of these chapters. They are divided here purely as an intellectual convenience.

The present chapter concerns the *processes* that tend to modify and change the organization from the way it is "officially" set up as a hierarchy of job tasks. Some of these processes involve but a few members of the group in interaction; others involve many and seem very impersonal and "abstract." All of them, however, are the result of different ways of studying group behaviors of individuals, and each is useful in reaching a total understanding of organizations.

The next chapter deals with the *goal systems* which operate within an organization, partially coinciding with its formal aims and partially modifying its formal structure. One group of goal systems is represented by the individual personality with its own set of norms; the small group is a second; and the organization as a social institution is a third. These goals naturally play their part in the processes to be described, although full consideration of this interplay must be brought out slowly and in line with further discussions.[1]

---

[1] While we avoid trying to postulate any all-inclusive scheme into which can be fitted all the elements of complexity from all possible viewpoints, it should be observed that, despite its present inadequacy to such a task, organization theory is being made more rigorous and inclusive all the time. See Chapters 20 and 21, below.

I • MODIFYING PROCESSES AS OVERLAYS ON FORMAL STRUCTURES

The formal structure of an organization represents as closely as possible the deliberate intention of its framers for the processes of interaction that will take place among its members. In the typical work organization this takes the form of a definition of task specialties, and their arrangement in levels of authority with clearly defined lines of communication from one level to the next. (See Chart 2-1.)

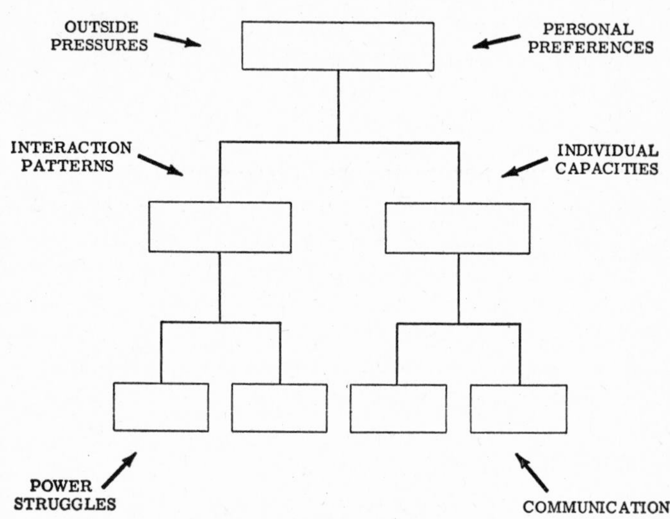

CHART 2-1. *The typical job pyramid of authority and some of its interacting processes.*

It must be recognized, however, that the actual processes of interaction among the individuals represented in the formal plan cannot adequately be described solely in terms of its planned lines of interaction. Coexisting with the formal structure are myriad other ways of interacting for persons in the organization; these can be analyzed according to various theories of group behavior, but it must not be forgotten that in reality they never function so distinctively, and all are intermixed together in an organization which also follows to a large extent its formal structure.

These modifying processes must be studied one at a time; a good way to do so without forgetting their "togetherness" is to consider each as a transparent "overlay" pattern superimposed on the basic formal organizational pattern. The totality of these overlays might be so complex as to be nearly opaque, but it will still be a closer approach to reality than the bare organization chart so typically used to diagram a large group structure.

Five such overlay patterns will be considered here; many more or less might be chosen from the kinds of studies that have been made, but these five might well be considered basic:

- The sociometric network
- The system of functional contacts
- The grid of decision-making centers
- The pattern of power
- Channels of communication [2]

The idea that these processes are overlays upon the conventional job-task pyramid does not require that the latter take a subordinate position, although much of the research in organization might give this impression. The overlay approach aims to be realistic in recognizing that organization also consists of a wide variety of contacts that involve communication, sociometry, goal centered functionalism, decision-making, and personal power. Let us consider this complex of processes one at a time.

The Job-Task Pyramid

The job-task pyramid constitutes the basis from which all departures are measured. It is the official version of the organization as the people in the organization believe that it is and should be. It would be correct to say that in most production organizations today, whether private or public, this official version of the organization-as-it-should-be reflects the view of those in the top echelons of the job-task pyramid. The actual operating organizations may differ in some respects from the formal organization;

[2] For much of the conceptual underpinnings of this chapter we are indebted to John T. Dorsey, Jr., "A Communication Model for Administration," *Administrative Science Quarterly* 2:307-324, December 1957. While Dorsey would seem to view communication as the central component of administration, we would put it on a level with others dealt with here.

this difference can be expressed by showing the manner in which the other networks vary from the job-task hierarchy.

Job-task hierarchy as foundation. Variations of the other networks from the job-task hierarchy should not be taken as an indication that the latter is being undermined or has no acceptance in the organization. It is well recognized in practice that there is an operating organization that varies from the chart with the full knowledge of those in authority. Day-to-day and hour-to-hour adjustments must be made, and there is no need to revise the chart for each of these. Nevertheless, the job task hierarchy as depicted by the organization manual does set forth the grid of official authority as viewed by those in the organization. Without it the other networks would simply not exist.[3]

The Sociometric Overlay (See Chart 2-2a)

In any organization there is a set of relationships among people which is purely social in nature; it exists because of a net feeling of attraction or rejection. This pattern of person-to-person contacts is called sociometric because it is revealed in the kind of group

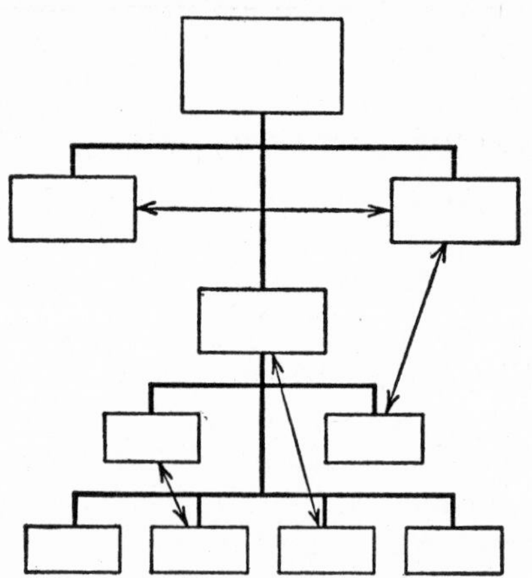

CHART 2-2a. *Social overlay—the special friendships in the organization. ("I'll talk to my friend George in Purchasing. He'll know what to do.")*

[3] William Brownrigg deals with the job-task hierarchy most provocatively in *The Human Enterprise Process and Its Administration* (University, Ala.: University of Alabama Press, 1954).

testing that was given that name by its originator, J. L. Moreno. Some investigators have felt that individual attitudes lending themselves to sociometric measurement include as many as the following:

1. The *prescribed* relations, which are identical with the official or formal organization.
2. The *perceived* relations, which consist of people's interpretation of the meaning of the official network.
3. The *actual* relations are those interactions which in fact take place among persons.
4. The *desired* relations are people's preferences regarding interactions they want with other persons.
5. The *rejected* relations are the relationships with other people which are not wanted.[4]

It is, however, the last two categories that are primarily sociological in nature, and it is these that will be considered sociometric here. Desired and rejected relationships are fairly easy to ascertain with statistical reliability, and are found to be very responsive to the other dynamics of the group. Ohio State studies of naval leadership have effectively utilized sociometric charts (sociograms —graphic representations of social relations) superimposed on the traditional job-task charts.[5]

The Functional Overlay (See Chart 2-2b)

There is in the organization a network of functional contacts that is important to and yet different from the formal authority structure. Functional contacts occur most typically where specialized information is needed; through them the staff or other specialist, the intellectual "leader," exerts his influence upon operations without direct responsibility for the work itself. This relationship, something like that between a professional man and his client, is a phenomenon of the twentieth century, and more markedly of the mid-century period.

---

[4] Fred Massarik, Robert Tannenbaum, Murray Kahane, and Irving Weschler, "Sociometric Choice and Organizational Effectiveness: a Multi-Relational Approach," *Sociometry* 16:211-238, August 1953.

[5] Ralph M. Stogdill, *Leadership and Structure of Personal Interaction* (Columbus: Ohio State University, Bureau of Business Research, Monograph No. 84, 1957), p. 10.

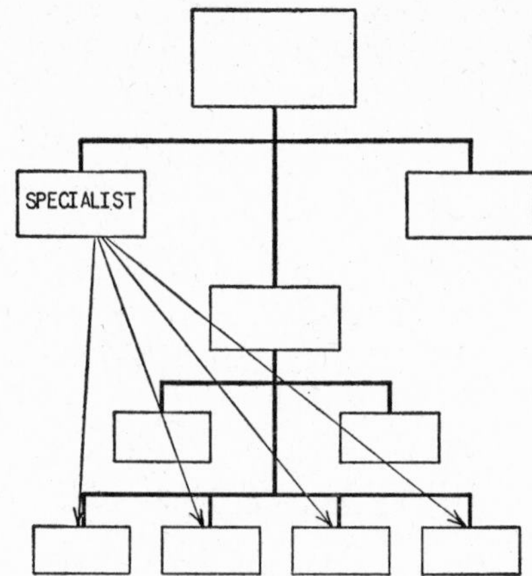

CHART 2-2b. *Functional overlay—the direct relationships between the specialist assistant and the operating departments. ("You have to see Personnel for approval to take that training course.")*

Frederick Taylor was so perceptive as to understand the importance of the network of functional contacts in a management institution. Taylor called these functional contacts "functional supervision"; this term upset many theorists who worshipped the concept of clear cut supervisor-subordinate authority relationships.[6] While Taylor's original concept of multiple supervision was rejected as a theoretical instrument at the time, it is still true that most organizations exhibit a system of functional supervision. Many charts of formal authority structures, such as those of the military, also show functional contacts through such devices as broken connecting lines.

The Decision Overlay (See Chart 2-2c)

Simon maintains that the best way to analyze an organization is to find out where the decisions are made and by whom.[7] It can

[6] A collection of excerpts from the literature of the early scientific management movement relating to staff specialization and functionalism is contained in Albert Lepawsky, *Administration* (New York: Alfred A. Knopf, Inc., 1949), pp. 299-306.

[7] Herbert A. Simon, *Administrative Behavior,* 2nd edition (New York: The Macmillan Company, 1947), p. xix. Simon's decision model is discussed in detail in Chapter 21.

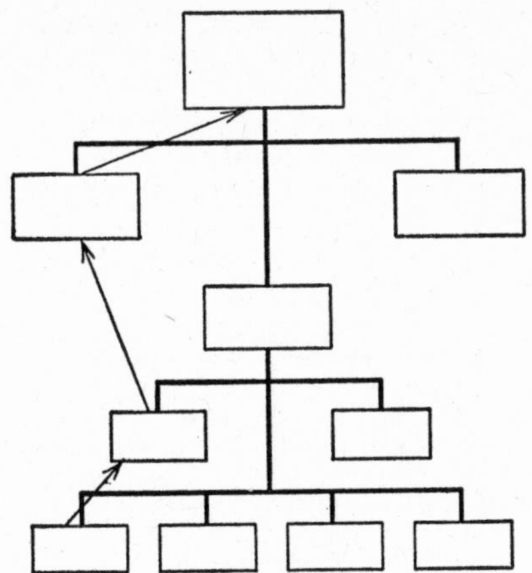

CHART 2-2c. *Decision overlay—flow of significant decisions in the organization. ("Don't worry about Joe. He doesn't concern himself about this. Our next step is to go topside.")*

perhaps be assumed that normally in an organization the decision pattern follows the structure of the formal hierarchy, that is, the job-task pyramid. However, the power and authority network, together with the functional network, may cut across hierarchical channels. It is in this sense that they take on the configuration of a grid or network. Thus the network pattern of approach is helpful, not in undermining the concept of hierarchy but in conveying the picture of actual practice. It modifies the harsh overtones of hierarchy by pointing out that actual organizations permit a great many cross-contacts.

Network of influence. It might be more correct to say that there is a network of influence, not a network of decision. This, of course, depends upon one's definition of decision-making and if one insists upon there being a clear cut choice between alternatives by a person in authority, then decision-making usually follows clear hierarchical paths and channels. However, if we think in terms of a decision *process* rather than a decision *point*, the sense of interaction and influence is more appropriately conveyed. In this connection it is helpful to refer to Mary Parker Follett's concept of order giving in which she says "an order, command, is a step in a process, a moment in the movement of interweaving experience. We should guard against thinking this step a larger part of the whole process than it really is."[8]

The Power Overlay (See Chart 2-2d)

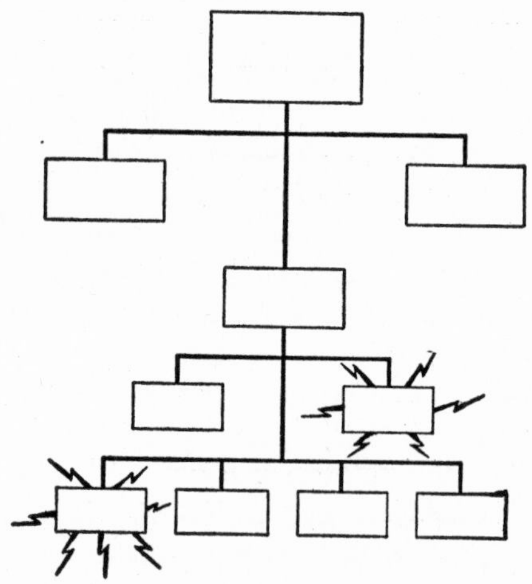

CHART 2-2d. *Power overlay—centers of power in the organization. ("Before you go further, you had better clear that with Jack in Production Planning.")*

Any discussion of power as a factor in organizational dynamics rather quickly encounters difficulties of definition and terminology. Since this is a subject upon which there will be considerable discussion at a later point in this book, let it be noted here that many of these problems arise from a confusion of the terms *power* and *authority.*[9] They are not necessarily synonymous; yet there has been a tendency to look at the organization chart, note the various status levels, and to assume that power increases as one rises in the pyramid. Much of this attitude is based on old concepts of authority as they are found in jurisprudence. Within this framework there is an assumption that a rule laid down by a political superior who is ultimately sovereign can be enforced by

[8] Henry C. Metcalf and L. Urwick, editors, *Dynamic Administration: The Collected Papers of Mary Parker Follett* (New York: Harper and Brothers, 1940), p. 49.

[9] See Chapter 5, "Authority, Policy, and Administration as Organization Factors."

the imposition of sanctions. Translated into the terminology of management institutions, this means that authority, and hence power, rests with those at the top echelons of the job-task pyramid.

Power no longer viewed as synonymous with authority. However there has been a considerable rebellion against this narrow view of the power factor in organization environment. Almost everyone who has had any experience in a management institution has encountered a situation where the boss's secretary, or his assistant, or the executive officer, is the "person to see." For a great variety of reasons, these people may be effective decision-makers in the situation. Thus power is really personal; it is political; and it may or may not be legitimate in that it has been authorized by formal law or has achieved hierarchical legitimization. Involving a person-to-person relationship, power exists when one has the ability to influence someone to behave in a particular way or to make decisions. As a result the mapping of power centers would seldom follow the pattern of a typical hierarchy.

Management institutions are political. It seems desirable to emphasize that management institutions are political in nature and that the basis of politics is power. While the use of the adjective "political" may be jarring to students of business administration who regard politics and government as being synonymous, the fact remains that business organizations are also political to an important degree. The maneuvering for proxies to gain control of an industrial corporation is certainly a political act and the same is true of struggles on the part of individuals to "build empires," or the use of artifice to gain the ear of the president.

The important consideration from the standpoint of organization theory is that there is a network or a grid of personal power centers, though sometimes latent and not expressed.[10] They may or may not coincide with the official structure of authority. Power is not institutionalized in the sense that one can look in the organization manual and find out where it resides. As a matter of fact one might find it in unsuspected places. The person of comparatively low status may be a power center because he has been

---

[10] Robert Dubin, *Human Relations in Administration: The Sociology of Organization* (Englewood Cliffs, N.J.: Prentice-Hall, Inc., 1951), p. 173. See also Dubin, *The World of Work* (Englewood Cliffs, N.J.: Prentice-Hall, Inc., 1958), pp. 47-54.

around so long that only he knows the intricate rules and the regulations well enough to make immediate decisions.

The Communication Overlay (See Chart 2-2e)

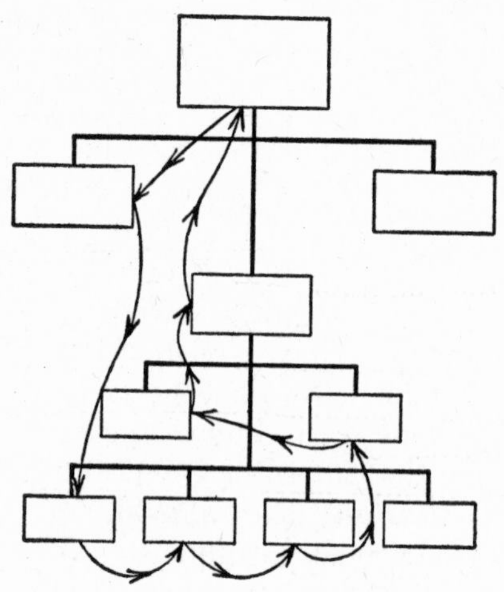

CHART 2-2e. *Communications overlay—the route of telephone calls on a particular matter. ("If we had to go through channels, we never would get anything done around here!")*

Perhaps nowhere is the inter-relationship of the various overlays more clearly to be seen than in communication. As will be observed at countless points in this book, the information process is central to organizational system. It affects control and decision-making, influence and power, interpersonal relationships, and leadership, to name only a few facets. Dorsey, in making a case for the significance of communications, says that "power consists of the extent to which a given communication influences the generation and flow of later communications. Points in the patterned flow where this occurs . . . are positions of power. . . ."[11] Furthermore, the communication net "consists physically of a complex of *decision centers* and *channels* which seek, receive, transmit, subdivide, classify, store, select, recall, recombine and retransmit *in-*

[11] Dorsey, "A Communication Model for Administration," *Administrative Science Quarterly*, p. 310.

formation."[12] This net consists not only of the technical information apparatus, but also of the human nervous systems of the people who make up the organization.

It is important to recognize that communication is itself a clearly identifiable facet of behavior. Redfield tells, for example, of the consultant who "starts his studies in the mail room, for, by plotting the lines of actual communication, he can sometimes build a more accurate organization chart than the one that hangs on the wall in the president's office."[13] Such a chart is, of course, one of communications. And it may tell a great deal more about how life is really lived in an organization than the formal authority picture. Thus an important and useful means of taking a look at an organization is to ask the question, "Who talks to whom about what?"

Answers to the question will often reveal that patterns of communication are at variance with official prescriptions. That is something the consultant mentioned in the previous paragraph frequently found. Furthermore there have been enough experiments with small groups to give great strength to the proposition that "the mere existence of a hierarchy sets up restraints against communication between levels."[14] Gardner has pointed out that factory production reports on productivity are sometimes rigged in order to give higher echelons the type of information which will make them happy.[15] Such blockages and distortions are certainly frequent enough to force us to recognize that the communications overlay represents an important dimension of organization analysis.

II • ORGANIZATION DEFINED

Since the word organization is so much a part of the vocabulary, it is possible to conduct a reasonably intelligent discussion of this subject without hair splitting definitions. In the preceding pages,

---

[12] *Ibid.*, p. 317.

[13] Charles Redfield, *Communication in Management* (Chicago: University of Chicago Press, 1953), p. 7.

[14] Burleigh B. Gardner and David G. Moore, *Human Relations in Industry*, 3rd edition (Homewood, Ill.: Richard D. Irwin, Inc., 1955), pp. 213 ff.

[15] Leon Festinger, "Informal Social Communication," in Dorwin Cartwright and Alvin Zander, *Group Dynamics* (Evanston, Ill.: Row Peterson, 1953), p. 201.

therefore, an attempt has been made to introduce the dimensions of the question before getting down to specifics.

Why do we worry at all about definitions?

Not so they can be committed to memory, to be rattled off later at appropriate time and place. The importance of the definition comes from its role as reference setter, as the basic guide post in sorting out that information which is relevant to our discussion and that which is not. In some cases definitions can be very precise; and hence information pertinent to the subject may rather easily be screened. The broader the concept involved, on the other hand, the less amenable the definition is to specific statement. For example, the editors of *Fortune* once noted that no one could agree on a definition of *free enterprise.* Without such a definition who knows what we are trying to destroy and what we are trying to protect?

Many dictionary definitions of organization are redundant—e.g., organization as the state of being organized. It has also been suggested that organization *is* coordination. Admittedly, the broader the definition the less the possibility of disagreement. Nevertheless we do have to make some decisions as to what will be considered under the label of organization; and those determinations must be made in reference to our conception of the word.

Underlying Assumptions

There are, then, certain assumptions underlying this work; and they in effect lead us back to a definition.

First, it may be observed that the state of being organized does occur in every relationship. Some individuals can order their time more effectively than others, as C. Northcote Parkinson has noted in enunciating his famous "law."[16] Certainly the mother of five small ones who still has time for the church, P-T.A. and bridge is "organized." Yet such individuals are not the focus of interest in this book; this suggests, therefore, an important point of reference: *size.* We are concerned with entities of scale; and

---

[16] A "total effort that would occupy a busy man for three minutes all day . . . may . . . leave another person prostrate after a day of doubt, anxiety, and toil." C. Northcote Parkinson, *Parkinson's Law* (Boston: Houghton Mifflin Company, 1957), p. 2.

these may roughly be identified as those associations of people which are too large to permit immediate, face-to-face leadership by a single individual. A *group* may gather around a table; some *organizations* couldn't crowd into Yankee Stadium.

Complexity. A second element in the development of our definition is complexity. Task specialization, as has already been noted, represents one of the most significant factors in twentieth century management. It is doubtful that a really *simple* organization exists today.

Conscious rationality. There is an assumption of conscious rationality implicit in the study of organization. To be sure, the overlays indicate clearly that this goal of rationality is not always achieved, but it is nevertheless there. Argyris has called it the "most basic property of formal organization";[17] he has quoted Herbert Simon approvingly:

> Organizations are formed with the intention and design of accomplishing goals; and the people who work in organizations believe, at least part of the time, that they are striving toward these same goals. We must not lose sight of the fact that, however far organizations may depart from the traditional description, . . . most behavior in organizations is *intendedly rational* behavior. By intended rationality I mean the kind of adjustment of behavior to goals of which humans are capable—a very incomplete and imperfect adjustment, to be sure, but one which nevertheless does accomplish purposes and does carry out programs.[18]

Presence of purpose. Finally, the significance of rationality to organization theory suggests a fourth major point, the need for a purpose. Relatively artificial accumulations of people exist to accomplish something, even though it may be so mundane as survival. As these purposes grow dim, the prospects of rationality decline; and if they disappear, the chances are that the consciously-created organization will also cease to exist. It is important to remember that the need for purpose perhaps exists only in organizations rooted in rationality. Smaller social groups, such as families, are held together by emotional, kinship ties; and who can say

---

[17] Chris Argyris, *Personality and Organization* (New York: Harper & Brothers, 1957), p. 54.

[18] Quoted by Argyris from Herbert A. Simon, "Recent Advances in Organization Theory," *Research Frontiers in Politics and Government* (Washington: The Brookings Institution, 1955), p. 30.

what lies behind the phenomenal organization of parts of the animal kingdom?

The Definition

On the basis of these assumptions (and their limitations), a definition may be attempted of organization as it will be used in this book:

> *Organization is the pattern of ways in which large numbers of people, too many to have intimate face-to-face contact with all others, and engaged in a complexity of tasks, relate themselves to each other in the conscious, systematic establishment and accomplishment of mutually agreed purposes.*

Edwin O. Stene about twenty years ago prepared a definition of organization which at first glance would not appear very different from that above. He said, "Formal organization is a number of persons who systematically and consciously combine their individual efforts for the accomplishment of a common task." [19] But note some important differences: (1) the point at which "numbers" become organization is not specified, and (2) the concept of task complexity is not introduced.

Universality of Organization

While organizations have a great diversity of objectives and operate in a multitudinous variety of environments, the existence of a common core of practice and pattern in organizations seems to have achieved reasonably substantial consensus. Note that the definition above does not prescribe boundaries of a geographic, public, or functional character. The purpose of earlier scholars in this field has been to pick from a variety of environmental experiences those patterns of behavior that recur regularly. This has been done on the assumption, obviously, that there are certain universal patterns in organizing management institutions.

Thus the problems that Pope John faced in 1958 in the management of the Roman Catholic Church are not appreciably different from those encountered by General George Marshall in assuming

---

[19] Edwin O. Stene, "An Approach to a Science of Administration," *American Political Science Review* 34:1127, December 1940.

command of the U. S. Army in 1939, or by Charles Thomas in accepting the presidency of the Trans-World Airlines in 1957. An oil company, a university, a department store, a child welfare unit, a newspaper, a mine, a municipality, a public utility, a hospital, or an ocean liner all have a place in these discussions.

III • SUMMARY

One way of attempting to develop a "feel" for the interaction processes which modify our traditional image of the formal job-task hierarchy is to think in terms of transparent *overlays.* This helps to convey the notion that no process is more important than the others. The formal authority pyramid is there and functioning. Operating simultaneously, however, are a number of other social processes which also clearly leave their mark on organizational behavior. The overlays which provide some indication of these modifying forces are:

(a) *The sociometric overlay,* which consists primarily of the contacts people have with each other because of personal attraction. These relationships exist in every organization and may or may not approximate the pattern postulated by the job-task pyramid.

(b) *The functional overlay,* which arises out of the relationships created by technical experts who exercise a type of authority because of their superior knowledge and skills. These relationships are unique in depending in such large measure on intellectual factors.

(c) *The decision overlay,* which evolves from the conceptualization of orders and commands as steps in a process, moments in the interweaving of experience. Decisions are part of a network of influence and in this sense are related closely to patterns of power and authority.

(d) *The power overlay,* which in organization life is frequently summed up by the expression, "the person to see." Power in the past has often been regarded as synonymous with authority. In more recent years power has been viewed in more personal terms; and it may or may not be legitimate in the sense of having formal sanction.

(e) *The communication overlay*, which involves the entire process by which information and perceptions are transmitted throughout the organization. Some writers consider the influence of communication so great as to dominate all organization theory.

Definition of the term organization ultimately becomes necessary as an aid toward segregating what is pertinent to the purposes of this book. However it is important to remember that a semanticist would regard "organization" as a "high level abstraction," far removed from measurable objects, and that precise definitions would therefore not be appropriate. The definition suggested in this chapter is based on the following assumptions:

(1) Organizations are large and do not permit face-to-face leadership.

(2) Organizations are complex.

(3) Organizations are attempts at "conscious rationality."

(4) Organizations must have a purpose, though it may be mundane, such as survival.

(5) Organizations as such are universal and would include an oil company, a university, a hospital, an ocean liner, and innumerable other human enterprises.

The definition proposed is: "Organization is the pattern of ways in which a large number of people, of a size too great to have intimate face-to-face contact and engaged in a complexity of tasks, relate themselves to each other in the conscious, systematic establishment and accomplishment of mutually agreed purposes."

THREE

Complexity of Organization: Man, Groups, Institutions

What to Look for in This Chapter . . .

Individual involvement complicates the organization on three levels:

- Level of individual personality
- Level of the groups he belongs to
- Level of the organization

How each level of involvement has its own peculiar properties, and offers unique options for individual behavior.

How these differences can cause conflict, within each level of involvement, and between them.

A useful way to think about an organization is as a universe with its full complement of solar systems, galaxies, and individual planets. Such an analogy may be helpful because it emphasizes that any large scale entity must be composed of a series of subsystems.

So it is with organization, as it has been defined in this book. The organization is really an uneasy holding company of individuals reacting as individuals; individuals reacting as parts of small face-to-face groups, and individuals reacting also as parts of smaller organizations. Always there is the individual as an adaptive organism at one end of the scale—and the organization at the other. In between there may be an infinite number of constellations which influence the total behavior of an organization. The point deserves to be emphasized. Individuals do not divorce themselves from their own norms, attitudes, and personality needs simply because they join an organization; neither do they necessarily sacrifice their own dependence on various types of group and associational memberships. Only if we understand the full range of loyalty options open to an individual in the average situation do we begin to sample the complexity of organization and the patterns of behavior within it.

Categories of Involvement

To simplify our thinking about the various behavior options available to the individual, three categories may be identified:

- The individual.
- The small, face-to-face group.
- The organization, which we may think of as a social institution.

Conflict Areas

Why do these categories of involvement levels pose problems?

Goals. A basic reason is that each level suggests its own system of responsibilities, loyalties, and commitments. In short, each has its own goals, and thus within the organization there will be need requirements as between individuals, as between individuals and groups, as between groups and groups, and as between groups and the organization. Hence the opportunities for divergence in aspirations, and, as a consequence, in goals, are almost infinite.

However, as March and Simon have pointed out, it is not enough to think of conflict in the organization as simply a matter of strife over consciously-considered goals. It is suggested that at least two other factors have great importance: (1) differences in perceptions of reality; and (2) the degree of felt need for joint decision-making.[1]

Differences in perception. There are many factors which influence individual perceptions of a situation. No one looks at things with complete objectivity. Decisions are taken and attitudes are formed on the basis of perceptions of reality that are shaped by experience, the environment, and indeed by the goals and expectations one holds consciously or unconsciously. In addition, March and Simon point out that information plays a highly important part; the greater the number of independent information sources, they emphasize, the greater the differentiation in perceptions within the organization. "Thus we would expect less perceptual conflict in an organization when one outside individual or group of individuals holds an acknowledged monopoly of relevant information than where there are a number of external sources."[2]

Need for joint decision-making. There is a substantial body of research to indicate that people are not concerned only about the satisfaction of their goals; they are deeply worried about the *processes* by which decisions are taken.[3] Simon and March argue that participation in decisions becomes the more critical under two circumstances:

(a) where there is a mutual dependence on a limited resource and everyone has to share it;

(b) where there is interdependence in the timing of activities.

In both cases individual well-being is tied up in group and organization operations; and the reasons for the desire of involvement are quite apparent. Thus, the existence of differing goals, perceptions of those goals, and aspirations for participation in the decision-making process help us to form a perspective on our problem. It cannot be seen in such simple terms as John Doe wanting one thing and the company for which he works wanting another. In the remainder of this chapter, therefore, we will look at the three major levels of involvement—individual, group, and

---

[1] James G. March and Herbert Simon, *Organizations* (New York: John Wiley and Sons, Inc., 1958), pp. 121 ff.

[2] *Ibid.*, p. 127.

[3] See the writings of Rensis Likert, F. J. Roethlisberger, and John M. Pfiffner in support of this point.

organization—as a further examination of the complexity of organization behavior.

I • THE INDIVIDUAL

In a few short pages it is obviously impossible to delve very deeply into the complicated world of the individual personality, but the reader should be reminded that such a world does exist. It is a world in which men are in some ways alike and in other ways quite different. How an individual organizes his conscious

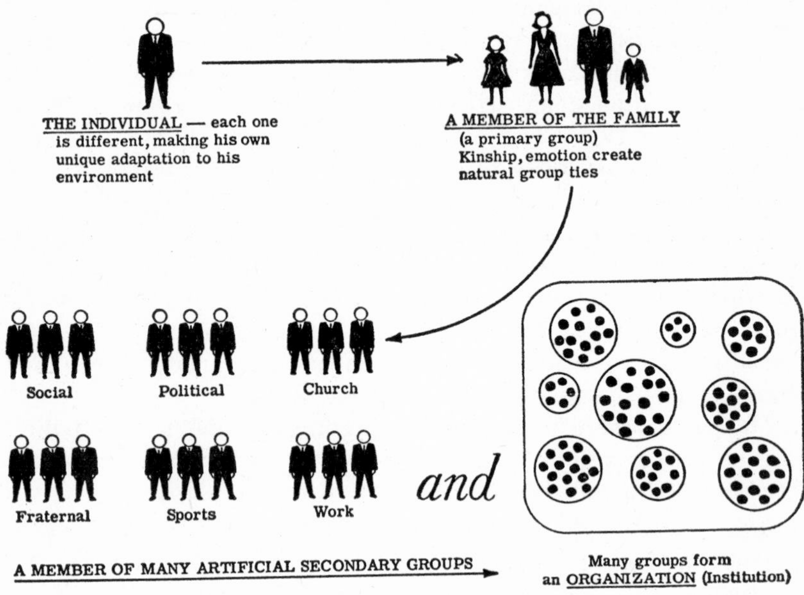

CHART 3-1. *The individual's inter-relationships.*

and unconscious needs, his social needs, and his physiological needs determines his personality; and his unique ways of arranging these requirements are conditioned by the interaction of his physical characteristics and the cultural milieu in which he finds himself. Thus the personality is not something ordained at birth.

Rather it is dynamic and reflective of the changing orientation of the organism to its environment.

Experience tells us that each person arrives at his own individual integration of his needs; and in order to satisfy them, he must fashion his own set of goals and aspirations. Furthermore because each individual's goals and experiences are different, his perception of situations will also vary. Where, then, do the similarities lie?

Personality Characteristics

Argyris has prepared an excellent summary of this problem in *Personality and Organization.*[4] The ideas expressed in the following paragraphs are taken largely from that source and suggest that personalities are *similar* in the following respects:

1. Personality must be viewed *as a system of organizing drives and predispositions.* The parts, such as honesty, loyalty, and initiative, cannot be taken out of the system and viewed independently.

2. The parts of the personality *stick together* because each part "uses" one or more other parts in order to exist. This occurs both internally and externally. Internally a balance exists when the parts of the personality are in equilibrium with each other; externally the balance occurs when the personality as a whole is in equilibrium with the outside environment.

3. The personality *manifests energy.* In Argyris' view the expression of this energy has significance to the administrator for these reasons:

- Everyone has such energy.
- This energy is indestructible.
- The extent to which this energy is manifested depends on the individual's attitudes at any particular time.
- If the expression of this energy is blocked, the individual will seek its expression in some other way.
- If the expression of the energy is channelled in an unsatisfactory way, there will be an attempt to express it elsewhere.[5]

---

[4] Chris Argyris, *Personality and Organization* (New York: Harper and Brothers, 1957), pp. 20 ff. (Chapter 2).

[5] *Ibid.,* p. 25.

4. The energy of the personality *comes from the individual's need system.* The extent to which energy is expressed in any one direction depends on the intensity of the need and the degree to which satisfaction is achieved.

5. The personality *has abilities,* of which three types may be noted. These are (a) the knowing (cognitive) abilities; (b) the doing (motor) abilities; and (c) the feeling abilities.

6. Personalities have *common mechanisms for dealing with threats.* One of these is to change one's self in a fashion necessary to eliminate the threat. The other is to deny or distort that which is threatening.

7. As the individual matures, he not only *acquires more parts* (i.e., more needs, abilities) but he also deepens many of them. These new additions must be so arranged in the total personality system as not to destroy its essential balance.

Individual Maturation

The concept of individual maturation seems a particularly important one. Here is a growth process which is common to all people but whose rate and character of development differs from individual to individual. It is also worth noting that in the maturation process, there is conveyed a real sense of a dynamic organism which is growing and changing, reacting to new stimuli, and creating new equilibrium patterns. As a consequence it is not surprising that Argyris has accorded this concept very considerable significance in his theory of organization behavior.

Dimensions. He suggests that there are certain dimensions to this maturation process which apply generally in the American culture. We all start at zero on the scale of each of these dimensions and reach varying points along the scale in the process of growth and development. The dimensions identified by Argyris are:

- The development from a state of dependence upon others as infants to a state of relative independence as adults.
- The development from a state of passivity as infants to a state of increasing activity as adults.
- The development from behavior capabilities in only a few ways as an infant to behavior capabilities in many ways as an adult.

- The development from erratic, casual, shallow, quickly dropped interests as an infant to deeper interests as an adult.
- The development from short time perspective (i.e. the present largely determines behavior) as an infant to a much longer time perspective as an adult (i.e. where the behavior is more affected by the past and the future).
- The development from a subordinate position in the family and society as an infant to a position equal to one's peers or higher than them.
- The development from a lack of awareness of one's self as an infant to an awareness and control over one's self as an adult.[6]

Concept of Role

Definition. This brief discussion of Argyris' estimate of the elements inherent in individual personality adjustment suggests their relevance to present organization norms and especially the significance of another important concept in the social sciences, that of *role.* A role is commonly defined as a set of behaviors which is expected of everyone in a particular position, regardless of who he is. These behaviors are of course socially ordained; and the role therefore sets a kind of a limit on the types of personality expressions possible in any given situation.

Obviously the motives and attitudes of some individuals enable them to fit more easily into some roles than into others. As we shall see later, the person with passive inclinations has many roles to play in a bank. But even within that organization, there are some places where the outgoing, directive type would find the adjustment to role demands easier. In all this it must also be added that the playing of roles has its effect on personality. Nobody remains quite the same in the process of adjustment. Thus *role*, which is social, and *personality*, which is individual, are important concepts in helping us understand the relationship of the individual to the organization.

Relationship between role and personality. In David Riesman's writings particularly, there is an indication of the extent to

[6] Argyris, *Personality and Organization,* p. 50.

which cultural demands, expressed through role prescriptions, provide shape to personality.[7] Conversely Riesman points out that certain components of the personality play the "principal role" in the maintenance of social forms; and these are learned in the lifelong process of socialization.

The inter-twining of social role and personality is to be found in Riesman's postulation of three different patterns in the organization of the individual's drives and satisfactions. These are:

Tradition-direction, in which the main forms of control over individual behaviors within the society come from taboo, myth, and other forms of cultural belief systems. In this pattern, which is to be found in primitive societies, the individual personality lives in a narrow, prescribed world.

Inner-direction, in which we see the locus of control shift to the family. Here the limits of personality expression are imposed through one's relationship with his parents. They become the gyroscope of right and wrong where life has become more industrialized, more mobile. It must be remembered here that the inner-directed person is conforming to social norms in his own way; the conformity is simply not as visible as in the tradition-directed personality.

Other-direction, which Riesman regards as largely an American phenomenon, but spreading to other countries as their capital wealth grows, and industrialization and urbanization proceed. A product of an affluent and mobile society, the pattern of other-direction shifts the locus of control from the family to one's peers and contemporaries in the society. This is partially necessary because the family no longer exists as a tight unit. Also, the system of mass communications and education rather successfully challenges any prescriptions instituted by the family. In Riesman's view, there is an "insatiable force of . . . psychological need for approval that differentiates people on the metropolitan, American upper middle class, whom we regard as other-directed, from very

---

[7] Riesman actually uses the term *character* which he considers "less inclusive" than *personality*. However, his definition of character as "the more or less permanent, socially and historically conditioned organization of an individual's drives and satisfactions," seems little different from some definitions of personality. See his *The Lonely Crowd* (New Haven: Yale University Press, 1950), p. 4. (Also available in the Anchor paperback series.)

similar types that have appeared in capital cities and among other classes in previous historical periods."[8]

Thus the nature of the adjustment between personality and role is a product of time and culture. An organization pattern which prescribed roles requiring abject subordination to authority might have been appropriate for the personality patterns of the late nineteenth century. These same prescriptions may be quite out of keeping with aspirations and needs of "other-directed" personalities at this juncture in the twentieth century.

In this section emphasis has been placed on the *common* processes of personality development and adaptation. However it should be borne in mind that though the processes are common, the results are different. The individual remains an individual; in this respect individual differences will always have to be considered as modifying generalizations about organizations and their behavior. Indeed the relationship of the individual to the organization is one of our most baffling problems, as later chapters of the book reveal. For the moment, however, it is enough to bear in mind that individuals are complex in their own way and that they continue to exist *as individuals* in the organization.

II · THE SOCIAL GROUP

A second level of involvement for the individual may be classified as the social group. At this point we see the individual in the process of dealing with others. The social group may be regarded as the smallest unit in which this interaction occurs. Furthermore it is an involvement which the individual cannot avoid. He is, in the last analysis, a social animal who depends on the people around him for his psychic sustenance and in many respects for physiological support. In short, during most of his life the individual acts not purely as an individual but as a member of a group. As one writer has put it, the groups to which a person belongs are "the ground on which he stands."[9]

---

[8] *Ibid.*, p. 23.

[9] Kurt Lewin, *Resolving Social Conflicts* (New York: Harper & Brothers, 1948), p. 82.

Concept of the Social Group

Definition. For our purposes the most important aspect of this significant human involvement arises from the fact that a group must be considered a dynamic whole with properties of its own. This means that a social group is something more than a sum-total of individuals, each acting in his own way. Hence we say that a social group exists when people share common values about something and when their social roles closely interlock.[10] In other words, there is developed a system of relationships and expectations which weld the members of the group together and which give them a "personality" separate and distinct from that of any particular member or members.

Relationship to large-scale organization. The significance of the social group to large scale organization was given great impetus by the now-famous Western Electric studies. One of the findings in this research was that a small group of highly skilled men—fourteen switchboard bank wiremen—could rather effectively subvert the efficiency goals and the formal organization of the company. Membership in the social group demanded conformance with the production levels set by the group; and excessive claims of delay could only be questioned by the supervisor at the risk of alienating the entire group. Thus the supervisor was at the mercy of his men, even though he had technical authority. The head foreman found it difficult to plan production schedules because of the inaccurate information he received; and there was almost no opportunity to increase the norms of production which had been set by the group.

Special properties. From the foregoing it is quite apparent that the social group has special properties. This is different from a work group in which individuals are brought into close contact on the basis of the jobs they are expected to perform. Such a work association does not necessarily mean that a social group has been formed. The sharing of common values may not occur; and if not, we can simply say that here are individuals who are in association with each other. In many cases, however, there will

---

[10] Theodore M. Newcomb, *Social Psychology* (New York: Dryden Press, 1950), p. 492.

develop a set of group values to which all members can subscribe and which then become the basis for group behavior. In some cases a natural leader may arise and the agreed-upon patterns of conduct may center on him.

Some Characteristics of a Social Group

Naturalness. A social group is natural and spontaneous; it does not ordinarily take on the characteristics of a social group as the result of an order or edict from higher hierarchical authority.

Interaction. Group members interact with each other because they want to; they have a natural and spontaneous desire to do so. Thus a group of people called together to hear the boss tell them "what's what" might not interact at all and hence would not constitute a social group.

Empathy. Members of a social group have a high degree of attraction and sympathy for each other. They like to be with each other and they enjoy the resulting intercourse. Their social inhibitions are at a minimum and they feel lack of that type of restraint which results from expected disapproval of one's associates. While some members of a social group are attracted to each other more than others, the general level of mutual attraction is high.

Social distance. Members of a social group do not feel too much social distance, that is, they do not feel that there are status or other barriers between themselves and other members. Social distance is the reason why interaction often fails to take place in a management conference attended by persons from several different hierarchical levels.

Democratic orientation. Social group theory has a strongly democratic orientation. The very essence of social group action is the attraction which members have for each other, supplemented by uninhibited communication and self-expression. Naturalness and freedom characterize effective social groups.

Leadership. Leaders tend to emerge naturally from the group itself. However, this does not mean that social groups cannot exist where leaders have been designated from the outside. Much depends on the characteristics and behavior of the leader. When an aggregation of people begins to become a social group, some people initiate interaction more than others and they are usually attractive to a large number of people. These are the natural leaders, but they may not necessarily also be designated as hierarchical leaders.

Group pressures. One aspect of the social group is the pressure exerted to get the members to conform to group standards in thought and action. The phenomenon can be used either to thwart the goals of management or facilitate their achievement.

Cohesiveness and unity. In order to endure, a social group must have a certain amount of cohesiveness. Members must have sufficient desire to belong to keep the group together and in continued existence. In short there must be enough attractiveness in group goals and associations to insure their observance as a means of maintaining the group.

Classification of Groups

Primary-secondary. One way in which these social groups are frequently classified is in terms of their immediacy and closeness to the individual. In the primary group, then, we would expect to find almost continued, face-to-face contact on the part of its members; and out of this high frequency of interaction, there would develop a rather strong loyalty to the group. Hence the family stands out as our best example of the primary group. It may be noted, too, that the ties which bind the family group are largely non-conscious and emotional. There is no questioning of the value of membership in such a group. Most groups fall into the *secondary* category. They do not involve such frequent interaction and the bonds of association are not as firm. However the concept of the social group would suggest that in both instances there is a sharing of values, and the size is not so great as to preclude a certain amount of face-to-face contact.

Organized-unorganized. Another way of classifying groups is in terms of those which are (a) organized and (b) unorganized. Here social groups may be differentiated on the basis of the number of specialized positions in the total membership. In a highly organized group, nearly every member will have a position with a special function which he is expected to perform as part of his role. In a loosely knit group, roles will not be as highly structured and there will be few specialized functions performed.

Within every organization we would expect to find the variations in types of groups suggested in the preceding paragraphs. Furthermore it is very important to remember that people do not belong to a single social group. They frequently belong to many, of which the primary groups are the most important because of their influence over members' lives. The other groups will from time to time have varying degrees of influence. Yet they are always present as another "pull" on the individual's loyalty and responsibility.

Group Process

Definition. As we have come to understand the nature of social groups, increasing attention has been given to the style of behavior which has been elicited by member interaction. This has commonly been called *group process*. It is most frequently seen as an aggregation of individuals are transformed into a social group; and the characteristics of the group, noted earlier, do much to explain the nature of group process. The concept is important because many have felt that it is through such group problem-solving that the best long-run solution to many of the dilemmas of organization behavior lies.

Hierarchical inhibitions. Again we find that the traditional concepts of hierarchy seem to be an inhibiting influence upon group process. Therefore a fundamental question of the future is how to reconcile the traditional concepts of hierarchical authority with the new democratic group processes. At first sight, for example, it may seem that there is no relationship between traditional job analysis and social grouping. On closer scrutiny, however, it will be observed that the nature of the job arrangement or layout can either discourage or encourage the transformation of work groups into social groups. An example of the discouraging type of mechanical layout is the automobile assembly line where the teamwork is almost entirely of a mechanical sort with a minimum of social interaction.

That is one reason why there is such large turnover on these jobs, and why those filling the jobs desire to get off the line into other jobs in the plant, although it may be noted that fatiguing work is also a causal factor. A study of the situation suggested that the amount of desirable social interaction could perhaps be increased on the line, and "that the engineering department restudy jobs and layouts with these factors in mind."[11]

There are, of course, other situations where the conditions of employment do not seem to encourage the generation of group process. Thus group factors were found to be rather low in an aircraft factory, a fact explained by officials as due to the frequent reassignment of workers. Workers did not stay on one assignment long enough to develop social groups. The same was found to be true of a shipyard devoted dominantly to the repair of vessels.

III • THE ORGANIZATION AS SOCIAL INSTITUTION

Thus far we have observed that each individual tends to develop his unique system of goals and values; secondly, the society is rife with social groups which have properties separate from those of their individual members. The individual may be considered the single star in orbit, the group would be the galaxy of stars, and finally there is the universe, the structure within which all these activities occur. In the analogy the organization is the universe. As such it contains unique properties which differ from those of the individual members and from the groups operating within it.

Concept of Social Institution

In these terms the organization is more than a mechanical edifice. It is a sociological whole and could appropriately be considered a social institution. While the term institution has often been used in broader context to describe systems of belief and loyalty within a society, such as free enterprise and the family, its application here to the idea of organization has considerable support. It is particularly noteworthy that some anthropologists, most importantly Bronislaw Malinowski, have sought to capture the concept of an organization as something more than a collection of small groups. As a consequence Malinowski used the term social institution to describe "a group of people united in a common task or tasks, bound to a determined portion of the environment, wield-

---

[11] Charles R. Walker and Robert H. Guest, *The Man on the Assembly Line* (Cambridge: Harvard University Press, 1952), p. 157.

ing together some technical apparatus, and obeying a body of rules."[12] According to such a definition a social institution could be a hospital, a department store, a school, a steel mill, a government bureau, an industrial corporation or a municipality.

Another anthropologist, Radcliffe-Brown, has essentially made the same point in suggesting the analogy between biological structure and social structure. Just as animal structures are composed of cells bound together in an organic whole, so are organizations composed of human beings "connected by a complex network of social relations."[13] Structure is the most fundamental part of social science because "the social phenomena which we observe in any human society are not the immediate result of the nature of the individual human beings, but are the result of the social structure by which they are united."[14]

Thus the anthropologists have contributed an important conceptual framework for studying modern management institutions—they have realized and expounded the idea that an organization is more than a mere collection of individuals or an assembly of small natural groups. As Malinowski has written, ". . . to study details detached from their setting must inevitably stultify theory, field work, and practical handling alike."[15]

From Structure to Institution

Infusion of value. The best general statement on the institutionalization of organizations, however, has been provided by Philip Selznick in his book, *Leadership in Administration*.[16] Selznick points out very appropriately that the mere creation of a formal structure does not automatically mean that an institution has been created. He chooses to limit the idea of organization to

---

[12] Bronislaw Malinowski, Introduction to H. Ian Hogbin, *Law and Order in Polynesia* (New York: Harcourt, Brace and Co., 1934), p. xxxiii; also Malinowski, *A Scientific Theory of Culture and Other Essays* (Chapel Hill: University of North Carolina Press, 1944), pp. 43-51.

[13] A. R. Radcliffe-Brown, *Structure and Function in Primitive Society* (London: Cohen and West, Ltd., 1952), p. 190.

[14] *Ibid.*, pp. 190-91.

[15] Bronislaw Malinowski, *The Dynamics of Culture Change* (New Haven: Yale University Press, 1945), p. 41.

[16] Philip Selznick, *Leadership in Administration* (Chicago: Row, Peterson, 1957).

the "rational instrument" of formal organization. Then, as it achieves natural dimensions, and becomes "infused with value," he ascribes to it the status of an institution.[17] An institution, therefore, is a product of social needs and pressures and is itself an adaptive organism. We can tell most easily that an organization has become "infused with value" by the test of expendability. If an organization is regarded merely as a technical instrument, it will survive only until a more efficient device has been uncovered. There will be little concern over the loss.

When value infusion has taken place, organizations are not so easily abolished. They now involve emotions and aspirations; and consequently there develops a genuine concern for the continuation of the institution for its own sake. Thus in the taking on of values, that is, ways of acting and believing that are deemed important for their own sake, organizations develop a strong "sense of self-preservation." This is more than a simple problem of survival; it is also a struggle to preserve the uniqueness of the organization in the face of new problems.

Organization character. Central to the Selznick concept of the organization as an institution is the idea that it acquires a self, a distinctive identity, which might be labelled "organization character." The existence of organization character is to be seen in the frequency with which new organizations are created to administer new programs, for the chances of adjusting the character of old organizations to new requirements are remote indeed. Selznick suggests further that the character of an organization develops through the same general processes as that of an individual.

Dependence on interaction. A final and important point is that the degree to which an organization develops character, and thus becomes institutionalized, depends on how much leeway there is for personal and group interaction. "The more precise an organization's goals, and the more specialized and technical its operations, the less opportunity will there be for social forces to affect its development. A university has more such leeway than most businesses because its goals are less clearly defined and it can give more free play to internal forces and historical adaptation. But

[17] *Ibid.*, pp. 16 ff.

no organization of any duration is completely free of institutionalization."[18]

Selznick's view of the organization as a "natural community" with its own social properties thus provides a further dimension to the complexity of the total organization process. Note also that the process by which these properties are developed is one that depends on the interaction of persons and groups. Organizations may at times be ripped asunder by conflict between individuals and groups; but it is also obvious that organizations cannot fulfill themselves without these vital components.

IV • SUMMARY

In the previous chapter some of the ways in which the various social *processes* affect organization behavior were explored. In this chapter the complexity of organization is revealed further in the existence of various levels of involvement for the individual. The analogy of the stars, galaxy, and universe was used. Although a planet is a part of a solar system and the universe, it still travels in its own orbit and has its identity. Another way of thinking about this aspect of the organization problem is to recognize that there are varying types of social organisms. The individual is one, with his own unique means of organizing his needs and responses; the small face-to-face groups of which he is a member are others; and the organization as a social institution is still another. In each case social interaction produces its own system of integrating behavior; and as this occurs, each of these levels of involvement acquires its own particular properties. Thus the character of a group or an organization is something different and apart from that of the individual members or the sum of those members.

Thus a simplified view of these levels of involvement suggests three major categories: (a) the individual; (b) the social group; and (c) the organization as a social institution.

Why does the existence of these various levels of involvement complicate the organization picture? Three factors seem most sig-

---

[18] *Ibid.*, p. 16.

nificant: (a) the development of various need patterns inevitably will result in the establishment of a unique set of goals to accomodate those needs; (b) perceptions of situations will differ to a considerable extent on the basis of goal-orientations; and (c) these various levels of involvement inevitably will come into contact at the point of joint decision-making.

There can be little question that organization patterns will always be affected by the differences among the people who live within them. However it is also good to remember that there is much that people have in common. For example the general nature of personality, which may be defined as the individual's organization of his predispositions to behavior, is in broad outline common to all. Argyris has summarized those characteristics. The same may be said of the process of maturation. We all move from infancy to adulthood and in the process make certain adjustments within ourselves and within the environment. The difference is not in the nature of the process but in the degree to which people move to adulthood along a number of different dimensions. This, in turn, relates directly to the nature of the culture in which a person finds himself. As Riesman has pointed out, there is a significant interlocking of personality and culture; and this is particularly important as we look back upon the roles individuals might have been willing to play in our own culture 100 years ago, or are still willing to play in some societies of the present-day world.

A social group exists when people share common values about something and when their social roles closely interlock. From this it would seem to follow that social groups must be relatively small and that in general they involve face-to-face relationships. Such social groups must exist; they are sometimes referred to as the ground upon which the individual stands. There are many types of groups, of which the family is the most generally important one. Commonly an individual will be a member of many groups, each of them having claims upon him of varying intensity. In recent years we have learned a great deal about the functioning of groups. This has caused particular interest in the idea of "group process," which involves the way in which people in intimate relationship arrive at consensus. There are many who believe that this small group approach, which is democratically oriented, has broad application to organization behavior.

Much has already been written about the concept of organization. Social scientists suggest that as the organization matures and as the opportunity for interaction among individuals and groups occurs, the organization itself takes on an identity. Selznick calls it a character. This results in a unique "organizational" way of thinking about things in which the idea of self-maintenance assumes increasing importance.

FOUR

An Introduction to Formal Organization Theory

What to Look for in This Chapter . . .

The climate that bred formal organization theory, especially the lure of the "machine model"

Weber's bureaucratic "ideal," applying to public and private organizations alike

Mooney and Reiley's four "principles"

- coordinative
- scalar
- functional
- staff-line

Public administration model—integration of agencies to fight tendency toward bureaucratic proliferation

Four types of formal hierarchies

- job-task
- rank
- skill
- pay

It has been said that organization structure "consists simply of those aspects of the pattern of behavior in the organization that are relatively stable and that change only slowly."[1] There are two types of structure, often referred to even in the scientific literature as formal and informal, although such a precise distinction constitutes an oversimplification. The formal structure is the official organization as viewed by those who are in ultimate authority. It is the *official* structure, and as such it is *legitimate*.

But here one runs into semantic difficulties, illustrating why the model builders among the behavioral scientists use such austere language. They are struggling for precision while confined to symbols (words) which are inherently ambiguous. The use of the word *legitimate* above is an illustration of this confusion because the informal organization also has its legitimacy—the legitimacy of social sanction. Certain aspects of the informal organization may be quite stable. They may modify the formal organization in practice.

Before proceeding to a description of formal organization, then, it seems desirable to emphasize that it is composed of a set of relationships officially approved by those in ultimate authority. Normally, therefore, one would look for by-laws, charters, manuals and charts. Obviously this is only one aspect of the total organization, but nonetheless a very important one. The attempt at this point will be toward objective description rather than criticism. We shall try to say what constitutes the traditional concepts of formal organization theory. How they are being modified by contemporary thought and research is an important theme of this book.

I • THE CLIMATE

Traditional organization theory is derived philosophically from a combination of absolutism, laissez-faire economics, rationalism, and an interpretation of human behavior based upon the automaton.

This climate was pre-democratic in the sense that nineteenth

---

[1] James G. March and Herbert A. Simon, *Organizations* (New York: John Wiley & Sons, Inc., 1958), p. 170.

century industrial institutions were pre-democratic. The validity of this observation is attested by the nomenclature of traditional organization theory: command, control, direction, and communication through channels. The flavor was authoritarian and the basic concepts were derived from institutions which were autocratic: the military, the Roman Catholic Church, the industrial corporation. The resistances of the Stuart Kings to Parliament's invasions of the royal prerogative were not different in kind from twentieth century management's defense of management prerogatives against the labor unions.

The machine model. Traditional organization theory of that vintage has recently been referred to as the "machine model" because it views workers as automatons. The worker must adjust to the job and the task; labor is a commodity which can be bought and disposed of at management's discretion. Organization is based upon jobs and tasks and the basic unit of organization is the position, which is composed of the tasks that are to be performed by a single worker. In establishing or studying organizations, the orientation therefore is the job. The personalities in the jobs should be ignored. People should adapt themselves to organization needs; and those who are unable to meet job demands are to be discarded. Leaders are chosen competitively on the basis of merit, and production workers take directions from such leaders without talking back. Orders go downward and reports of accomplishment constitute the sole upward communication. To sum it up, men are machines.[2]

Rationality and motivation. Formal organization theory is rational in both temperament and process. The administrative man maximized productivity on a rational basis just as did the economic man of classical economic theory. Administrative decisions were to be made on the level of full consciousness and presumably with a complete knowledge of alternatives.

Traditional organization theory assumed that workers were motivated by rational choice which caused them to behave as would economic man when faced with alternative choices. Thus workers on incentive pay would produce at their fastest rate in order to maximize earnings. The fear of job loss and hunger in

[2] *Ibid.*, p. 36.

an economy of scarcity would cause workers to put forth their utmost in a spirit of competition. The industrial engineers would rationalize the productive process through their search for the "one best way" to do each job, and workers were expected to conform to this rationalized behavior in performing job operations. Thus the theory of motivation which underlay most orthodox organization thought ignored man as a very complex human organism. It excluded most of the behavior variables except those pertaining to economic maximization.

II • THE WEBER MODEL

The model of formal organization most familiar to social scientists (but not to vocationally-oriented students of management) was postulated by the German, Max Weber, who was most productive at about the turn of the century.[3] Weber had a great interest in uncovering the "laws" of social behavior. Most of his research was historical; and hence he is frequently considered an historian.

Three Power Centers

In the course of his inquiries, Weber directed much attention toward the function and exercise of power in society; and this research led him to conclude that there were three major points of influence:

1. The law and the traditional taboos of the society.
2. Individual leadership, largely emotional, which he labeled "charisma."
3. The mass of administrators who carried out the laws and policies of the government. In short, the "bureaucracy."

Weber's classification is particularly interesting in terms of power centers 2 and 3, for one symbolizes irrationality and the other

---

[3] The best known translation of Max Weber's writings on bureaucracy is in H. H. Gerth and C. Wright Mills, translators, *From Max Weber: Essays in Sociology* (New York: Oxford University Press, 1946). For brief excerpts which bear directly on the subject, see Robert K. Merton and others, editors, *Reader in Bureaucracy* (Glencoe: Free Press, 1952). A recent paperback which is an excellent statement of many of these theoretical propositions is Peter Blau, *Bureaucracy in Modern Society* (New York: Random House, 1956).

rationality. There are occasions in history when the "great man" comes along; and because of immense personal magnetism, he can dominate decision-making regardless of the logic of his position. Such a man, in Weber's terms, is a charismatic leader. Adolf Hitler is perhaps the best modern illustration of such a person. But normally power is not exercised through the "great men." It is the product of a host of decisions at many points in a chain. Weber saw in this process an opportunity for the functionaries of government as a collective entity to dominate. It was assumed, too, that logic and reasoning would underlie their behavior patterns.

From this brief summary it is understandable why the *idea* of bureaucracy, which as used here is essentially synonymous with "large organization," was central to Weber's interests. He was one of the first scholars who was concerned with probing this phenomenon and in discovering the relationship of structure to accomplishment of bureaucratic goals.

Bureaucracy as an Ideal Type

The chief feature of his analysis was the postulation of an "ideal type" of bureaucracy. Here the term was not used to suggest goodness or badness. Rather it was used to suggest a standard, or a model. Weber did not expect that any bureaucracy would have all the features he cited. The essential idea was to see whether a large scale organization, possessed of enough of the features to assume a power role in the society, might then operate as a rational solution to the complexities of modern problems.

What was this ideal type?

- *Emphasis on form.* Its first, most cited, and most general feature has to do with its emphasis on *form* of organization. In a sense the rest are examples of this.
- *The concept of hierarchy.* The organization follows the principle of hierarchy, with each lower office under the control and supervision of a higher one.
- *Specialization of task.* Incumbents are chosen on the basis of merit and ability to perform specialized aspects of a total operation.
- *A specified sphere of competence.* This flows from the pre-

vious point. It suggests that the relationships between the various specializations should be clearly known and observed in practice. In a sense the use of job descriptions in many American organizations is a practical application of this requirement.

- *Established norms of conduct.* There should be as little as possible in the organization that is unpredictable. Policies should be enunciated and the individual actors within the organization should see that these policies are implemented.
- *Records.* Administrative acts, decisions, and rules should be recorded as a means of insuring predictability of performance within the bureaucracy.

Bureaucracy as a universal phenomenon. A *second* aspect of Weber's theory of bureaucracy is its emphasis on the universality of the phenomenon. Though his interest was largely in seeking out the power centers in the society, the elements of the form he postulated are as applicable in the private as in the public sphere. For example, he thought that big city party organization in the United States at the turn of the century was a masterpiece of bureaucratic development. Note that this was intended as a compliment. Weber wanted rationality in human behavior; he believed that bureaucracy was the best means of achieving it at the institutional level. This, of course, is a difficult point for many Americans to grasp. The labels "bureaucracy" and "bureaucratic" have been used so long to connote government red tape that their more neutral application to business represents a real departure from traditional attitudes.

Assumption of man's freedom. The *third* aspect of Weber's theory relates to the general conditions of human labor presented in the introductory chapter. Essentially his ideas as to form arose from his insightful recognition of the changing nature of society. These were based solidly on the assumption that man had to be a free agent, perhaps not in the sense we use the term today, but most emphatically different from the master-slave relationship. He did *not* consider that large agglomerations of people who worked as slaves constituted a bureaucracy. The complexity of society, and hence of organization, was also recognized. For example, Weber did not believe that bureaucracies could exist except in a money economy. The idea of the bureaucracy, as a complex organism, depended on a whole series of transactions among its members and the society. These could not be accomplished on a barter basis.

Professional management. Finally, Weber suggested a rough kind of separation of policy and administration, in which the idea of professional management is emphasized. He was concerned that the predictable, decision-making processes of the bureaucracy not be subverted by a non-professional. Thus the bureaucratic hierarchy should be peopled entirely by professionals. The king, who rules by divine right, lies outside this framework. He is not a part of it. The same could be said for the popularly elected president or mayor.

Weber's Impact

There have been many criticisms of Weber's concepts. Some have argued about his method, others about his purposes, and still others about his model. Most frequently, he has been accused of taking the autocratic, Prussian bureaucracy and making this the standard by which the world's organizations should be judged. Without doubt there is considerable truth in this; yet his writings form the conceptual core of a large part of social science research in this field. In this respect it is only fair to say that Weber's chief function in more recent years has been to serve as a departure point. Most typically, the social scientists will establish that a bureaucracy does exist in Weberian terms, then the research will concern itself with events that occur under this so-called rational system.[4]

While Weber has had substantial influence on social scientists, it is noteworthy that he has had relatively little impact on the more vocational management literature. Only in more recent years, as the social scientists have used his model as a basis for empirical research in large scale organization, do we find his name and writings assuming reasonable familiarity.

---

[4] A classic essay which follows this general line is Robert K. Merton, "Bureaucratic Structure and Personality," *Social Forces* 18: 560-568, May 1940; reprinted with "minor modifications" in Merton and others, *Reader in Bureaucracy*, p. 361-371.

III • THE MOONEY AND REILEY MODEL

In the early 1930's two General Motors executives—James D. Mooney and Alan C. Reiley—attracted considerable attention with the publication of a book, *Onward Industry,* which was soon sold out, but which reappeared in 1939 under the title, *The Principles of Organization.*[5]

A Note on the Problem of Terms

The pioneer formulators of organization theory often characterized their major ideas as "principles," a practice which brought much criticism from later writers. Perhaps unfortunately many of these attacks rested on disagreements over definitions. We have in this book been rather reluctant to spend much time on definitions; however it may at this point be appropriate to indicate generally how we regard certain terms.

We consider a principle synonymous with a law; and both should embody a high degree of regularity. This consistency should provide reasonable predictability, as with the law of gravity or the principles of thermodynamics. We have generally refrained from talking about principles in this book because we have not been able to identify such regularities in organization practice.

The term *theory* involves the total framework in which all facets of the organization phenomenon, internal and external, are placed in meaningful relationship. We talk of *models*—the Mooney and Reiley model (for internal organization), the decentralization model, the decision model, and so forth—as a somewhat lesser order of theory. Models are really simplified images of what we think life is really like. Basically we have tried to suggest models of some

---

[5] James D. Mooney and Alan C. Reiley, *The Principles of Organization* (New York: Harper and Brothers, 1939). It is currently in print in the form of a revised edition issued by Harper in 1947 under the sole authorship of Mooney. The changes are rather slight.

This book did not purport to be a treatment or description of the organization of General Motors although obviously the authors were influenced by their experience in that organization during the formative years of Alfred P. Sloan's leadership. See Ernest Dale, "Contributions to Administration by Alfred P. Sloan, Jr., and General Motors," *Administrative Science Quarterly* 1:30-62, June 1956.

of the important processes in organization life. The term *construct* is used as a synonym for model. Finally, we have thought of *concepts* primarily as ideas upon which models and theory are built. Thus we think of authority as a concept and an important part of the decentralization model.

In the Mooney and Reiley model four major categories of "principles" were proposed. These were (1) the coordinative principle, (2) the scalar principle, (3) the functional principle, and (4) the staff phase of functionalism.

- *The Coordinative Principle* (see Chart 4-1a) is the first and all-inclusive principle which provides unity of action in pursuit of a common purpose. It embodies the need for authority and leadership. But coordination comes about not only through the manipulation of hierarchy; its fruition depends also on the unifying forces of doctrine, spirit, and morale.
- *The Scalar Principle* (see Chart 4-1b) is the form of organization sometimes called hierarchical. (We have called it the Job-Task Pyramid.) Sub-processes are (1) Leadership, (2) Delegation, (3) Functional Definition. The scalar principle really refers to the vertical division of authority and definite assignment of duties to organization units. As such it differs from "The Functional Principle" which follows.
- *The Functional Principle* is really the concept of specialization. The following example is offered: ". . . the difference between generals and colonels is one of gradations in authority and is, therefore, *scalar*. The difference between an officer of infantry and an officer of artillery, however, is *functional*, because here we have a distinct difference in the nature of these duties."[6]
- *Staff and Line.* The line represents authority and the staff advice and ideas, although this dichotomy should not lead to a double-track concept of organization. A unifying rather than divisive interpretation of staff and line is counseled.

This outline is the bare skeleton which in the book is expanded and interpreted in some detail, but for our purposes it suffices in imparting an over-all impression of the model. The authors then

---

[6] Mooney and Reiley, *op. cit.*, p. 25.

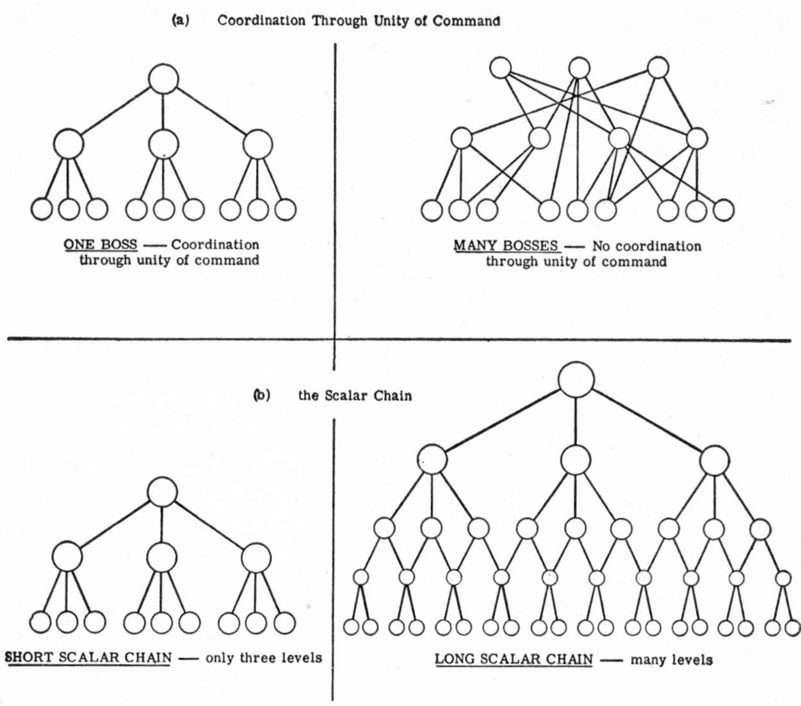

CHART 4-1. *Mooney and Reiley concepts.*

go to to discuss the principles of organization revealed in history, particularly as applied to the institutions of state, church, army, and industry. The church and the military are regarded as the most efficient and the state the least.

The Catholic Church as prototype. The supreme coordinating authority of the Roman Catholic Church resides in the Pope. While he has a world-wide hierarchy to aid him, his real coordinating power, according to Mooney and Reiley, is the doctrine that he is infallible. This doctrine must be "strong enough, in its hold on the faithful, to overcome all centrifugal tendencies."[7] The church's scalar chain is quite familiar with its Pope, cardinals, bishops, heads of orders and priests.

The Catholic Church has fewer levels than most other world-

[7] *Ibid.*, p. 103.

wide organizations, largely because the coordinating force of doctrine is so strong. In addition to possessing formal staff institutions, such as the consistory and Curia, church practice calls for everyone in the chain to act in a "compulsory staff" capacity. This simply means that superiors must consult subordinates to obtain facts, opinions, and advice before making decisions. Advice need not be followed, but consultation is required. There is also considerable delegation of both authority and responsibility to the bishops, who may decide many rather fundamental questions of policy and doctrine as they see fit.

The military prototype. All four of Mooney's "principles" are found to a marked degree in the military. He spent a part of World War II with the Navy, which accounts for the fact that most of the new material in the 1947 edition had to do with military organization. Here again he emphasized the importance of doctrine as a coordinating force. Here the development of an understanding of the reasons for U. S. participation was considered essential to organization spirit.

The evolution of military organization during World War II offered new insights into the working of the scalar principle. Mooney as a consequence suggested that as organizations grow beyond a certain size, coordination by one man becomes more difficult. This problem is aggravated in the military by an especially long scalar chain (number of levels)—from the squad leader in Normandy to the President in Washington. The contrast with the short scalar chain from the Pope to the parish priest is particularly marked. This means that the military has had to develop the distinction between rule and principle. The necessity for decentralization in handling huge masses of troops has necessitated a greater area of discretion in decision-making at the lower echelons, and hence reliance upon flexible principles instead of rules. "Experience has proved that no unit of all arms and functions larger than a division can be efficiently handled under a single command." [8]

Mooney gives credit to the military for originating the general staff principle. While armies going back to antiquity have always had to perform the quartermaster function, which is staff in na-

[8] *Ibid.*, p. 137.

ture, the modern concept of the general staff is a product of the nineteenth century brought to fruition by the Prussians under von Moltke in 1870. (The leading modern advocate of the general staff principle as applied to civilian operations was President Eisenhower whose administration of the Presidency secured some notoriety on this score.)

The industrial prototype. The discussion by Mooney and Reiley of their own industrial field does not contain the sharp conceptualization characteristic of their writings on the Catholic Church and the military. It is said that "the main problem in modern industry is the decentralization of command through line delegation and the encouragement of individual initiative, even in the smaller units of command."[9] This is to be accomplished through "indoctrination," a process which has been practiced more successfully by the church, and even the military. It is thought that the labor revolt of the 1930's could have been avoided had industrial management not failed at "indoctrination"—an application of the coordination principle through moral and spiritual means as well as by structural arrangements.[10]

IV • THE PUBLIC ADMINISTRATION MODEL

There is considerable uniformity in the structural arrangements for governmental reorganization recommended by management consultants, academic specialists and citizen reform groups.[11] (See

---

[9] *Ibid.*, p. 173.

[10] It is also worthy of note that the 1920's and 1930's, especially the period 1926 to 1939, constituted a period of great intellectual ferment in formulating organization concepts into systematic form. It seems ironic that during the period when the credos of formal organization were receiving their most literate conceptualization (by Mooney, Urwick, White, Willoughby, and Gulick) the seeds for its decline were being laid by Mayo, Roethlisberger, and Barnard. It was as though a patriarch was being prepared for burial at the time of his birth. However, the point should be made here that the patriarch did not die; he merely metamorphosed.

[11] The literature on governmental reorganization is so extensive that there should be no difficulty in locating it by author in any central library. Look under Leonard D. White, W. F. Willoughby, and A. E. Buck. Consult the publications of the National Municipal League, particularly the Model City Charter and Model State Constitution. For the recommendations of the Brownlow and First Hoover Commissions relative to federal reorganization see

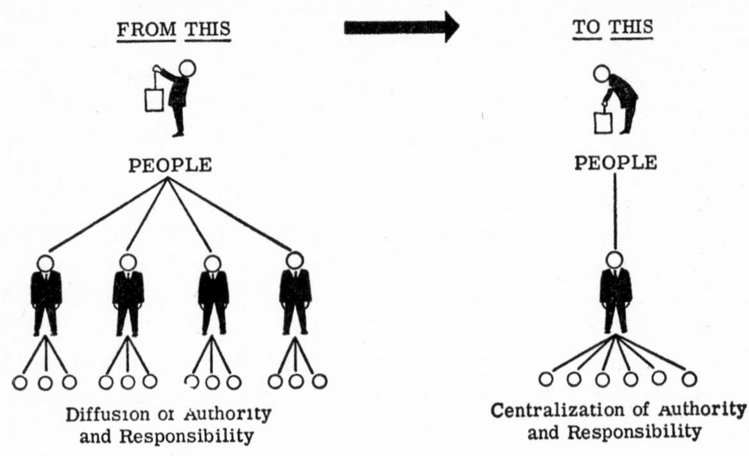

CHART 4-2. *What government reformers have wanted.*

Chart 4-2.) As a preliminary to the understanding of the public administration model, a brief description of organization pathology, i.e., "what's wrong," in American government seems desirable. Our fear of arbitrary power, and our concern that our democratic way of life be preserved, have resulted in a proliferation of governmental agencies. These often tend to go their own way without central executive direction, many being semi-autonomous under their own governing boards. Thus the federal government has around 75 separate agencies which are in many cases only nominally under presidential control. But the situation most abhorred by the professionals prevails in the states, where frequently the governor has slight coordinative authority over upward of 150 agencies. This situation formerly prevailed in the cities (and still does in some) but elements advocated in the model described below have been more widely adopted at the municipal level in recent years.

The following are the main features of the governmental reorganization model:

Report of the President's Committee on Administrative Management (Washington, D.C.: Government Printing Office, 1937), and reports of the Commission on Organization of the Executive Branch of the Government (1949). The second Hoover Commission (1955) bore the same title.

- *Executive leadership of administration.* The objective is to make the President, governor, or mayor an administrative leader as well as political chief. In council-manager cities the manager would become chief administrative officer.
- *Unity of command.* This is but a corollary of the point made earlier that someone should have sole ultimate responsibility for coordinating all administrative agencies.
- *Hierarchical conformation.* The channels of administrative authority would follow the hierarchical pattern, making everyone in the pyramid administratively answerable to the President, governor, or mayor.
- *Span of control.* The number of departments reporting to the chief administrative officer should be small enough so that he can give each adequate attention.
- *Coordination through the budget* by the chief administrative officer.
- *Boards for advice but not for administration.*
- *Staff as instrumentality for coordination and control.* Central budget, accounting, and personnel units maintain rather detailed supervision over line activities.
- *Departmentation by general purpose.* All of the activities devoted to the same end such as public works, health, or agriculture, should be grouped in the same department.
- *Separation of politics and administration.* This concept was originally intended by reformers as a means of combating the corruption existing in state and local government fifty years ago. Politicians were "bad guys" and administrators "good guys;" hence the way to get good administration was to keep the politicians out of it. The concept has come under severe criticism from contemporary political scientists who claim that the dichotomy is artificial and unrealistic. It is included here because: (1) it was a vital part historically of the model under discussion; and (2) it continues to be featured, at least implicitly, in the reports of management consultants and the utterances of some reform groups.

V • TYPES OF FORMAL HIERARCHIES

As the foregoing sections reveal, the last half century has resulted in the development of a very substantial body of literature dealing with the formal hierarchy. This is essentially a structural concept in which jobs, positions, processes, and procedures are dominant. It is concerned with operations and things as distinct from people. It is established on the basis of duties, activities, and tasks. People are secondary in the structural hierarchy; they are fitted into it on the basis not of their own desires and needs, but according to the demands and requirements of the hierarchy itself.

But it is something of an oversimplification—one to which we have perhaps contributed in the beginning parts of this book—to assume that there is only one kind of structure and only one kind of formal hierarchy. Actually there are several of which we should be aware and which are commonly institutionalized. (See Chart 4-3.) These are:

- *The Job-Task Hierarchy*, to which attention has previously been called.
- *The Rank Hierarchy*, which is unique in that status attaches to the individual and not to the job.
- *The Skill Hierarchy*, in which the various knowledges and competences are accorded differing levels of organizational status.
- *The Pay Hierarchy*, which is not exclusive of those noted above but does in many instances provide a different perspective of the formal organization.

The Job-Task Hierarchy

Although Chapter 2 provided an introduction to the idea of a job-task hierarchy, it would seem appropriate to explore further this concept since it is so central to much of the management literature. We tend in this perspective to think of people as working at specialized tasks, or in social science terms, as playing different roles. There is a division of labor, which in the assembly line process is broken down into minute and repetitive operations. In small businesses and primitive hierarchies these roles develop

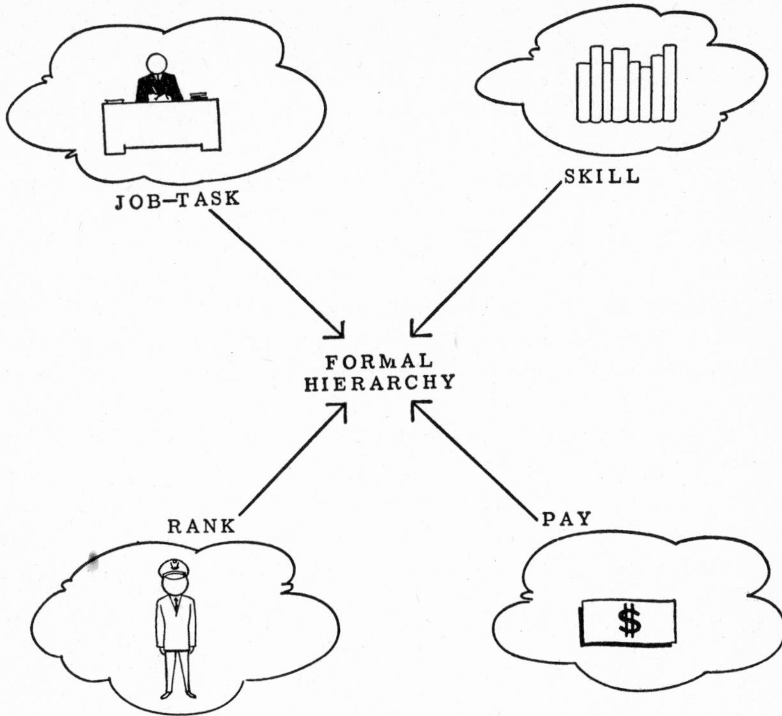

CHART 4-3. *Types of formal hierarchy—all may be legitimate, official parts of the organization structure.*

rather naturally and are not formalized in the sense of being written and published. As management institutions become larger and more complex two developments tend to take place. There is (1) a classification of duties and (2) a centralization of the authority to establish new jobs and positions.

The concept of the formalized job hierarchy in public administration grew out of the abuses connected with pay favoritism under politically dominated administrations. Two stenographers in the same building might be receiving $1200 in one case, and $4000 in the other. Hence, position classification became an integral phase of civil service reform under the battle cry of "equal pay for equal work." Today the well-administered governmental units have effective systems of position classification under which those having similar duties and responsibilities are grouped under job categories having identical descriptions. Every worker, whether bureau chief or janitor, is operating under a set of job specifications standardized to fit his specialized duties. Under typical civil service rules an individual cannot work "out of class," that is, he cannot perform duties not germane to the class descriptions.

The job hierarchy is thus a version of the structural hierarchy. Job descriptions spell out roles and give official authentication and stability to hierarchical structure.

Study of tasks rather than persons. A basic tenet of job analysis or position classification is that the determinations shall not be influenced by the persons occupying the positions. It is an analysis of work and not of people. This does not mean that individual skills and aptitudes are ignored in the management process. Individual differences are taken into account in the selection and placement phases. Once in a job, incumbents are expected to carry on the tasks alloted to it. It is well known, of course, that the duties and tasks of jobs change, sometimes as the result of technological events, but often because the human beings in a job alter its duties and responsibilities.

Job descriptions in industry. Recent years have seen the acceleration of job formalization in industry. It has come about for different reasons and at different times at the managerial and production levels. The writing of job descriptions at the production level came about during the late 1930's and World War II.

Unionization first brought pressure to obtain "equal pay for equal work"; jurisdictional disputes between rival unions and crafts also necessitated the spelling out of duties in many areas. Then a widespread movement toward job standardization and written job descriptions gained impetus at the beginning of World War II. In order to assure an equitable distribution of labor, especially in war industries, and in order to counteract the hoarding of scarce labor, the government instituted manpower controls. This necessitated the preparation of manning tables, and employers were required to justify their avowed needs for labor. Their justifications had to have a factual basis which naturally meant the spelling out of duties and tasks. The result was that many firms developed written job descriptions for the first time, and some continued to use them after controls were removed.

Advent of organization planning. The 1950's witnessed a growth in organization planning among business corporations. It was motivated by two interlocking developments: *first,* the popularity of administrative decentralization, and *second,* an expanded interest in planned executive development. It was found that in order to obtain decentralization in practice it was necessary to spell out the boundaries of decision-making as between headquarters and the decentralized units. It was furthermore discovered that planned executive development could not proceed without analyzing and writing down the roles to be played by the various members of management. This mapping out of the management roles has been called "organization planning."

The Hierarchy of Rank

The hierarchy of rank refers to an elite officer class, the most obvious example being the military. However, there are also examples in civilian bureaucracies such as the United States Foreign Service, a municipal police department, and the British Administrative Class. A hierarchy of rank differs from the job hierarchy in that status does not attach to the particular job; a colonel is a colonel whether he is commanding an infantry regiment or pushing papers in Washington. He will remain a colonel until he becomes a brigadier general or is retired. The job hierarchy places emphasis upon the duties to be performed while the concept of rank is based upon the personal status, pay and prerogatives of the individuals. This is not to say that the latter has no relation to function and level of responsibility; a naval captain, for instance, is supposed to command a fighting ship of the line, but many a captain attains such a command either not at all or only briefly. The rank concept is characteristic of most European civil service systems.

The Hierarchy of Skills

An organization is based also upon a hierarchy of skills. The job descriptions used for personnel administration contain a statement of the required training and experience for each position, in addition to a statement of the duties to be performed.

Management ladder. At the top of each hierarchy are the jobs demanding the administrative skills: strategy, planning, public relations, and over-all coordination. These are the attributes of the generalist, the person who can see the forest as a whole. He sees individual trees, but only as units in the whole. He has the ability to organize the work of others on a grand scale. He may also possess professional skills as a lawyer, engineer or chemist, but his duties as administrator are not based upon them.

Below the administrator come the operating managers, the people to whom British governmental terminology refers as "executives." They are the plant superintendents, division heads, and general foremen. These men are also coordinators, but their objectives are supervising day-to-day production and not high policy. Beneath them are the immediate supervisors of the rank and file. This is the hierarchy of managerial skills.

Professional and technical ladder. There is also a hierarchy of professional and technical skills. In any industrial organization these could be listed along a continuum with the research scientist at the top. Then would come the production engineers, management engineers, a galaxy of functional specialists such as accountants, personnel technicians, and statisticians. These skills would be based upon college training, but another sub-hierarchy would require sub-college training, e.g.: drafting, business machine operation, X-ray technique, and engraving. Then there are the manual crafts requiring apprenticeships: machinists, plumbers, sheet metal workers, and printers. Below them is the force of semi-skilled labor which constitutes the great bulk of labor today. These are the people working at jobs which require skill and experience that can be learned rather quickly.

Emphasis on jobs, not people. The thing to remember is that the theory of formal organization looks at this hierarchy of skills as job requirements. Individuals are placed in the jobs because they are thought to possess the indicated skills, or have the potential for acquiring them in reasonable time. In modern mass production organizations the tendency is for shop skills to gravitate from the level of the manual artisan to that of the laboratory scientist and production engineer. Even the craft skills are being broken down so that fewer all-round mechanics are needed; they are being replaced by persons who perform only one phase of a mechanic's job. The same thing is happening in the clerical field.

Office machines are replacing bookkeepers, a fact validated by the perpetual shortage of key-punch operators. Clerical and bookkeeping operations tend to take on an assembly-line aspect. The punch card and other machine processes are minimizing the old manual clerical skills.

The Pay Hierarchy

Large scale organizations tend to have a standardized pay hierarchy, often referred to as a compensation plan. Indeed, salary and wage administration has become a specialty of its own, demanding the skills of trained and experienced analysts. Public administration sets up more formal controls for administering compensation than does industry, except where the latter is operating under a tight union contract. In these instances the great preponderance of formal grievances concerns the protests of individuals against their job and pay status.

Salary and wage administration takes on some of the elements of scientific method, utilizing statistical approaches. Manufacturing operations make considerable use of time-and-motion study to establish standards for incentive pay and bonus systems. Moreover, salary administration tends more and more to be based upon so-called "factor" and "point" evaluation systems which attempt to quantify the elements which make up a job. Levels of difficulty are established, which in turn facilitates the internal comparison of various kinds of jobs. This method is less widely used in civil service where the comparative evaluation of different classes of jobs is based largely upon the subjective judgment of skilled analysts.

VI • SUMMARY

It is frequently written that organizations contain two types of structure, the *formal* and the *informal.* Actually there is no such easy distinction; organizations are a great deal more complicated than that. Nevertheless, thinking of those aspects of the organization which are official as the *formal* hierarchy and those which are legitimatized by social sanction as the *informal* hierarchy does provide us with a useful means of conceptualizing some important aspects of organization theory. In this chapter we have been concerned with theories about the *formal* hierarchy, for a considerable body of literature has been developed around the basic problem of developing a command and authority structure.

The orientation toward command and authority is in keeping with the social climate at the time when problems of large scale organization began to occupy attention. The flavor was authoritarian and the basic concepts were derived from institutions which were autocratic: the military, the Roman Catholic Church, and the industrial corporation. It was a period when a "machine model" was tenable because workers were viewed as automatons and as persons who behaved rationally in pursuing their best economic interests.

Max Weber, a German sociologist, may be considered the father of our modern concept of "bureaucracy," which we may here think of as synonymous with "large scale organization." The chief feature of his analysis was a postulation of an "ideal type" bureaucracy. Its most cited features emphasized form of organization and included (1) the concept of hierarchy, (2) specialization of tasks, (3) specified spheres of competence, (4) established norms of conduct, and (5) records. Weber believed these features applied as closely to private as to public bureaucracies. In other words, business organizations might as easily attain these qualities as governmental units. Weber's conceptualization is also noteworthy because of its emphasis on professional management.

An important landmark in the literature of formal organization is *Principles of Organization,* written in the 1930's by two General Motors executives, James D. Mooney and Alan C. Reiley. Like other early authors, Mooney and Reiley characterized many of their propositions as "principles," a claim which many later critics were to condemn as presumptuous. The General Motors executives argued that there were four main principles which were basic to the effective functioning of organizations; and they supported their case by analyses of the Roman Catholic Church, the military, and government and industrial organizations. The four "principles" advanced were (1) the coordinative principle; (2) the scalar principle; (3) the functional principle; and (4) the staff phase of functionalism.

The field of governmental reform affords a particularly good opportunity to view formal organization dogma. Our fear of arbitrary power and our concern that our democratic way of life be preserved, has resulted in a proliferation of governmental agencies. From the very beginning we placed emphasis—negative—on the structure of authority. Since then, much of the concern in governmental reform has been directed toward providing for integration of the authority structure. Some of the features of this public administration model are (1) executive leadership of administration, (2) unity of command, (3) hierarchical conformation, (4) span of control, (5) coordination through the budget, (6) boards for advice but not for administration, (7) staff as instrumentality for coordination and control, (8) departmentation by general purpose, and (9) separation of politics and administration.

The structural concept is one in which jobs, positions, processes and procedures are dominant. But it is an oversimplification to assume that there is only one kind of formal structure. Actually there are several of which we should be aware and which are commonly institutionalized. These are (1) the *job-task* hierarchy, in which the job is central; (2) the *rank* hierarchy, in which the person is central; (3) the *skill* hierarchy in which knowledge and competences are central; and (4) the *pay* hierarchy in which money is central.

FIVE

Authority, Policy, and Administration as Organization Factors

What to Look for in This Chapter . . .

- AUTHORITY as the *right* to command, *vs.* POWER as the *capacity*
- Policy *vs.* administration as a useful distinction in structuring democratic institutions
- Ambiguities in the policy-administration distinction
- Efforts to embody the distinction in governmental organizations
- In business organizations, the problems in the growing separation of management (*administration*) from ownership (which should provide the *policy* but lacks adequate representation to do so)
- Policy-administration distinction as applied in other organizations of scale

Perhaps nowhere do we see more clearly the present state of human organizations in all its ramifications than by considering problems of power and authority. In our day people who are members of organizations expect that they shall have something to say about the nature of their performance and goals. Furthermore that concern is not just restricted to those who are the immediate parts of the organization. People outside, for a variety of reasons, make up the many "publics" which also affect organization processes and structure.

As a result one of our most significant problems in modern organization—and the subject of this chapter—is the way in which fundamental goals and values are determined. This has been a centuries-long issue in government, particularly in the generations since democracy has gained a relatively firm foothold. In brief, how can we create organizational units that will reflect the people's will, and be responsive to their needs and desires? In more recent years, the same kind of questions have begun to plague nearly all large-scale organizations—business corporations and religious and other voluntary associations. In each instance the question is fundamentally the same: *to what extent shall the constituent members of the organization have a say in its affairs and how shall that say be provided organizationally?*

I • THE CONCEPT OF AUTHORITY

Before considering the basic problem of the chapter, however, it is necessary first to look carefully at the terms which are commonly used in such considerations, notably "authority" and "power."

Distinction between Power and Authority

The traditional concept of hierarchy, as has been previously observed, finds its essential rationale in the idea that someone has the *right* to command someone else and that the subordinate person has the *duty* to obey the command. This is implied in the notion of official legitimacy, legal in nature rather than social and informal. Note, however, that the *right* to command does not necessarily connote the *capacity* to command. The Hungarian revolution is a good illustration of the point. The government of

Premier Imre Nagy clearly had the *right,* but the Russian army and its puppets had the *capacity.*

Legitimacy as a power attribute. That a confusion should have developed, though, is not surprising. In an earlier, simpler society official legitimacy carried with it tremendous resources of power. As a dogma, the "Divine Right of Kings" did much to add *capacity* to monarchical authority. With control absolute and unchallenged from any other islands of strength, the hierarchical lines tended to be neater and cleaner. Even the decline of personal prerogative and its replacement by the rule of law did not change this pattern greatly. Behind the "legitimate" exercise of control lie important social agents of enforcement. Without the law concepts of hierarchical authority hold little meaning. In the United Nations, for example, there can be no such hierarchical approach because all nations are assumed to be equal and there is no unifying agency with the right to command. Nevertheless it is quite obvious that certain nations, notably the United States and Russia, have a *capacity* to secure their will which is far greater than that of the other nations.

Authority-power continuum. The reasons then, that official hierarchical authority has been a consistent part of organization literature and thought lies in the existence of certain resources of power, sometimes subtle, which stand behind the matter of *right.* In actuality, of course we may expect to find a continuum. At one pole right and capacity would be as one, such as probably was the case in the Henry Ford empire at one time. At the other extreme, hierarchical legitimacy and capacity would be completely separable, as was true in Hungary. Between these two extremes it is possible to find an infinite number of variations. The management of a division of the Army comes quite close to combining right and capacity, excluding such external factors as a more powerful enemy. Near the other end of the scale is the situation in a printing plant, where the foreman's hierarchical status provides little in the way of capacity. Frequently the veteran printers are unwilling to assume the foremanship and lose some of their prestige as journeymen because the wage differential is so slight.

Definitions. Indeed, whatever terms we may choose to use, it seems quite apparent that the key analytical question is: Who, in fact, sets the goals and allocates the resources for their accomplishment? If we permit ourselves to dwell only on the official and the prescribed, it seems apparent that a myopic view of the organization reality will be obtained. Having thus emphasized that the important key here is the focus of analysis and not its label, definitions strictly for the purpose of convenience may now be ventured. It is suggested that:

(a) *Authority* be regarded in the official hierarchical sense as the *right* to command; and

(b) *Power* be regarded as the *capacity* to secure the dominance of one's values or goals.[1]

Top-Down vs. Bottom-Up Authority

Although definitions have been suggested in the preceding paragraph, it is important to recognize that much of the controversy surrounding *right* and *capacity* to control has involved a certain degree of semantic confusion. Much heat has been generated, for example, as to whether authority, defined to include capacity, really flows down from the top in traditional fashion or whether it rises from the bottom as a kind of "consent of the governed." Here, then, is another dichotomy in the management literature which carries with it the usual risks of seeing everything in complete blackness or whiteness.

Barnard's challenge. The challenge to the belief in traditional *top-down* authority came most resoundingly from the pen of an eminent industrialist, Chester I. Barnard. In his series of lectures at Harvard University in the mid-'thirties, Barnard built very considerably on the philosophy of Mary Parker Follett, on the then-recent findings of the social psychologists, and on his own perceptive insights. One of the most significant contributions

---

[1] The definitions are very close to those of Mary Parker Follett, who has written: "Power might be defined as simply the ability to make things happen. . . . Control might be defined as power exercised as means toward a specific end; authority, as vested control." Later she suggests that power is "self-developing capacity" and suggests that "authority which has not been psychologically developed, which is not an expression of capacity, is an empty ethics." Henry C. Metcalf and L. Urwick, *Dynamic Administration* (New York: Harper and Brothers, 1940), pp. 99 ff.

of this former president of the New Jersey Bell Telephone Company was an onslaught on "divine right" authoritarianism in American management philosophy.

The essence of the Barnard thesis was that people differ in the degree of effort they will contribute to achieve the objectives of an organization. Hence at any given time the individual members will be putting forth varying percentages of effort, with a consequent effect on their production. The organization must in some way secure their willingness to cooperate, and financial incentive is not the important way to do this. The degree of effective authority possessed by a leader is measured by the willingness of subordinates to accept it; and the acceptability of orders to the individual member can be graded on a time-point scale. There are those which are clearly unacceptable, those on which there is a neutral attitude, and those which are unquestionably acceptable.

Authority, then, is in a sense delegated upward. The web of authority is maintained by a system of communications which is in turn supported by the willingness of individuals to cooperate. Even in the military—Barnard argues by quoting a famous general of World War I—authority is based upon the willingness of members to accept it.[2] Indeed, there are many inducements and compulsions to cooperate in an organization, not the least of which is our long training in the significance of hierarchical status, as Simon, Smithburg, and Thompson have pointed out.[3]

Impetus for authority-upward idea. Support for the *authority-upward* idea has come also from those who are loosely known as the "human relations" researchers; and in a sense their logic returns us to the fundamental question of this chapter. Who, in the last analysis, should determine the goals and values of the organization? As one human relations writer, Robert Tannenbaum, has said, ". . . an organization doesn't mean anything very much apart from the people who comprise it."[4] Tannenbaum has argued that the organization must be so molded as to provide for the

---

[2] Chester I. Barnard, *The Functions of the Executive* (Cambridge: Harvard University Press, 1938), pp. 92-94.

[3] Herbert Simon, Victor A. Thompson, Donald Smithburg, *Public Administration* (New York: Alfred A. Knopf, Inc., 1950), pp. 180-201.

[4] Frank P. Sherwood, editor, *The Status of Organization Research* (Los Angeles: University of Southern California, 1955, mimeo.), pp. 19 ff.

satisfaction of individual needs. William B. Given of the American Brake Shoe Company has made approximately the same point in his writing.[5] This approach brings us very close to the basic philosophy of democratic government, in which the state exists to serve its members. Those in leadership positions are there by consent of the governed; and ultimate sovereignty must rest with the people.

Upward-downward dichotomy oversimplified. There is no doubt that the debate over whether authority goes upward or downward has been healthful. Nevertheless it is equally apparent that the upward-downward dichotomy is an oversimplification of the complex dynamics by which goals are determined in any major organization. Indeed there are increasingly few situations where all the critical decision centers rest within the organization itself. As an open system, interacting with many other facets of the society, the larger organization has become increasingly vulnerable to power centers which are external to it. This, of course, has long been true of government; but it is becoming a factor in private organizations as well. As we shall see later, the structuring of governing boards and bodies bears heavily on this point.

Administrative Politics

In reality, capacity to control and work one's will, and indeed the *right to* do so, may move upward, downward, sideways, outward, or in any combination. Today there is perhaps less concern with the ideal flow of authority or power, whether it be upward or downward, and more concern with behavior in the organization. The sociologists have been particularly helpful in exploring these new avenues of analysis; and the empirical evidence strongly indicates the danger of relying solely on the picture of prescribed official authority or in following any preconceived notion as to the direction in which power and control will travel.

Studies of power and politics. Dalton found, for example, that power did not flow downward automatically when attempts were made to impose certain controls on a subordinate, decen-

---

[5] William B. Given, *Bottom-Up Management: People Working Together* (New York: Harper and Brothers, 1949).

tralized unit.[6] Lipset's study of political change in a Canadian province also indicated that major resources of power rested with the career bureaucracy in dealing with a newly elected leadership,[7] and Selznick's study of the Tennessee Valley Authority suggested that the determination of the Authority's goals lay outside the government itself.[8] Thompson's analysis of two identical wings in the Air Force revealed marked differences in the exercise of power within two agencies having exactly the same table of organization.[9]

In a later chapter, power and politics as conditioning factors in organization behavior will be discussed in greater detail. For the present it is sufficient to beware the limitations of vocabulary. The idea of authority has been much confused; and while no one has a corner on its correct use, it is important that everyone be agreed on a definition before meaningful discussion can take place. Here it is vital to recognize that the *right* to command or control does not necessarily carry with it the *capacity*. Who actually *does* the controlling is the really critical question. Beyond that, the achievement of capacity for such control must be the product of a host of factors operating in the total organization universe . . . in the broad sense, politics.

II • THE POLICY AND ADMINISTRATION CONCEPT

While it must always be recognized that the struggle for control over an organization cannot be legislated in the formal legal sense, the existence of hierarchical legitimacy is in itself an important power attribute. In short, the structuring of an organization is one of the battlefields on which the power struggle is waged. The avenues to control are enhanced when formal arrangements are favorable.

---

[6] Melville Dalton, "Managing the Managers," *Human Organization* 14:4-10, Fall 1955.

[7] Seymour Lipset, "Bureaucracy and Social Change," in Robert Merton, *et al., Reader in Bureaucracy* (Glencoe, Ill.: Free Press, 1952), pp. 221-232.

[8] Philip Selznick, *TVA and the Grass Roots* (Berkeley: University of California Press, 1949).

[9] James D. Thompson, "Authority and Power in Identical Organizations," *The American Journal of Sociology* 60:290 f, November 1956.

Who Determines Organization Goals?

The point at which this problem becomes critical is in the determination of the broad goals of an organization. Reflect for just a moment on your attitude toward the organizations to which you belong. For an American it is almost inconceivable that he should not at least have the opportunity to make his will known on the major issues confronting the organizations of which he is a part.

How and what? The dilemma arises, however, in (1) the development of instruments by which this will may be appropriately expressed; and (2) determining what particular types of decisions do concern the setting of basic organization goals. Assume, for example, that you are a member of the American Legion. How would you feel about your membership if the organization consistently behaved in a manner contradictory to your belief system? To what extent would you feel that formal opportunities for the expression of your feeling should exist? What kinds of activities by the Legion would most concern you?

Bigness means restricted participation. It is quite clear that the individual member of a large organization cannot expect to play a direct and personal role in all the affairs of such an institution. That is true whether we are talking about the voter in a national or even a city government; about the shareholder in a large corporation; or about the individual member of a labor union. Obviously it has been necessary, particularly as organizations have grown and specialization has occurred, to depend on certain persons to do the real work.

By force of circumstance, then, it is suggested that the most that can be controlled by the total membership of an organization is the determination of ends. The means by which these goals are to be accomplished are left to special workers. The English political philosopher, A. D. Lindsay, put this means-ends rationale in government terms by suggesting that the most the average voter could expect to influence public events was by indicating through his ballot when the shoe pinched. Beyond that, the basic directions of a democratic government had to be determined at a level below the electorate.

The Policy-Administration Line

In the literature of administration, this means-ends approach has become the *policy-administration* dichotomy. In this concept *policy*, as the Pigors have written, "is a general direction as to how to go about thinking when decisions are to be made that ought to be valid for the company as a whole." [10] Administration, then, consists of everything except the setting of these general directions. In briefer terms, it is often said that policy is the *formulation* of goals and administration involves their *execution*. As with all attempts to package the totality of organization processes neatly, however, this precise division has proven difficult to apply.

Attacks on the administration-policy idea. Some, such as David Lilienthal, have attacked it on the ground that the selection of means is fully as important to the constituency of any organization as the ends; and in a sense the distinction is unimportant because either or both may sabotage the democratic society.[11] Others, such as Paul Appleby, have taken a more operational view. They have argued that policy-making is a *continuum*. That is, it does not occur at a single point but at many levels. Furthermore the points at which policy is made will shift as time, circumstance, and political behavior demand.[12] Selznick, too, has pointed out that application of the policy-administration dichotomy even to the political-military relationship is no longer tenable.[13]

Difficulty of using dichotomy in organization structuring. Here, then, is the nub of the problem: Members of a democratically oriented organization *do* want to have some say about its general directions. It would be most convenient if structural arrangements could be built on a mechanistic application of the means-ends (or policy-administration) dichotomy. Yet such pre-

---

[10] Paul and Faith Pigors, "Let's Talk Policy," *Personnel* 27:5-14, July 1950.

[11] "Working at the grass roots is the surest guarantee of that day-to-day adjustment to the needs and aspirations of the people which is the liveliest form of public accountability." David Lilienthal, *TVA—Democracy on the March* (New York: Harper and Brothers, 1953), p. 184.

[12] Paul Appleby, *Policy and Administration* (University, Alabama: University of Alabama Press, 1949), p. 15.

[13] Philip Selznick, *Leadership in Administration* (Evanston, Ill.: Row, Peterson and Co., 1957), pp. 74 ff.

cise distinctions do not in fact exist. Constituent members, or their representatives, cannot make all the policy in an organization; and, as Lilienthal suggests, there are occasions when the *way* in which a task is being undertaken may be of greater significance than the end being pursued.

Problems involved in the policy-administration dichotomy will concern us throughout the book, but we should indicate at this point at least the operational problems involved in its application. These questions multiply as the organization becomes more complex, grows in scale, and occupies a sensitive niche in the total society. Nevertheless it is obvious that the membership of an organization is not going to be any the less interested because a distinction between policy and administration cannot be drawn. The fundamental issue remains; and from the point of view of shaping an organization, it is a basic ordering element. It is a matter of vital concern because every organization that is in any sense democratic must establish an appropriate role relationship between the constituent membership and those who serve as its hirelings.

III • POLICY AND ADMINISTRATION IN GOVERNMENT

Perhaps the importance of this problem can best be seen by looking at its relevance to government organization. Here the problem becomes really significant as the principle of popular sovereignty, or consent of the governed, is recognized. As noted earlier, there is no issue when the monarch is omnipotent. He decides everything, big and small, policy or administration. Until 1955 in one of the Middle Eastern nations, for example, the head of the local city government was appointed by the Central Ministry. Subject to orders from the top, he made all the decisions and saw that they were carried out. There was no local city council, no expectation that the citizens should have anything to say about their own affairs.

Then a new law was passed which gave the citizens such power, councils were elected, and the head of the city government was then chosen by that body. What was to be their relationship? What decisions, what types of matters were to be referred to the legislative body? As might be expected, the discovery of an appropriate association has been very difficult.

Early Emphasis in U. S. on Policy-Making

The early post-Revolutionary War experience in the United State also suggests another way in which the emergence of democratic institutions literally forced some attention to a rationalization of the relationships between administrator and policy-maker. When first freed from the British yoke, the Americans were concerned in the main with legislative institutions and policy-making. At first the execution of these goals was left to temporary committees of the Continental Congress, there being no real administrative apparatus. Even though later the Continental Congress did establish standing committees to supervise the major functions of the government, it seems fairly clear that one of the major shortcomings of the period was the absence of adequate administrative institutions. In contrast to the situation in the Middle Eastern country where the executive had been supreme, the United States experience revealed a central legislature which had not successfully determined what it could and could not do effectively.[14]

The separation of powers. Since Roman days, the argument has been made that the functions of government are divisible and that this distinction should be reflected in the organization structure. The Baron de Montesquieu, in Book XI of *L'Esprit des Lois,* is particularly known for the development of a philosophy which has become a cornerstone of American government. Montesquieu argued that liberty could only be assured by separating three basic functions of government: legislative, judicial, and executive. The placement of all power in one man could lead only to absolutism and dictatorship.[15] In the United States Constitutional Convention there were, of course, many other factors at work besides this theory. Nevertheless it is significant that this type of

---

[14] Alfred H. Kelly and Winfred A. Harbison, *The American Constitution: Its Origins and Development* (New York: Norton, 1948), pp. 100 ff.

[15] See Herman Finer, *Theory and Practice of Modern Government,* revised edition (New York: Henry Holt and Co., 1949), pp. 94 ff.

policy-administration separation has been reflected in institutions of government at all levels in the United States. All the states follow the pattern of the national government.

The Council-Manager Form

The separation of policy and administration has been the primary theoretical underpinning for another form of local government, the Council-Manager plan. By January, 1959, a total of 1,550 local governments had adopted this system, representing a population of 32,000,000 people.[16] Here the essential idea is that the elected Council shall be the governing body, and thus set policy; the manager shall be responsible for the administration of the policy.

Historically, the Council-Manager form evolved out of a pattern of local organization which was not greatly different from the old Continental Congress: the Commission type. Under this system all power rested with an elected Commission, which functioned both in a legislative and an executive capacity. As Thomas Reed has written, "The chief defects of the commission system were found to center about the absence of a distinctive executive authority and the obvious remedy was to add to the board of directors or commission, a manager, selected by them because of his professional qualifications, to perform their executive functions." [17] Curiously enough, the resulting Council-Manager model was consciously borrowed from what was considered a democratic form of business organization. As Reed, writing in 1926, said, "The director-like commission, with its emphasis on business methods in municipal affairs, inevitably suggested the completion of the analogy between city and business organization." [18] Reed pointed to the inherent democracy in the plan which he said was usually employed in private corporations. ". . . the stockholders choose directors," he wrote, "the directors select a manager, the directors settling questions of *policy* and the manager *carrying out* all

---

[16] The International City Managers' Association, *Recent Council-Manager Developments and Directory of Council-Manager Cities* (Chicago: The Association, 1959), p. 5.

[17] Thomas H. Reed, *Municipal Government in the United States* (New York: The Century Company, 1926), p. 219.

[18] *Loc. cit.*

decisions. The circumstance that the manager may have recommended the policy to the board does not at all diminish the fact that the board adopts the policy and is responsible to the stockholders for its success or failure."[19]

Public School District Organization

In much of the United States the public schools operate separately from other units of local government. These independent school districts thus carry on a reasonably technical and professional form of activity and at the same time are responsive to the desires of the citizens of the district. To meet these needs, an organization pattern similar to that of the Council-Manager form and built on the familiar policy-administration dichotomy has been universally adopted. School board members, most of whom are popularly elected, determine "the policies for the operation of the school system. . . ." and the superintendent of schools is ". . . the chief executive and administrative officer . . . responsible to them for the administration of the school system.[20]

Other examples of the manner in which American governments have organized under the policy-administration rationale might be advanced. These, however, would only labor the obvious; for it is quite clear that the problems of building responsiveness into these democratic structures has been a major element of the structuring process. In each case there have developed two major segments of the organization, one, the policy-making or legislative unit, and two, the executive or administrative unit.

Thus government organizations reflect in very marked degree the consequence of popular responsibility. In many respects the most significant aspect of this structural development is its inevitability, despite the shortcomings of the policy-administration dichotomy as a base for organization. The resultant structure has provided all the contradictions we might expect, the legislative and executive always being in a tenuous and volatile relationship. The grounds between the governor and the legislature, the city manager and the council, and the superintendent of schools and

---

[19] *Ibid.*, p. 220; italics added.

[20] Harold F. Alderfer, *American Local Government and Administration* (New York: The Macmillan Company, 1956), p. 635.

the board constantly shift. However no structural alternative has gained currency. Policy and administration, whether it be myth or reality, is deeply imbedded in our governmental forms of organization.

IV • POLICY AND ADMINISTRATION IN BUSINESS

It is somewhat amusing that students of local government, such as Thomas Reed, looked to business to provide them with a prototype of democratic organization. For while the corporation with its board of directors has long been a legal organization pattern in the United States (but not in many other parts of the world), business for many decades was not troubled with problems of democratic responsibility. As Cameron Hawley's *Executive Suite* so well suggests, the typical business organization has until recent years been dominated by the single individual.[21] In Hawley's novel, Avery Bullard made *all* the decisions; and the principal problem of the book arose precisely because Bullard had not designated his successor before he died. Bullard ran the organization totally and the Board of Directors served at his convenience. The shareholders existed only as a silent group with no more important function than to receive their quarterly dividend, *if* the President decided the company could afford to pay it.

The Significance of Constituencies

The proxy fights. But times are changing. The most dramatic evidence of the trend has been in the great proxy fights of the 'fifties, particularly in the New York Central Railroad and the Montgomery Ward Company. These are colorful chapters of political electioneering, of attempts to vote new members to the Board of Directors, and of insistence that organizational policies be changed.

Smiths in the Telephone Company. But these are only the surface manifestations. More significantly, the major corporations are acquiring constitutencies of shareholders that number in the

---

21 Cameron Hawley, *Executive Suite* (Boston: Ballantine Books, Inc., 1952; paper).

millions. The stock of the American Telephone and Telegraph Company is reported to be held by so many people (1,619,-397) that more than 15,000 are named Smith. The dimension of size is further to be seen in the Telephone Company's total of 725,000 employees, many of them having a stake in the organization not only because of their jobs but because of the stock they possess.[22] In addition the rise of institutional investment trusts, pension funds, and similar programs representing countless numbers of individuals have contributed to the shift in ownership of our large private organizations.

Relationships between ownership and management. It can be said truly that the divorcement of ownership from management in our large businesses is complete. As illustration, Chairman Frederic G. Donner of the vast General Motors Corporation in 1958 owned about one-hundredth of one per cent of the company's stock.[23] Standard Oil Company of New Jersey's entire Board of Directors possessed only about one-tenth of one per cent of the company's stock.[24]

Courting the shareholders. While the involvement of millions of Americans in these organizations through shareholding could in itself be expected to raise major questions of corporate responsibility, there has also occurred a "revolutionary change since the 1930's in the concept of social, political, and economic responsibilities of the corporation. These responsibilities present a challenge . . . but they have only recently emerged. . . ."[25] The companies themselves have courted the shareholders in a variety of ways, not, however, to win votes in the usual sense. Rather the courting has occurred because the stockholders themselves represent a very sizable market for many concerns, as one testified at the Standard of New Jersey's annual meeting, saying, ". . . I want all the stockholders to know that when I go on the road sometimes

---

[22] *Time* 73:94, February 23, 1959.

[23] Donner held 26,080 shares. Robert Sheehan, "GM's Remodeled Management," *Fortune* 56:123, November 1958.

[24] Standard Oil Company (New Jersey), *Report of the 76th Annual Meeting* (New York: May 28, 1958), p. 23. The Directors held 210,000 of approximately 200 million shares.

[25] E. Everett Smith, "Put the Board of Directors to Work," *Harvard Business Review* 36:42, May-June 1958.

I go ten miles with only one gallon of gas, to look for the Esso sign. I hope other stockholders will do the same thing." [26] In a period of great economic growth, business concerns have also sought to maintain the favorable support of their stockholders because of their significance as a source of further capital.

As a consequence of these changing perspectives, the 1959 annual meeting of the American Telephone Company attracted more than 10,000 people, by far the largest in its history.

Stockholder involvement in policy questions. The effect of these developments may very well be that large business organizations will in future face government's problems of building democracy into the organization pattern. It certainly does appear that some shareholders, at least, are tending through their participation at annual meetings and in the range of their interests to expect a larger role in policy matters. At the 1958 meeting of New Jersey Standard, when over 4,000 people made it the biggest in the company's history, the gamut of questions put to the Chairman of the Board and the President was great indeed. Criticism of a $250,000 donation to Radio Free Europe, of the nature of the company's advertising program, of debt policies, and of the President's speaking in favor of the Reciprocal Trade Agreements Act in Washington, D. C., provided a lively interchange between the "citizens" of the company and the officers. In 1959 the City of Los Angeles witnessed a very considerable controversy over the purchase of foreign generators for the municipally-owned power department. The General Electric Company published advertisements in the city's newspapers protesting this purchase, even though the foreign prices were said to be lower, on the grounds of an adverse effect on national security. One G. E. stockholder, a former head of the Economic Office of the State Department, thereupon indignantly wrote to the Los Angeles *Times* that he was protesting the use of company funds to finance the campaign against foreign purchases.

Is the board of directors a "tired fiction?" Despite these protests, it appears to remain true that boards of directors as a whole do not play a significant role in most businesses. While pointing

---

[26] Standard Oil Company (New Jersey), *op. cit.*, p. 17.

out that legally the board is considered to be representative of the owners and thus has all the power, Drucker pronounces this a "tired fiction."[27] Some of the reasons advanced for this situation are curious: (a) complexity of modern business operations; (b) difficulty of finding good men; and (c) the divorce of ownership from management which now "makes it absurd that the business enterprise be directed by the representatives of the shareholders."[28] Smith, on the other hand, sees the decline of the board's role as due (a) to a lack of recognition in management circles of its importance, and (b) the "fact" that "for all practical purposes the board is a creature of the chief executive."[29]

Nevertheless the board is still considered to lie at the heart of corporate organization. Drucker has strongly argued for a policy and administration separation, under which the board would not be an "organ of action" but an organ of review, of appraisal, or appeal. "Somebody," he has written, "has to approve the decision what the company's business is and what it should be."[30] Aside from the board's role in helping to shape better policy, there is no question in Smith's mind that corporations must move with the times. If for no other than public relations purposes, the managements of large private organizations cannot afford to allow themselves to become self-perpetuating.

The stockholder with his vote is regarded by Smith as one of the "last of the Indians," and distrust could generate quickly from this sector. Because business does not have as good a "public relations posture" as do such monopolistic and powerful groups as labor unions, American management "must evolve a better system of checks and balances to satisfy the public interest."[31] Smith sees the board as a major factor in this development.

This is on the assumption, however, that the board is reasonably representative, particularly of shareholders and of the public. In those organizations where the board is made up exclusively of

---

[27] Peter Drucker, *The Practice of Management* (New York: Harper and Brothers, 1954), p. 177.
[28] *Ibid.*, p. 178.
[29] Smith, "Put the Board of Directors to Work," p. 43.
[30] Drucker, *op. cit.*, p. 179.
[31] Smith, *op. cit.*, p. 45.

members of management, it is obvious that the quality of representativeness is removed from policy making and advice. At the New Jersey Standard Oil meeting previously referred to, one stockholder made his "customary objection" to the absence of an "outside director" among the board of fifteen.[32] All the company's board members are full-time management people.

The General Motors Case

Leadership by the board. Because of the company's size and its influence on the American economy, leadership and control of General Motors is a matter of immense public interest. Well known for its outstanding management, General Motors is unique in that a major share of its ownership rests in relatively few hands. The Du Pont corporation, as of November 1958, owned 23 per cent of its stock; and another 3 per cent was owned by five men, making a total of 26 per cent.[33] This pattern of ownership undoubtedly has had an influence on the system of organization control in the years of Du Pont's involvement in G. M. It has been a guiding precept, *Business Week* reported, "that the ultimate responsibility for the conduct of General Motors' affairs lies in the board of directors." [34] Also fundamental has been the assumption that the board is responsible to the owners; thus large shareholders have had seats on the board and participated in its policy deliberations.

V • POLICY AND ADMINISTRATION IN OTHER ORGANIZATIONS

Since the policy and administration question tends to become more pressing in proportion to an organization's commitment to the democratic idea, organizations that profess to be controlled by their membership find the question of establishing appropriate

---

[32] Standard (New Jersey), *76th Annual Meeting*, p. 21.

[33] Sheehan, "GM's Remodeled Management," p. 124. Charles F. Kettering, the largest single shareowner, died after the appearance of the article.

[34] "GM Board Heads for Big Shifts to Meet Changing Auto World," *Business Week*, April 18, 1959, p. 143.

relationships between the goal-setters and the doers the most pressing. Yet we have seen that this is not always the case. No one can claim that American business organizations have really been premised on the democratic ideal. Nevertheless there are various interest groups at work within almost every hierarchy which find themselves in conflict and which seek to control the ends of the organization. In a completely authoritarian organization these pressures may not be visible in a formal way; but in other instances, such as in our large corporations, it appears that we may be moving toward a decision-making process which will encompass in more systematic fashion these contending forces.

The Church

The Pope and the College of Cardinals. Even in quite authoritarian settings, many of the same pressures are at work but there is less need to rationalize them. For example, the experience in the Roman Catholic Church in the fall of 1958 was in some respects similar to that of General Motors. Under Pope Pius XII the traditional Senate of the Catholic Church, the College of Cardinals, apparently met seldom and had essentially lost its policy-advisement function. In fact many of the vacancies in the College had not even been filled. However the importance of the College was made quite clear when it had to assume the responsibility of selecting Pius XII's successor. Once having made the appointment, the College's future importance rested with the new Pontiff. John XXIII brought the College up to strength, and "let it be known that he intended to revitalize the College and make it function as it traditionally is supposed to function—as the Senate of the Church." [35]

Thus, intermittently at least, the College of Cardinals makes major policy when it selects the new Pope. It is rather too early to tell whether the Catholic Church, with 400 million members, has passed beyond the point of complexity and size where one

---

[35] Robert Neville, "Pope John," *Harper's Magazine* 218:32, April 1959. James D. Mooney points out that in appointing the Pope, the College of Cardinals is simply acting as an intermediary of God, who actually makes the selection. The College has no power in its own right. James D. Mooney, *Principles of Organization* (New York: Harper and Brothers, 1947), pp. 53 ff.

man can provide the necessary policy leadership. Certainly there was criticism of Pius XII on this score; and there is some indication that a revitalized College of Cardinals drawn from many geographic parts of the Catholic world may have an important influence on the policy role of the College. As long as the Pope is omnipotent in Church affairs, it is obvious that questions of constituent representation could not arise in any institutional sense.

The Mormon approach. Within the United States the commitment to democratic processes is of course very strong. In some instances organizations have been able to satisfy the demand for popular sovereignty with very little disturbance of the traditional structure of hierarchy. The Mormon Church, for example, places all power in its President; but this is tempered by a highly institutionalized system of policy advice down through the echelons and by the use of plebescites on official appointments and on policy matters. Thus are "the people, men and women, under God, the rulers of the Church." [36]

Voluntary Associations

Other organizations, particularly those which are essentially voluntary associations, frequently rely on annual or bi-annual conventions to establish the fundamental guidelines. This is essentially the way basic decisions are made in the AFL-CIO, which has 15,000,000 union members, and in the United States Chamber of Commerce, which represents about 2,500,000 businessmen.

VI • SUMMARY

The experiences of government, business, and other types of organizations all seem to demonstrate that the processes of large-scale human cooperation with which we are concerned do not involve just the "doing." *What to do* is of first importance. Here is where the basic values of the organization are involved; and here is where the struggle for control, power, and authority is at its rawest.

---

[36] John A. Widtsoe, *Priesthood and Church Government, revised* (Salt Lake City, Utah: Deseret Book Co., 1954), p. 234.

The principal purpose of this chapter has been to explore these questions in terms of their impact on organization structure. First, however, it is important to realize that formal authority alone may not provide the capacity to determine goals. One aspect of the continuing ferment over these questions is the contention that authority actually flows upward and that in a real sense the workers are sovereign.

This brings us back to the fundamental question of the chapter. We have developed many large organizations in the society, in business, in government, in the churches, and at many other points. Each of them has a constituency. The AFL-CIO has 15,000,000 members; the City of New York has over 8,000,000 citizens; and the American Telephone Company has nearly 2,000,000 stockholders. To what extent are individual voices to be heard in such mammoth units? How are they to be heard?

There are differing views as to the right of individuals to participate at all. In the authoritarian setting no right would exist; as we move toward the concept of democracy, which is based in popular sovereignty, this right becomes increasingly significant. It is not surprising, then, that governments have been the organizational units where the problem of building into the structure an opportunity for some type of popular participation has been considered most critical. Even in governments, however, it has been recognized that citizens could participate in large-scale organizations in only the most modest way. This has led to the application of the policy-administration distinction to questions of governmental organization. Citizens, through their legislators, presumably have the most active interest in establishing goals and policies; bureaucrats, who have a less direct relationship to citizens, are the paid functionaries assigned to carry them out.

Various aspects of this same general approach are to be found in other organizations. In the field of business, for example, new questions are being raised about the role of boards of directors. Drucker has called them a "tired fiction" and yet at the same time there seems no alternative to such an organization arrangement.

It would seem fair to say that as of the present time we know very little about how to provide a system of popular representation in our large-scale organizations. Our reliance on the policy-administration distinction has been far from satisfactory; for in actual fact such a precise gulf does not exist. Inevitably, then, attempts to apply the distinction with any rigorousness are bound to create conflict and tension. Yet all along the line the demand for participation seems to be on the increase. The broadening base of ownership in American business is a particularly striking feature of this development. How we meet this problem will do much to set the tone for organization behavior in the latter half of the twentieth century.

SIX

The Metamorphosis of Organization Theory

What to Look for in This Chapter . . .

Traditional theory emphasizes authority

Traditional theory emphasizes efficiency as the single criterion for decisions

Traditional theory emphasizes universalized "principles"

Revolt against traditional theory includes:

- Research findings in motivation, decision-making, and leadership
- Revival of planning and control as central themes

The late 1930's marked the emergence of a revolt against traditionalism in organization theory. This revolt came from a number of sources, movements, and schools, some of them highly critical of each other. But they had in common an agreement that traditional concepts of organization held by management people were too narrow and limited. A thorough discussion of this revolt ought to begin with a brief survey of what the revolt was against.

I • THE NATURE OF TRADITIONALISM

Dehumanization of Organization

Perhaps the most salient point of attack was the view, at least implicit, of the traditionalists that the job was separable from the man. The task was all important; labor had always been in surplus supply and it was the duty of the worker to adjust himself to the job. If he did not do so, someone else was available to take his place. Perhaps the rebels are most united, in this age of more humane industrial relations, by their common revulsion from the concept of man the worker as a mere commodity. In a positive view, this is the recognition that workers are human beings with the right to work and live in dignity.

The job-task hierarchy. The job-task hierarchy was referred to in Chapter 4 as embodying such concepts as the unity of command, superior-subordinate echelons of supervision, limited span of control, staff and line distinctions, and control from the top down. Traditionalists tended to view the job-task hierarchy as the major, if not the only, dimension of organization. It involved an approach which was strongly authoritarian because it originated in authoritarian ages and had its immediate historical sources in authoritarian institutions, namely the military, the Catholic Church, and the business corporation as it came to full flower during the period from mid-nineteenth to mid-twentieth century.

For the job-task hierarchy, traditionalism was characterized, *first,* by the study of tasks and jobs and work to be done and their relationship to each other; *second,* by a failure to recognize the people who fill those jobs as human beings; and, *third,* by a spirit of authoritarian control from the top down which was at variance with the concepts of democracy in our political and social institutions.

The analysis of work. The scientific management movement which originated in the opening decades of the twentieth century under Frederick Winslow Taylor had as its principal objective the division of work into its component parts. These scientific managers worked at the shop level and were not interested in hierarchy and institutions. They concentrated mainly upon ascertaining what constituted a fair day's work and on the arrangement of tasks into sequences so as to produce the most effective production operations. One aspect of this approach was the breaking down of jobs into tasks so small that the operators would spend their entire working day on one very repetitive operation.

The reorganization movement in public administration pursued the concept of work division in the theories of departmentalization as stated in the writings on state reorganization, and in Luther Gulick's famous essay on organization. Thus departmentalization by function came to be one of the cardinal "principles" in the organization theory propounded by the pioneers.[1] Closely allied to the concept of departmentalization by function was that of span of control, according to which the number of departments under any leader should be small enough so that he could give them the attention necessary. This concept has perhaps come under greater attack than any of the traditional "principles."

Financial incentive. Management values have leaned heavily upon the concept of financial incentive as the major motivator of man at work. Measured production, piece work, time and motion study have formed the basis for what is known in management parlance as incentive pay.

Productivity: A single standard of value. Until the third decade of the present century organization theory was wedded to the single value system of productive efficiency and maximization of financial return. In industry this took the form of increasing productivity per manhour, a movement which has certainly yielded a tremendous social dividend as evidenced by the fact that American industry has increased this productivity steadily for practically half a century. The manifestation of this value system in public administration came through the reorganization movement represented by the rash of efficiency and economy commissions beginning in the second decade of the twentieth century.

It is difficult to criticize on logical grounds the concept of increased productivity—getting all you can for your money. However, the fact remains that the word efficiency has acquired a

[1] Luther Gulick, "Notes on the Theory of Organization," in Luther Gulick and L. Urwick, editors, *Papers on the Science of Administration* (New York: Institute of Public Administration, 1937), pp. 1-45.

stigma which causes it to be avoided in many circles, principally because of its association with the single value system. This was a philosophy of human motivation which viewed labor as a commodity, each individual being his own agent operating within the laws of the marketplace. Under this single system of values, owners and managers did not view themselves as their brother's keeper and regarded themselves and their enterprises as insulated from the broad problems of human welfare.

Anti-Democratic Bias

The one-way street. As we have noted, management ideology has been traditionally authoritarian and undemocratic, even anti-democratic. Orders always went down, policies were generated at the top, and communication was one way except for the upward reporting of results. No one communicated upward in the spirit of criticism or protest. All wisdom resided in the top of the hierarchy and any resistance to its edicts was regarded as subversive. It was a sign of hierarchical weakness for a leader to permit questioning of his orders or opinions by a subordinate. While not all leaders behaved in this way, they were common enough to reveal one of the reasons why the new organization theory rebels against much of what formerly was regarded as gospel.

Management prerogative. The concept of management prerogative is *prima-facie* reasonable. It merely states that a manager wants his superiors to define his mission and then leave him alone to choose his own methods for achieving that goal. In this sense it involves the concept of freedom in performing one's job which receives support in the findings of modern social science research. However, the more sinister aspect of management prerogative is embodied in its extension to hire-and-fire, with the implication that the manager can dispose of people as he would of goods and property. Thus the concept of management prerogative has taken on the flavor of unhampered authority to deal with personnel and labor problems without interference from labor unions or civil service laws.

II • THE ESSENCE OF THE CONTROVERSY

The traditionalists tended to take the viewpoint that there were certain universals in administrative behavior which were principles. Thus there were specified rules of conduct with regard to unity of command, span of control, departmentalization by function, distinction between staff and line, and the policy-administration line. In a 1936 discussion of this subject Leonard D. White insisted that principles are tested hypotheses.[2] Ten years later one of his former students, Herbert A. Simon,[3] blasted the so-called principles stating that they were merely proverbs which had never been scientifically tested. He referred particularly to span of control, which has since become a whipping boy. There has been a running controversy on this subject between Simon and Lyndall Urwick, a British management authority, in which the latter has upheld the traditional point of view.

In public administration the revolt against the principles approach resulted in part from the rejection of the politics-administration idea, in which administration was regarded as a technical process separate and insulated from the political process. The administrators were the professionals who carried out the mandates of the politicians. They were to be political eunuchs who exercised no value judgments upon their own; as neutral servants they merely possessed an administrative know-how enabling them to carry out whatever their political masters decided. As seen in Chapter 5, this sharp separation of the decision-makers from the doers is now regarded as unrealistic in business management as well as in public administration.

The revolt against principles by the more theoretical students of administration had emotional roots in the social philosophers' distrust of techniques; the management developments of the twentieth century have been dominantly technical. They were influenced

---

[2] John M. Gaus, Leonard D. White, and Marshall E. Dimock, *The Frontiers of Public Administration* (Chicago: University of Chicago Press, 1936), pp. 13 ff. A best selling text in management is based largely on the statement and explanation of "principles." Harold Koontz and Cyril O'Donnel, *Principles of Management* (New York: McGraw-Hill Book Co., Inc., 1955).

[3] Herbert A. Simon, "The Proverbs of Administration," *Public Administration Review* 6:53-67, Winter 1946.

by industrial engineering in the opening decades of the century and more recently by the emerging electronic communications of mid-century. This domination by people who have largely ignored human values thus was challenged by the social scientists whose interest obviously would run to the human dimension. It is only natural that when the social scientist enters the field of management he should examine it from the viewpoint of his own value standards.

It is extremely important that the contemporary student of organization have this insight because the organization theory of the future will be influenced by the behavioral sciences. The behavioral scientists who enter the management world will bring with them a humanistic value system which cannot but have a profound effect.

III • THE IDEOLOGICAL REVOLUTION

The year 1920 seems a significant date, though perhaps an arbitrary one, to mark the beginning of the ideological revolution in organization theory. It was during the 1920's that the principal researches of the Hawthorne experiment took place, even though results were not published until a decade later. The Hawthorne experiment was basic to the new ideology because it established in the minds of management people the concept of an organization as a social institution. It was also during the 1920's that Kurt Lewin came to this country and began his experimentation at the State University of Iowa. Lewin was in many respects the godfather of the group dynamics movement which has had such profound effect upon the theories of authority and motivation.

The Hawthorne Experiment

Provided respectability. The Hawthorne experiment provided an aura of respectability to the ideological revolution for two reasons: *first,* because it was carried on in a corporate environment, and *second,* because it was sponsored by the Harvard Business School. The Hawthorne plant was (and still is) a manufacturing unit of the Western Electric Company, part of the American

(Bell) Telephone and Telegraph Company system, and certainly among the most respectable of our private enterprises. The experiment had the backing of management, members of which actually participated at the plant level. Management respectability was also gained by the cooperation of the Harvard Business School, under the leadership of Elton Mayo. The book by Roethlisberger and Dickson reporting this experiment still stands as a classic which combines empirical research with a high order of social theory and philosophy.[4]

Two contributions. The two significant contributions of this study to the ideological revolution in organization and management were:

- A challenge to the physical or engineering approach to motivation.
- The first real assault on the purely structural, hierarchical approach to organization.

The experiments showed definitely that people do not respond in any predictable fashion as physical or environmental incentives are applied; i.e., motivation cannot be engineered. The response to piece work incentive is distorted by other factors related to the element of change itself and secondly to the social climate. Studies a quarter century later were to confirm the latter point by showing that supervisory training will not change behavior unless the social climate to which the trainee returns is ready for such change.

The challenge to the purely hierarchical concept of organization was furnished by the demonstration that a factory is a social institution, and that the influence of the supervisory hierarchy is modified or limited by the extent to which the members of the factory society will accept its edicts.[5]

---

[4] F. J. Roethlisberger and W. J. Dickson, *Management and the Worker,* (Cambridge: Harvard University Press, 1939); see also Elton Mayo, *The Social Problems of an Industrial Civilization* (Boston: Harvard Business School, 1945).

[5] It should be noted that the "human relations" movement spawned by the Hawthorne study has itself come under considerable attack. For an excellent statement of the nature of the issues generated, see Henry A. Landsberger, *Hawthorne Revisited* (Ithaca, New York: Cornell University, 1958), particularly Chapters 3 and 4.

Leadership

The new concepts of authority and the group dynamics movement, together with the advent of widespread collective bargaining, have occasioned a new approach to leadership. The old authoritarianism permitted of no questioning or talking back to the boss. Furthermore, the former concepts of motivation were based upon what Elton Mayo called the *rabble hypothesis*, namely that people are animalistic in their individual drives for a share of the world's scarce goods. It followed that only a forceful driving type of leadership could keep them in their proper position. Otherwise the slothful would not work and the over-ambitious would take more than their share. Today the group-centered concepts of leadership and authority call for a type of leadership which will stimulate group as well as individual response. The result is that most supervisory training tries to condition supervisors to behave as though they were group leaders rather than to drive with the whip.

It should be said in passing that the new sociological concepts of group process do not go unchallenged. This is evidenced by such criticisms as those of William H. Whyte, Jr., who in *The Organization Man* decries the possible adverse effect of group values upon our supply of future strong leaders.[6] The new procedure of making decisions by groups is charged with inhibiting the emergence of the risk-taking, free-wheeling entrepreneur of the past. There is also some apprehension that the emphasis upon group process will increase the tendencies toward conformity in a society which is alleged to be magnifying the pressures against individualism.

Decision Theory

Another break with traditionalism in the last twenty years has arisen from a new emphasis upon decision theory. Simon, following Barnard, regards the decision, or rather the points at which decisions are made, as representing the actual outline or structure

---

[6] William H. Whyte, Jr., *The Organization Man* (New York: Simon and Schuster, 1956), later republished in paper covers by Anchor Books.

of the organization.[7] It has now become a mark of sophistication among organization theorists to refer to decision-making and the decision process, a subject seldom if ever heard in the literature of traditionalism. While decision theory is still in an embryonic state, the student of organization can expect to hear a great deal more of it in the future, especially in view of the emphasis being placed upon decentralization, group process, and delegation. Under traditionalism there was no question about where decisions were made. They were the prerogatives of the man at the top, subject to minor processing decisions by his subordinates in the chain of command. It is now suggested that the decision-making process is much more subtle and complex than that.

The Planning Renaissance

It may be difficult for members of the present generation to understand the opprobrium in which the words planning and control were held even a quarter century ago. The economics of the market place and the ideology of the uninhibited free price system were so deeply ingrained in the American ethos that planning had become virtually a subversive word. This spirit of individualism and of unrestrained economic enterprise was useful in developing an unexploited continent. When it came to an end with the vanishing of the frontier, on the one hand, and the catapulting of the United States into world leadership, on the other, we were forced to plan for resources which were no longer present in abundance. Thus, lumber companies are maintaining vast tree farms which will not yield marketable timber for over half a century and steel companies must go to Labrador and Venezuela for raw material. A nation which previously took its wars in stride without a professional military establishment has been forced into strategic planning by the threat of international communism.

Every large-scale organization today, whether public or private, utilizes planning as a natural process. There has been a tremendous emphasis upon staff work. The troubled condition of world affairs has forced our national government into world planning and the population explosion has compelled state governments to plan high-

---

[7] See Chapter 21, "The Decision."

ways and city governments to struggle with rebuilding of deteriorated downtown sections.

Co-plan. Planning is such an all-pervading influence in the organization processes of today that we have felt obliged to coin a new word, namely co-plan. Planners of today are not isolated "pure" staff people who dream up ideas in their own ivory towers, although there is some of that and it is very necessary. The planning to which we refer is an integral part of the whole production process in which the planners are in constant contact and association with line people. That is where the "co" part of our coined word comes in: communication, coordination, consultation and control. Planning is wired into the communication and decision networks described in Chapter 2. Control is here used in the sense of feedback (see below) rather than in its more traditional connotation of coercion. The principles of such control have long been known but what is new is the information revolution brought about by technical progress in the electronic processing of data.

The information revolution. Control as the communication of information about organizational operations and accomplishments was discussed by Fayol early in the century, and Holden, Fish, and Smith emphasized it about 1940.[8] The principal technical advance resulting from the information revolution is the fact that it is now possible for a headquarters establishment in Chicago, New York, or Washington to receive production data pertaining to the previous day's business and have it upon the executives' desks at the beginning of business the next day. It has long been possible to communicate such data over long distances but now we are able to analyze these data by means of the new electronic computing machines, and also to highlight the most pertinent points in such a manner as to draw immediate attention to danger spots. This is where control and feedback come in.

Cybernetics. The discipline of cybernetics has made two ideological contributions to the theory of organization.[9]

---

[8] Henri Fayol, *General and Industrial Management* (London: Pitman, 1949); Paul E. Holden, Lounsbury S. Fish, and Hubert Smith, *Top Management Organization and Control* (New York: McGraw-Hill Book Co. Inc., 1951).

[9] That this terminology is beginning to enter the literature is illustrated in Kenneth E. Boulding, "Evidences of an Administrative Science," *Administrative Science Quarterly* 3:1-22, June 1958; on page 12 he refers to the "cybernetic model" as a "great step forward in organization theory."

The first contribution is to relate the information and control patterns of organizations to that of the new automatic machines. In these machines the goals and patterns of performance are set by the minds and hands of man, but electronic controls keep the machines on the "paths of righteousness." This results from a combination of planning, communication, and decision similar to that which goes on in an organization. The decision centers plan and establish tolerances within which performance is acceptable. The performers communicate their accomplishments back to the decision centers but the deciders are alerted only when corrections need to be made. This is the time-honored "exception principle" of management theory. Only that data which is needed for corrective decision is fed to the executive or manager.

The other contribution of cybernetics pertinent to organization theory has to do with biological analogy. The human brain is the planning and decision center which communicates goals and directives through the nervous system to other parts of the body. These in turn communicate back their accomplishments which lead to new messages from the brain to continue, adjust, or discontinue the initial action.

Thus control through feedback is a circular process; and this give-and-take of goal setting, communication, and continuous correction is not only the essence of feedback but also comprises the heart of coordination in large scale organizations. Insofar as the metamorphosis of organization theory is concerned, it is probable that we have only begun to see the impact of these new information developments and ideas on our traditional ways of doing things.

Studies of Bureaucracy

Whereas students of the traditional concepts of organization have become familiar with such names as Mooney, Gulick, Fayol, Urwick, and others, the sociologists have until recently concentrated their attention on the model suggested by Max Weber and described briefly in Chapter 4. Their interest, however, has not been so much in refining the model as it has been in testing the hypothesis which lay behind it. Weber, it will be recalled, believed that his model of bureaucracy was the most rational means of attaining certain ends in the society.

Rather strikingly, the interest of American sociologists in this hypothesis appeared to develop at about the same time that big government of the post 1933 period became a part of the national landscape. Many organizations were being created in rough accord with the Weberian notion and yet they behaved on numerous occasions in an apparently most irrational fashion. Thus the sociologists became interested in discovering what the "unanticipated consequences" of bureaucratic organization were.[10]

In general they have discovered that Weber's single dimensional view of organization has all the limitations one might expect of any failure to see such social institutions in their total context. It has been found that many of the organization's prescribed goals have been accomplished but in the process other events have also occured. In many instances these unanticipated consequences have appeared to be antipathetic to the prescribed goals of the organization. Thus the sociologists have suggested a fundamental problem: the attempt to pursue one goal rationally may result in the unleashing of social forces which may result in irrational behavior patterns relevant to the accomplishment of other organization goals. Furthermore, there is evidence that the natural bureaucratic response, on the part of leaders and participants, is to tighten controls and become even more rigid in adherence to prescribed patterns of behavior as threats occur.

As a consequence of such studies and analyses, it has become increasingly clear that the traditionalism of the past, whatever its impetus, has been far too limited in view. The sociologists have been important in the revolt against such traditionalism by providing empirical evidence that the problems of human behavior in large-scale organizations stem from the operations of sub-systems

---

[10] Among the important pioneer works in this field are: Robert Merton, "Bureaucratic Structure and Personality," *Social Forces* 18:560-568, May 1940; Philip Selznick, *TVA and the Grass Roots* (Berkeley: University of California Press, 1949); Reinhard Bendix, "Bureaucracy: the Problem and Its Setting," *American Sociological Review*, 12:493-507, October 1947; Alvin W. Gouldner, *Patterns of Industrial Bureaucracy* (Glencoe, Ill.: The Free Press, 1954), and Peter M. Blau, *The Dynamics of Bureaucracy* (Chicago: University of Chicago Press, 1955).

TRENDS IN ORGANIZATION THEORY

A Quick View

From	To
Traditionalism	Social Dynamics
Job-Task Hierarchy	Social Process
Efficiency as a Mechanical Process	Efficiency as a Human Process
Organization as a Bureaucratic Structure	Organization as a Social Institution
Control through Command	Control through Communication
Authority from the Top Down	Authority from the Group
Leadership by Authority	Leadership by Consent
Decision as an Individual, Highly Centralized Act	Decisions as Collegial, Situational
Regimented Work Environment	Democratic Work Environment
Technological Change by Fiat	Technological Change by Consultation
Social *or* Financial Incentive	Social *and* Financial Incentives
Job as Subsistence	Job as Satisfying Experience
Planning as Crisis Technique	Planning as Formalized Process
Incomplete and Delayed Information	Complete and Current Information
Policy and Administration Dichotomy	Policy and Administration Continuum
Profit with Buccaneering	Profit with Social Responsibility

SOURCE: Developed by Emery E. Olson on the basis of materials prepared by John M. Pfiffner. Some modifications have been made by the authors.

within the total. They have indicated "the ways in which the needs of individuals, the primary work group, and the large organization interact to affect each other." [11]

IV • SUMMARY

In earlier chapters we saw that present thinking—and certainly the emphasis of this book—tends to conceive of the organization as a total social entity. Yet we found in Chapter 4 that most of

[11] James G. March and Hubert A. Simon, *Organizations* (New York: John Wiley and Sons, Inc., 1958), p. 47.

the early literature concentrated on the formal, authoritarian aspects of organization. By the very nature of things, then, it was inevitable that a reaction would develop to this single-dimensional view of a process which is so obviously complicated.

To recapitulate, traditional organization theory tended to "dehumanize" the individual by assuming that one man was pretty much the same as another. Any minor differences would cancel themselves out. Secondly, it leaned heavily on the marketplace theory that man would rationally pursue his own self-interest. Thus, to get more production was to boost the payoff. Thirdly, a single standard of value, variously known as efficiency or productivity, pervaded the literature.

A tremendous number of variables which serve to complicate organization behavior were thereby removed from consideration by the traditionalists, in whose picture there was also implicit the expectation that anyone who deviated from the simplified picture established should be dealt with summarily. This was the heart of managerial prerogative.

The conflict that developed centered in very considerable part on the question of "principles," but implicit were the assumptions noted in the previous paragraphs. The principles, it was discovered, only had predictive value when nearly all the key variables in organizational behavior were excluded. Any new theory therefore had to comprehend the totality of organization as a social organism.

In some respects it might be said that the ideological revolt which developed was fed largely by the social scientists' discovery of organization as an intriguing area of inquiry. The management revolution of the twentieth century had been dominantly technical; and the persons who propounded the theorems and the principles were largely engineering-oriented. When social scientists began to involve themselves, they brought with them a philosophical bias rooted in the dignity of the human being. Thus we find an important change in research focus. The Hawthorne studies are one important manifestation of this. They are important for having (1) challenged the physical or engineering approach to motivation; and (2) made the first real assault on the purely structural, hierarchical approach to organization.

Other facets of this general trend appeared in new concepts of authority, in motivation research, in decision theory, and in analysis of leadership behavior. Studies of bureaucracy, which have been particularly undertaken by the sociologists, have assumed importance because they sought to identify the "unanticipated consequences" of so-called rational patterns of organization. What has been found is that pursuance of one goal in a rational manner may trigger all types of irrational behavior with reference to other goals.

Part Two

ORGANIZATION STRUCTURE

SEVEN

Specialization and Work Division

What to Look for in This Chapter . . .

Traditional structuring of organizations on a twofold basis
- Division of work
- Integration of work

Grouping of activities—basic process in structuring
- Effects of technological change on groupings
- Struggle for status in grouping
- "Adjective" tasks increase

Individual jobs and work division

The metamorphosis of organization theory has been particularly successful in planting seeds of doubt about traditional concepts; it has been somewhat less successful in coming up with a systematic theory which embodies all the variables operative in the organizational situation. Obviously there have been a number of proposals for that theory. Yet we are far from consensus; and indeed it may be that this is too much to expect. As a matter of fact our knowledge of organizations may be so sophisticated that we never again will see a comprehensive theory acceptable to a major portion of the students of the subject. As with social theory generally, there are a number of different perspectives from which these complicated processes may be approached.

As one perspective, the theoretical orientation of the traditionalist is useful. Although it is structural and mechanical to a considerable degree, it provides a generally understood point of departure for further elaborations of organizational behavior. This traditional frame of reference appears to have two essential elements:

- The division of work into its most economic parts; that is, pursuant to the ideal of task specialization which has been so central to managerial philosophy.
- The patterns of integrating the voluminous behaviors and actions of the specializations into one combined effort.

Sargent and Belisle have explained these two reference points in traditional organization theory in the following terms:

> . . . the primary principles . . . might be identified as *specialization* on the one hand and *coordination* on the other. The application of the scientific method, in terms of observation, data gathering, analysis and measurement, test, hypothesis and experiment, depended upon using and developing *specialists*. The findings then needed to be organized, applied and coordinated. It might be further noted that, of the two principles, specialization sprang from science above and beyond the necessity for the division of responsibilities in the organization, while coordination sprang exclusively from the necessities of the organization of human effort.[1]

Drucker has used the same theoretical framework in describing one of the major production feats of World War II.[2] Those were days when the United States was desperately short of airplanes, including a carrier based type needed by the Navy. At the time of Pearl Harbor only one test model existed; and it had been hand-built. The Navy needed thousands as quickly as possible. One of the large industrial organizations of the United States took on

---

[1] Cyril G. Sargent and Eugene L. Belisle, *Educational Administration: Cases and Concepts* (Boston: Houghton Mifflin Company, 1955), p. 433.

[2] Peter Drucker, "The New Society, I: Revolution by Mass Production," *Harper's Magazine* 199:21-30, September 1949.

the task of making these planes—a job which could not have been done by the small firm which originated the plane.

What separated the large from the small was not size so much as it was production organization know-how, that is the ability to break down the complex job of building an airplane into its individual economic parts and then to relate each of these specialized operations in such a way as to end up with a completed airplane. Drucker describes the following planning steps: (a) analysis of the plane; (b) breakdown of the plane into component parts; (c) breakdown of sub-assemblies into individual operations and motions; and (d) reintegration of operations into sub-assemblies, sub-assemblies into parts, parts into planes. Thus, "it was work done entirely on paper—with some hundred tons of blueprints as the final yield—and it was done *entirely on the basis of general principles*," Drucker notes.[3] So skilled were the planners that five weeks after the final blueprints had been made, the plant was operating at its full production rate of 6,000 planes per year.

Because of the continued applicability and hence importance of these traditional concepts, therefore, it has seemed appropriate to use them as the primary orienting point for a major section of this book. This and the following three chapters particularly fall within this well-established frame of reference.

In this chapter we shall look at the general problem of dividing work at the broad organization level.

In Chapter 8 the concept of layers in organization will be discussed. Here it will be noted that such layering suggests another dimension of specialization as it is viewed from the top down and of integration as it is viewed from the bottom up.

Chapter 9 will deal primarily with the broad problem of organization integration, particularly focussing on the concept of span of control. Finally in Chapter 10 the development of staff and functional specialization as a means of bringing about organization integration will be reviewed. The remaining chapters of the section will also be directed along structural lines and will consider such matters as decentralization, formalization, and organization planning.

One caveat deserves re-emphasis. We follow some of the tradi-

---

[3] *Ibid.*, p. 24.

tional concepts of organization in this section because they seem as useful a means as is available for categorizing the knowledge we presently have about certain aspects of organizations. No suggestion is made that this the only way of organizing such knowledge. Neither is there in the use of such a framework any suggestion of a prescription or dogmatic guideline for the eager person who wants "answers" to all his organizational dilemmas.

I • GROUPING OF ACTIVITIES AS A BASIC STRUCTURING PROCESS

Work Division and Grouping

Whenever a job involves more than one operation, or more than one person, there will be different possible ways of grouping the operations and the operators. The grouping may be extremely primitive, as in the case of the shoe factory whose only subdivision was between those who made men's shoes and those who made women's, or it may be very complex, as in the case of nearly all manufacturing and processing operations in our society.

Importance of system. Since grouping is inevitable in organizations, it is important that it occur according to plan, and not be allowed to grow fortuitously. The basic values of systematic grouping are those of coordination, as can be illustrated by a domestic example. Suppose a parent, having assigned each child the task of cleaning his own room, also assigns an older one that of vacuuming the entire house. Does he have to "do" the rooms of the other children, too? That requires a separate parental decision, because natural and easily definable boundaries have not been set up.

The object of grouping and organizational structuring according to a system is to reduce these special interventions to a minimum, so that, as much as possible, coordination occurs automatically. In the example, tasks were not classified systematically. For the children generally, a geographical boundary was assigned; for the older one, a work process boundary.

Centrifugal tendencies. Added importance is given to the factor of natural, self-regulating coordination by the contrary tendency of groups in an organization to become separated from one another and from the central lines of authority. Centrifugal forces in groups seem to be associated with their self-preservation; the forces in a group that resist change and aim at the status quo also tend to find ways of isolating themselves from the rest of the organization. An exciting example of this is set forth in Dalton's case study of a regional branch of an industrial firm where local management deliberately set up dummy staff units for the purpose of hoodwinking headquarters, protecting privileged empires, and resisting coordination from above.[4]

The thrust for autonomy in a group naturally interferes with the need for *centripetal,* uniting forces of coordination and control. Since these forces often require changes, existing groupings, in preventing change, find it sometimes necessary to set up mechanisms to prevent accurate information from ever being obtained. An outstanding example is the well-known difficulty of coordinating the bureaus in the great executive departments of the federal government, but the problem is not at all absent from industrial affairs. In the late 1950's the general slump in the electrical appliance industry necessitated an overhauling of the hierarchical structure of the Philco Radio Corporation. Investigation disclosed excessive autonomy in its divisions, so that reorganization was possible only by reducing their number and integrating them with new lines of coordination.[5]

Classification approaches. Grouping as a centripetal force is at the heart of (1) span of control, (2) unity of command, (3) the structuring of official authority, and (4) maintenance of channels of communication. Its relevance to them derives, as we have noted, from the need for grouping of work divisions to take place in a systematic and orderly way. The process of classifying work groups systematically, it should be noted, may proceed from the whole to the parts, or from the parts to the whole. Whether the subject be viewed as a *macrocosm* (beginning with the whole) or as a *microcosm* (beginning with the parts), depends on its nature and the purposes of the study. A living organism, for ex-

---

[4] Melville Dalton, "Managing the Managers," *Human Organization* 14:4-10, Fall 1955.

[5] Edward T. Thompson, "The Upheaval at Philco," *Fortune* 59:113-116, 206 f, February 1959.

ample, cannot be separated without depriving it of the essential characteristic of life; therefore living things are studied as a whole before the attempt is made to distinguish and classify their parts. The animal kingdom as a whole, however, cannot be considered all together, so that classifying its larger groups must wait until the smaller ones have been appropriately compared.

The proper approach to classifying and grouping organizations has been much debated, probably because the solution is not so clear cut as it is in the previous cases. Governmental reorganization schemes have usually proceeded from whole to part: beginning with a regrouping at the top to conform to some desired new system of coordination for the highest executive levels, and then and only then deciding how best to fit smaller units into the over-all scheme. Basic industrial reorganization, on the other hand, cannot take place effectively until each necessary task has been worked out in detail; when all the microrequirements are known, then the best ways of coordinating them can be worked out.[6]

In this chapter we shall be dealing mainly with the groupings depicted in official charts and manuals—the broad macrocosmic arrangements of organizations. Microcosmic classifications—the province of the industrial engineer and the time-study specialist—will however concern us somewhat later in the chapter.

Two rules for classifying. It is important to remember that work division and grouping is far from the precision of an exact science. It is perhaps best to consider it as both art and science; as the latter, it has evolved certain broad norms to guide it reliably, but as the former, all procedures must be flexible and defer to judgments that cannot be justified rigorously by the norms. With that in mind we list two rules that are most commonly followed:

- Be consistent in following a single guide, or basis, of classification.
- Make your categories mutually exclusive—that is, set up your classification system in such a way that any particular part will fit in only one niche.

---

[6] For the manner in which industrial management consultants approach a reorganization problem, see *Management Survey of Activities of the Veterans Administration by the Firm of Booz-Allen-Hamilton,* 82nd Congress, 2nd Session, House Committee Print No. 322, (Washington, D.C.: Government Printing Office, 1952).

Basic Concepts of Grouping

Gulick's essay. Luther Gulick's essay on the theory of organizing stands as a classic in this field.[7] He says that every individual worker can be characterized by:

- The major *purpose* he is serving, such as furnishing water, controlling crime, or conducting education;
- The *process* he is using, such as engineering, medicine, carpentry, stenography, statistics, accounting;
- The *persons* or *things* dealt with or served, such as immigrants, veterans, Indians, forests, mines, parks, orphans, farmers, automobiles, or the poor;
- The *place* where he renders his service, such as Hawaii, Boston, Washington, the Dust Bowl, Alabama, or Central High School.[8]

Gulick goes on to point out that departments organized on the basis of general purpose may also have subgroupings on the basis of *process,* particularly such management processes as clerical, finance, personnel and supply.[9]

Newman's elaboration. The basic approaches are similar in government and industry, as pointed out by Newman, who cites Gulick.[10] Newman lists the following bases for grouping: products or services, locations, customers, processes, and functions. He states that most schemes of departmentation are a composite of several of these, but goes on to say that there is no ideal pattern to suit all occasions and situations. The organizer must take into consideration the peculiar circumstances of his firm. However, Newman does list and discuss in some detail what he calls key factors in departmentation. They are as follows:

- Take advantage of specialization
- Facilitate control

---

[7] Luther Gulick, "Notes on the Theory of Organization," in Gulick and L. Urwick, *Papers on the Science of Administration* (New York: Institute of Public Administration, 1937), pp. 1-45.

[8] *Ibid.,* p. 15.

[9] This he depicts graphically on p. 17.

[10] William H. Newman, *Administrative Action: The Techniques of Organization and Management* (Englewood Cliffs, N.J.: Prentice-Hall, Inc., 1951), pp 125 ff.

- Aid in coordination
- Secure adequate attention
- Recognize local conditions
- Reduce expense

Program, Purpose, and Function in Grouping

As is the case with most areas of management, the grouping of tasks suffers from ambiguous terminology. Take the word "function," for instance. As a verb, "to function" means to perform, to operate, to carry on. As a noun, it has a technical meaning in mathematics. In organization a function has such variable meanings that one can seldom be sure of its use. In one sense it is applied to an over-all general purpose such as law enforcement or fire protection; in another application it means a specialized process, such as welding, key punching, or typing. In general, however, when an activity is described as "functional" the connotation is that of specialization: *functional* supervisors, following Taylor's terminology, are technical staff people who have specialized knowledge and skill.

Unifunctionalism. It is frequently stated that the principal organization subunits should be unifunctional in nature. In governmental reorganization this means that activities should be grouped into a few major departments, each of which is concerned with a single over-all objective or general purpose. Examples are law enforcement, public health, education, and public welfare. In a farm machinery company it could be tractors, plows, and reapers, although some would call this organizing by product. Some federal departments have been referred to as "holding companies" because they house diverse activities; the Department of Commerce includes, for instance, subdivisions for aeronautics, patents, weather, and the Bureau of Standards.

The Booz, Allen, and Hamilton report on the Veterans Administration recommended that the major subunits be established on the basis of product or program, terming it a "program-department type of organization." [11] These consisted of five operating departments to correspond to the five fundamental benefits afforded to

---

[11] *Management Survey of Activities of the Veterans Administration,* p. 21.

veterans: medical, insurance, vocational rehabilitation, loan-guaranty, and claims.

Process and Function in Grouping

The question of whether general purpose departments should have process units of their own keeps recurring in most reorganization studies. Perhaps the most familiar examples are posed by stenographic or motor pools. Strong arguments for economy can often be advanced and substantiated in favor of such separate process departments. One should hasten to say that the process designation applies not only to such pedestrian tasks as stenography and automotive services, but also to such highly professionalized "processes" as medicine, finance, and engineering. Should a general purpose department be required to patronize a central process unit for such services, or should it have its own physicians, accountants, and engineers? Contention often arises when an attempt is made to require purpose departments to patronize central duplicating and mimeographing services.

Again the only generalization which seems to bear up is that such determinations should be made upon the basis of studying the variables in the local situation. The economies to be realized by centralizing process activities may be offset by the greater possibilities for coordination and accomplishment of mission if the purpose agencies are allowed to have their own.[12] There are strong arguments for organizing purpose departments so that they will be self-contained, subject of course to functional coordination from above.

This latter point raises a question about the organization of legal services which will be discussed here briefly, and more fully below, in the chapter on decentralization. Let us suppose that there is the office of corporation counsel at the corporate level, but that there are also lawyers on the staffs of the general purpose department heads, and perhaps even on the subordinate echelons. Should the lawyers in the departments have a direct responsibility relationship to the department head or to the corporation counsel? A parallel study of industrial controllers seemed to conclude that

---

[12] James G. March and Herbert A. Simon, *Organizations* (New York: John Wiley & Sons, Inc., 1958), p. 29.

some companies had worked out a satisfactory *modus operandi* which virtually amounted to dual responsibility.[13] The accounting units at subordinate echelons operated in such a manner that they "belonged" to the factory managers while still subject to supervision from the corporation controller.

II • SPECIAL PROBLEMS OF WORK DIVISION AND GROUPING

Relationship Between Hierarchy and Process

The concept of organization as being dominantly vertical and hierarchical is being subjected to some questioning. As we have seen, a number of factors are causing this reassessment. But it is interesting that a purely technical factor has also brought the matter to the fore. Modern production processes tend to flow horizontally, and to cut across vertical structuring of authority. This is particularly true of assembly line operations where the work flows through the jurisdictions of a number of foremen. A recent study points out that there is much bickering between foremen on the automobile assembly line who are in direct contact with each other. They are so apprehensive of the higher command levels of the traditional hierarchy that the settling of disputes at the level dictated by technology is not possible.[14]

Whyte's study of restaurants showed that, even in such a traditional organization, the work flow also cuts across vertical channels of authority. While the waitress is administratively responsible to the hostess, her most immediate and irritating relationships are with the counterman and customer. In many industrial activities the maintenance people in an area are under different supervisors than those engaged in direct production, and the same is true of those who furnish materials to the productive processes. The spectre of hierarchy has been so strong that traditional concepts of formal organization have not yet been adapted to the needs of

[13] Herbert A. Simon *et al.*, *Centralization versus Decentralization in Organizing the Controller's Department* (New York: Controllership Foundation, 1954). See Chapter 21.

[14] Frank J. Jasinski, "*Adapting Organization to New Technology*," *Harvard Business Review* 37:79-86, January-February 1959.

the new technology. The result is that horizontal coordination has been brought about by the growth of informal relationships which get the job done.

The question arises as to whether or not we may have reached the point where a restatement of organization concepts is due. One author has suggested the following steps to be taken to ameliorate the problem in particular situations:

1. Examine the work flow of the technology to determine what relations are required.
2. Identify the points where the formal organization meets these requirements and where it does not.
3. Discover what nonformal relationships exist at present to meet the technologically required relations which are not encompassed by the formal organization.
4. Determine what formalization does exist to cope with relations falling beyond the traditional vertical planes.
5. Decide which of the nonformal relations might be profitably formalized.
6. Provide measures to facilitate the nonformal relations which are still required but which may best remain nonformal.[15]

The Struggle for Status

The members of a vocation tend to constitute a social in-group which becomes organizationally myopic; that is, they view organization decisions from the standpoint of their effect upon the fortunes of their vocations. If each specialty could have its way, it would be in a separate department, thus increasing infinitely the number of units on the same echelon. This is one reason why one so often hears emotional outbursts against organization charts and the management consultants who want to streamline organizations.

Three reasons. There are three principal reasons why vocational groups want to have departments of their own:

First, they want attention—to avoid being lost in the maze. They want to report directly to the chief executive officer in the first instance without going through intervening echelons. On the national level an example is the effort of educators who have lobbied for many years—so far unsuccessfully—for a separate department of education with cabinet rank, instead of a present first-echelon

[15] *Ibid.*, p. 86.

status in the holding-company Department of Health, Education, and Welfare.[16]

This tendency may be accentuated in government where pressure group politics have freer play, but it is not absent in voluntary and industrial organizations. The more obvious examples in the latter have to do with staff services, such as personnel and training. There is a tendency to group such activities as personnel, salary administration, training, industrial relations, and organization planning under a vice-president for administration. Training staffs have sometimes wanted independent status because they thought they could obtain greater acceptance of training if they were not associated with the negative and repressive control aspects of the personnel unit. They also felt that training would receive greater prestige by being associated with the top echelon.

This brings us to the *second* factor making for a large number of departments, namely the desire for status and prestige.

This second factor of group pride is directly connected with the *third,* which is inter-vocational conflict. We should not overlook the empire builders who utilize the fundamental human motivations of pride and loyalty to one's calling in order to resist being combined with another department.

Examples of conflict. More difficult to explain is the antagonism which often prevails between groups which would seem to have similar vocational objectives and background. Two examples may be noted which involve traditional antagonisms. In each case attempts at federal reorganization have been successfully resisted. One concerns the Forest Service of the Department of Agriculture. It administers large sections of the public lands, as do several units in the Department of Interior. Yet proposals that the Forest Service should be transferred to Interior arouse emotional opposition on the part of Forest Service personnel. The same situation applies to the Corps of Army Engineers and the Bureau of Reclamation of the Department of Interior, each of which builds and operates large hydroelectric projects, sometimes at the same site with carefully demarcated jurisdictions, as at Bonneville, Oregon.

---

[16] How bitter feeling can become is illustrated by the resistance of the educationists to having their library integrated into a departmental library. Harold Stein, editor, *Public Administration and Policy Development* (New York: Harcourt, Brace and Company, 1952), p. 31.

III • ADJECTIVE TASKS AS AN ASPECT OF WORK DIVISION

As an illustration in support of his famous "law," Parkinson pointed out that during the period 1914 to 1928 the number of ships in service in the British Navy had *decreased* by two-thirds and the military personnel by one-third. The total of blue-collar civilians who maintained the ships remained fairly constant with about a ten per cent increase, but the shipyard officials and clerks *increased* by 40 per cent and the officials at departmental headquarters by 78 per cent.[17] Parkinson went on to state the pertinent law, which runs to the effect that the number of workers increases irrespective of the work to be done, that superiors create subordinate positions to enhance their own status, and that people in an expanding organization create unneeded tasks for each other.

Increase in "Adjective" Tasks

The point in Parkinson's law which concerns us here has to do with the increase in the proportion of indirect to direct workers. In short, there has been an increase in "adjective" tasks. The word "adjective" describes these indirect types of activities and is taken from jurisprudence, wherein a distinction is made between substantive and adjective law, the latter being in a sense a synonym for "procedural." American large-scale organization has been increasing the adjective tasks while the substantive or direct jobs have been remaining fairly constant. This is demonstrated by the revolution that has taken place in the composition of American society since World War II. During that period the professional, managerial and technical labor force increased by approximately two-thirds, at the same time becoming one-fifth of the working force. While this was going on the number of blue-collar workers remained fairly constant.[18]

Labor statistics. The Bureau of Labor Statistics reported sig-

[17] C. Northcote Parkinson, *Parkinson's Law* (Boston: Houghton Mifflin Co., 1957), p. 39.

[18] Reece McGee, "White Collar Explosion," *The Nation* 188:112-115, February 7, 1959.

nificant increases in the number of persons employed in professional, clerical, sales, and administrative jobs during the decade 1947–1957. At the end of the decade they accounted for 42 per cent of all persons in the civilian labor force, and during the specified decade the rate of growth for nonproduction workers was fifteen times as great as for those in direct production.[19]

These new managerial, technical, and professional workers constitute an intellectual class in that they are educated, many of them having graduate degrees. They work for great corporations; they are propertyless in the sense that their incomes derive from salaries rather than ownership; and they tend to be mobile, meaning that they move from one corporate installation to another. The revolutionary feature of this phenomenon may well be that their "services involve primarily the manipulation of ideas and abstract concepts rather than machines or materials." [20]

A task revolution. It is this latter point which is significant to the study of organization. Along with the revolution which is taking place in social structure, there has been a corresponding revolution in texture of tasks performed. Today one can hardly pick up a management periodical without finding an article on research and development ("R & D"). Industry is combing the universities for their brains and luring away many of the most promising potential teachers of the future. This is not happening in the areas of engineering and natural science alone. There is the case of the young assistant professor of English with a growing family who felt compelled to become a technical writer in a factory at double his academic pay. Also there comes to mind the chairman of a department of philosophy who had on his desk a half dozen inquiries for Ph.D.'s in philosophy who were needed as logician-programmers for automatic data processing.

Nature of Adjective Tasks

Excursion into terminology. We have used the word "adjective" in order to find a catch-all designation for those tasks often referred to as indirect labor, which has been defined as "labor

---

[19] "Nonproductive Workers in Factories," *Monthly Labor Review* 80:435-440, April 1957.

[20] McGee, *loc. cit.*

which is not engaged in changing the form of the product directly or in creating any other customer utility. . . ."[21] Whatever term we employ, however, we should recognize that all such labels are being used to distinguish between those activities which directly contribute to the accomplishment of stated goals and those which support such efforts. Very often we find the term "staff" used to characterize these supportive activities; but it has developed so many meanings as to lose much of its usefulness. While Chapter 10 will be devoted to staff activities and will consider these questions in detail, it seems desirable at this point to make a preliminary foray into this jungle of terminology.

A limited usage of the word "staff" refers to those activities, advisory in nature, which have to do mainly with specialized intellectual activity. Staff is often distinguished from line in that the latter has command functions while the former does not. Nevertheless, staff people are closely associated with production and exercise the authority of expertise which frequently falls little short of command. Another term for the latter is "functional" supervision, using functional in Taylor's sense of being specialized. Functional supervisors are sometimes referred to as technical staff.

Auxiliary or service activities. There is a special type of staff activity coordinative in nature, often referred to as "auxiliary" or "service" activities. These include finance, personnel, supply and maintenance of physical plant, and transportation. In an American industrial corporation they may be grouped together under a vice-president for administration. As will be pointed out in Chapter 12, organization planning is becoming one of his principal responsibilities. British public administration refers to the whole group as "establishment" services, while in American public administration the terms "business" and "administrative" are often utilized. From the standpoint of hierarchical structure the main problems connected with these staff services have to do with: (1) centralization versus decentralization, and (2) their relations to the line departments, matters that are discussed in later chapters.

---

[21] Alton W. Baker and Ralph C. David, *Ratios of Staff to Line Employees and Stages of Differentiation of Staff Functions* (Columbus: Ohio State University Bureau of Business Research, 1954), p. 3.

The Relation to Division of Work

The reason for going into some discussion of the various types of "adjective" tasks springs from the perennial speculation as to whether they are increasing too rapidly. The almost instantaneous response to Parkinson's Law when it was first published in the London *Economist* testifies to rather universal apprehensions concerning the burgeoning of bureaucracy. But industrial managers are not without their own anxieties relative to the growth of adjective activities in their own bailiwicks. For the direct production activities they have the broad guides of measured work, but for the other activities they have only the over-all measures of profit and loss. They have a vague suspicion that Parkinson's Law may be at work in their organizations, especially in times of prosperity when economizing pressures are in the background.

One index which tends to allay such apprehensions is the trend in national productivity, which continues to rise both absolutely and per worker. Moreover, it is an accepted fact that automation brings about a decrease in direct production workers and an increase in the engineering, technical, and managerial tasks. This may have been the principal factor in the rise of unemployment early in 1959, when total national production was on the increase. The point is also made that employment is more stable for the new managerial-technical jobs than for the blue-collar, because the former deal with long-term plans which are not affected by short-term oscillation of the business cycle.

IV • A FURTHER LOOK AT THE JOB AS AN ASPECT OF WORK DIVISION

It has been pointed out that the division and grouping of work within an organization can start either at the top or the bottom. The bulk of this chapter has been devoted to the "top-down" approach because this is the perspective which most frequently concerns organization theory. Nevertheless the *microcosmic* view is also important; and it is in this area that scientific management has made the significant contribution.

Importance of Scientific Management

Scientific management has emphasized the division of work into its irreducible elements, much as has been done by the scientists in classifying physical phenomena.

Therbligs. At one time it was thought that there was "one best way" to perform every operation, and the objective of the analyst was to search for it. This was accomplished by breaking the operation down into simple movements which were called therbligs, examples of which are search, find, select, and grasp, among many others. These movements are timed by a stopwatch, thus leading to the setting of a standard time. From an organization standpoint this breakdown of work into simple movements and operations has been the basis for the assembly line. When coupled with the concept of interchangeable parts and the moving line, specialization reaches the point that a particular operative can confine his activities to one or two simple operations, often merely tending a machine. After he has finished his unitary task, the piece is transported to the next operator who does something else to it.

The origin of the assembly line method of production on its modern large scale is often popularly attributed to Henry Ford, but there is a story to the effect that Eli Whitney, inventor of the cotton gin, utilized it in the manufacture of rifles in a government arsenal many years before.

Methods-time-measurement. While the work of Taylor and Gilbreth took place at the opening of the twentieth century, a more recent development is an attempt to develop not only universal therbligs, but universal time standards for jobs. A well-known venture in this direction is *Methods-Time-Measurement.*[22] Two principal difficulties have been encountered in traditional time and motion study. One is that it is not economical for small organizations and for jobs that do not last long enough. The cost of making the study is too great. Another is the resistance and opposition encountered from both workers and supervisors, not to mention union difficulties, when making the study.

Methods-Time-Measurement attempts to overcome these obsta-

---

[22] Harold B. Maynard, G. J. Stegemerten, and John L. Schwab. *Methods-Time-Measurement* (New York: McGraw-Hill Book Co., Inc., 1948).

cles by establishing prefigured time standards. They have been standardized by studying the time required for the same motions (therbligs) in a large enough sample under varying conditions to be statistically significant. The next step is to train the line organization in methods so that a foreman can lay out the job, designating the motions required and their sequence. This has the advantage of involving the line organization in the setting of standards, and it is said that arguments are largely avoided. When they do occur, they deal with what motions are necessary rather than how much time is required. Given the motion sequence, those writing the job instructions can refer to the standard time tables and come up with expected standards.

Job Enlargement

Modern industrial psychology has established that one of the greatest needs is to find ways to motivate the people who work at these simple repetitive tasks. They become "frozen" in the sense that their work is merely to be endured as a means for receiving a pay check. They receive no satisfaction from the work itself; most of them have achieved their job ceilings, and the competitive motivation postulated by management ideology has little if any effect upon them. Instead they look for rewards in the intimacy of the primary group composed of their peers, and these all too often take the form of resisting management's lures.[23]

In an attempt to break through this ice jam there has been some recent experimentation with "job enlargement" which aims to have the worker perform several operations which will result in a completed assembly, even though it is only a sub-assembly which goes into a larger one. The assumption is that it may be possible to restore at least some of the personal satisfaction which allegedly accrued to the skilled artisan who made the whole shoe.[24] But work satisfaction is a product of both individual and social factors, which gives rise to the speculation that assembly lines

---

[23] A. Zaleznik, C. R. Christensen, and F. J. Roethlisberger, *The Motivation, Productivity, and Satisfaction of Workers* (Boston: Harvard Business School, 1958); Eli Chinoy, *Automobile Workers and the American Dream* (New York: Doubleday & Co., Inc., 1955).

[24] W. Lloyd Warner and J. O. Low, *The Social System of the Modern Factory* (New Haven: Yale University Press, 1947), pp. 66-89.

might be organized so as to foster more social interaction.[25] It has even been suggested that industrial engineers collaborate with social scientists in laying out production processes.

Job Analysis

Most managerial and technical positions are analyzed, and the analyses recorded and filed in the form of job descriptions. Job descriptions are also often prepared for nonsupervisory direct labor jobs, especially in those organizations which have standardized salary and wage plans. Indeed, until quite lately job descriptions were used almost entirely for the purpose of wage setting and standardization and as a basis for determining jurisdictional questions—that is, the boundaries between classes of jobs. However, job descriptions have more recently become a principal device for outlining the organization structure (the job-task pyramid). One of the most remarkable contemporary developments in large corporations is the emergence of organization planning units, whose duties include the preparation and maintenance of job descriptions for all managerial positions.

The significance of this development to the main theme of this chapter—the division of work—is that modern management ideology has found it advisable to rationalize, describe, and differentiate the structural fabric of managerial positions. In doing so it enlarged upon the original concept of job descriptions as tools for wage setting and developed a new variety which goes more deeply into the limits of decision-making and areas of responsibility.[26]

V • SUMMARY

This chapter is the first of a group in this Part Two that approaches the phenomenon of organization in rather traditional terms. This is done because the traditional framework, though mechanistic, provides (1) an important perspective, (2) a con-

[25] Charles R. Walker and Robert H. Guest, *The Man on the Assembly Line* (Cambridge: Harvard University Press, 1952), pp. 141-163.

[26] C. L. Bennett, *Defining the Manager's Job* (New York: American Management Association, 1958), pp. 9-40.

venient means of classifying present information about organizations, and (3) a way of conveying that information in terms that are generally familiar. This traditional approach tends to revolve around two basic concepts: (1) the division of work into small, single-task units; and (2) the reintegration of work into a cohesive whole so as to move the total organization toward its basic mission.

The grouping of activities is viewed as basic to this structuring process, since the division of work is essentially a problem in classification. If we start at the level of total activity of an organization, we find that our first task is to identify the major categories of activity. If we start from the very bottom, we even more clearly are concerned with the problem of grouping individual operations, then jobs, then groups of jobs, and so forth. The rational grouping of activities is particularly important because of its relationship to "natural" coordination within the organization. Where the grouping of activities does not follow a systematic and understandable pattern, personal leadership intervention to settle boundary disputes becomes much more common.

The basic concepts of grouping seem to be applicable in almost every organization situation, private or public, large or small. Four bases for grouping have been most typically suggested: (1) purpose, (2) process, (3) persons or things served, and (4) place where services are rendered. In these concepts there is, unfortunately, a considerable amount of ambiguity. This is to be seen particularly in the use of the term function. It has come to mean a great many things. Though it is perhaps best to think of it as a synonym for specialization, it is often used to describe organization structuring based on purpose or program. Similar ambiguities exist in that organizations based on the processes involved, such as engineering, medicine, stenography, and so on, are often considered functional units.

As might be expected, the structuring of these work relationships does not go on in a vacuum. The way in which work is divided and the effect of the resultant grouping on hierarchical status are matters of great consequence in organization life. They may have a very real impact on the manner in which a program is conducted. As a consequence, administrators seek to secure for their particular activities recognition as the prime element around which grouping should occur. This is done to insure that they will be close to top management, will have status and prestige, and will prevail over other vocational groups who seek to have their goals and ideologies dominate. The struggle between vocational groups to maintain their identity is of particular relevance here. This suggests some of the obstacles that exist in attempting to provide a rational distribution of activities within an organization.

An aspect of work division which has caused considerable concern in recent years is the growth of nonproductive specializations within the organization. Bureau of Labor Statistics figures show that in the decade 1947–1957 the rate of growth for nonproductive workers was fifteen times greater than for those in direct production. This is in part a result of the tremendous technological changes in American industry; nevertheless there is also the lurking fear that we may have gone too far in this movement toward a specialization which is sometimes labeled staff services but which might more properly be called adjective tasks.

The job remains a key consideration in any discussion of work and its division. Here the contributions of scientific management have been particularly relevant in providing a framework within which tasks at the microcosmic level might be ordered into a rational pattern. More recently, however, organization planning has reached down to the individual job level; and job descriptions, which were once used almost entirely for wage setting, have become a principal device for outlining the total organization structure.

EIGHT

Levels of Specialization and Coordination

What to Look for in This Chapter . . .

Channels and chain of command in the formal authority pyramid
Unity of command in the hierarchy
Task and responsibility differentiation at four levels in the organization:
- Corporate
- Top production management
- Middle management
- Supervisory management

Behavior-task guides for each level

I · THE PYRAMID

The heart of formal structure is the job-task-pyramid, which consists of tasks grouped into jobs (more accurately, positions), and jobs grouped into functional units, or boxes as depicted on the organization charts. These boxes are arranged into the pyramid both horizontally and vertically. The pyramid may be steep, in which case there are many echelons or horizontal levels, or it may be "flat," meaning that there are fewer horizontal levels but larger numbers of units on each echelon.

Unity of command. According to formal organization theory the lines of official authority run from boxes on a subordinate echelon to boxes on the next higher, and so on until they all converge at a single box at the top. At each level there are evidences

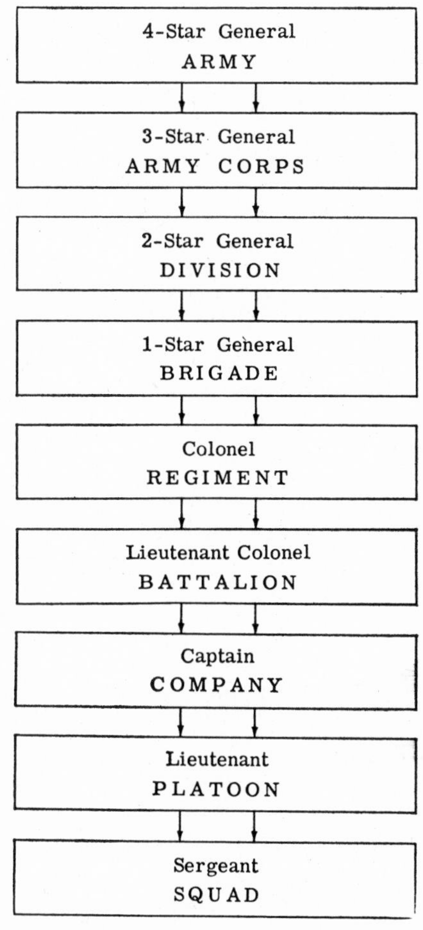

CHART 8-1. *Traditional Army line of command.*

of *unity of command,* meaning that subordinates formally report to only one boss. Ultimately all authority and responsibility rests in the top box. This is the supreme coordinating entity with official authority to impose its fiat upon all subordinate echelons. Sociological concepts of authority as advanced by Barnard and Simon throw doubt upon the validity of this extreme view of unity of command, but here we are attempting to set forth the main precepts of traditional organization theory as they apply to superior-subordinate relationships. The myth of unity of command, using the term "myth" as a bit of folklore widely believed rather than in its vernacular meaning as being at least partially false, constitutes a major concept of the theory of formal organization.

Inasmuch as the term came (at least presumably) from the military, perhaps the traditional infantry regiment would be an example familiar to most male readers.[1] At the bottom is the squad led by a sergeant; three or four squads constitute a platoon led by a sergeant or lieutenant; two or more platoons make a company led by a captain; three or four companies form a battalion led by a lieutenant colonel; and several battalions go to make up a regiment commanded by a colonel. In the composition of a traditional division two or more regiments make a brigade commanded by a brigadier general and two or more brigades comprise a division commanded by a major general. Above these is the corps, a grouping of divisions, and the army, a grouping of several corps.

Channels and Chain of Command

The chain of command constitutes the conduit through which commands and communications travel between superior and subordinate commanders. According to traditional organization theory, commands flow downward and information relative to achievement against prescribed goals flows upward. Communications and orders flow "through channels"; that is, they do not skip levels or echelons. On the plus side this pattern strengthens the positions of subordinate commanders by assuring them that their own subordinates will not receive orders directly from someone on a different level, a very demoralizing practice. The requirement that orders and

---

[1] The exigencies of mechanized and atomic warfare may be modifying this traditional organization so that it may be not so familiar to younger readers.

communications go through channels also makes for coordination because everyone on the chain of command will have seen the communication and thus be "in the know."

Communication aspects. One of the principal disadvantages of the requirement that communications go through channels is that it slows down communications by requiring them to pursue a circuitous route. This is particularly aggravating in a situation where a communication to an office nearby has to go up through several echelons and back down through a branch chain. Those familiar with the military will perhaps have had experience with the system known as "endorsements" wherein a communication is added at each successive level and "endorsed" by the appropriate commander. If such a communication has to follow a long hierarchical route it may become a thick bundle of endorsements; furthermore, its travel time may have been slowed down considerably by waiting for attention at the several endorsing echelons.

As will be pointed out later in the chapter on communication, modern hierarchies, both military and civilian, provide for channels of communication that follow oblique and horizontal lines without infringing upon the integrity of the unity of command concept. Nevertheless, the folklore of formal organization theory is so strong that the organization analyst is likely to discover slavish adherence to "channels" in many cases where it is not necessary and where streams clogged with the debris of correspondence can be cleared by redirecting the flow through shorter conduits. With the "exception" principle and modern concepts of communications as a circuit rather than a pyramid, it is not necessary for a commander on each echelon to have seen and read every message, but only those which require his attention for purposes of information or decision.

Upward focus. In the theory of formal organization the attention of subordinates is toward the boss and higher echelons, in general. Everyone is busy watching the boss and he in turn is observing his boss.[2] Orders flow downward as does the dispensation of rewards and benefits. Recent researches have indicated that this is perhaps more true of the mobile members of the organization

---

[2] Burleigh B. Gardner and David G. Moore, *Human Relations in Industry*, 3rd edition (Homewood, Ill.: Richard D. Irwin, Inc., 1955), pp. 91-92.

than of those who have become "frozen," that is, who have reached their ceilings. The latter tend to seek rewards which management cannot give, namely, the social group membership dispensed only by their fellow workers.[3] Indeed, perhaps the major problem of motivation is to devise ways and means of "unfreezing" the workers, that is, in a sense, to get them to look more eagerly upward.

Nevertheless, the dominant spirit prevailing in most organizations is that of the pyramid rather than the circle. Significant decisions tend to be made on the higher echelons; the important orders emanate from there; the formulation of major policy originates there; and personnel actions affecting the personal fortunes of individuals are taken by bosses rather than peers. Hence the focus upward prevails.

II • THE VERTICAL GROUPING OF ECHELONS

We have noted that it is common to distinguish between direct and indirect labor, and suggested that the terms *substantive* and *adjective* were perhaps most descriptive of these two broad categories of tasks. Such a distinction is also important here. Most substantive (direct) workers are located on the bottom rung of the pyramid. This important point is rather frequently overlooked because of our emphasis on the supervisory and management echelons.

Differentiation of Tasks by Level

The significance of this observation lies in the fact that there is a differentiation of tasks and hence of behavior at the several managerial levels. Assuming that all leaders are generalists, the activities engaged in by leaders at the different hierarchical levels differ in degree if not in kind. Thus a president and a foreman each do some planning, but a president's planning is strategical and long-run whereas that of a foreman is operational and short-run.

[3] A. Zaleznik, C. R. Christensen, and F. J. Roethlisberger, *The Motivation, Productivity, and Satisfaction of Workers* (Boston: Harvard Business School, 1958).

Importance to selection and training. This differentiation of task between echelons is of more significance to the selection and training of leaders at the several levels than may be indicated by the attention accorded it in the past.[4] The psychological adjustment necessary when one goes from one level to another is often difficult because of the tendency to continue former behavior patterns. In illustration, two of the largest psychological jumps take place: (1) when a journeyman or operator is promoted to full-time supervision, and (2) when a production manager is advanced to corporate management. This is sometimes referred to as the problem of working at the proper level.[5]

Role of job descriptions. At first glance this might appear to be a problem of human relations rather than of formal organization, but such a conclusion would be only partially true. Good job descriptions should reflect task differentiation at the various echelons. It is a matter of tasks combined with behavior, and tasks make up the basic elements of formal organization. According to the classical theory of formal organization people are expected to adjust to jobs rather than vice versa, and one of the principal reasons for failure on the part of supervisors and executives is that they have been unable to perform the tasks (behave, if you will) in the manner called for at that particular level.

Experiences in Two Organizations

Social Security. The problem is well illustrated by a study conducted in the district offices of the U.S. Bureau of Old Age and Survivor's Insurance (a unit of the Social Security Administration), which is more familiarly known as the social security agency. In the beginning the district offices were rather small, having six to a dozen people plus a single supervisor known as a manager. The manager functioned at a level of immediate supervision in a field office. One must bear in mind that this might be different from functioning at this level in a factory or home office. At this level

---

[4] The Ohio State Group has done some research bordering on this point but not directly applicable. See Ralph M. Stogdill, *Leadership and Structures of Personnel Interaction,* Ohio State University Bureau of Business Research, Research Monograph No. 84, 1957.

[5] Paul Appleby, *Big Democracy* (New York: Alfred A. Knopf, Inc., 1945), p. 65.

the social security manager sometimes carried a case load himself and his management problems were those of close association and face-to-face supervision. The problems encountered were not the problems of hierarchy so much as those of individual failure to deal with people in the face-to-face relationship.

The problem changed, however, when many of these offices grew to 25 or 30 people and the positions of assistant manager and supervisor of case workers were added. Noticeable stresses appeared in two particular areas. The *first* was the relationship between the manager and his assistant manager, the *second,* the manager's continued pattern of participating in cases himself. The study found a considerable number of the managers in conflict with their assistant managers because they did not know how to use them. They were apprehensive of the assistants and distrusted them. The other problem, which is related to the first, arose from the fact that the managers continued to operate at the journeyman's level by interfering in the interviews of case workers and receptionists with their clients, often giving incorrect information. The managers had failed to keep up with the intricacies of a very complex and rapidly changing set of regulations, and were actually no longer competent to give advice to clients about their rights to social security. These managers did not know how to operate at the managers' level with the result that they occupied their time by interfering needlessly and detrimentally in the work being performed by the journeymen.

Lifeguards. One of the most difficult adjustments to make for one who has been an active agent in the field is to be transferred to a job where he is supposed to supervise. An example given by a student who had functioned as a lifeguard illustrates this point. In this particular case the former lifeguard, who had been promoted first to supervisor and then field supervisor over several beaches, nettled and annoyed both the supervisors and the guards of particular beaches by coming in and taking over a beach and running it for a day. Apparently he enjoyed the emulation accorded his status by running up and down the beach in a jeep and by giving orders directly to lifeguards. Nevertheless, demoralization resulted and the beach supervisor survived only by staying in his office and exercising the utmost self-control.

III • AN OUTLINE OF TASK DIFFERENTIATION BY ECHELON

Large-scale organizations may have as many as a dozen supervisorial levels or echelons between the person performing "direct labor" in the factory or the field and the top echelon at headquarters. However, it is our hypothesis that these levels of leadership and sub-leadership can be divided into four distinct categories on the basis of similarity of task. These are (1) corporate management, (2) top production management, (3) middle management, and (4) supervisory management. Obviously what people do, the tasks they perform, differs from one of these management levels to another.

Furthermore, a person who performs well on one of these levels may not do equally well on another. This may be because of inherent personal qualities which cannot be altered or because of a failure to perceive the need to change behavior which one has followed in the old job. For example, the corporate level is a relatively new organization device. While it may have existed in organizations of the past, American corporations are just beginning to adjust themselves to the realization that the tasks of corporate management differ from those of production management. The corporate executive committee, which tends to be the power center at the corporate level, spends a great deal of time in reading reports, digesting information, deliberating, planning, and formulating over-all long-range policy. The natural place to look for corporate managers is at the production management level, but that is a place of action rather than of deliberation, with the result that the transition from production management to corporate management may be difficult.

Similarly, the supervisory management level often requires a behavior in which, in order to get things done, the supervisor seems to compromise. He is often referred to as a "double talker." He must have one ear cocked to the sentiment of the work group while listening to the production logic of management with the other. In order to preserve a desirable equilibrium he attempts to mollify both sides, but in doing so he fails to manifest the ascendancy traits which attract the attention of higher-ups. The levels above him call for a management ideology characterized by a rational emphasis on maximizing productivity, and upward social mobility. These are values which the environment of the production levels does not foster.

The Corporate Level

In smaller organizations there may be no distinction between corporate management and production management. But as organizations grow beyond a certain size, stresses and strains develop because people at headquarters continue to function as though they were production managers. There is a tendency in such an organization toward line functionalism, that is, the headquarters people deal with manufacturing, supply, engineering, and marketing as though they had to assume control and direction at the operating level.

Experience of the aircraft industry. One of the best laboratories for observing the emergence of the corporate level is the aircraft industry, where in the fifteen years from 1940 to 1955 there took place an evolution which in most organizations lasts for several decades. They started out in limited quarters with a few hundred employees, and were led by flying or engineering enthusiasts who had little or no managerial background. The experience of one such company may be typical. From 1936 to 1943 it jumped from 5,000 to 90,000 employees. When the government began to ask for cost figures and more production, the existing system would yield neither. Management, experimentation, and production tended to operate together at the shop level. Then size and government pressure forced the adoption of system (bureaucratization). But top management continued to be housed on the factory premises, where it concerned itself with the minutiae of day-to-day operations.

Then came three developments which forced the recognition of the corporate level as a distinct entity in itself. The first was geographical decentralization by the establishment of plants at different locations, some hundreds or thousands of miles away, such as Lockheed in Georgia and at Sunnyvale, California, and Boeing in Seattle and Wichita. The second was diversification, such as North American's move into the field of atomic energy. The third was the need for administrative decentralization because of size and bureaucratic ponderousness. This trend was capped by the erection in 1957-58 of buildings devoted exclusively to corporate activities for two of the California aircraft companies.

Other perspectives. Management below the corporate level tends to be parochial; it is composed of people who are unifunctionally oriented, that is, they have one objective such as making a particular automobile, paint, or fabric. As organizations grow there is a tendency at first to have production executives double in brass as members of the corporate executive committee. This has two disadvantages, in addition to overworking the individual involved. In the first place, production executives tend to have an eye cocked toward the interests of their own separate bailiwicks in making decisions which should be based on broader considerations. Secondly, their habits, visions, and outlook are focused toward day-to-day productivity rather than planning and general guidance. The result is that it has been found advisable to relieve members of executive committees from operating duties, a step which took place at DuPont twenty or more years ago and in the Bank of America in the 1950's.

Drucker's study of General Motors describes central management's role as "to weld several hundred aggressive, highly individual and very independent divisional top executives into one team." [6] He goes on to state five main ways in which this is accomplished: (1) setting goals, (2) defining limits of authority, (3) constantly checking on divisional problems and progress, (4) relieving divisional management of problems not strictly a part of production and selling, and (5) furnishing staff advice and service.

The problem of the corporate level is to boss without seeming to boss; to watch productivity without taking over direct responsibility—therefore, to know what takes place without seeming nosey; and to maintain control without stifling initiative and self-reliance.

It is not only a matter of giving up power, but learning to

---

[6] Peter Drucker, *The Concept of the Corporation* (New York: The John Day Company, 1946), p. 49.

operate in a different manner (changing behavior). The new dispensation in organization behavior aims to reverse the cultural values extant in the world throughout human existence. It seeks to modify the hierarchy wherein a great Caesar at the top directs the most minute actions of a chain of little Caesars beneath him. The hierarchy is retained but its harsher features are disguised. Each echelon of leadership leads without seeming to; each leader is encouraged to make decisions on his own responsibility. Indeed, the whole effort is directed toward developing strength and resourcefulness at the operating levels. That is why, when a production manager is promoted to the corporate level, he finds it difficult to adjust; he is not used to a role characterized by planning, deliberation, review, reading, and long-run perspective. The result is that he sometimes disturbs subordinate echelons by his tendency to reach down into production as an agent for action and trouble-shooting.

Application to government. While it may be difficult to apply the corporate level concept to specific governmental institutions, it surely has relevance to the behavior of specific units. Thus, in federal administration it would seem that both the presidency and the top echelons of the great executive departments are essentially corporate from the standpoint of differentiation of tasks. One could say the same of the office of governor in the states and mayor in the larger cities. Each of these positions embraces tasks that require a behavior essentially corporate rather than productive in nature. These include: (1) coordinating a wide variety of agencies with separate and distinct technologies and objectives, (2) doing this without making operating decisions, (3) planning for the long run, (4) evaluating results without constantly "telling how" to do it, (5) developing policy which has over-all implications, and (6) providing and allocating finances.

Top Production Management

By top production management is meant the leadership jobs at what is known as the division level in industry and perhaps the bureau and regional office level in the federal government. These are at the top of a unifunctional sub-hierarchy, such as production of a particular brand of automobile or administering the national forests. At the top of the production hierarchy is found a replica of the subunits at corporate headquarters. In industry these would include manufacturing, sales, engineering, and finance.

Since present management philosophy calls for the decentralization of decision-making at all levels, production management, like corporate management, must condition itself to a hands-off type of behavior, in this case toward middle management. But top production management differs from corporate management in other respects. First, it is nearer to the scene of production. Second, while a "breathing down the necks" type of supervision may be frowned upon, production management is nevertheless directly interested in production and the chances are that it gets daily feedback reports that are closely scrutinized and questioned. This means, third, that the prevailing psychological atmosphere is centered upon operations and what goes on in the factory or field.

Middle Management

Middle management is a generic term that may be difficult to apply to positions in specific organizations. It includes the echelons of leadership immediately below those of top production management. The terminology used may be department head or division head, and also included are those staff, technical, and engineering personnel who are production-centered.

A psychological study of how top and middle management looked at itself demonstrated marked variations between the two.[7] Individuals in the top management group perceived themselves as active, self-reliant and willing to act on the basis of their abilities. They were ready to take risks. They possessed confidence that their decisions would lead to success, and their interpersonal behavior was characterized as candid and straightforward.

Middle managers saw themselves as careful planners who displayed well controlled behavior and whose actions were carefully thought out. They seemed to place more reliance on operating within the rules and conditions of the system than in plunging ahead on their own ideas. They wanted to avoid the appearance of

---

[7] L. W. Porter and E. E. Ghiselli, "The Self Perceptions of Top and Middle Management Personnel," *Personnel Psychology* 10:397-406, Winter 1957.

being controversial personalities. They saw themselves as stable and dependable persons who tended to hew to the line.

Supervisory Management

Supervisory management embraces what may be three or four levels, constituting those jobs whose duties typically involve immediate and continuing contact with production workers. It should be noted, however, that there may be some supervision on virtually all levels, including the top where a head clerk is in charge of clerical help in an executive suite. However, we ordinarily think of supervisory management as being in charge of direct labor in the factory or field. Foreman is the term most generally applied to the lowest level of full-time supervision. He may have an assistant foreman and may himself report to a general foreman.

The tasks of supervisory management are in many respects similar in kind to those of management on other levels, because supervisors plan, implement policy, and organize—and would seem to be acquiring increasing duties in the realm of budgeting and finance.[8] Indeed, the prevailing climate of decentralization tends to picture the foreman's bailiwick as a microcosm wherein he exercises a maximum of decision-making authority, a situation which is perhaps more of an aspiration or virtuous avowal of intent than it is an actual achievement in most organizations.

But perhaps the distinguishing feature of the supervisory level is propinquity to the mass of production workers. A recent study of the foreman's tasks discovered the three broad areas of critical competencies to be in administrative matters, in supervising subordinates, and in relations with equals and superiors. The second category was broken down into the following six: (1) development of subordinates, (2) correction of undesirable behavior, (3) giving credit where due, (4) equality of treatment, (5) concern for employee's welfare, and (6) keeping subordinates informed. Of the 16 critical factors in the three broad categories, ten were based directly on *interpersonal relations.*[9]

---

[8] Chester E. Evans, *Supervisory Responsibility and Authority*, American Management Association, Research Report No. 30, 1957.

[9] Brian R. Kay, "Key Factors in Effective Foreman Behavior," *Personnel* 36:25,27, January-February 1959.

IV • BEHAVIOR-TASK GUIDES FOR EACH ECHELON

Each of the four managerial levels has tasks which are essentially alike in kind but vary in degree. And much of the difference in degree lies in the extent to which decision-making is decentralized. Though the idea of levels in organization is old, present theories as to the nature and function of these levels derive clearly from the decentralization concept. This general question of relating levels to the new decentralization trend is a timely one, which is attested by the appearance of three studies almost simultaneously. Each describes the problems encountered in industrial organizations undergoing decentralization where relations between the various functional specialists and the operating people was particularly delicate.[10] In each case one of the major problems encountered was the inability or unwillingness of people who had previously been in positions of operating control to change over to specialist advisory positions.

It might be argued that in such cases the problem is primarily behavioral, rather than one of formal organization. However, an equally cogent argument can be made for an opposite view. Tasks embody a major element of behavior, whether it be the operator manipulating a lathe or the district superintendent visiting a store manager. The point is that the behavior of the managers at the several scalar levels should be spelled out in the job descriptions and organization manuals. In short, executive tasks and executive behavior are inseparable.

As a concrete means of identifying the nature of these responsibilities at the various levels, a set of broad behavior-task guides for the four levels are suggested. They assume the existence of a philosophy of decentralization within the organization and a full complement of functional specialists.

---

10 Eli Ginzberg and Ewing W. Reilley, *Effecting Change in Large Organizations* (New York: Columbia University Press, 1957); George Albert Smith, Jr., *Managing Geographically Decentralized Companies* (Boston: Harvard Business School, 1958); Paul R. Lawrence, *The Changing of Organizational Behavior Patterns* (Boston: Harvard Business School, 1958).

Corporate Management Level

Spends comparatively more time in reflection and deliberation; reads staff reports.
Attends many meetings.
Meticulously avoids becoming involved in day-to-day operations at production levels.
Specialized units act in pure staff relationship to subordinate echelons.
Contacts with operating officials deal with over-all and long-run goals rather than day-to-day problems and achievements.
Makes long-range plans.
Makes policy which serves as guides rather than directions.
Sets goals and devises feedback control in such a way as to stay out of day-to-day operations.
Has public relations contacts with government officials, national pressure groups, and client (customer) organizations.
Travels a great deal; visits to branches consultative rather than punitive; inspection.
Evaluates personnel from standpoint of choosing future executives.

Top Production Management Level

Focus is on immediate production, whether manufacturing, sales, or service.
Makes policy decisions within framework laid down at corporate level, but does not hesitate to plow new ground when circumstances warrant.
Gets daily feedback on productivity and takes personal and immediate interest in trouble spots.
Lets subordinates handle trouble, but makes his own interest felt.
Specialized units act in staff capacity, but have intimate and constant contact with production.
Engages in long-run planning which is synchronized with corporate level.
Evaluates personnel for promotability.

Middle Management Level

Maintains closer contact with day-to-day results.
Participates in operating decisions.
Evaluates production results rather than program.
Evaluates personnel from standpoint of immediate usefulness rather than future potential.
Press of events minimizes time spent in reading and reflection.
Deliberation with colleagues more likely to be spent in solving urgent and immediate problems.
Makes plans for achieving goals established by corporate level.

Implements policy decisions within the limitations set by higher echelons.

Supervisory Management Level

Plans day-to-day production within goals set from above.
Assigns personnel to specific jobs and tasks.
Watches hour-to-hour results.
Reports feedback information daily.
Takes corrective action on the spot.
Maintains personal and immediate contact with production personnel.
Evaluates personnel from standpoint of immediate needs.
Implements policy decisions within the limitations set by higher echelons.
Informal custom not prescribed or proscribed.

V • SUMMARY

Specialization in an organization occurs on at least two planes. In the previous chapter we saw that division of work, hence specialization, takes place *vertically*. The total organization mission is sliced from top to bottom or bottom to top—but not from side to side. Nevertheless, as we have discovered in the present chapter, a different kind of specialization does take place on the *horizontal* plane. We find that *levels* appear in the formal authority structure of any large organization. These levels actually represent differentiated task responsibilities in the total job of coordinating organizational activity. Perhaps the best illustration of this point lies in the fact that nearly all the substantive (direct) labor occurs at the bottom-most level. From that point upward, the organizational participants are largely engaged in adjective (indirect) labor. They are, in short, taking on various specialized portions of the total coordination responsibility. Ultimately the top echelon is reached and here the final responsibility for coordination rests.

The traditional pyramid of organization authority is built on concepts presented in this and the preceding chapter. As we move from the top down we observe an increasing division of work. At the same time, each division of work seems to involve a new echelon of activity and thus *layering* (levels) becomes a part of the hierarchical concept. Unity of command contributes directly to the pyramid by forcing an integration of authority and responsibility from the bottom-most levels of coordination in the organization to the uppermost. The pyramid is really created by the unity of command concept. Finally, the chain of command idea suggests the appropriate pattern for order-giving and communication within this structure.

The rationalization of the various levels of coordinative responsibility within the organization has taken on increased significance because of current trends toward decentralization. In this present movement it is particularly striking to note that many large business organizations are creating for the first time separate, top level coordinating units. This new echelon is the corporate headquarters staff; and its principal mission is to deal with over-all and long-run goals rather than day-to-day problems and achievements.

The problems encountered in articulating the function of this new corporate level only serve to illuminate a long standing difficulty. Many people find it difficult to make the adjustment required in moving from a role of action responsibility and immediacy at a lower hierarchical level to one which involves long-term coordinative and planning duties at a higher level. In large part this is a behavioral question, having real implications for the selection and training of management people. However it is also a place where organization planning has a role. Good job descriptions should reflect the differentiation in task-behavior patterns at the various echelons of the organization.

It is suggested that there are four levels within the administrative organization in which task-behavior patterns might be appropriately differentiated. The levels and their patterns are, in brief:

Corporate level. Officials have no direct contact with immediate operating questions in the organization. Their principal function is the continual reassessment of organizational status and goals. They are responsible for long-range planning rather than immediate order-giving.

Top production management level. Officials are the organization leaders immediately responsible for the accomplishment of stated goals. Their area of responsibility is typically less broad than that of the corporate leaders since they are involved in the performance of only a part of the total corporate mission.

Middle management level. Officials are involved in a smaller area of responsibility. Consequently they have an even more immediate concern with day-to-day performance; and they tend to be engaged in evaluating production results more than program objectives. They are participants in operating decisions.

Supervisory management level. Officials have the immediate, day-to-day contact with those who are actually doing the work. Their appraisal of performance is on an hour-to-hour basis and corrective action is taken where necessary on the spot. Their concern is largely with immediate needs.

NINE

Coordination at the Top

What to Look for in This Chapter . . .

Span of control—the number of persons formally supervised by another
Small span is a central "principle" of traditional theory
Large span is a necessity for most political executives in government
Size of span helps determine levels in hierarchy and its shape
Large span tends to require delegation and decentralization
The committee in top-level coordination

The idea of the organization pyramid postulates a convergence of authority and responsibility at the top. It follows, then, that the leader's task of coordination should be a matter of central concern. This interest is in accord, too, with the traditional concepts of management which have been discussed earlier. To repeat briefly, the man who sits at the top of the pyramid is regarded as an omniscient father figure with superior judgment and knowledge. He maintains a firm rein on the organization and the major decisions are essentially his. This leader has subordinates but he is supposed to interact with them individually, not as a team.

With this philosophical underpinning, questions concerning control by the leader have been posed in largely mechanical terms. How many people can a leader efficiently supervise? When is the point reached that these supervisory responsibilities involve too many contacts for a single person to handle comfortably? What is to be done when that point has been reached? Is there any way of extending the executive's "personality" and therefore his capacity for control? In all the traditionally raised questions, coordination is seen in large part as a function of executive capacity, and that capacity is fairly well dictated by organization structuring rather than by program and behavioral factors.

This way of looking at structuring has caused *two* basic concepts to dominate much of organization theory and planning.

The first is that of the executive's *span of control,* which simply refers to the numbers of persons he supervises. Implicit here is the notion that coordination in the organization rests largely on the executive's direct relationship with his subordinates; and these should not be so numerous or so few as to handicap seriously his control potentialities.

The second idea has to do with the extension of the executive personality. It may be labeled the *staff concept.* It proposes essentially that the executive can be given more eyes and ears, and these should not interfere with his basic command (hence control) relationships.

In this chapter we shall consider the span of control concept, with a slight diversion to discuss committees as an element in top management coordination. In Chapter 10 the staff idea will be considered.

I • SPAN OF CONTROL

There is perhaps no more hoary artifact of organization folklore than the notion of span of control. Many a reorganization has taken place almost entirely in terms of the number of people an executive should supervise. Prescriptions as to number abound. Sometimes it is three; seldom does it exceed twenty. In most instances the reduction in numbers of people supervised has been looked upon as *good in itself.* Thus executives pride themselves that somehow the organization process has been "streamlined" when their span of control has been reduced from twenty to twelve, twelve to seven, or whatever.

Perspectives

Has such emphasis on the idea of span of control been appropriate? Does it deserve a prime place in our thinking? Certainly its dominance as a theme of traditional organization theory is not hard to understand. Its relationship to the hierarchical structure is clear-cut. It has a quantitative aspect which can result in concrete proposals for organization reform. Finally, the span of control notion fitted well with earlier ideas of "principles" for organization behavior.

Nature of attacks. In the past fifteen years, many writers have questioned the usefulness of span of control as an avenue to a real understanding of organization processes. Although it was not the first, Herbert Simon's essay in 1946, "The Proverbs of Administration," was particularly successful in bringing these questions to a focus.[1] In the first place, no one really seems to know what the magic number of persons supervised should be. Secondly, it appears that such factors as the personality of the executive, the routine or varied nature of the work, the degree of geographic dispersion, the need for immediate decisions, and the type of program administered, are all factors of prime importance in defining the supervisory relationship. They have much to do with the number of persons who might be included in the executive's span of control. As a consequence there is no quick and sure formula which can be used to determine the appropriate span.

Bias in the concept. The traditional bias in most of the literature on this question is also worth noting. It emphasizes the small span. Seldom even today do executives state publicly and proudly that the number of persons they supervise has been *increased* from

[1] Herbert A. Simon, "The Proverbs of Administration," *Public Administration Review* 6:53-67, Winter 1946.

12 to 20. It must be assumed that the almost unconscious reluctance to broadcast such heresy is based on the traditional theory that the small number permits the executive to obtain more intimate control. Further ambiguity in the concept is added also by the fact that some social scientists would probably argue for a small span but for different reasons. They would likely say that modern teamwork patterns of executive leadership work better with a small group of people interacting.

Relation to hierarchical conformation. The span idea is important not only in terms of executive relationships with subordinates; it is also significant because of its influence on the conformation of the hierarchy. It can do much to determine the number of levels in the organization pyramid, and in doing that it can impose a mushroom-like flatness or a cone-like depth on the structure. Put another way, an organization is in many ways like a rubber ball. If you squeeze it in one place, it bulges somewhere else. Thus, if 20 department heads all report to the president, the organization tends to "flatten." In such a circumstance there are only two levels. If on the other hand only three report to the president and the others report to the three, more levels have been added to the structure. It has "deepened." In the process of deepening, it is assumed that problems of communication become more difficult. In the first instance, everyone talks to the boss. In the second, seventeen talk through someone else, with consequent difficulties of blockage and distortion that inevitably occur.

In this introductory section of the chapter, we have sought to provide a perspective in which the span of control idea may be viewed. It has occupied an important niche in traditional theory. It has a significant bearing on the number of organization levels and hence on the coordinative system. On the other hand, there are many reasons why it is less of a specific guideline to structuring than many have claimed. Much blood has been let to reduce the executive's span with inconsequential results to administrative performance. Yet span of control sails merrily on. There is much written about it. Most consultants tab this as an essential in reform proposals. Students sweat over its definition, mainly because they assume the concept should be more complicated than it really is.

Thus, regardless of what its merits may be, span of control is so entrenched in the administrative culture that it must be accorded a prominent place in any book on organization.

Research on the Problem

Graicunas. There has been relatively little, if any, empirical study of span of control. Perhaps the most influential paper in the past generation was that of Graicunas who carried out a mathematical projection of what would happen to an organization by manipulating the span of control at the top.[2] The general import was that as the span at the top is increased mathematically, the complexity of relationships at subordinate echelons grows geometrically. Along with that of Davis, this study was *not* based upon empirical observation but rather upon theoretical projection by mathematics. This approach is not to be condemned out of hand: after all, modern nuclear physics is based upon theoretical assumptions and projections. In nuclear physics, however, the assumptions are subsequently tested by experiment. The study of organization is now perhaps approaching a stage of maturity, through the emergence of the behavioral sciences, wherein such theoretical projections will be subjected to experimental, or at least observational, test.

Baker and Davis. An example of an empirical study of this nature is offered by the investigation of Ohio manufacturing companies by Baker and Davis. The inquiry was designed to test Davis' previously expressed "law of functional growth," which maintained that "as line [substantive] personnel increases in arithmetic progression, staff [adjective] personnel tends to increase in geometric progression."[3] The results did not support the validity of this so-called law, because it was found that the

---

[2] V. A. Graicunas, "Relationship and Organization," in Luther Gulick and L. Urwick, editors, *Papers on the Science of Administration* (New York: Public Administration Service, 1937), pp. 183-187. See also Ralph C. Davis, *The Influence of the Unit of Supervision and the Span of Executive Control on the Economy of Organization Structure* (Columbus: Ohio State University, Bureau of Business Research, 1941).

[3] Alton W. Baker and Ralph C. Davis, *Ratios of Staff to Line Employees and Stages of Differentiation of Staff Functions* (Columbus: Bureau of Business Research, Ohio State University, Research Monograph No. 72, 1954), p. 57.

number of indirect employees expanded arithmetically, instead of geometrically, at approximately the same rate as direct employees. An incidental result of the study, however, presented data which supported generally-held ideas about span of control.

> These data confirm the contention that there is a unit or span of operative supervision, and that it exists regardless of the industry. These data indicate that the average unit of supervision is 100/6, or 16.7 operatives per supervisor. This is almost exactly in the center of the generally accepted range of units of operative supervision, 10 to 30 employees. These data also confirm the contention that there is a unit or span of executive supervision. They indicate that the average span of executive supervision is six subordinates, approximately. This is also in the center of the generally accepted range for units of executive supervision of 3 to 8 or 9 subordinate executives.[4]

Relation to decision-making. Other writers, notably Waino W. Soujanen, have emphasized the impact of changes in decision-making practices on the span of control concept.[5] The replacement of the omniscient father figure with the management team has changed the whole system of communication and contact within the organization. Inevitably it has affected attention paid to the way the executive controls in the command sense. As Soujanen has written:

> The most striking feature in the recent development of the large well managed, contemporary American corporation is the variety of decision-making processes that have been incorporated into its structure and philosophy. Hierarchy, or control by leaders, still remains the most significant decision-making process. To an increasing extent, however, other decision-making processes have become important. In the control of the operating divisions of the large corporation, the price system, or control of and by leaders, is replacing hierarchy at a very rapid pace. Similarly, voting or control by the led, is being increasingly incorporated into the decision-making structure of the progressive organization. Finally, bargaining, or control of leaders by leaders, has shown a phenomenal growth in recent years.[6]

---

[4] *Ibid.*, p. 31.

[5] See Waino W. Soujanen, "The Span of Control–Fact or Fable?" *Advanced Management* 20:5-13, November 1955.

[6] Waino W. Soujanen, "Leadership, Authority, and the Span of Control," *Advanced Management* 23:17, September 1957.

Urwick's reaction. Soujanen's contention that modern social science concepts have seriously modified the traditional underpinnings of the span of control drew a sharp retort from Lyndall F. Urwick.[7] Urwick's article, despite emotional overtones, was more than a mere diatribe because it was exceptionally well-documented. It is not easy to categorize Urwick's points. In general he felt that Soujanen was giving social science credit for a maturity that it had not attained. The claim was made that Soujanen had deliberately distorted Barnard, as well as Dale's study of corporations,[8] in order to support his point.

Urwick also took issue with Herbert Simon. Here he was concerned mainly with Simon's contention that a short span of control at the top must necessarily increase the number of horizontal echelons. Urwick seems to admit that such echelons are created, but he asks, "What of it?" A steep hierarchy with many echelons is not necessarily a bad thing if it offers the opportunity of access to higher authority with key levels where personal leadership stands out. Urwick says that the critics of the short span have failed to make a distinction between "access to" and direct supervision. Span of control applies only to direct supervision and it does not necessarily prohibit "access to" on the part of people not in the formal pattern.

Experience in Government

Forces in the situation. The span of control in most American governmental jurisdictions is large because there are certain and almost irresistible forces which make it so:

First, there is a tendency toward a large number of separate departments because the "empire builder" type of department head wants to be answerable, if at all, only to the chief executive or governing body. *Second,* each pressure group desires its own pet administrative activity to be set up in an independent department rather than embodied as a bureau or division in another depart-

---

7 Lyndall F. Urwick, "The Span of Control—Some Facts about the Fables," *Advanced Management* 21:5-18, November 1956; Herbert A. Simon, "The Span of Control: A Reply," *Advanced Management* 22:14, April 1957.

8 Ernest Dale, *Planning and Developing the Company Organization Structure,* American Management Association, Research Report No. 20, 1952.

ment. *Third,* every functional chief desires access to the seat of authority without going through intervening hierarchical steps. *Fourth,* each functional chief desires such access to the legislature or governing body as may pertain to the position of department head. *Fifth,* those interested in particular governmental activities fear that inept and dilatory handling of functional affairs may result if they are placed in what is merely one of the many units in a large department. They are apprehensive of possible frustration and of failure to achieve desired ends because of the inertia and lack of enthusiasm of departmental officials.[9] *Sixth,* the sponsors of new administrative activities do not want to become units in an old department because they imagine that they will become stifled in the red tape of an organization which they believe already too large for effective action.

Criticism of President's span. The Brownlow Committee in 1937 and the Hoover Commission in 1949 criticized the huge span of control exercised by the President. The former found upward of one hundred separate agencies "presumably reporting to the President," while the latter listed sixty-five,[10] not including the independent regulatory agencies, which partially accounts for the discrepancy. Both reports insisted that the President could not possibly give proper attention to this number of agencies even if he had legal authority to do so. In many instances, the agencies were not legally amenable to his supervision or anybody else's. The Brownlow Committee recommended the regrouping of these agencies into twelve major departments, each headed by a cabinet member responsible to the President, the independent regulatory commissions to be attached to a department for housekeeping convenience, but the commissions to remain autonomous. The Hoover Commission contented itself with a recommendation that "these various agencies be consolidated into about one third the present number," which would amount to something over twenty, not including the independent regulatory agencies.

---

[9] James Landis, *The Administrative Process* (New Haven: Yale University Press, 1938), pp. 24 ff.

[10] President's Committee on Administrative Management, *Report with Special Studies* (Washington, D.C.: Government Printing Office, 1937), p. 32. Commission on Organization of the Executive Branch of the Government, *General Management of the Executive Branch* (Washington, D.C.: Government Printing Office, 1949), pp. 35, 47.

Pressure groups, vested interests, and legislative distrust will always operate against establishing a smaller span of control for a political executive. A governor or a mayor might be able to supervise fifty departments through budgetary control if he possessed it, but he is frustrated here also by permanent and continuing appropriations which may exempt as much as two thirds of the budget from annual executive review. Nevertheless, efforts are constantly being made to counteract these tendencies and considerable success has been achieved in some states and cities.

II • SPAN OF CONTROL AND DECENTRALIZATION

Traditional concepts of hierarchy were built upon a philosophy of decision-making which was dominantly characterized by centralization. Decisions were made at or near the top even on matters of minor detail. Today the emergent philosophy of hierarchy emphasizes decentralized decision-making supported by a fabric of group process. Thus two elements are raising a sharp challenge to the standard proposal of a short span: (1) the trend toward decentralization; and (2) the new pattern of leadership evolving from a growing acceptance of group process as a way of life in management institutions.

Hierarchical Flatness as a Means of Forcing Delegation

The most widely publicized arguments in favor of a wider span of control have emanated from the utterances of James C. Worthy, a sociologist who became an executive of Sears Roebuck and Company.[11] Worthy took a stand against the excessive elaboration of organizational arrangements in general, maintaining as one might expect of a person who was sociologically trained that the proper integration of organizations could better be brought about through sociological rather than mechanical approaches.[12] The essence of the "heresy," which attracted widespread attention,

---

[11] He also served as Assistant Secretary of Commerce in the Eisenhower administration.

[12] James C. Worthy, "Organizational Structure and Employee Morale," *American Sociological Review* 15:169-179, April 1950.

was advocacy of a wide span of control at the top and middle echelons, primarily to enforce delegation and decentralization.

Sears, Roebuck. It was alleged that this pattern of organization, often referred to as "flat," was in successful operation at Sears, Roebuck. It grew out of the need to build self-reliance into the retail store manager's job, particularly to protect him against the over-solicitous, clucking-hen type of supervision which previously had been practiced by the area chiefs. In other words, one device for keeping the area offices from exercising too detailed a supervision of the stores was to give them so many stores to look after that they would not have time to devote to inconsequential matters.

> . . . the company has gone directly counter to one of the favorite tenets of modern management theory, the so-called "span of control," which holds that the number of subordinate executives or supervisors reporting to a single individual should be severely limited to enable that individual to exercise the detailed direction and control which are generally considered necessary. In an organization with as few supervisory levels as Sears, it is obvious that most key executives have so many subordinates reporting to them that they simply cannot exercise too close supervision over their activities. By this means, substantial decentralization of administrative processes is practically guaranteed.[13]

Bank of America. A less publicized but nevertheless noteworthy example is offered by the Bank of America, which has over 600 branches throughout California, each of which reports directly to corporate headquarters at San Francisco. There is no intervening area structure with directive powers over the branch offices.

When officers of the bank are questioned about this seemingly unorthodox setup, their response is that they do not want to risk setting up an echelon that would take authority away from the branch managers. They want them to be self-reliant local business men with a maximum opportunity for making decisions on their own. An intervening layer of district offices would, in their efforts to justify their existence, inevitably invade the sphere of discretion of the branch managers.

---

[13] James C. Worthy, "Factors Influencing Employee Morale," *Harvard Business Review* 28:61-73, January 1950.

Chain merchandising. As will be pointed out in Chapter 11 which deals with decentralization *per se*, there is now a strong movement in the chain merchandising field to alter the role of the local managers. In general the change makes the managers citizens of the local community, rather than puppets manipulated by functional and staff controls from above. This has been partly motivated by a resurgence of competition from locally-owned independent merchandisers who have drawn at least a part of their strength from success in identifying themselves with their communities. Thus the decentralizing forces in chain merchandising have emanated from the felt need to build the local branch-managers into resourceful and self-reliant entrepreneurs socially integrated into the communities they serve. This has required a change in philosophy away from central attention to detail toward a more general type of supervision by headquarters. The lengthening of the span of control has been one device sometimes utilized to accomplish this purpose.

Government. One might speculate as to any possible lesson this might have for public administration. Apparently the overriding motivation in chain merchandising has been the need to strengthen local managers so that they could play the role of independent business men in competition with strong people who were just that. In general public administration does not have this competitive motivation to decentralize. Nevertheless the social security district offices are a good example of the way in which strengthening of local managers occurs in government as well.[14]

Communication and Span of Control

If the principal ideological underpinning for the short span of control is the need for frequent communication, will the development of electronic communication modify this need? Electronic data processing can place on the executive's desk up-to-date information on what is happening. As one writer has recently stated,

---

[14] John M. Pfiffner and Frank V. K. Mason, "Personnel Management at the Grass Roots," *Personnel Administration* 20:25-33, May-June 1957.

it will widen the executive's "reach." [15] This writer even went so far as to call for the abandonment of organizing by horizontal functional departments. He would substitute organization by "action" centers based upon the flow of information. In his mind this would mean recognizing the informal organizations that now exist and building the information system around the people who are now taking needed action irrespective of their formal authority. This would in turn magnify the "reach" of top executives by building the information system so as to facilitate management by exception. They would be fully informed about those matters that need executive attention.

Other writers have suggested that the ever-increasing emphasis upon scientific and technological development will create a sort of "oval" organization at the top.[16] Middle management, as composed of persons of executive calibre, will tend to disappear. Their function of decision will gravitate upward because of the need to centralize information under electronic data processing. Some will be downgraded into low-grade standby supervisors and others who possess intellectual skills will be upgraded toward the top echelons. It is here that a permissive atmosphere of social and professional interaction will replace leadership by hierarchy, the top echelons coalescing into a group that will be social in Lewin's sense rather than scalar as that term was used by Mooney. Presumably, if this should come to pass, the traditional concept of span of control would have little if any application.

Conclusion

For the present the concept of span of control cannot be relegated to limbo. Rather it is necessary to take the temperate view expressed by Urwick that it may be a valuable diagnostic instrument in certain cases.[17] It seems more realistic to approach the problem by asking how much supervision is needed in each particular situation. By acknowledging that circumstances may differ,

[15] Stahrl Edmunds, "The Reach of an Executive," *Harvard Business Review* 37:87-96, January-February 1959.

[16] Harold J. Leavitt and Thomas L. Whisler, "Management in the 1980's," *Harvard Business Review* 36:41-48, November-December 1958.

[17] Lyndall F. Urwick, "The Manager's Span of Control," *Harvard Business Review* 34:39,41, May-June 1956.

and inquiring to ascertain the pertinent variables, an attitude of research will be engendered. Instead of a preconceived formula, people will begin to inquire into the factors which apply in each new supervisory setup. Perhaps after a number of analyses of this kind, empirical evidence will emerge and point to the variables operating. Then it may be possible to begin to establish norms for determining how much supervision is needed.[18]

III • COMMITTEES

Committees are coming to be recognized as belonging to the formal structure, particularly in those organizations which have organization planning departments where the creation, functions, and jurisdiction of committees have often been made the subject of planning and control. This development has been hastened by the emergence of group management in recent decades. Committees have become a major instrumentality of coordination in those huge organizations having a great diversity in both product and geographical location, such as DuPont and Standard Oil. Even such a single purpose entity as the Bank of America operates almost wholly through a series of committees.

While this committee system is essentially horizontal in that each committee is composed of representatives from the functional departments which are concerned with the subject matter under its jurisdiction, the emerging pattern tends toward a hierarchy of functional committees headed by an executive committee. The latter usually operates at the corporate level and is headed by the chief executive officer. At both DuPont and Bank of America this person is the president. The Standard Oil companies operate under an inside board of directors composed of full time executives, and this body resembles an executive committee.

The executive committee has decision-making powers and its formal leader is *primus inter pares,* first among equals, a term frequently applied to the British Prime Minister. Other units in the hierarchy of committees incline more toward an advisory ca-

---

[18] See the section entitled "Criteria for Determining the Span of Control" in Dale, *Planning and Developing the Company Organization Structure,* p. 53.

pacity, although there are functional committees with final authority, usually spelled out, such as a loan committee in a bank.

The AMA Survey

The American Management Association's study of organization practice found that 110 of the 150 companies surveyed reported one or more committees meeting regularly. Half of the companies have a general management committee, usually consisting of working directors and heads of departments. Many companies also have functional committees in such areas as production, sales, or personnel. The following four requirements were laid down for successful operation of committees:

> . . . (1) Work of committees should justify their costs. (2) The principles of effective group action should be applied. (3) Committee mechanics should be arranged so that meetings will not be hampered by procedural difficulties. (4) Only subjects that can be handled better by groups than by individuals should be selected for committee discussion.[19]

Costs. A quick and fairly accurate way of arriving at the cost of a committee is to ascertain the number of man-hours put in by both members and secretarial staff and multiply this by an average hourly salary cost.[20] This numerical result should then be balanced against the contributions which the committee has made to cost-reduction or to increased revenue. The quest for such data may be found in committee contribution to solving knotty problems, coordination, communication, better acceptance of decisions, and executive development and training.

Group effectiveness. The AMA report covers essentially the same ground and states conclusions similar to the norms of group process set forth earlier in this book. To be effective, committees should become social groups rather than gatherings of individual executives. The group sociologist's advice to compose committees of persons who have strong attraction for each other may be difficult to achieve in administrative organization. Furthermore, might it not lead to undue conformity? Don't organizations need a

---

[19] *Ibid.*, p. 86.
[20] *Ibid.*, p. 88.

maverick or two in order to upset the inertia of complacency which develops naturally in all institutions?

Committee mechanics. Factors to be considered include size, proper person to act as chairman, a suitable secretary, agenda and reports, and scheduling of meetings. A committee fewer than six or seven may be too small, for example.

Subjects handled. In the words of the report,

> Committee action seems to be definitely superior in settling questions which may give rise to jurisdictional disputes within the company; individual action seems to be superior in providing leadership, in organization structuring, in execution, and in decision making." It was also reported that committees seemed "slightly better in communication, but not as good in planning, formulating objectives, and administration. Committee action was judged approximately equal to individual action in control, technical innovation, and advisory activities.[21]

Harvard Research

An experimental investigation of committee action and behavior have been carried on at the Laboratory of Social Relations at Harvard University since 1947.[22] An excellent summary of the Laboratory's findings on committee functions and mechanics has been prepared in "how to" terms by the editors of *The Management Review:*

1. Avoid appointing committees larger than seven members unless necessary to obtain representation of all relevant points of view. Try to set up conditions of size, seating, and time allowed so that each member has an adequate opportunity to communicate directly with every other member.
2. Avoid appointing committees as small as two or three members if the power problem between members is likely to be critical.
3. Choose members who will tend to fall naturally into a moderate gradient of participation. Groups made up entirely of high participators will tend to suffer from competition. Groups made up exclusively of the opposite type may find themselves short on ideas.

---

[21] *Ibid.*, p. 93.

[22] Robert F. Bales, "In Conference," *Harvard Business Review* 32:44-50, March-April 1954; digested under title of "Ten Guides to Better Group Decision-Making," *The Management Review* 43:410, July 1954. For a more technical treatment see Talcott Parsons, Robert F. Bales, and Edward A. Shills, *Working Papers in the Theory of Action* (Glencoe, Ill.: Free Press, 1953).

4. Avoid the assumption that a good committee is made up of one leader and several followers. Laboratory findings, while still tentative, indicate that the man who is judged by the group members to have the "best ideas" contributing to the decision is *not* generally the "best-liked." There are two separate roles: task leader and social leader. Try to provide the group with leaders to fill these roles who will support one another.
5. In actual procedure, start with facts if possible. Even where the facts are thought to be well-known to all the members, a short review is seldom a waste of time. A good general procedure is probably to plan to deal with three questions on each major agenda item:
   "What are the facts pertaining to the problem?"
   "How do we feel about them?"
   "What shall we do about the problem?"
   This is probably the preferred order. Take time to lay the ground work before getting to specific suggestions, the third stage. It may be noted that the order recommended is the exact opposite of that which is characteristic of formal parliamentary procedure.
6. Solicit the opinions and experiences of others, especially when disagreements begin to crop up. People often think they disagree when actually they simply are not talking about the same experiences. Try to get past the words and general statements the other man uses for the experiences he is trying to represent.
7. When somebody else is talking, listen, and keep indicating your reactions actively. Most people are not much good at reading your mind. Besides that, they need the recognition you can give them by your honest reaction, whether positive or negative.
8. Keep your eyes on the group. When you are talking, talk to the group as a whole rather than to one of your cronies or to one of your special opponents. Search around constantly for reactions to what you are saying. A good deal of communication goes on at a subverbal level. Nothing tones up the general harmony of a group like a good strong undercurrent of direct eye contact.
9. When you scent trouble coming, break off the argument and backtrack to further work on the facts and direct experience. In some instances the best way to get started on a cooperative track again after a period of difficulty is to agree to go out and gather some facts together by direct experience.
10. Keep your ear to the ground. No recipe or set of rules can substitute for constant, sensitive and sympathetic attention to what is going on in the relations between members. Do not get so engrossed in getting the job done that you lose track of the first prerequisite of success; keeping the committee in good operating condition.

IV · SUMMARY

The span of control idea is central to formal organization theory. This is so because traditional concepts greatly emphasize coordination exercised through the leader at the top. Much interest has therefore centered on the number of people a leader can supervise effectively, that is, his span of control. The bias in the traditional theory has been that a small span is better than a large one because an executive must have intimate and direct contact with his subordinates.

The number of persons an executive supervises also has an important influence on the nature of the hierarchical structure. If the span is large, this means that fewer levels are needed in the organization. The structure would then tend to be wide and flat. Presumably the possibility of communication blockages would be lessened because more people would report directly to the top. If the span is small, the structure would narrow and deepen. There would be more levels. More people would have to communicate to the top through intervening layers of officials. The possibility of communication blockages and distortions would therefore be increased.

In recent years there has been considerable question raised as to the true significance of the span of control concept to organization theory. Partly this has been due to many pragmatic experiences where organization reforms have been built largely on reducing executive span with little ultimate impact on administrative performance. Scholars, particularly those who are behaviorally oriented, also have suggested many limitations to the concept. Finally, it may be noted that the entire culture of management has been changing. The image of the leader as father figure is no longer so prevalent. This transformation in the style of decision-making has had an inevitable bearing on questions relating to the number of people an executive can supervise.

In at least one way, however, the span of control idea has had a resurgence because of its relationship to the number of levels in an organization. The tenor of management philosophy today is delegation and decentralization. And it is argued that a large span of control is an effective means of forcing executives to delegate. It is contended that if an executive has enough people to supervise, there is a point beyond which intimate control becomes impossible. Hence the large span is an effective mechanical means of forcing delegation and decentralization. The experience of Sears Roebuck and Company has been particularly cited in this regard.

The span also tends to be large in governmental organizations. However here we find it is a traditional arrangement and one in which a number of forces operate to keep it that way. The President of the United States, for example, is said to have approximately 100 separate agencies reporting directly to him. Pressure groups, vested interests, and legislative distrust operate against establishing a small span at this level, as well as with most political executives.

On balance it is probable that the span of control idea will occupy a role of lessening importance in organization theory in future. Partly this is due to the general management climate and to the tendency toward group decision-making. Also technological changes in communication, which loom so large in many phases of organization behavior, will probably reinforce this trend. For the present, however, the span of control idea must be taken seriously, if for no other reason than that it is taken seriously by so many practitioners, consultants, and planners. It still seems to have usefulness as a diagnostic instrument in an organization culture in transition. Thus it seems more realistic to approach the problem by asking how much supervision is needed in each particular situation.

Committees represent a different approach to the problem of coordination at the top. As we would expect, they have become increasingly important and are now recognized as belonging to the formal structure. A survey by the American Management Association showed that committees were best utilized in settling questions which may give rise to jurisdictional disputes within the organization.

TEN

Staff and Functional Aspects

What to Look for in This Chapter . . .

Staff as an attempt to extend the executive's capacity to coordinate

Staff work as an intellectual process involving:
- fact-finding
- planning
- organizing

Categories of staff units:
- general
- technical
- coordinating and auxiliary

Effects upon the nature of organizations of the staff concept of functional specialization

---

The staff concept rests essentially on the same theoretical basis as span of control. As in the preceding chapter, the problem remains one of creating a system in which coordination at the top will be most effective. One way, as we saw, is to keep the number of people supervised down to a modest number. Another way is to extend the executive personality. Perhaps the nature of this second alternative can best be explained in the fact that the President of the United States and the Presidency are two different things. In the first instance we are talking about an individual—Roosevelt, Truman, Eisenhower, and so on. In the second we are talking about an institution which in 1959 numbered more than 2000 people. The institution of the Presidency has arisen because the supervision of an executive establishment employing more than 2,000,000 people is an impossible task for any one individual. Thus the President no longer does all the coordinating at the top himself; and it is therefore necessary to distinguish between what the President himself does and what occurs under the Presidency as a corporate entity. This, then, is the staff concept at work. The basic command structure of our national government has changed little in the last half-century; yet the President's executive personality has been extended far beyond anyone's wildest dreams of 1900.

The traditional concept of staff is aid to the executive. This is presumably to be done without disturbing the formal command relationships in the hierarchy. Yet increasing specialization in the organization and growing pressures on the top executive have complicated this initially simple concept greatly. As a result the use of the term staff has become quite ambiguous. Similarly authority and responsibility lines within the organization have seemingly become confused.

Today it is more useful on many occasions to think in terms of two types of activity within the organization: (a) that which is *substantive* (direct) in its contribution to the organization's overall objectives, and (b) that which is *adjective* (indirect) in its contribution. Such a way of thinking removes some confusion and permits us to define staff in somewhat different terms. Staff should be thought of as a *process* occurring around the executive. This process involves thinking, planning, and organizing.

And the question of who gives the orders and who gives the advice becomes a matter of decidedly secondary importance. The advice-authority concept does not really appear to be the keystone of the staff idea. It is much more appropriate to think in terms of the basic problem of extending the executive personality and the processes by which this is done. Bear in mind, too, that the shift in approach suggested here is in accord with the more general metamorphosis in organization theory. With a more collegial style of decision-making, the old problem of who gives the advice and who gives the command seems markedly less relevant.

I • THE STAFF CONCEPT

There is, of course, an abundant literature on the idea of staff and line in the conventional sense. In this construct the line activities are those associated with order-giving in the line of command, on the one hand, and with direct labor or production work on the other. In a relatively small organization, in which all the participants can be coordinated at the top by a single person, everyone would be in the order-giving chain and would be engaged in direct labor.[1] Hence this would be a line type of organization. Such a structure is rare today because few organizations are small enough to permit this kind of coordination at the top.

Origins

Military antecedents. To this basic structure is then added the notion of extending the executive personality. This idea is often thought to have had a military origin and its beginnings are sometimes attributed to the Prussian general staff, which goes back to the days of Frederick the Great.[2] This military background does serve to explain the seeming insistence that the introduction of helpers around the commander should in no way affect the formal command relationships. Thus it developed that staff people were to be regarded as very different from line people. They were to be purely advisory in nature. They were not to give orders. Yet it is doubtful if this presumably clear-cut distinction ever did work in practice. Indeed the very idea of staff work suggests a closeness

---

[1] E. H. Anderson and G. T. Schwenning, *The Science of Production Organization* (New York: John Wiley and Sons, Inc., 1938), p. 125.

[2] Walter Gorlitz, *History of the German General Staff, 1657-1945* (New York: Praeger, 1953).

and a comprehensiveness of view of the top executive's problems that makes informal authority almost inevitable. Added to this is the fact that staff work is really characterized by its intellectual underpinning. Line administrators tend to be conservative, pragmatic, and inclined to make decisions on the basis of their experience and accumulated value systems. The staff person has his time freed to gather data, study, reflect, and come up with solutions arrived at through intellectual processes. He is the thinking and planning arm of the organization. He must inevitably wield power.

Basis in intellectual process. Furthermore the relevance of the intellectual process to staff work becomes more pronounced as time goes on. It has become an intrinsic phase of organization life. For instance there has been a veritable rash of studies and reports dealing with the problems of administering many types of "egghead" activities in modern organizations, particularly military research installations. The research scientist and member of the learned professions does not conform to the behavior pattern which administrative man postulates for him. He is a maverick and outlaw, administratively speaking. In those instances where business competition has forced the constant generation of new ideas and of new products, companies have to make their environment congenial to the intellectual. Thus the Standard Oil Development Company premises ". . . may look rather like a school; its offices, with their blackboards chalked with chemical equations, resemble classrooms. Many of the calm, pleasant men who work here are former professors, or men who once thought of being professors."[3]

Reasons for Growth

It has already been pointed out that as organizations grow they require more record keeping. In a manufacturing company there seems to be a marked jump in the percentage of record keepers at the point of about 150 employees. There also comes a stage of growth at which some necessity arises for the *specialization of the intellectual function*. Why is this so? Does it mean that those already on the job are no longer capable of thinking? Not at all!

---

[3] "Research: The Long View," *The Lamp* 36:2, June 1954.

The reasons for this metamorphosis are perfectly natural and logical.

Specialization of knowledge. One of the principal reasons for the rise of special staff units is the heightening complexity of knowledge. While organizations need generalists, the fact remains that it is increasingly difficult for the generalist to make decisions in subject-matter fields on the basis of his own knowledge alone. Hence he finds himself more and more dependent upon the advice and counsel of specialists. Indeed, in businesses whose processes are based upon chemistry, physics, and engineering the specialization of the intellectual function is a paramount consideration. In those instances where business competition has forced the constant generation of new ideas and new products, companies have had to make their environment congenial to the intellectual.

But not all specialization of intellectual function is at the exploratory or developmental level. Much of it has to do with such operating activities as accounting, engineering, law, organizing, design, and advertising. Indeed, considerable staff work is performed at the operating level by people whose main concern is getting out the goods, even though they do not directly perform the necessary manipulative tasks. The point of distinction is that their work has a strong intellectual ingredient. Modern organizations will neither run nor survive unless they provide for free play of intellect. Yet there is a strong normal drag for organizations to suppress intellect.

The people who rise to executive posts have in their personalities marked components of aggressiveness, compulsiveness, and the need for action. Around them something must be happening, not next week, not tomorrow, but today. Their preferences lie in the direction of quick and on-the-spot decision rather than more deliberate studied solutions. Often persons with exceptional native endowment, they may have a high batting average in getting along without much staff service. But as the organization becomes more mature and complex, conditions arise which require carefully developed solutions rather than the hunch and intuition of a "superman."

A primary executive function is to do that sort of thinking on which major policy decisions are based. But executives become so bogged down in trouble-shooting and on-the-spot emergency decisions that they do not have time for studying basic policy problems. So they farm out a portion of their intellectual activities to staff assistants. In gathering the information needed for their studies the assistants must contact other members of the organization, including department heads. As the operating officials learn to have confidence in and respect for the staff representatives, many of the vexing day-to-day problems are settled on the spot without need for going to the boss, with the result that the latter's time is released for more important matters. One of the most fruitful methods of relieving executive overload is to furnish the boss staff assistance, provided he will use it.[4]

The coordinating impetus. The multiplication of specialists in growing organizations places new emphasis on the problem of coordination. The specialist tends to be a myopic and provincial fellow who regards the boundaries of his specialty as the organization universe. So we create a new genus of coordinating staff specialist to get the other specialists to work together as members of the larger community. A whole new galaxy of management analysts has emerged recently: organization analysts, budget analysts, and 57 varieties of staff assistants. Their primary purpose is to aid the officers in creating a smooth working management machine, bringing about standardization and uniformity of practice where desirable, and minimizing duplication, overlapping, and waste. The staff's coordinating job involves a peculiar combination of fact-finding and management ability, on the one hand, with conference and face-to-face negotiation on the other. So, staff work varies from the search for theoretical truth in the laboratory to the rough-and-tumble of negotiating a labor contract.

II • NATURE OF STAFF WORK

Since we regard staff work as essentially an intellectual process, it follows that its primary ingredients derive from that point of reference. In short we are suggesting that the essence of staff

---

[4] Ernest Dale, *Planning and Developing the Company Organization,* American Management Association, Research Report No. 20, 1952.

work is thought. And it is thought directed toward making sure that the various parts of the organization mesh as effectively as possible. It therefore appears that three basic elements are involved. These are: (1) fact-finding, (2) planning, and (3) organizing.

Elements in Process

Fact-finding. The essence of staff work is fact-finding which may take a wide variety of forms. Basic research in the structure of long molecules over an extended period of years led to DuPont's thriving business in new textiles. This required a great deal of what the practical man of the market place has been known to condemn as mere "theory." Because a long molecule is a theoretical construct no one has ever seen one. On a somewhat lower intellectual but nonetheless worthy level, the assembling of operating data, as characterized by administrative analysis studies, seems to have similar aspects. Would it be more or less advantageous to have company-owned autos or to compensate drivers for using their own? Would it be cheaper to rent office space or to have a company-owned building? Should an incentive pay plan be adopted and, if so, what form should it take?

A great deal of staff work consists of arranging data and writing it in such form as to be most useful. Thus statistical work looms large in the operation of many organizations. Whole suites and buildings are devoted to installation of computing machines or "mechanical brains." Some people devote their entire time to writing and maintaining standard practice manuals. Others do likewise with job descriptions, production specifications, and various types of standards. In other words, the staff man on whatever level needs to be literate in one or both of the two basic modes of recording and communicating: (1) statistics, and (2) the written word. Statistical solutions are increasingly sought and relied on in struggling with the increasingly complex problems of large-scale organizations. Prediction of things to come can hardly be attempted without consulting the mathematical laws of probability.

Planning. All of the ingredients of staff work blend together instead of being separate entities. Thus there can be precious little planning without fact-finding, yet the latter will not in itself tell what facts mean in terms of the future. Planning, like research, embraces a wide spectrum of duties and functions. Some are rather pedestrian such as laying out work flow in an office or scheduling the completion of specific phases of production. Others utilize the higher intellectual capacities by attempting to predict needs, exigencies, and the scale of operations several years hence. Thus forest managers acquire the right-of-way for a lumbering road that may not be used for ten years. War planners must be expert in geopolitics as well as the probable future development of battle techniques if they may hope to anticipate all probable war situations a quarter century hence.

Organizing. There is a large sector of staff work which is concerned with organizing in the broad sense. A study of critical incidents in the district ranger's job in the United States Forest Service revealed close similarity between the dimensions labeled "organizing" and "planning." An organizer breaks down jobs into their component tasks, assigns jobs, lays out the work, fixes responsibility, and follows up to see that things get done. But in order to do so he must also plan and schedule work.

What does the staff man do as an organizer? He makes, analyses, and formulates plans for improving organization. But he does not do all of this in the vacuum of his private office. Instead he confers, negotiates, and even wheedles. Thus the staff approach to organizing takes on a color akin to "coordinating"—getting the various parts of the mosaic to dovetail and synchronize. As organizations grow larger, the basic management functions tend to become specialized: personnel, accounting, stores and warehousing, maintenance of property and equipment. Operating or line departments are supervised by central units or relieved entirely of such functions.

Two fundamental points come out of this discussion. *First,* the idea of staff as an intellectual process is further underscored. Its basic elements are fact-finding, planning and organizing. This may involve far more than the mere giving of advice and even go so far as entering the realm of command and authority, as will be pointed out in the next section. *Second,* while it is correct to speak of certain units and individuals as having predominantly staff duties, a great deal of staff work may be carried on by people whose assignments are essentially line. Therefore, understanding will be promoted by talking about staff work, rather than about individuals or units as staff or line.

Staff Authority

It is customary to say that staff people have the authority of ideas. By this is meant that they may have superior knowledge as a result of both their training and their fact-finding. They may or may not have superior brains, but the staff process compels them to use constantly what they have. Hence they are likely to be up-to-date in their information about techniques, procedures, and productive processes. It has been said that effective staff persons think of themselves primarily as catalysts. "They stimulate and ensure proper emphasis on management planning, spotlighting deficiencies and problems that might otherwise be ignored. They organize the participation of all interested parties in the solution of problems, and help train the line organization in the application of better administrative practices. They supplement the line organization. . . ."[5]

Ernest Dale has pointed out that there are at least five ways in which staff people actually do exert influence or "command authority":

1. *Superior Articulation.* Staff men are generally articulate and skilled in persuading others to accept their ideas, while the line executive is often less vocal.
2. *Technical Competence.* Since the staff specialist has technical skills and knowledge not possessed by the line department, his advice, like legal counsel, may have to be accepted.
3. *Command Through Status.* Many staff specialists are considerably higher in the management hierarchy and in the salary scale than the executives they advise, and are able to obtain acceptance on that account as well as because of their technical competence. [A corollary of the third point is propinquity to top management. The staff specialist has many opportunities for association and contact with persons in legal authority.]
4. *Command Through Sanctions.* If a line executive does not agree with the staff proposals, the staff men may appeal to the line executive's superior and then to the president, who could force the line to accept the staff counsel (advice).

---

[5] E. W. Reilley, "Why Short-Change the Chief Executive on Staff Assistance?" *Personnel* 24:85, 89, September 1947.

5. *Command by Default.* Important problems may exist on which no line actions have been taken—personnel problems, for example. This may be due to lack of time or interest on the part of the line. More seriously, it may be difficult for top executives to arrive at agreement in open negotiations without "losing face." Consequently, the line executives may depend upon lower ranking staff specialists to reach agreement in informal discussions.[6]

Categories of Staff Units

There are so many logical ways to classify staff agencies that one is privileged to choose his own. Here we see no reason to alter the threefold classification used in our previous writings:

- General staff
- Technical staff
- Coordinating and auxiliary staff

This is not original with us, having been suggested by various writers in public administration,[7] rather than industrial management.

General staff. The general staff consists of the people who work on over-all plans and policies. They are usually thought of as related immediately to the chief executive, but the general staff function may exist further down in the hierarchy. Again, much confusion would be avoided by thinking of the general staff function rather than whether particular individuals are members of the general staff. It is quite possible that the operating vice-president, a line official, may act in a general staff capacity to the chief when he sits as a member of a policy committee. He may also have a general staff of his own. The term has a distinct military flavor, the most common connotation having to do with preparing war plans, in times of peace as well as war. It received widespread public attention during the tenure of Elihu Root as

[6] Dale, *Planning and Developing the Company Organization,* pp. 73 ff.

[7] John M. Gaus and Leon P. Walcott, *Public Administration and the United States Department of Agriculture* (Chicago: Public Administration Service, 1940), pp. 289-377; Arthur W. Macmahon, John D. Millett, and Gladys Ogden, *The Administration of Federal Work Relief* (Chicago: Public Administration Service, 1941), p. 245; W. F. Willoughby, *Principles of Public Administration* (Baltimore: The Johns Hopkins Press, 1927), pp. 143-149; Luther Gulick and L. Urwick, *Papers on the Science of Administration* (New York: Institute of Public Administration, 1937), pp. 30, 49-88.

Secretary of War under President Theodore Roosevelt. It is interesting to note that Root virtually forced adoption of the staff organization of the Army over the strong opposition of the military brass, who, just like civilians of comparable status, did not want to be coordinated.[8]

Technical staff. The distinguishing feature of technical staff is specialization. These people possess knowledge and skill that is unique. Not all of them are in a purely advisory relationship, a fact which gives rise to most of the difficulty to be discussed shortly. As most organizations grow—especially those whose production processes are based on scientific, professional, and technical developments—they find it desirable to set up research and advisory units which specialize. Thus an automobile manufacturer has a body design unit, a school district has specialists in the teaching of reading; a social agency has a group specializing in psychiatric case work; the military has researchers experimenting with new weapons and ordnance. Such technical staff units devote their time principally to development, training, and advice, although they sometimes engage in "functional supervision." Their distinguishing feature is that they are specialists, that they have skills not possessed by the line or program units, and that they have been set up primarily with the mission of "spreading" their unique knowledge to the line organization.

Coordinating and auxiliary staff. The coordinating staff is mainly interested in patterns of management control, organization structure, budgeting and accounting, personnel and industrial relations, management planning, and administrative analysis. Closely related and overlapping are a series of activities which American writers sometimes call "auxiliary" and which are referred to by the British as "establishment" services. They embrace such activities as property management and maintenance, real estate, warehousing and supply, insurance, automotive shops, and transportation. There are logical reasons for not using the term "staff" in designating these activities and such writers as Leonard D. White refrain from doing so. However, there is strong logical ground for

---

[8] See Otto L. Nelson, Jr., *National Security and the General Staff* (Washington, D.C.: Infantry Journal Press, 1946).

including them because the essential approach is characterized by staff work.

The element which coordinating activities and auxiliary services have in common is that both are forms of centralization, in which organization-wide approaches would seem better than each subunit's performing such activities itself. Thus the centralization of real estate activities or bus transportation is in a sense a coordinative step based on specialization of function. It does not matter particularly whether the term "staff" is used in describing them.

III • STAFF AND FUNCTIONAL RELATIONSHIPS

It should be re-emphasized at this point that the term "functional" has many shades of meaning, but that one of them comes close to being synonymous with "staff." Reference to functional contacts, functional authority and functional relationships really suggests those specialized activities attached to the line but not necessarily exercising command authority.

The principal problem of functional relationships in large-scale organizations is the structuring of formal authority. At the headquarters echelon there will be a number of specialized departments. In industry these will probably include manufacturing, sales, finance, research and development, and industrial relations.[9] The problem centers around the degree of line or command authority that is given to these specialized units over their counterparts on subordinate echelons. The functionalists at headquarters want direct line authority but the traditional command structure seeks to place them in an advisory capacity.[10]

Types of Organization

This results in two principal types of organization that constitute the main choices available to organization planners. These are the

[9] *Improving Staff and Line Relations,* National Industrial Conference Board, Studies in Personnel Policy No. 153, 1956.

[10] For a case study where functionalists seem to have won out, see Herbert Kaufman, *The New York City Health Centers,* ICP Case Series No. 9, (University, Alabama: University of Alabama Press, 1952).

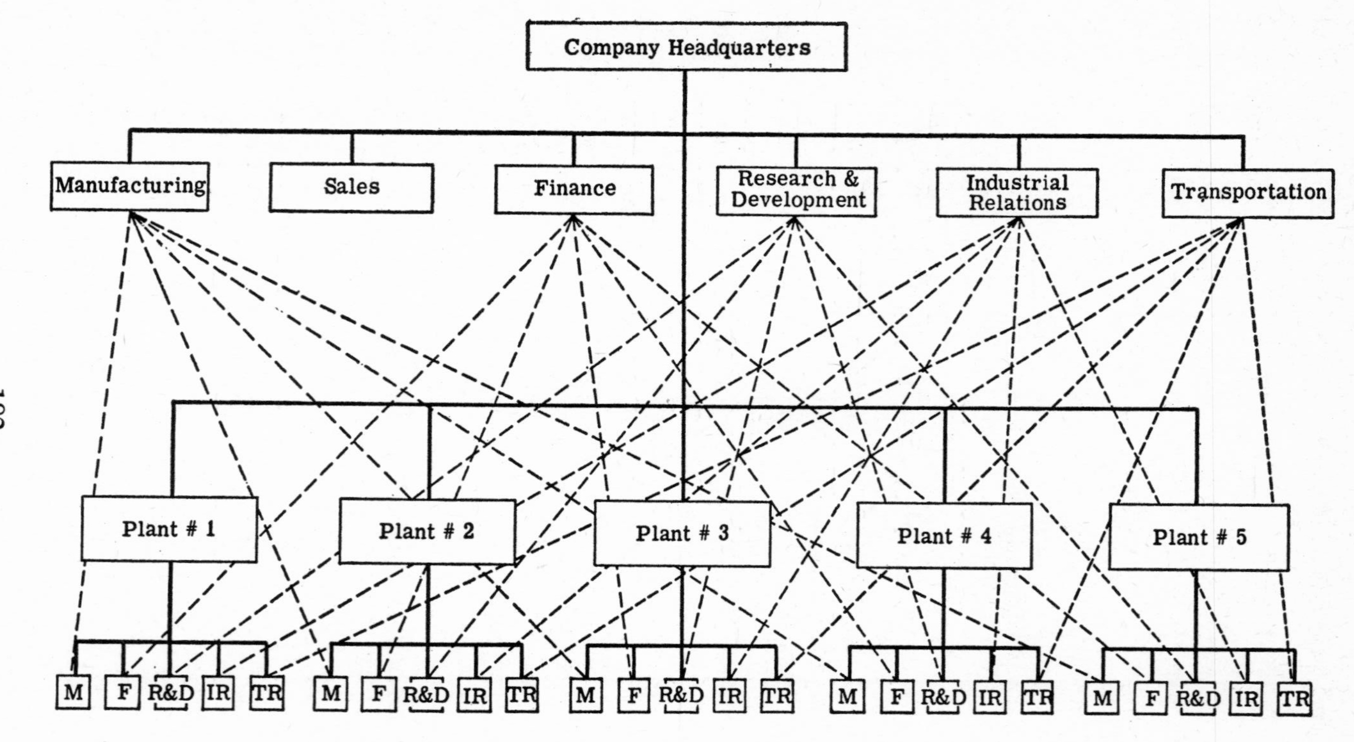

CHART 10-1. *Staff-and-line type of organization* (—— = *line relationship*; - - - - - = *staff relationship*).

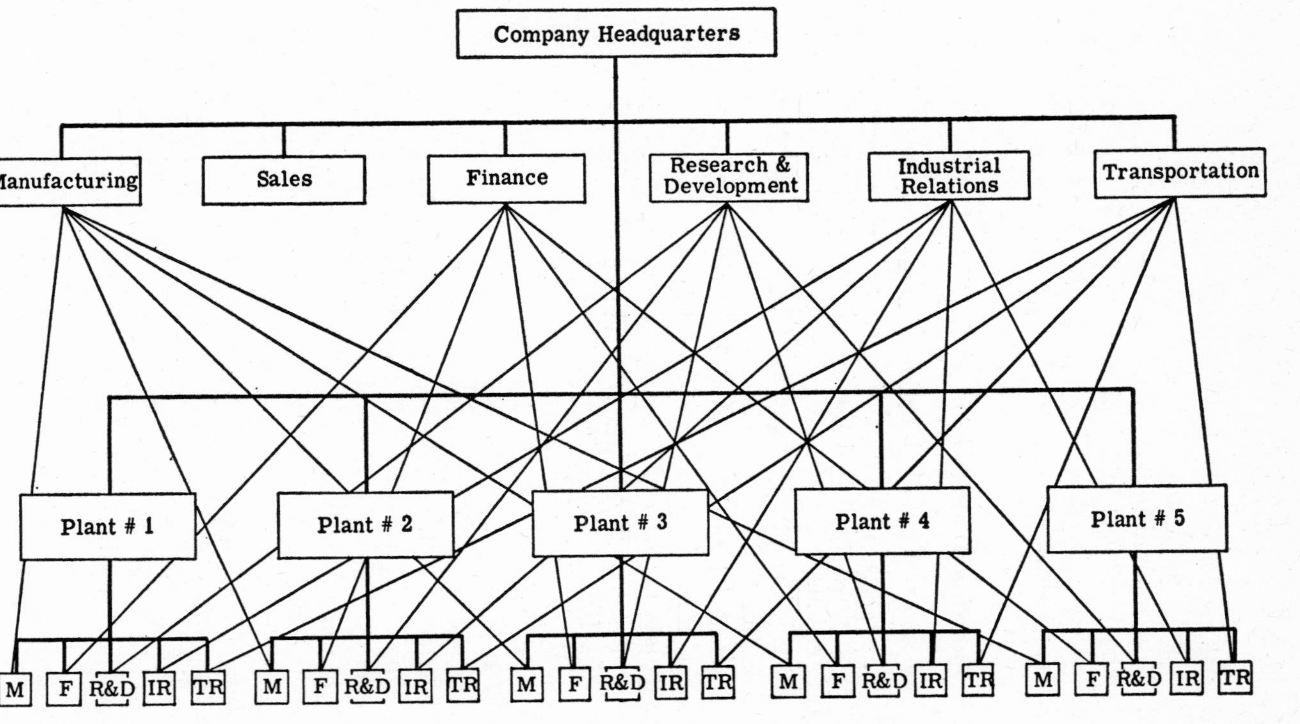

CHART 10-2. *Functional type of organization—multiple or dual supervision. Line of command shares line authority with specialized sub-units.*

line-and-staff model and the functional model, depicted in Charts 10-1 and 10-2. In the line-and-staff type, as we have indicated, authority is structured to flow along a unity of command pattern. The functional units act in a staff capacity. In the functional type, the specialized units share line authority, resulting in dual or multiple supervision.

Taylor's Functional Supervision at the Shop Level

The term and concept of "functional supervision" was originated by Frederick Winslow Taylor, who described it in his *Shop Management.*[11] Basically, he felt that the job of supervision was too complicated to be handled effectively by one foreman and should therefore be parceled out to as many as eight specialized foremen, as depicted in Chart 10-3.

This functional idea, however, did not take root, probably for two reasons. *First,* the concept of multiple supervision seemed to outrage the sacred *unity of command* precept so deeply ingrained in management lore. *Second,* specialization had not reached such a point as to force attention to this question. However specialization of tasks has been increasing at such a steady geometrical ratio in recent years as to raise forcibly the problem of functional influence. It can no longer be "swept under the rug" because of an uncongenial or, in the eyes of some, a sinful connotation.

As a matter of fact, an examination of the tasks and duties of Taylor's functional foremen will reveal that their counterparts actually do exist in today's manufacturing organizations. Modern systems of production control have shop planners, clerks, and timekeepers located right in the shop. Taylor's "shop disciplinarian" is the counterpart of the decentralized personnel supervisor. The "gang boss" is of course the line foreman, the "speed boss" the time study man, and the inspector is the same as ever. The "repair boss" has his contemporary counterpart in the maintenance foreman, who it is said will become more important in the age of automation. Taken all in all, Taylor's functional supervision

---

[11] Frederick Winslow Taylor, *Shop Management* (New York: Harper and Brothers, 1911). All of *Shop Management* is to be found in Taylor, *Scientific Management* (New York: Harper and Brothers, 1947), pp. 17-207.

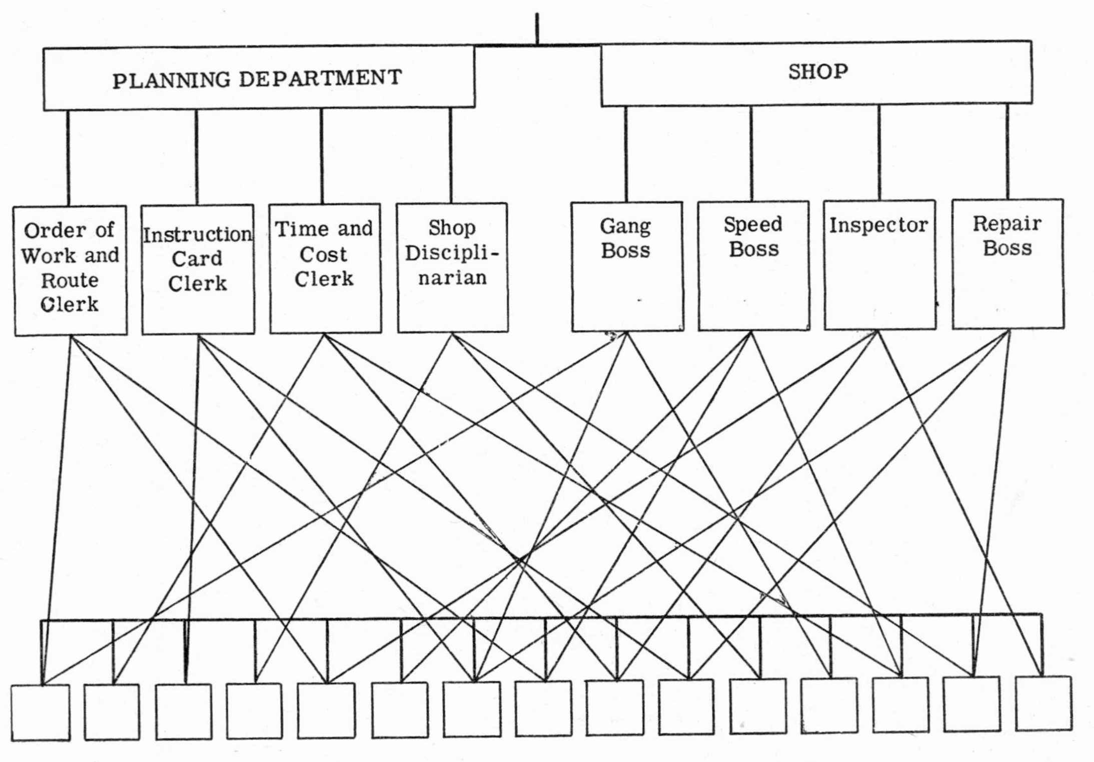

CHART 10-3. *A graphic example of Taylor's functional foremanship.*

has come to pass, thus confirming what his disciples have always said: that he was a prophet not wholly honored in his own time.

Tension Points

A sociological study of several industrial plants revealed the existence of a "general conflict system."[12] Part of this was due to the tendency of staff people to occupy higher status levels in the social hierarchy than shop people. Staff members were more highly educated. They were more concerned about dress, the daily shave, the weekly haircut. They used better English in speaking and in writing reports. They were more suave and poised in social intercourse. The staff people chose to eat together rather than to lunch with the line. Staff members were usually more mobile, both socially and vocationally. They were ambitious, restless and individualistic. Their desire for personal distinction often prevailed over sentiments of group consciousness. There was also some age conflict, particularly where a young staff officer studied the work of an older line supervisor.

It might also be added that staff people are likely to be more theoretical and bookish. They place greater emphasis upon the niceties of paper work and record-keeping. They are more likely to have an idealistic approach to problem-solving which involves changes in methods and therefore alteration of long-established habits. The line people, on the other hand, tend to have a preference for pragmatic on-the-spot solutions, often belittling the theoretical approach of the staff.

Part of this conflict can be related to aggressiveness on the one hand, and defensiveness on the other. The staff function by its very nature must question the status quo. A staff man is a professional critic, and nobody likes to be criticized. Hence the line thinks that the staff criticizes existing practices to make themselves (the staff) look good. The staff has to justify its existence and to do so it points out defects at the expense of the line. It is small wonder that line people become apprehensive and defensive. This, of course, is only one of many tension points built into any structuring of organizations. It suggests in only slightly different

---

[12] Melville Dalton, "Conflicts between Staff and Line Managerial Officers," *American Sociological Review* 15:342-351, June 1950.

terms how human interactions will ultimately determine the degree to which these conflict areas will become serious organizations problems.

IV • SUMMARY

The staff idea has occupied a very prominent place in the literature of organization. In many respects it represents an attempt to superimpose on the traditional command structure the benefits of specialization and expertise. This has seemed necessary because in large, complicated organizations, it has no longer been possible for the man who sits atop the hierarchical pyramid to provide in an intimate, personal way the necessary coordinative facilities. In short it has been necessary to extend the executive personality. The traditional thought has been that such specialist abilities could be made available to the leader without disturbing the unity of command in the organization. As a consequence much emphasis has been placed on the staff man's authority relationships within the organization. The doctrine is that the staff man is an adviser, an aide with no authority.

But in actual experience the theory has been hard to square with the practice. This is due to the fact that staff work is essentially an intellectual process. Its purpose is to provide thinking, planning, and organizing support to the executive. Hence it follows that anyone with such capacities and with access to the top would have real power in the organization, whether it shows on the organization chart or not. It is our contention that the debate over the authority relationship between the line officer and the staff man has been an essentially fruitless one. It has missed the main point that staff work is essentially an intellectual process.

Three basic elements of staff work may be identified: (1) fact-finding, (2) planning, and (3) organizing. The objective of such efforts is to facilitate the coordination of the various units of the organization. It is also apparent that this concept of the nature of staff work requires that it be performed in operating units as well as those specialized sections of the organization which are frequently labeled staff.

Within organizations it has of course been necessary to set up units that specialize in various aspects of the staff process. These so-called staff specialists may be classified in a number of different ways, each of which has its own brand of logic. In this chapter we suggest three categories which have long had currency in the literature of public administration. These are:

(1) *General staff*, which involves those who work on over-all plans and policies.

(2) *Technical staff*, in which the key features are specialization and possession of knowledge and skills in the organization that are unique.

(3) *Coordinating and auxiliary staff*, which concerns such matters as patterns of management control, budgeting and accounting, personnel and industrial relations, and so forth. Of an auxiliary nature are property management and maintenance, warehousing and supply, insurance, and so forth.

Some have contended that this latter category is not appropriately a staff activity. While a strong argument can be made for this view, it may also be contended that such activities qualify because they involve essentially the same intellectual processes. However the labeling of coordinating and auxiliary staff services does serve to point up some of the basic semantic difficulties in these concepts. For here the essence of the staff idea seems to be synonymous with functional specialization.

The idea of functional authority and functional contacts represents a fundamentally different approach to organization structuring from that of the traditional hierarchy. In the latter instance the authority pyramid is actually created by rigid adherence to the unity of command precept. An organization structured on the functional principle, on the other hand, violates unity of command. A number of specialists are permitted to exercise authority within their areas of competence, thus resulting in multiple supervision rather than unified supervision. Such an idea was first proposed by Frederick W. Taylor and aroused little interest. Today the functional concept is really operating, though there is still a rather general reluctance to recognize its existence.

ELEVEN

The Decentralization Pattern

What to Look for in This Chapter . . .

Contemporary trend toward decentralization in large scale organizations

The decentralization pattern includes these elements:

- formal structure
- executive behavior
- policy and decision
- social climate

Decentralization can take place by:

- functions
- geographic regions
- product divisions

Delegation as a part of executive behavior in the decentralized situation

The mixture of competition and freedom in the social climate of decentralization

The contemporary trend in large-scale organization is toward decentralization, but we must realize that decentralization is several things to different people. There are those who view it entirely in terms of decision-making; others see it from the standpoint of geographical dispersion of plants and installations; and still others approach it as a philosophy of corporate life, a set of organization values with sociological, psychological and spiritual facets.

Although the current wave of conversions to the "gospel" of decentralization seems to have started during and after World War II, there was a flurry during the 1920's [1] marked by the emergence of perhaps the greatest of the prophets, Alfred P. Sloan, Jr., and his enduring monument, General Motors.[2] Industrial decentralization seems to have continued apace during the 1950's. One of the most vocal practitioners has been Mr. Ralph J. Cordiner, President of the General Electric Company, who is the author of a plan that embraces the current philosophy of decentralization.[3] As further evidence that a move toward decentralized organization is emerging, it is no happenstance that three studies setting forth and spelling out the decentralized way of corporate life should have issued from the nation's foremost business schools almost simultaneously in 1957–1958.[4] Decentralization is truly in the air!

I • THE GOSPEL OF DECENTRALIZATION

In some respects decentralization has come to be a "gospel" of management. First, leaders like Sloan and Cordiner have regarded it as a way of life to be adopted at least partially on faith; secondly, it is an idealistic concept with ethical roots in democracy. Thirdly, it is in the beginning a more difficult way of life because it involves a change in behavior running counter to

---

[1] Alfred O. Chandler, Jr., "Management Decentralization: A Historical Analysis," *The Business History Review* 30:111-174, June 1956.

[2] Ernest Dale, "Contributions to Administration by Alfred P. Sloan, Jr., and G.M.," *Administrative Science Quarterly* 1:30-62, June 1956.

[3] Ralph J. Cordiner, *New Frontiers for Professional Managers* (New York: McGraw-Hill Book Company, Inc., 1956).

[4] George Albert Smith, *Managing Geographically Decentralized Companies* (Boston: Harvard Business School, 1958); Paul R. Lawrence, *The Changing of Organizational Behavior Patterns* (Boston: Harvard Business School, 1958); Eli Ginzberg and Ewing W. Reilley, *Effecting Change in Large Organizations* (New York: Columbia University Press, 1957).

historically-rooted culture patterns of mankind. That is why the new literature of decentralization dwells on how to bring about change in organization behavior. Men find it difficult to delegate, to think in terms of the abstractions required by long-term planning, to listen rather than to give orders, to evaluate other men and their work in terms of over-all results instead of the irritations and tensions of the moment. Yet this is the very key to the behavior required of leaders in a decentralized organization.

Cultural Aspects

The point has been made above that the decentralized way of life is not an easy one. The same can be said of political democracy as witnessed by the difficulties it has encountered in those parts of the world where it has not sprung up indigenously and developed as the result of centuries of experience. Decentralization will always experience a certain amount of endemic conflict between those whose purpose is to coordinate and those who resist coordination. What is needed is to learn a way of life in which the coordinating process will be the least restrictive, in which people can pursue their individual goals to the maximum and yet work in harmony toward group goals with others who look upon things differently. It takes considerable experience and organization maturity to do this.

Experience in Public Administration

World War II. One cannot gainsay the fact that public administration is in some respects unique, the leading responsible factor being the political nature of its environment. Nevertheless, industrial models have always had their influence on organization reform in the public realm. The most gigantic decentralization actions, perhaps, in the history of mankind, were taken in connection with military administration during World War II, and among these was the establishment of the Army Service Forces, which reversed the flow of paper work away from Washington to the field. In addition, it kept thousands of people out of Washington who had no need to be there, often much against their desires. After the war ended, the Army Service Forces was abolished as a single entity, but it was immensely successful during the war in decentralizing finance, supply, personnel, property maintenance, and dozens of other auxiliary activities, as noted by Ginzberg and Reilley.[5]

The fact that the Army Service Forces organization was abolished at the close of hostilities need not be related to its effectiveness; it was made up in the beginning by combining fifty lesser empires. One need only to refer back to the opposition encountered by Elihu Root when, at the turn of the century, he pushed through a reorganization of the War Department and inaugurated the general staff idea. Decentralization is a way of organization life which cuts deeply into the fences erected to protect personal empires.

Proposals of consultants. During the last 20 years consulting firms in the field of industrial management have been engaged to study the organization and administration of many federal agencies, and they have in general tended to recommend a greater degree of decentralization. Thus since World War II such decentralization in formal structure has taken place in the Post Office, the Internal Revenue Service, and the Veterans' Administration. Studies are needed to ascertain how these moves are working out, whether they actually conform to the pattern presented below, or whether decentralization has taken place in form only. The traditional literature in public administration has tended to emphasize geographical area rather than the dynamics of administrative action and decision.[6] It should be pointed out in passing that some federal agencies, notably the United States Forest Service, have operated effectively for many years in general accordance with the decentralized pattern to be suggested. However, perhaps the greater number have functioned according to a rather highly centralized pattern, just as in industry.

Present Status

While the tenor of the remarks thus far would undoubtedly so indicate, it should nevertheless be pointed out that the pattern described below is only partly an achieved fact and that in many

---

[5] Ginzberg and Reilley, *Effecting Change in Large Organizations,* p. 111.

[6] The standard work has been James W. Fesler, *Area and Administration* (University, Alabama: University of Alabama Press, 1949).

organizations which have professed the gospel, achievement of the goal has been but partial. Cordiner estimated that it would take five years to make the changeover in General Electric, and experience proved this to be true.[7]

Decentralization requires maturity and character, not only on the part of the individual members of the organization, but also in the culture of the larger society as well as the subculture of the organization itself. The fact that so many large industrial corporations have professed this gospel and are endeavoring to practice it should give some comfort to those who view the twentieth century bureaucratization of life apprehensively. The fact that decentralization seems to be profitable financially is of course a primary consideration, but should not blind one to the less mundane values involved.

II • THE DECENTRALIZATION PATTERN IN OUTLINE

An overview in outline at this point may give the reader an understanding of the whole pattern of decentralization before we proceed to a fuller discussion of its parts.

I. The Formal Structure
  A. A flat job-task pyramid
    1. Minimize number of horizontal levels
  B. Distinguish between corporate and production levels
    1. Corporate level keeps out of production
    2. Establish semi-autonomous subsidiary corporations or divisions as the principal operating units
  C. Staff-and-line
    1. Structure formal authority according to the staff-and-line model postulated in the preceding chapter
  D. Set up organization planning as an instrumentality of dynamic growth and change

II. Executive Behavior
  A. Corporate executives
    1. Major efforts devoted to planning, policy-making and evaluation of results
    2. Refrain from that type of interference in current production matters which weakens subordinates
      (a) Keep from seeming too interested in details of production

[7] Cordiner, *New Frontiers for Professional Managers*, p. 54.

(b) Give advice to subordinate echelons in such a manner as not to constitute an order or decision
(c) When asked for advice, "return the ball" instead of answering categorically
3. Set broad goals and targets
4. Control by remote feedback rather than immediate supervision

B. Production Executives
1. Function as autonomous head of own unit
2. Operate on flexible budget making executive virtually an entrepeneur; cost centers, allocating profit-and-loss, extend down into the plants
3. Make and implement policy subject to guide lines established at the corporate level
4. Delegate and then absorb heat generated by subordinates' errors
5. Plan production goals and controls by feedback
6. Generate atmosphere of self-reliance within a framework of freedom in which the main sanctions are results

III. Policy and Decision
A. Broad guide lines are established at corporate level
B. There is a policy continuum in which each subordinate level determines policy in line with that set by superior echelons
C. Decisions are made at the lowest level consistent with the situation
D. Decisions are arrived at only after completed staff work and consultation, *but* the responsibility for decision resides with the appropriate executive
E. The superior behaves in such a manner as to encourage subordinates to make decisions, parrying attempts to evade responsibility

IV. The Social Climate
A. Relaxed freedom within the rules of the game
B. Communication is two-way, oblique, and horizontal
C. Democratic consultation and interaction without undermining the essential needs of leadership and discipline
D. Individual self-expression and self-development are encouraged within the limits imposed by organization's resources and needs

III • THE DECENTRALIZATION PATTERN IN DETAIL

The Formal Structure

Two general approaches. There are in general two ways of decentralizing an industrial structure. One is by leaving the decentralized units as integral divisions, there being only one corporation. In general this is the policy followed by General Motors. The other is to decentralize by the organization of subsidiaries, or affiliate companies. The Standard Oil companies have tended to follow the latter method. Indeed, the patriarch of the Standard Oil world, Standard Oil (New Jersey), is entirely a holding company with no operating functions. The way such a corporation operates through affiliation is explained by Robert Johnson, of Johnson and Johnson. The subsidiaries are called associate companies.

> Each associate company has its own president and board of directors. They run their own show, making their own decisions on matters affecting the operation of their own corporation. Matters that concern the whole organization, such as financing or completely new products, are discussed in each company. They are referred to the Board of Johnson and Johnson, which reaches a final decision and assumes final responsibility.
>
> This may seem difficult and complicated, yet it really is simple. Each member of the Executive Committee is responsible for contacts with one group of associate companies. Their presidents report to him, which means that they tell him how their companies are getting on and bring him their plans or problems. He presents their needs to the entire Board, thus saving its time and the time of people in his group of associate companies.
>
> We have said that the president and directors of each associate company make their own decisions. Their authority to do so, however, comes from the Board of Johnson and Johnson. Since the Board gives them the right to act, it therefore accepts their acts as its own. Moreover, since the Chairman of the Board is the executive officer, he becomes responsible for the acts of management throughout our whole family of companies.[8]

Three bases of decentralization. Smith's study found three general types of decentralized structure in American industry: (1) by functions; (2) by geographical regions; and (3) by product divisions.[9] Firms organized by function tend to have one main product. In them the decentralized factory manager and sales manager each report to separate functional executives at head-

[8] *Robert Johnson Talks It Over* (New Brunswick, N.J.: Johnson and Johnson, 1949), pp. 6-7. A letter from Mr. Johnson, dated March 28, 1958, stated that this pattern of decentralization was then still in force.

[9] Smith, *Managing Geographically Decentralized Companies,* pp. 25-33.

quarters, as would other functional people, such as finance. This type of organization has three vertical levels, and the people working in it seem to be less confused about status because it is clear to whom they report.

In the second, an organization based on geographical decentralization, everyone reports through the regional manager. Functional lines to headquarters are purely staff, similar to the line-and-staff model postulated in the previous chapter. Such organizations tend to have four levels. In spite of the fact that this is the type of organization postulated by our model for large companies with diversified products, Smith points out that it seems usual "to have strong differences of opinion between the headquarters officers, on the one hand, and the branch officers, on the other, as to who should have authority to do what."[10] This is only one more example of the fact that the decentralized way of life may not be the easiest one.

Organization by product line is represented by the Ford Motor Company, General Motors, and Du Pont. In each case a major division is devoted to making and selling a single product. Each division is organized as an independent unit and the structure of the field units may be functional, geographical, or a mixture of the two. Committees at the corporate level work toward desirable standardization and uniformity.

The government corporation. The government corporation is an instrumentality for decentralizing administration utilized more frequently in times of emergency, its birthrate having increased rapidly during both world wars and the New Deal era. The basic objective is to give government industrial operations some of the flexibility of decision, coupled with fiscal accountability, commonly associated with private business measures. The current generation of readers will be familiar with the Federal Deposit Insurance Corporation, the Commodity Credit Corporation and the Tennessee Valley Authority. At the state and local levels the Port of New York Authority is a particularly good example. It is chartered by two states, New York and New Jersey.

Congress has not looked upon the government corporation with

---

[10] *Ibid.*, pp. 28-29.

wholehearted approval, as evidenced by the reduction in number of such corporations after each emergency, and also by enactment of the Corporation Control Act of 1945. The latter requires the budget of each corporation to be reviewed by the Bureau of the Budget and then to pass through congressional appropriation procedure.

Executive Behavior

The principal reason why decentralization is so difficult to accomplish is because it calls for a pattern of executive behavior which on first sight seems in many respects to be opposite to the stereotype of model executive behavior. What is this stereotype? The successful executive is expected to be a forceful man of action: decisive, commanding, ambitious, and very much the central figure.

Planning responsibility. The new approach calls for the top executives to follow a radically different type of behavior, which poses quite a problem for successful production executives who have been elevated to the corporate level. Their very success which has led to promotion has been based upon a lifetime of acting like a clucking brood hen. This is exemplified particularly with regard to the production executive's habit of continuous follow-up of operations and results, accompanied by his own participation in on-the-spot trouble-shooting. When he gets to the corporate level, he must change these ingrained habits of a lifetime. First, so that he will have time to engage in the planning function which is the heart of his new job, even if he is corporate vice-president for manufacturing. Secondly, if he continues to function in the clucking hen fashion toward those on the production echelons he will influence them to behave likewise toward their subordinates, a mode of behavior which runs contrary to that required by the decentralized model.

Evaluation of personnel and results. The corporate executive does things other than planning. One of the most important of his activities is evaluation of both executive personnel and results. But this takes place on a long-range basis and involves a more remote point of vantage than day-to-day trouble-shooting. The keystone of executive behavior under decentralization is to push decision-making down, and this cannot be done if top executives are not operating at their "proper level."[11] If a top executive behaves like a shop superintendent, the whole organization will adapt to him and do likewise. The major problem in decentralization is to get top executives to stop being shop superintendents and begin acting as planners, philosophers, and evaluators in-the-large.

Implications for delegation. A company operating a chain of successful supermarkets decided nonetheless that it was time to change from a highly centralized to a decentralized organization. The momentum for decentralization came from the president, which was a promising beginning because the type of change required would not come to pass without the rigorous leadership of the man at the top. He had been influenced in his decision by two factors: first, by his belief that the climate of American management was changing and that steps should be taken to adapt to it; and secondly, by a resurgence of locally-owned competition. The strong local independent achieved success in considerable part by his ability to identify with the community and assume the role of local citizenship. It was felt that chain stores would have to go farther than in the past toward strengthening local managers so that they also could play an appropriate community role.[12]

In changing to decentralized management the greatest obstacle was encountered in the behavior of the district managers. Each formerly exercised line authority over several stores. The type of supervision previously exercised was closely akin to military inspection, with its hunt for imperfections. Layout and standard practice were handed down from headquarters. Communication was entirely one-way with the local store personnel acting largely as puppets manipulated from above.

The new type of behavior postulated for these district managers in the decentralized organization deprived them of their line authority. They had to learn to act in a staff capacity. They were to build strength and self-reliance into store personnel, and in

---

[11] Paul Appleby, *Big Democracy* (New York: Alfred A. Knopf, Inc., 1945), pp. 65-77.

[12] Paul R. Lawrence, *The Changing of Organizational Behavior Patterns.*

doing so they had to refrain from making decisions, taking action, and issuing orders as they had formerly done. They had to do the most difficult thing a dynamic and aggressive person can do—that is, refrain from immediate corrective action when something goes wrong. Under a decentralized system people must be allowed to make mistakes.

This calls for a new type of superior-subordinate relationship in which Fromm's distinction between rational and inhibiting authority seems apropos.[13] He gives the archetypes of each as, first, the teacher-student relationship (rational authority) and, second, the master-slave relationship (inhibiting authority). In the one, superiority has the function of helping, and if teaching is successful the authority relationship tends to dissolve itself. In the other the authority function is based on exploitation, and the distance between superior and subordinate becomes intensified.

But organizations have production goals and deadlines that must be met. This means that pressures toward these ends are bound to be felt, and these pressures must inevitably enter the superior-subordinate relationship on all levels. How can a proper balance be achieved so that people will be motivated by their own awareness of organization imperatives instead of the inhibiting type of authoritarian behavior on the part of their superiors? In general it would seem to call for Fromm's teaching type of behavior in which the social distance between superior and subordinate tends to disappear. It takes the form of questioning, listening, advising without admonishing, and the clinical type of evaluation wherein criticism, when necessary, become developmental rather than punitive.

The compulsive, hyperactive type of superior must be conditioned to stay out of situations which cause him anxiety until the operator has had time to make things right himself. One of the worst sins of the nondelegator is to step in and do things himself when a job is not being accomplished fast enough to suit him. One method is to allow a previously set period of time to elapse before instituting follow-up. Some large-scale organizations are experimenting with counseling such leaders, often by the devel-

---

[13] Erich Fromm, *Escape from Freedom* (New York: Rinehart and Company, Inc., 1941), p. 164 *passim.*

opmental psychologists in the personnel department. This fits in with the new clinical evaluative approach to executive development. It may very well be that in order to run our great organizations of the future it will be necessary to provide, as a regular phase of training, the type of psychological counseling which will curb those behavioral habits destructive to others.

Policy and Decision

Decision and decentralization. In this chapter an ideal pattern of decentralization is being postulated, in which decision-making is the basic ingredient. The first thing to be remembered in this connection is that a decision may not be a rational choice between alternatives supported by all the knowable facts. Thus Simon says that it is often impossible to know who makes the decisions because a complex organization resembles a great stream drawing its premises from many tributary sources. "Many individuals and organization units contribute to every large decision, and the problem of centralization and decentralization is a problem of arranging this complex system into an effective scheme."[14]

Two considerations. While the proposition prevails that decision-making should be pushed down to the lowest practicable level, there are certain modifying factors encountered in practice. Two of the determining considerations are the existence of (1) skills and competence, and (2) information at the point of decision.[15] The newer approaches to organization planning and executive development are tackling the first by estimating the quantity and quality of executives who will be needed and maintaining development programs which will produce decision-makers.

The second problem concerns the availability of information upon which to base decisions. Here again we see electronic data-processing as as significant factor. It has been predicted that large industrial organizations will recentralize and that many operating decisions formerly made at the lower levels will become routine, all of this because of the greater availability of information through

---

[14] Herbert A. Simon, *Administrative Behavior,* revised edition (New York: The Macmillan Company, 1957), p. xii.

[15] Harold F. Smiddy, "Managerial Decision-Making," *Advanced Management* 23:5-13, November 1958.

electronic data-processing. The routinizing of decisions will also result from the operations research solutions. The centralizing tendency will be a by-product of the centralization of information under the contemporary practice of installing large computers at headquarters. However, could it not very well be that the communications networks of the future will provide for transmission and storage of data at subordinate centers as well as at headquarters? Computer technology seems to be in such a state of flux that, if decentralization has other enduring values, the communications system will be adapted to facilitate its objectives.

Other factors. One of the factors that seems to influence the degree of centralization is the amount of stress which the organization is undergoing. Thus during a recent period decision-making tended to be recentralized in an airplane company because of the transformation of operations brought about by the changeover from propeller to jet planes on the one hand, and the military emphasis on missiles on the other. It could perhaps be stated as a general proposition that decision-making will evidence a disposition to drift toward the center (1) in times of general stress, and (2) in those areas where stress is greatest.

Dale's study of 20 companies having from 4,000 to 20,000 employees indicated that centralization was greatest in such activities as financial, legal, and industrial relations problems, and less in manufacturing and marketing.[16]

Social Climate

The fourth major ingredient of the decentralization pattern is a social climate which is congenial. Such a social climate is difficult to describe because it is full of contradictions and enigmas. On the one hand it would seem to be welfare-centered, with a certain flavor of devotion to human uplift. On the other it retains the production drive and competitive atmosphere so characteristic of the industrial scene in the past. Surely no one would characterize such industrial giants as Sloan and Cordiner as lacking in drive and willingness to make the hard decisions of the market-place and those affecting the careers of personnel. The successful man

---

[16] Ernest Dale, "New Perspectives in Managerial Decision-Making," *The Journal of Business of the University of Chicago* 26:1-8, January 1953.

in these positions must possess a certain element of flint in his make-up because his decisions will inevitably hurt people, often those to whom he may be socially near.

Need for security. But the social climate of a truly decentralized organization must provide for a feeling of security on the part of decision-makers. This security comes from a feeling that they will be judged on their batting average rather than for a single strike-out. They will be evaluated on the basis of objective data and information rather than arbitrary whims. Above all, they will be protected from petty interference on the part of an over-anxious supervisor. They must feel assurance that in the case of honest error they will have the protection of a superior who will share responsibility and take at least part of the heat from above instead of hunting for a scapegoat.

Freedom and competition. The decentralization pattern suggests a competitive climate with the spirit of evaluation permeating the air. Yet, strangely enough, it is characterized by the relaxed freedom of the good athlete. People are under organization discipline yet they feel it as a constructive and motivating force rather than as restrictive and inhibitive. Two-way communication prevails, and democratic consultation and interaction accompany decision and action. Individual self-expression and self-development are encouraged within the limits imposed by the organization's resources and needs.

IV • PERSPECTIVES

There will be those in whom the behavior patterns sketched will arouse apprehension for the future strength of our institutions. Among them will be the social Darwinists and those who esteem the Spartan ideal of boot-camp discipline. We believe that the latter has its very proper place in training soldiers for combat, but only limited usefulness in the free civilian society. It is interesting to note that when the German general staff looked for the reasons for defeat in World War I it came up with the conclusions that leaders at the company and platoon level had not been trained in taking responsibility on their own. This was reversed in the training of Hitler's army with the result that sergeants and company officers were given rigorous exercises in which they had to make decisions in the field, often on the spur of the moment. The beneficial results are well known, because Hitler's army fought on at the company and platoon level after the larger units collapsed.

It is very probable that the type of behavior called for in the decentralized pattern will strengthen our institutions rather than weaken them. It will give a larger number of people training in decision and responsibility. Furthermore, it will foster culture change in which people will become more sensitive to the effect of their behavior on their fellow men, and this will help to ameliorate and minimize the individual's subordination to large-scale organization as a standardizing enemy of human dignity. For those whose values tend toward the virtues which make for economic survival, it should be pointed out that the contemporary movement for decentralization is emerging from the great industrial corporations which have proved beyond doubt their capacity to survive in a competitive milieu.

It should also be emphasized that behavior in a decentralized organization cannot be described as laissez-faire and hence overly permissive. People are expected to devote themselves wholeheartedly to the accomplishment of organization goals, but the manner of motivating them to do so is different. The pace does not slow down, nor are the dynamic pressures for accomplishment absent.

IV • SUMMARY

Since World War II there has been a very strong trend toward decentralization in large-scale organization. Actually the movement is somewhat older than that, for Alfred P. Sloan, Jr., developed the General Motors philosophy of decentralization in the early 1920's. There is no doubt that the Sloan model, which achieved such brillant success, has inspired events of more recent years.

In some respects decentralization has come to be a "gospel" of management. It is considered to be a way of life, an end in itself. It is, in some respects, an idealistic concept, with ethical roots in democracy. This is so because it suggests a system in which the coordinating process will be less restrictive and in which people will be given an opportunity to pursue their individual goals to the maximum. Local autonomy, beginning with the individual, thus is an important credo of decentralization.

The decentralization pattern, as it is ideally set forth by both practitioners and academic theorists, seems to have four major parts: (1) the formal structure, (2) style of executive behavior, (3) policy and decision facets, and (4) social climate.

The formal structure of a decentralized organization tends toward hierarchical flatness, i.e., the number of levels are kept to a minimum. Specialized support to these operating levels is provided on the basis of the line and staff pattern identified in the previous chapter, i.e., the lines of command and responsibility are kept as "clean" as possible to expedite the evaluation of performance. Finally, it is to be noted that in industrial organizations the corporate and production levels are emerging as quite distinct entities with very different responsibilities.

In government a facet of decentralized formal structure has been the semi-autonomous corporation, which has been removed from the main stream of legislative and executive control. It is supposed to function with greater independence and flexibility—hence better business management—than the traditional agencies of government. The Tennessee Valley Authority at the national level and the Port of New York Authority at the local level are probably the best examples of this form.

Perhaps the greatest change implied in the move toward decentralization is in executive behavior. Here again we see that the familiar father figure of organization lore has little place. This problem becomes more pronounced as an executive ascends the hierarchial ladder. By the time he reaches the uppermost echelon, he is no longer an active participant in day-to-day affairs. Now he is mentor and judge. His biggest job is planning and his next most important task would seem to be evaluation of personnel and results, if the two can be separated.

Thus delegation must be a real part of the ideal decentralization philosophy. Decisions are supposed to be pushed to the lowest practicable level, which emphasizes again how far this concept of decentralization moves from the notion of one man sitting at the top pulling all the wires. There are of course factors which importantly condition the degree to which decision-making is delegated in an organization. Two particularly important considerations are: (1) the skill and competence available at a certain decision center, and (2) the amount of information which can be made available at that decision center.

Environment, or social climate, has a great deal to do with styles of decentralization. For example one study showed that there is disposition to drift toward the center (1) in times of general stress, and (2) in those areas where stress is greatest. Beyond this the appropriate climate would seem to be a curious admixture of seemingly contradictory elements. On the one hand it should be welfare-centered with a certain flavor of devotion to human uplift. On the other it retains the production drive and competitive atmosphere of the industrial past.

While decentralization is now an important feature of organization philosophy, it should not be assumed that the pattern suggested in this chapter is an achieved fact. There is a long road ahead for those who accept this "gospel." It not only exacts maturity and character from the individual members of the organization, but also requires that they be present in the culture of the larger society. The fact that so many large industrial corporations have professed this "gospel" and seem to thrive financially would indicate that we shall see more, rather than less, of its pattern.

TWELVE

Formalization

What to Look for in This Chapter . . .

Importance of formalization for organizational stability
Types of formalization and legitimacy
Formalization as a measure of organizational maturity
Role of job descriptions in formalization
Use of charts in defining formal relationships

As seems inevitable in any organized body of knowledge, there is a tendency in the study of organization and administration to build iron-tight categories. This process of simplification frequently reaches the point that there are only two major clusters, one black and one white. Then a great deal of argument ensues as to where certain specifics belong, even though the categories have long since become oversimplified. We have dealt in earlier parts of the book with two related sets of these: (1) policy and administration, and (2) staff and line.

Now we turn to a third, the *formal-informal* dichotomy. Let it be said that such a categorization has its usefulness as a conceptual tool. The trouble is that its face validity often induces to a false and elusive security, for reality behaviors cannot be governed on the assumption that such absolute categories exist. Nevertheless this distinction has become so ingrained in popular parlance and in the professional literature that it is impossible to avoid its use.

I • THE CONCEPT OF FORMALIZATION

Perhaps the easiest definition of formalization would be: "that which has been written down and authenticated by the policy makers." But we know full well that organizations do not operate as the official writings say they should. Hence we acknowledge the existence of informalization, which consists of all that behavior which varies from the official writings. Chart 12-1 refers back to Chapter 2, in which it was postulated that organizations are multidimensional, by depicting three main categories of organizational phenomena: (1) the operating organization, (2) the job-task pyramid, and (3) the system of sociological, psychological, and ideo-

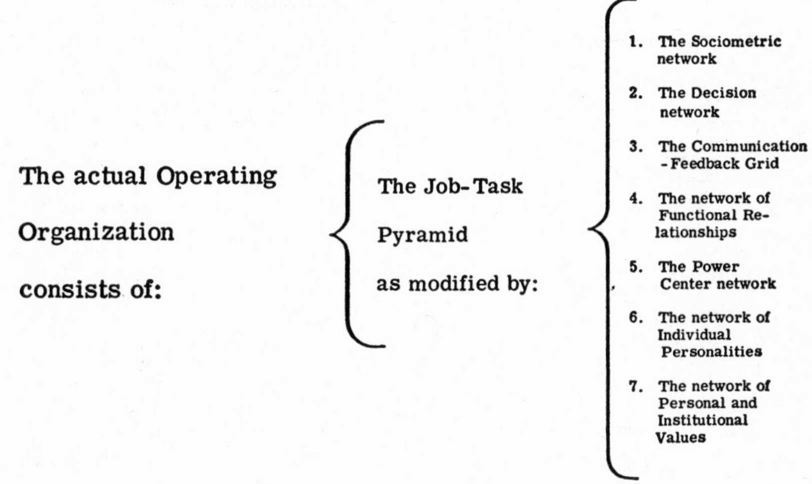

CHART 12-1. *Multi-dimensional aspects of organization.*

logical networks.[1] The job-task hierarchy, (2) refers to the features that are included in the formal organization; the other two embrace the behavior patterns ordinarily referred to as the informal organization.

These several dimensions of organization are not isolated entities; they are in mesh with each other. Indeed they modify one another. As an articulated totality they comprise the *operating organization.* Nor is it correct to view the informal organization as consisting entirely of social phenomena because there are behaviors which vary from the written hierarchy. Some behaviors are job-centered and do not have important social connotations. For example, the infantry regulations of some years ago required the soldier to use a sling when firing a rifle, at least in many situations. But the sling was uncomfortable to many, with the result that the regulation requiring its use was often honored in the breach. There are countless examples of this kind where practice varies from regulations because of the individual operator's choice or habit. The same variations prevail in the realm of relationships with other workers.

Meaning of Formalization

Writing and formalization. Formalization has to do with writing and legitimacy. An organization is formalized to the extent that the behavior expected of members has been written down in accordance with the desires of those who make policy and has been authenticated by them. The phrase "those who make policy" should be noted here in the light of previous discussions of the policy continuum, a concept which recognizes that policy is made and implemented on all levels of the hierarchy. In other words, the foreman who prepares and issues a written work order is indulging in formalization, as is the officer on the top echelon who authenticates a job description for a vice-presidency.

Legitimacy and formalization. In order to become formalized, organization relationships must have been authenticated, that is, have someone's stamp of approval. It would be simple to say that

[1] For research evidence as to how these operate in mesh with the formal organization see Everett E. Hughes *et al.*, *Twenty Thousand Nurses Tell Their Story* (Philadelphia: J. B. Lippincott and Company, 1958), pp. 62-82.

all such authentications must come from the policy-makers on the top echelons. This would be in accordance with traditional organization theory, but would not take into account, first, the policy continuum, and second, and more important, the existence of two varieties of legitimacy. One is the legitimization that results in official writing: a statute, a charter, a manual, or a chart. The other is the sociological legitimizing process. Inasmuch as the first is simple and well understood, we will confine our discussion here to social legitimacy.

Social legitimacy. In oversimplified terms, the concept of social legitimacy refers to group acceptance of norms of behavior through accepted practice, precedents, and values. Weiss has, for example, shown this type of legitimacy operating in job and personnel evaluation in a research laboratory. There women who possessed higher professional skills were assigned jobs of lower status. While the job specifications did not exclude women, the social group had decreed that women were to be assigned more routine tasks. They accepted these low status roles without apparent protest.[2] This concept of the *social legitimacy of roles* underlies much of the behavior in organizations, especially evident in jurisdictional disputes in labor relations. It is important to the understanding of formal organization, because the job-task pyramid must eventually recognize it. The clamor of social forces will put the social group's desires into the official writings, as when a collective bargaining contract spells out the agreement arising from a jurisdictional dispute.

Formalization without writing. While we advance in broad outline the concept that formalization is usually represented by official writing, there is nevertheless a variety of formalization that does not involve writing. The British constitution and English common law are excellent examples. Neither will be found in one writing or set of writings: indeed some parts are not embodied in any official writing. They exist only in the minds and intuitive behavior of men, passed on from generation to generation. Yet it would not be entirely correct to say that they are not formalized, because they are stable and predictable.

---

[2] Robert S. Weiss, *Processes of Organization* (Ann Arbor, Mich.: Survey Research Center, 1956), p. 25.

Linton, the anthropologist, points out that certain African tribes have developed a high state of formalization without written prescriptions. They have developed law and legal procedure. A central government with defined duties and powers exists. Officials are surrounded with considerable pomp and circumstance.[3] It would seem that legitimacy is the crucial factor in formalization, and that only in literate societies is it evidenced in writing.

Charters and Organization Maturity

Certain functional and applied anthropologists have attempted to conceptualize the totality of an organization's character or personality. It is important to our consideration of formalization because it serves to identify the components that give an organization form. Malinowski's distinction between *activities* and *rules* is a classic statement. "The activities depend on the ability, power, honesty and good-will of the members. They deviate invariably from the rules, which represent the ideal of performance, not necessarily its reality. The activities, moreover, are embodied in actual behavior; the rules very often in precepts, texts, and regulations." [4]

Legal view. Those of us who have received our intellectual nurture from a legal or management viewpoint are accustomed to the use of the word charter in connection with a document which constitutes the basic writing of an organization: a city charter, corporation charter, or a charter issued by a national body to a local unit or chapter. In this sense we often refer to an organization as being "chartered" by some legal superior such as a legislature, the secretary of state, or the national governing body of a voluntary society. The superior sets forth in the charter the purpose, powers, duties, and restrictions placed upon the chartered organization. The powers granted are usually stated in plenary terms, that is, sufficiently inclusive to provide for all expected exigencies, but not in such detail as to hamper desirable discretion.

Anthropological view. The functional anthropologists have a

---

[3] Ralph Linton, *The Study of Man* (New York: Appleton-Century-Crofts, 1936), p. 500.

[4] Bronislaw Malinowski, *A Scientific Theory of Culture and Other Essays* (Chapel Hill: University of North Carolina Press, 1944), p. 53.

concept of charter much broader than this. "Roughly speaking it refers to the philosophy which underlies group behavior, the beliefs, purposes, guiding principles, and values which the group holds in common." [5] It really springs from Malinowski's concept of the institution, discussed in Chapter 3. The charter in this sense constitutes the institutional framework. Malinowski has depicted it graphically as in the accompanying illustration.[6]

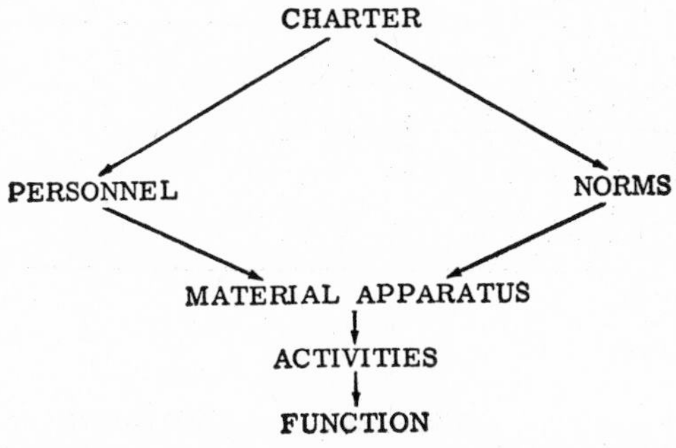

It should be remembered that Malinowski and his fellow anthropologists spent their working lives studying primitive peoples and societies. However, both Bakke and Ellsworth studied modern industrial institutions. Bakke researched a telephone company which was a member of the Bell System; Ellsworth traced the institutional history and development of a New England factory. The anthropologists have brought out into the open many facets of organization of which there had been vague awareness before, but which we had largely put out of mind as being perhaps "off limits." Will the sophisticated analyst of the future be more free to deal with the totality of organizational influences? Indeed, will his increasingly sophisticated bosses insist that he do so?

Organization maturity continuum. Formalization is in a sense a measure of organization maturity, as indicated by Chart 12-2, which is an Organization Maturity Continuum. The idea for the chart came from a book of readings in anthropology which graded

---

[5] John S. Ellsworth, Jr., *Factory Folkways* (New Haven: Yale University Press, 1952), p. 93; see also E. Wight Bakke, *Bonds of Organization* (New York: Harper & Brothers, 1950).

[6] Malinowski, *op. cit.,* p. 53.

1	2	3	4	5	6	7
Individuals interacting in same situation but no permanent pattern apparent.	Individuals interacting in same situation with pattern. Pattern breaks if new conditions arise.	Primary groups appear, such as family or isolated work teams.	Hierarchy first appears.	Hierarchy is given formal sanction.	Formally constituted hierarchy	Formally constituted hierarchy.
	Leadership not apparent but someone makes decisions occasionally.	Indigenous leaders appear, such as family head or leader of work group. Deliberate leadership.	Recognized leaders more or less formally selected appear.	Pattern of leadership is deliberately established.	Pattern of leadership is supplemented by duties statements for each post.	Formally constituted pattern of leadership, with clear channels of communication and authority.
	Individuals not a conscious group, but show in-group pattern.	Group may not be conscious of leadership, depending upon point of evolution of group—but conscious of group or clique membership.	Clusters of groups develop within the hierarchy. (Clique Structure)	Groups in the organization are formally delineated, but not highly "rationalized."	Groups in the organization are formally established and their relationships are states. May be written organization charts.	Groups in the organization are carefully established on basis of specific criteria such as stage in production process. Organization charts.
		Single level group.	Division of labor around a total production goal may be introduced, but simple independent processes.	Total production process is introduced where succeeding groups are dependent upon work of preceding groups.	Production is broken down into specific jobs and responsibilities of each person are carefully defined. Job descriptions of general nature.	High degree of "rationalization" job duties through such techniques as administrative analyses, time-and-motion study.
				Articles of incorporation or legislative act containing name, purpose, etc.; formally constituted organization in community.	Charter is supplemented by manuals or books of rules and regulations.	Comprehensive manuals of detailed formal powers. Charters of legislative acts.
				Formal basis for membership in group is specified.	Detailed specifications for membership are set down as criteria for selection.	Comprehensive testing program based upon careful job analyses used.
				Organization has legal relationships with other groups in community, thus formal status.	Organization so integrated into social and economic structure that it is subject to some pressure to coordinate its goals with other organizations.	Organization subject to formal control by state, or top of hierarchy if governmental organization, because its product is essential to the overall socio-economic system.
					Introduction of staff personnel who act in the name of constituted leaders.	Organization control appears in the form of official authorization of organization charts, job descriptions, standard practice manuals.
						Written objectives and goals resulting from and revised by staff planning agency.

NOTES:--1. Direct evolution of each factor through these stages is not implied. Only illustrative of different types of informality or formality.

2. Formalization of any organization at one time probably will not fall into any one column at one time.

CHART 12-2. *Organization maturity continuum.*

SOURCE: This chart was prepared by John M. Pfiffner and William J. Gore. The idea was in turn suggested by the

the organization of human cultures from the most primitive or simple to the most advanced and complex. Seven levels were there identified, including the apes in the trees at level zero. The categories are as follows:

- Level Zero—Life in the trees: The behavior and social relations of man's closest kin.
- Level One—Simple family bands (Seal Eskimos, reindeer herders).
- Level Two—The band contains several families.
- Level Three—The rise of specialization and multiple institutions.
- Level Four—The number of institutions per individual increases, and hierarchies begin.
- Level Five—Hierarchies and compound institutions.
- Level Six—One complex political institution (the Athenian democracy and the Roman empire).[7]

Our chart, while suggested by these categories, is not a direct transfer because we are dealing with modern management institutions, rather than with cultures. In reviewing the chart, it would be desirable for the reader to attempt to postulate examples of modern institutions in our culture exemplified by the vertical columns. Columns 1 and 2 are ignored because they represent such low levels of organization.

Column 3 suggests a one-man or family business, perhaps conducted in the home. Column 4 might be found when a one-man business hires a supervisor or when a simple partnership has grown to the point where it has to be put in writing. Column 5 could be represented in a small manufacturing plant that has introduced some of the aspects of scientific management piecemeal without rationalizing the whole setup. Columns 6 and 7 are the most mature and complex. In public administration they may be reached in metropolitan police and fire departments. Perhaps a new column 8 is now needed for those organizations whose productive processes embody automation and electronic data processing for feedback and control.

The reader should bear in mind that this attempt at charting

---

[7] Carleton S. Coon, *A Reader in General Anthropology* (New York: Henry Holt and Company, 1948).

and categorization is intended merely as a framework for thinking about the maturation process in organization.

Significance of Formalization to Organization Effectiveness

Research findings. How important is formalization to organization effectiveness? A study at the University of Southern California School of Public Administration, sponsored by the Office of Naval Research, indicated that it has a great deal more to do with performance than is often assumed. This was a research effort, undertaken over a four year period, which examined a great many dimensions having a possible relationship to effectiveness. These data were then treated statistically. It was found that one of the most significant dimensions—significant at the one per cent level in the statistician's terms—was formalization. This means that in this particularly designed study, there was little possibility that chance was operating. There were 99 chances out of 100 that formalization *was* having an effect on performance.[8]

Effective forest rangers, as an illustration, were found to furnish their subordinates not only with written job assignments but with charts showing interrelationships.

The specific items in the dimension were:

He has made available to his employees an up-to-date organization chart.

How many of his permanent employees have been provided with clear-cut written descriptions of their duties?

When work assignments are given, he provides a written copy for those involved.

He likes to have work plans written down.

He has provided employees with an adequate written statement of rules and regulations to be followed.

He makes available adequate written statements of procedures to be used in carrying out work assignments.

Relevance to supervision. People have higher morale when they know what is expected of them. In order to put forth their best efforts they must feel secure in their boss—secure in the sense that they know what he will do in particular situations. The studies at the University of Southern California suggested further that

[8] Andrew L. Comrey, John M. Pfiffner, and Wallace High, "A Survey of District Rangers," *Personnel Psychology* 7:533-47, Winter 1954.

the effective supervisor is consistent—people know what he will do next and where they stand. They know what they are to do; they do not receive conflicting orders; and there is no question in their minds about the source of orders.

II • MECHANICS OF FORMALIZATION

The General Pattern

The general rule to follow in formalization is that written prescriptions should be brief and general as they issue from the top echelon, and become more specific with descent down the scalar ladder. This is in accord with the concepts of the policy continuum, on the one hand, and of the decentralization of decision-making, on the other. It will be remembered that the policy continuum embraces the practice of implementing policy on all subordinate levels which fits in very practically with the contemporary move toward decentralization of decision-making.

Good organizing theory may find itself at loggerheads with the views of the organization's lawyers who by the very nature of their work must constantly have in mind the possibility of legal liability and litigation. In their zeal to protect the organization from future liability they tend to cover every known eventuality, with the result that documentation becomes bulkier. The current tendency to sue at the slightest provocation, together with the inflationary size of the awards for damages, may have accentuated these trends. This may also be one of the major deterrents in the path of decentralized decision-making in public administration, where officials are very sensitive concerning personal liabilities resulting from their decisions.

But here we are concerned primarily with the elements of good organization and thus the suggestion of increasing specificity in written formalization from the top down. A policy statement issued at the corporate level will ordinarily be very brief and general, leaving ample opportunity for the lower echelons to interpret and to meet the peculiarities of local situations and needs. Detail and specificity at the top hinders the exercise of discretion and the development of desirable self-reliance.

Job Descriptions

Two types. The basic writings are job descriptions and organization charts, but these are supplemented by, or are implementations of, various types of manuals, including the policy manual, the organization manual, and several forms of standard practice manuals. Perhaps the most prevalent form of writing relative to organization as such is the job description, of which there are two types. One is the job description intended to be used for pay-setting purposes, and the other might be referred to as the "responsibility and relationship" job description used for purposes of organization planning and management development. There has been a growing realization that the job descriptions developed for salary fixing may not be suitable for organization planning purposes.

The need for these two types of job descriptions first entered the literature with the publication of the Standard Oil Company *Management Guide.*[9] The specific weaknesses which these pioneer organization planners discovered in their own traditional job descriptions lay in the area of responsibility and authority.

> Management needs to know to what position specific responsibility for a particular portion of the enterprise's activities has been delegated, and, as a corollary, whom to hold accountable for its accomplishment. Management must know how far in a certain direction each of several similar positions may go, in order to know through which channels certain matters must be pursued and co-ordinated. Management must know how much authority has been delegated to various positions to determine the type and amount of effort each is capable of contributing to the solution of a problem.[10]

In other words the job descriptions that are needed for organization planning must be directed toward hierarchical relationships and responsibilities. The traditional approach dealt with tasks to be performed and qualifications desired for a single position or class of positions. They emphasized the "how to." On the other hand, the broader job descriptions recognize a position as a sociometric entity in the sense that it deals with the relationship between jobs, jurisdictional boundaries, authority, and delegation.

The AMA Study. In 1957 the American Management Associa-

---

[9] Franklin E. Drew and George Lawrence Hall, *The Management Guide* (San Francisco: Standard Oil Company of California, 1948, rev. 1956), pp. 7-9.
[10] *Ibid.*, p. 8.

tion surveyed a sample of industrial firms having 5.000 or more employees. The inquiry was concerned with what might be termed the philosophy of job descriptions, the extent to which they were being prepared and used, and the mechanics of their preparation and administration. Attention was directed primarily toward *managerial* job descriptions. Questionnaires were sent to 618 firms of which 140 returned usable responses, together with sample position descriptions and related exhibit material, some of which is reproduced in the report. Thus this document constitutes a commendable source of both the "why's" and "how's" of job description.[11]

The responses indicated that while managerial job descriptions were often originally inaugurated for the sole purpose of salary setting, the trend is definitely in the direction of utilizing them for organization planning, management development, and clarifying relationships and responsibilities. The impetus for inauguration usually came from the top executives. The prevailing and desired procedure is to have the executive for whose position a description is prepared participate in the process to the extent of writing the first draft himself. The inauguration of a job description program is not to be undertaken lightly because it will usually encounter some initial opposition or apathy, and it is costly. It takes about five hours of a staff man's time to prepare a job description, not to speak of the time of the incumbent himself. Ninety-five per cent of the companies responding professed to have some provision for review, maintenance, and revision, the interval most often mentioned being once a year.

The AMA Study suggests certain general conclusions:

- The industrial trend is definitely toward wider use of managerial job descriptions.
- They are increasingly used for purposes other than salary setting, including organization planning and management development.
- Their content more and more emphasizes relationships, authority and responsibilities, rather than a merely wooden enumeration of tasks.

---

[11] C. L. Bennett, *Defining the Manager's Job: the AMA Manual of Position Descriptions,* American Management Association, Research Study No. 33, 1958.

Readers desiring to know more of the "how to" should consult the volume itself which is a rich source of suggestive practice.

Job descriptions and personal security. There is an impression in some of the literature on bureaucracy, as well as in popular writings, that formalization may be a stultifying influence. Bakke's study of the Southern New England Telephone Company, however, reports one unexpected finding. In that organization detailed job descriptions were used for assignment purposes and as vehicles for drill during training sessions. The researchers expected that the workers would find such descriptions restrictive of freedom, but actually the effect was the opposite, for two reasons. *First,* knowing what is expected of him, the employee is subjected to less close supervision. Immediate supervisors have fewer excuses to interfere with what he is doing. *Second,* his knowledge of what is expected of him gives the employee sufficient feeling of security to devise and invent informal working patterns which are in harmony with the written word.[12] Thus, job descriptions facilitate delegation and operate to discourage that type of oversupervision manifested by a superior's undue interference in a subordinate's work. The latter has written authority for resisting such oversupervision.

Organization Charts

Typical shortcomings. It seems fashionable to begin any discussion of organization charts by noting their shortcomings. Thus it is said that they falsify through oversimplification.[13] The sanctity of the printed word tends toward inflexibility by making change more difficult.[14] Charts show the relationships which are "supposed to" exist, but which may not be the fact.[15] These cited statements are for the most part judicious words of caution from

---

[12] E. Wight Bakke, *Bonds of Organization* (New York: Harper and Brothers, 1950), p. 43.

[13] Herbert A. Simon, Donald W. Smithburg, and Victor A. Thompson, *Public Administration* (New York: Alfred A. Knopf, Inc., 1950), p. 173.

[14] William H. Newman, *Administrative Action: The Techniques of Organization and Management* (Englewood Cliffs, N.J.: Prentice-Hall, Inc., 1951), p. 311.

[15] Ernest Dale, *Planning and Developing the Company Organization Structure,* American Management Association, Research Report No. 20, 1952, p. 147.

persons who believe in charting but who see its pitfalls if charts are not well prepared and used with discretion. However, one occasionally runs across an emotional deprecation of organization charts based upon their failure to take human values into account.

Much of this desultory sniping at charts would be avoided if the basic concepts principally set forth were understood, not only by social scientists but by management people themselves. *Structure is plural,* but a chart is limited to a single set of relationships, namely the official structure. Some chart makers try to overcome this handicap by using dotted and hatched lines to show the different types of functional control, usually to the confusion of everyone.

Some critics of charts hit at the basic assumption of orthodox management theory that the position and its duties are established first and then people are chosen to fit the pre-established job specifications. They call this "blueprinting" an organization in mechanistic engineering fashion without reference to the real nature of human beings. They say that such blueprinting cannot be realistic because people cannot be fitted to positions according to precise engineering practice.

Some industrial sociologists recognize and admit the desirability of an official blueprint, which they call "formal" organization, but say that this should be supplemented by a set of sociometric charts. The latter depict the natural and spontaneous interaction which workers have with each other. For the preparation of a sociometric chart members of a group are asked to express their preferences for each other member, as well as their rejections of some.[16] The industrial sociologists would have workers placed in jobs in a manner conforming to social preference. That is, people who expressed a preference for each other would be grouped together for work purposes; indigenous leaders would be spotted and their leadership propensities capitalized. Rejected persons or isolates would either be given therapy to improve their attractiveness or placed where teamwork was not important.

Need for charting. In spite of their shortcomings, charts of the official organization are worthwhile. The fact that laws are

---

[16] Delbert C. Miller and William H. Form, *Industrial Sociology* (New York: Harper and Brothers, 1951), pp. 496-501.

not obeyed in their every detail is not considered sufficient reason for abolishing the rule of law in human affairs. Nor are charts impugned by the fact that the role of President Wilson's famous and shadowy Colonel House could not be pictured on a chart. Until more is known about organization dynamics, it seems desirable to proceed on the assumption that the official organization should be set down in official writing, mapped and charted. Certainly it has long been a credo of organization orthodoxy that authority and responsibility should be definitely pinpointed. There are several different kinds of organization charts but most of them fall into one of these categories: (1) skeleton, (2) functional, and (3) personnel.

Skeleton charts. A skeleton chart, as the name implies, is merely the graphic presentation of the essential hierarchical framework. It contains the principal subunits, usually depicted as hollow squares or rectangles. These are arranged in levels or echelons of hierarchical status, connected by lines suggesting the different types of authority. The line of command is usually indicated by a solid black line, while broken or hatched lines represent staff or functional relationships.

Functional charts. Functional charts usually apply to subunits, with the boxes showing smaller breakdowns into divisions, units, or sections. Sometimes they go down far enough to depict every first line supervisor. Each box contains a write-up of the duties, activities or functions of that particular subunit, executive or supervisor. In a sense, this prose material constitutes an abbreviated job description; by glancing at it one can get an over-all view of the mission of each organization cell. Sometimes the charts are a part of the organization manual, but in other cases the charts are bound together in a volume which in itself constitutes a manual.

Personnel charts. A personnel chart is of the same graphic design as the functional chart, but the boxes contain personnel information. This may consist of the job titles of the supervisor and each subordinate and in some cases the names of the incumbents are listed. Sometimes the authorized personnel is compared with actual personnel on a given date. In the latter case classification code numbers may be indicated, such as GS-5, GS-10, GS-12. It is fairly common practice to combine the personnel and functional charts with both types of information on the same document.

Wall charts. Combinations of the above charts are sometimes posted on office walls or bulletin boards. An example is the organization development control board used at Du Pont to keep track of the status, development, and potentialities of the engineering personnel. Traditional hierarchical organization charts are sometimes used to combine organization control with evaluation of the growth potential of executive personnel. In this case a commercially available visual ticket system permitted flexibility and aided in keeping the charts up to date.[17]

III • SUMMARY

The concept of a formal and an informal system within each organization has received considerable attention in recent years. Traditionalists have been accused of having concentrated entirely on the formal in the past. Some of the ardent human relationists have more recently gone to the other extreme and held that the whole of organization lies in its informal structure. In actual practice, of course, the formal blends into the informal. The sharp distinction so prevalent in the writings is only a conceptual tool which cannot serve as a guide to behavior in the real-life situation.

It does appear, however, that the greatly increased concern with the social elements of organization life has tended on occasion to obscure the great importance of striving for stability in organization processes. Formalization in a real sense is concerned with that problem. It seeks to secure a predictability of performance; and, in so doing, it has its human relations consequences. The consistency of treatment inherent in formalization has an effect on the individual's sense of security and confidence about his role.

There is some research evidence to support this general proposition. At the University of Southern California, it was found that

[17] Gerald L. Risser, "The Development of Technical Personnel," American Management Association, Personnel Series No. 148, 1952; see illustrations pp. 24-25.

formalization did correlate highly with effective performance. Forest Service supervisors, for example, not only provided subordinates with formal job descriptions but also with charts of organization relationships.

Formalization has essentially to do with writing and legitimacy. But we know that organizations do not operate as official writings say. Hence it follows that informalization—insofar as a distinction can be drawn—consists of all those behaviors which vary from official writings. The concept of legitimacy is very important. There is the legal, authority type of legitimacy. But in addition there is a social legitimacy which involves accepted practice, precedents, and values. Sometimes this social legitimacy is in conflict with the legal legitimacy. On other occasions, however, we find that such a sharp distinction cannot be drawn. Social legitimacy sometimes works to enforce that which is official and legal.

We have proposed that formalization is in a sense a measure of organization maturity. By this we mean that as institutions grow, role concepts and expectations become more sharply defined and understood. In the process a need is expressed to put these role definitions into writing, to make them official. Using anthropological categories, for example, it is possible to construct a *continuum* which moves from the absolutely simplest form of human interaction through seven levels to one which is highly complicated. In the latter instance we would find the greatest definition of role and the most formalization. In the continuum the family would probably be at level three and an organization like General Motors at level seven.

An important rule to observe in the process of formalization is closely related to the decentralization and delegation concepts discussed in the previous chapter. The dictum is that written prescriptions at the top should be brief and general; they should become more specific as they flow down the hierarchy. Thus a policy statement issued at the corporate level will ordinarily be very short and general, leaving opportunity for the lower echelons to amplify it.

Present mechanics of formalization are heavily dependent on the job description. Originally the job description was seen essentially as a device for rationalizing the wage structure. More recently it has been found that the job description is perhaps the best single means of getting at questions of formal responsibility and authority. Thus the traditional approach to a job description as a summary of tasks to be performed and qualifications desired has shifted. The "managerial" job description recognizes a position as a total entity in the sense that it deals with the relationship between jobs, jurisdictional boundaries, authority, and delegation.

Despite obvious shortcomings, the organization chart remains an important mechanic in formalization. It provides a good short hand picture of basic formal relationships. The difficulty is that many people expect it to do more than that. If it will be recognized for what it is, a single dimensional view of the organization, it can perform a useful function.

There are several types of charts: (1) skeleton, (2) functional, and (3) personnel.

THIRTEEN

Organization Planning

What to Look for in This Chapter . . .

Organization planning units as general staff aides to chief executive

Organization planning operations:

- job descriptions
- organization manual
- policy file or manual
- organization charts

Organization planning relationship to executive development

Absence of formal organization planning trend in government

In the affairs of mankind some slogan, phrase or movement occasionally catches the fancy of the public and spreads with epidemic haste. Management people are not immune from being bitten by bugs of enthusiasm; they often feel a compulsion to try out new procedural gadgets merely because they have a certain vogue. These developments are not always ephemeral passing fancies, one should hasten to add. They are often substantive and enduring, and it is believed that organization planning is in this category. Nevertheless the establishment of organization planning departments seemed to spread at such a rate in the late 1950's as to suggest that it may have been at least partially due to the dictates of fashion.

One of the earliest references to the term in the literature occurred in the Holden, Fish, and Smith study of corporate structure published just before the opening of World War II. A most significant statement in that volume declared that relatively little attention "seems to have been devoted to planning and designing the organization structure. . . ."[1] Prepared in the organization planning offices of the Standard Oil Company of California, a unit commonly given credit for the origin of the organization planning movement, the book had a very wide circulation and was undoubtedly influential in the spread of a formal approach to organization planning in the next decade. At any rate, more than half of the companies participating in the 1950-1952 AMA seminars on organization had a department or an individual in charge of organization planning.[2] Dale's survey of corporate practice in this field, published in 1952, may have triggered the popularity of the movement in the late 1950's. Organization planning has now become one of the most influential staff activities in the larger corporations, especially those which have diversified and decentralized.

I • THE NATURE OF ORGANIZATION PLANNING

A staffman for a rapidly growing company who was sent to observe organization planning practice in over a score of companies of various sizes arrived at the conclusion that as a national pattern, "organization planning is what you want to call it; an organization planning man is whoever you put to doing it; organi-

---

[1] Paul E. Holden, Lounsbury S. Fish, and Hubert L. Smith, *Top Management Organization and Control* (New York: McGraw-Hill Book Company, Inc., 1951; first published by Stanford University Press, 1941), p. 91.

[2] Ernest Dale, *Planning and Developing the Company Structure,* American Management Association, Research Report No. 20, 1952, p. 15.

zation planning work is whatever these people do."[3] After thus emphasizing the great diversity in practice which he found to exist, C. A. Efferson proceeded to recommend that his company establish an organization planning department because the management of the companies studied expressed a strong feeling "that somewhere in the general area of improved alignment of work of people and their work relationships, and somewhere in the general area of thinking through the future shape and form of the company's departments and activities lies something of extreme and growing importance."[4]

A prominent organization planning director has stated that planning departments lean in one of two directions, either "head-hunting" or executive development. The question to be decided is whether the organization planning unit is to operate in the realm of broad management strategy across the board, working in collaboration with top policy makers, or whether it is to be tied into an established function such as personnel. If organization planners join personnel, they cannot be management strategists because they are personnel men. If they look into systems and procedures, they become "head-hunters." It is difficult to be a "head-hunter" and also be a broad management strategist.

Characteristics

Broad planning. Hardly more than 20 years ago the ethos of economic individualism so dominated American business culture as to make planning virtually a proscribed word. However, the events which have transpired since 1940 have forced planning on business organizations.[5] This has been due to two types of competition, one for the share of the market and the other for dwindling supplies of such raw materials as iron, oil, tin, and bauxite. The result is that virtually every corporation today has its five year

---

[3] C. A. Efferson, "Basic Problems in Organization Planning," a paper read at the First Atlantic Meeting of the National Industrial Conference Board, on March 22, 1956. Efferson was Manager of Organization Planning, Kaiser Aluminum and Chemical Corporation, Oakland, California.

[4] *Ibid.*, p. 3.

[5] Students of public administration will remember the emotional onslaught against the New Deal Planning agencies in the late 1930's, particularly the abolition of the National Resources Planning Board and its counterparts in the states. Planning, as a word, was synonymous with socialism and communism.

plan and some are projecting for a quarter century. Thus Philco has at the corporate level a five-year planning committee composed of the president as chairman and several vice presidents. While this committee establishes the ground rules, each division has its own five-year planning committee made up of the managers of departments.[6] Westinghouse also has long-term planning departments decentralized to the divisions but subject to ground rules determined at the corporate level.[7]

There would seem to be a strong tendency among the most vocal of organization planners to regard their function as a top coordinating activity, a sort of global view in which organization planning becomes the focal point for all types of planning. Thus an industrial enterprise must constantly have its eye upon the state of the economy and business indicators; it must also have a focus upon competitors, what they are about to do and may do in the future; and it must constantly look toward its customers, the market.[8] But these matters are directly related to the internal organization of the company, because jobs and the people who fill them are responsible for what happens now and in the future. Hence the global role of organization planning.

A member of the new school of organization planning directors suggests that the organization staffman of the future must be something of a philosopher, a broad gauge fellow who is constantly ahead of the boss, or at least anticipates what he will next think about. He says that the management of the future will have an intellectual base; management decisions will stand upon an underpinning of social philosophy, rather than the cleverness of the old-time entrepreneur. Competition is becoming so keen that, in order to survive, the manager of the future will have to be something of an egghead. The freewheeling intuitor is *passé*. In the present competitive milieu errors are much more costly. For instance, the master plan of a metallurgical company showed that decisions had to be made almost at once relative to taking up

---

[6] Ernest F. Bareuther, "Budgeting Policy and Practice in a Decentralized Company," *N.A.A. Bulletin* 39:31-36, October 1957.

[7] Russell B. Read, "Planning in the Larger Company," *Management Review* 47:18-21, April 1958.

[8] Richard C. Anderson, "Organization of the Planning Process," *Advanced Management* 23:5, May 1958.

options on ore deposits in many parts of the world. An improper decision could be disastrous because of the disappearing frontier of world supply.

More than job analysis. The result is that organization planning consists of a great deal more than traditional job analysis, and that is undoubtedly what is bringing it to the forefront at this time. The techniques of organization planning have been practiced in one form or another for centuries, as pointed out by one of its more prominent directors, in referring to Jethro's biblical admonition to Moses that he divide the work and delegate.[9] Organization planning utilizes the old techniques of administrative analysis; the study of jobs is still basic, but from the standpoint of a broader focus and milieu. Thus organization planning is allied with economic planning because one cannot project the future conformation of hierarchy unless one makes some estimate of business conditions and the company's competitive position. What is more, organization planners must also be social planners because their plans must take people into account. They must think in terms of labor supply, the whims of consumer demand, the development of plant communities, and the housing of personnel, particularly in remote hardship posts. The actual studies and projections in some of these areas may be done by other specialized planning staffs, but organization planners will have to be in on it in order to project the organization of the future.

General staff. In other words, organization planning is becoming a general staff function rather than a housekeeping adjunct, as was the case with many management staff units in the past. The tendency is for the director of organization planning to be in constant and intimate contact with the top line officials and to be at the heart of decision-making. The major consideration has been the altered environment relative to the utilization of people, and people mean jobs, and jobs are the warp and woof of formal organization. The forces working in this direction have been categorized by Drucker as: (1) the transformation of labor costs from variable to fixed, (2) the scarcity of people skilled in the

---

[9] William R. Willard, "Organization Planning for Effective Management," *Advanced Management* 21:14, December 1956; also Exodus 18:13-22.

new technical tasks, (3) lengthening of the time span of managerial decisions, and (4) the advent of automation.[10]

Organizational arrangements. In large decentralized companies organization planning units are usually found at both the corporate and division levels. At the corporate level they tend to be under a vice-president for administration for the very largest companies, but may report directly to the chief executive officer in medium sized units. In some cases organization planning may extend to the individual plant. The corporate unit usually has no administrative authority over its counterparts at the division or plant level which is, of course, in accord with the contemporary decentralization trend. The organization planning people "belong" to the line command of the level in which they are located. However, a very intimate functional relationship usually prevails between the various levels.

Small staff. Organization planning units usually have relatively small staffs—a reflection of three concepts of contemporary organization. *First* there is the desire to be a good example. If they are to combat empire building, organization planners must not themselves become vulnerable to that charge. *Second,* there is the realization in all staff activities that acceptance of change must spring from the voluntary acceptance of people at the production level. Higher echelons can be catalysts but not actual manipulators. The single great truth relative to organization change is that it must meet the needs of the people of the organization in which change is sought. This means that it must come from within.[11] Based upon the best anthropological theory, which in turn springs from empirical observation of all types of human organization, the formal organization of management institutions is beginning to recognize and incorporate it into its structural arrangements. That is why the training function, for instance, has been decentralized with a small staff to give direction at the top

---

[10] Peter F. Drucker, "Integration of People and Planning," *Harvard Business Review* 33:35, November-December 1955.

[11] Bronislaw Malinowski, *A Scientific Theory of Culture and Other Essays* (Chapel Hill: University of North Carolina Press, 1944), p. 41; John S. Ellsworth, Jr., *Factory Folkways* (New Haven: Yale University Press, 1953), pp. 107-111.

COMPANY LEVEL

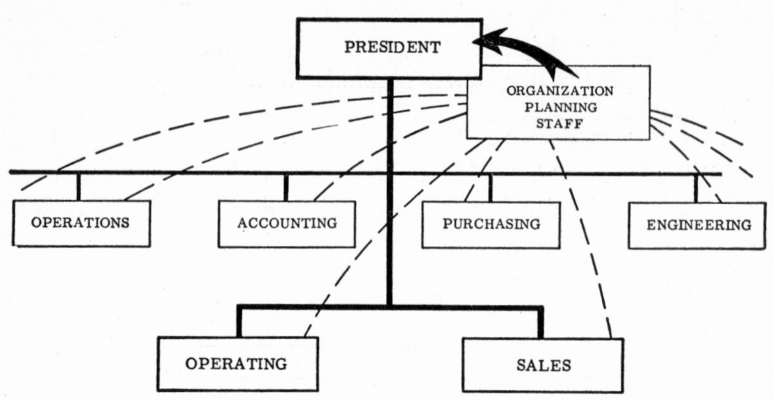

PLANT LEVEL

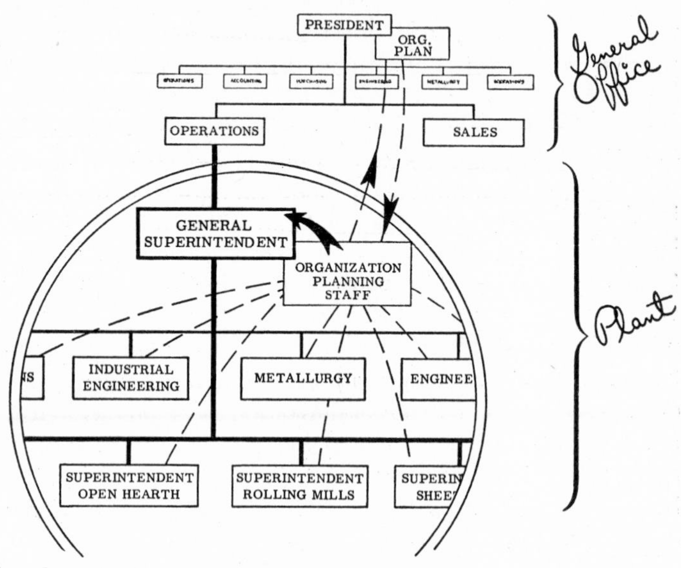

CHART 13-1. *Organization planning staff assistance* (Reproduced by permission of William R. Willard, "Organization Planning for Effective Management," *Advanced Management,* 12:14, 1956).

echelon, but with actual training being conducted at the operating levels.

But perhaps the greatest single reason, *third* in our series, for a small staff in these units is the emerging concept of that activity as concerned with strategy rather than techniques. If one accepts Efferson's concept that such a unit is to function as the organization's philosophers and global planners, it follows that it should not become bogged down in the details of map-making.

Closeness to top. It is remarkable in how many instances the organization planning unit seems to be close to the president of the company, both from the standpoint of hierarchical status and social and ideological nearness. This is not meant to insinuate that this relationship is wholly social or haloistic. Quite to the contrary, it probably indicates an underlying anxiety about the burgeoning of industrial bureaucracies. These presidents are aware of the empire-building and social stratification that goes on in all organizations, including the most efficient industrial enterprises. May they not place their trust in organization planning units in the hopes that they constitute the best promise to combat these tendencies? Perhaps the same metamorphosis is going on here as in the engineering profession where graduate engineers are no longer used as draftsmen, as they once were. Now they lay out the work for draftsmen and themselves engage in the higher level activity appropriate to their training and skills. It is true that the organization planning staff does prepare organization blueprints in the form of charts, manuals, and job descriptions, but these are the by-products of the strategy planning that flows from the decision network. Organization planning people are not technicians in the same sense as are personnel classifiers or time-study people. If they possess the technician's set of mind, they cannot serve well as strategists and planners. Their technical work is incidental; it flows from their own participation in the planning process.

II • OPERATIONS OF ORGANIZATION PLANNING UNITS

Program Orientation

The basic approach of organization planning units is in terms of programs and objectives, rather than individual jobs. C. A. Efferson has commented, "Once the programs of an organization are clear and acceptable, 90 per cent of the problem of setting organization structure is over. Organization charting itself is a relatively quick and easy chore. It is only when one is not sure what he wants the structure and the people in it to accomplish, that charting becomes difficult. Needless to say, much of our work is discussion of goals or programs with department heads."[12]

Efferson's unit prepares a number of charts showing alternative ways of organizing, leaving personalities out of consideration. The charts are then discussed with the unit head, trying to keep him from discussing personalities, and inducing him to select an ideal long-range structure. However, the organization planning people, at this point, do indicate rather emphatically which chart they believe to represent the best formal organization. Having reached agreement on an ideal organization the staff men begin to talk personalities with the head, with the result that finally there is evolved a structure which, while not ideal, is nevertheless workable. The organization people try to obtain the best possible structure after taking into account sociological, psychological, economic and engineering considerations. It contains compromises from the standpoint of theory, but it generally remains a good plan.

Another director states that an organization plan is not a straitjacket; it points out objectives and asks people to use their own initiative in achieving these objectives. A plan should leave freedom for thought on the part of operating people. It should permit them to go along parallel but different goals toward common objectives because excessive central procedures kill initiative. It is the function of the top echelon to lay down the basic philosophy which brings about balance and coordination among the individuals on subordinate echelons. This constitutes the foundation of large-scale modern organization: maximum individual self-reliance within the framework of the organization's need for coordination. Organization planning units seem to have accepted this philosophy as their *modus operandi.*

Types of Writings

Four categories. The organization planning unit is responsible for preparing and maintaining the basic writings relative to organi-

[12] Efferson, "Basic Problems in Organization Procedure," p. 6.

zation. These fall into four general categories: (1) the job descriptions for managerial positions, (2) the organization manual, (3) the policy file, book, or manual, and (4) organization charts. Not every company maintains all four of these. For instance, the organization charts and job descriptions may substitute for an organization manual. The latter, when it exists, may take the form of a prose description of the relationships between jobs. As such it becomes an elaboration of individual job descriptions or job descriptions of organization subunits. In an organization manual the jurisdictional limits of both individuals and subunits can be found. It also includes a statement of the duties, goals, and functions of a particular group of jobs. In other words, it tells who is to do what from the standpoint of activity groupings. Some organizations maintain functional charts whose boxes contain the descriptive material which otherwise might go into a manual.

Policy manual. Perhaps the most interesting phenomenon is the policy manual which seems to have gained its recent vogue coincident with two developments: (1) the recognition and demarcation of the corporate level, and (2) the rise of organization planning. There comes a time in the history of an organization when top management feels impelled to communicate what it believes should be the basic set of values guiding decisions on all echelons. In the beginning these communications may not be distinguished from the mine-run of memoranda; but ultimately they are numbered serially and punched for loose-leaf filing. Usually such policies are issued by the president upon the recommendation of a committee composed of officials on the top echelon. Representatives of the organization planning unit sit in on the deliberations of this committee and are responsible for the preparation, issuance, and distribution of management policy statements.

Salary Administration

The salary function does not seem to be included in the activities of many of the newer organization planning units. This also seems logical if one accepts Efferson's premise that the most desirable characteristic of an organization planning person is ability to think "big" and to think across the board. For the most part personnel people are technicians, and as such they are not accustomed to thinking big. That may be why management development programs have sometimes been taken away from them and put under organization planning.

It is interesting to note that the pioneering organization staff agency at the Standard Oil Company of California regards pay along with manpower, methods, and organization planning as a "package that ties together logically." The technique of job description varies as one goes up and down the hierarchy, the higher management positions calling for attention to the more intangible factors. However, the emphasis on all echelons in Standard Oil is placed fundamentally upon job description and job analysis, and pay is regarded as a necessary objective of study.[13]

Ancillary Activities

Efferson's survey of the practice of organization planning (1954) revealed that organization planning departments were either themselves conducting, associated with, or under the supervision of a wide variety of traditional management activities.[14] These included industrial engineering, industrial relations, salary administration, operations control, facility planning, economic forecasting, operations research, education, communications, manpower, and cost control. Efferson attributed this diversity to two influences: (1) the function was new and undergoing a period of definition, and (2) as often happens with capable people, the organization planning unit was given some of these important activities because no one else was doing them.

Participation in Management Development

But one striking fact seemed to stand out in organization planning departments on the West Coast, namely, that so many of the directors, including Efferson himself, had been running management development activities in their previous assignments. This is a perfectly logical move in the light of the form that manage-

---

[13] Department on Organization, *People and Pay Checks* (San Francisco: Standard Oil Company of California, 1957), p. 48. See also *The Management Guide* (San Francisco: Standard Oil Company of California, 1948, revised edition, 1956).

[14] Efferson, "Basic Problems in Organization Planning," p. 3.

ment development activities have taken in the last decade. Fundamentally the major mission has been to provide management manpower to meet future needs, which has required three major steps: (1) projecting the organization into the future so as to ascertain needs; (2) evaluation of present manpower to determine future availability and potential for promotion; and (3) taking steps to develop persons deemed to have such potential.

Not classroom exercise. Management development has not taken the form of group training so much as clinical evaluation. The reason so many management development programs are associated with organization planning rather than training may be to remove them from the stigma of a classroom approach. Management development is essentially individual and clinical in philosophy and technique.

Manning tables. The maintenance of manning tables illustrates one of the principal reasons why management development is so often either directly in the organization planning unit or closely affiliated with it. Although the manning table might very well be kept in the personnel department, it would seem logical that much of the basic data for its maintenance should come from the studies conducted by organization planning. These would project the future conformation of hierarchy, revealing the executive jobs that will exist in the future. As is the case with orthodox organizing procedure, these studies are made without reference to personalities. Then follows the task of determining how existing personnel will fit into the projected organization. Some organizations maintain manning charts in the form of traditional organization charts containing the names of the incumbent in each box, plus some desigation as to what is likely to happen to him. The latter information is often coded by meaningful variations of color, presumably identifiable by only a few of the insiders. These codes may indicate such likelihoods as early retirement, continuation in present job without promotion, or availability for promotion. It is obviously desirable to maintain security over the evaluation data in order that such information will not become common gossip.

In an organization like the Bank of America, with its 600 separate banking offices, many of the people on the banking floor can be regarded as possible future executives in contrast with a manufacturing enterprise where the blue-collar workers make up a larger proportion of the total. The Bank of America has been experimenting with a combination manning table and skill file containing data on each of the 3,000 employees classified as officers. These data, having to do with the promotability of officers on seven different items or characteristics, are identified by color. The material on a given officer or bank can be obtained readily by flipping over the search tabs on a Kardex® series. The file is in the form of a convenient console-like structure which the director of organization planning can manipulate from the swivel chair at his own desk. The data are obtained from evaluation questionnaires which are in turn interpreted by the organization staff so as to equalize the known differences in raters.

Relationships of Other Management Activities

Standard staffing tables. The Bank of America also maintains standard staffing tables for the banking offices, based upon time study and a record of the volume of transactions. While these studies are made by a unit separate from organization planning, the latter evaluates and interprets how these standards are being applied. The branch offices have to justify their requests for additional personnel on the basis of actual volume of work as compared with time standards.

Evaluation of personnel. It has already been indicated above that the evaluation of executive personnel has become the keystone of management development, which has in turn become either an integral phase of organization planning or closely affiliated with it. The difference between this and traditional personnel rating is that it is oriented more toward development and stimulating self-help than toward the punitive outlook of traditional practice. In a number of cases that is why it has been separated from personnel and training. The old "efficiency" ratings sprang from a philosophy and concept of human nature which saw man motivated only by a strong drive from above. It was furthermore assumed that all men were equally competitive by inherent make-up and that in a productive setting each would strive to outdo the other.

What does the evaluation of personnel have to do with organization planning? The organization planner is concerned not only with the structure *today* but with what form it is likely to take in the *future*. This is combined with a recognition that, while the job-task pyramid is the matrix of formal organization, the jobs still have to be filled by people. Hence it is only natural to follow up on a projection of the job-task pyramid five years hence by also planning for the people to fill the jobs. This necessarily entails making some judgments about the availability and competence of the people now in the organization, as well as giving some attention to what steps seem advisable in preparing individuals for future responsibilities. The latter is management development which, according to contemporary thought and practice, cannot be divorced from current and continuous evaluation.

Position control. The question arises as to whether or not the organization planning department should review all proposals to establish new positions, with the authority to approve or reject. Our survey of companies with corporate headquarters revealed only one that practiced position control through the organization planning unit. On the other hand organization planners are quite aware of the necessity to be watchful in evaluating the need for proposed new positions. With the one exception mentioned above, they felt that this could best be accomplished by effective staff work in which the organization unit maintained intimate relations with the line. However line managers make the ultimate decisions. In one case the line people were required to make a report on a special form whenever a new position was added. The report was merely explanatory and did not require central approval before hiring. One director stated that it might be desirable to pre-audit managerial positions and post-audit those for clerks and stenographers.

The objective of position control is of course to maintain the number and types of personnel needed at the point where the work must be accomplished. This is fairly easy for direct labor where output is measurable. However the problem often becomes baffling in the realm of adjective (indirect) labor. With the proportion of such labor becoming ever greater, position control becomes increasingly complex. It has been suggested that there is little to be accomplished by trying to control the establishment of individual positions; the critical questioning should be directed toward the establishment of a new activity or function. Once a new activity is authorized, the augmentation of staff naturally follows; but a rigorous examination of the actual need for a new activity may result in the decision to abandon it.

Reduction in force. The business slowdown in 1957-58 gave an opportunity to observe the reduction in force undertaken by two aircraft companies which experienced cancellation of government orders, and which had but recently inaugurated organization planning as a formalized activity. In one case cancellation came without warning. It necessitated the layoff of thousands practically overnight. In the other instance, the need was not so immediately pressing with the result that the reduction program could be extended over several months.

In the case where the cancellation was sudden, the organization planning unit at the corporate level took relatively little part. Instead an organization planning unit at the division level played a major role in the heavy cutbacks and layoff. Direct production personnel were reduced drastically all along the line, and only a skeleton organization of six supporting services was preserved. The management people in these units were downgraded from the standpoint of status and prestige, but salaries were maintained in all but one or two cases. Decisions were made at the division level, by the division head. In this company the need for reduction in force was confined largely to this single missile division.

A combination of circumstances required a cutback in personnel in several divisions of the other company with the result that the corporate organization planning unit took an active part. It acted as coordinator for what was done in the divisions. The executive vice-president issued a directive stating that the divisions should watch their superstructure to see that it was not out of proportion with the reduced number of direct workers. An historically derived index of the ratio of supervisory to nonsupervisory workers served as a useful guide. The divisions were asked to maintain the old supervisory ratio in planning their reduction moves. While the divisions had organization planning units of their own, the corporate people kept in constant contact with their counterparts in the divisions and sat in on planning meetings. A target date one year ahead was set for the completion of the reduction. Each division established its goals by function, such as manufacturing, engineering, and industrial relations, determining the number of positions to be abolished as well as the supervisory ratio to be achieved. Stabilization was reached six months ahead of the target date. The planned supervisory ratio was achieved and in some cases the number of supervisory levels was reduced. There was no emotional slashing of "fringe" activities; the reduction was orderly, and as a case the episode constituted an argument in favor of formalized organization planning.

III • ORGANIZATION PLANNING IN GOVERNMENT

It may have been noted that the emphasis in this chapter has been entirely on organization planning developments in the field of business management.

What about government? Here we find a curious circumstance. We do not discover the same flowering of enthusiasm in the government sphere, despite the fact that organization was a prime focus in many of the early reform movements. This interest in organization developed in the early part of the century. It was given rather lasting momentum by the creation of research bureaus under the auspices of large cities, universities, and private groups. World War I and the New Deal—both events which increased the size of the federal government very appreciably—further stimulated concern with problems of organization.

Pattern of Administrative Planning

By 1940 the essential pattern for administrative planning had been established. It differed in at least three important respects from the approach which was later to be taken in industry. These differences involved: (a) a broader definition of responsibility for administrative planning than organization analysis alone, (b) concepts of the organization planning function which were more generalized but perhaps differed in degree more than in kind, and (c) a closeness to the budget operation. This concept of administrative planning reached a maturity during World War II in the Division of Administrative Management of the U.S. Bureau of the Budget and in the Control Division of the Army Service

Forces.[15] Nearly 20 years of experience since that time has changed its character very little.[16]

Strategy and tactics. The responsibilities of administrative planning units were laid down in a speech given by Bernard L. Gladieux in 1939 and later printed in *Processes of Organization and Management.*[17] He stressed organization planning, but he also noted such other duties as simplification of procedures, preparation of administrative orders and their clearance, development of standards and measurement, and forms control. This indicated that such units were to have responsibility for broad strategy and *also* for rather detailed tactics. Such a mixture of breadth and detail has generally continued to characterize these units. For example, in World War II one of the spectacular achievements of the Budget Bureau's Administrative Management Division—far removed from large questions of strategy—was the development and dissemination of a work simplification program for supervisors. In New York State some of the recent accomplishments of the Administrative Management unit also have been at the detail level. They have included: (1) the development of office space standards, (2) establishment of a state-wide records management program, and (3) evaluation of fees paid for specific government services.[18]

Functions of administrative planning. One of the consequences of this very broad grant of responsibility has been a lessened attention to organization planning and strategy as such. It is paradoxical, too, that the organization planning function has continued to be defined in almost ambiguous terms. Indeed Gladieux's statement in 1939 contains about as high a degree of specificity as organization planning in public administration has achieved in the past twenty years. He pointed out that the big

---

15 For a brief but good description of this approach, see Donald C. Stone, "Administrative Self-Improvement," in Fritz Morstein Marx, editor, *Elements of Public Administration* (Englewood Cliffs, N.J.: Prentice-Hall, 1946), pp. 448 ff.

16 A recent essay that makes the same general points is Abe Lavine, "Administrative Management Units," Management Forum in *Public Administration News,* June 1959, unpaged.

17 Bernard L. Gladieux, "Administrative Planning in the Federal Government," in Cathryn Seckler-Hudson, editor, *Process of Organization and Management* (Washington: American University Press, 1948), pp. 172 ff.

18 Lavine, *op. cit.*

job was to study the basic plan of organization and "to develop improved plans." He said these studies would concern themselves with "the proper division and functional distribution of the work of the agency; the establishment of a sound structure of authority and control; the provision of appropriate staff facilities and services; the elimination of jurisdictional conflicts; and proper program coordination." [19]

Orientation toward mechanical. The product of this type of orientation over the last two decades has been an almost total concentration on the structural mechanical aspects of organization. The administrative planners have seen their role as an architectural one . . . designers of structure. This would seem to be far different from what has been occurring in industrial organization planning in the last decade. There organization has been used as the vehicle around which much of top policy planning evolves. Particularly is this to be seen with reference to executive development. In contrast to the situation in industry, there are few if any instances where administrative planning units have had any direct involvement in career development programs in government. These have typically been undertaken in the personnel units, which have most commonly operated quite separately from administrative planning. This has had a larger relevance, too, because it has meant that organization planning in government has not been viewed as involving the major strategies of executive placement and their implications for organization building.

Relationship to Budget

Perhaps the most significant difference between industry and public administration, however, has been the auspices under which administrative planning has operated in government. It has either been a function of, or closely tied to, the budget. Here we see a major environmental feature that separates most private business from government. Budgeting in the public service does not have any ready mechanical means of judging its resource allocations. Such allocations are wrapped up in the philosophy of the organization, judgments as to effectiveness of performance, and choices between alternative strategies. In short the budget has in

---

[19] Gladieux, *op. cit.*, p. 173.

many respects become the vehicle around which high level staff work moves in the government. Organization planning, as such, has not become the "top coordinating activity" and has not been in "constant, intimate contact at the heart of decision-making," because the budget has already been there.

It is important to realize, of course, that this has not meant the sharp difference in actual operations that might be suggested. Take Donald C. Stone's statement of the budget function as an illustration and compare it to some of Efferson's comments cited earlier:

> The budget office, for example, in the formulation of work plans with the operating bureaus or divisions deals with two general classes of problems: first, the character and extent of operations that are proposed—that is to say, the program; second, the organization and methods to carry out the program. . . . Because of this interrelationship of budgeting and administrative planning, the two are often combined under the same head. If separate the two groups must work together very closely.[20]

Thus in government the focus has been primarily on the budget as the central coordinating device. In industry it seems to be shifting increasingly toward organization planning. Consequently it is to be expected that in the future excitement about the role and function of organization planning will continue to come from business and industry, as it has in the last decade.

IV • SUMMARY

One of the striking management developments of the decade of the 'fifties was the appearance of formal organization planning units. It is safe to say that by 1960 organization planning had become one of the most influential staff activities in larger organizations, especially those which have diversified and decentralized.

Despite the popularity of organization planning units, there has not yet developed consensus as to their precise area of responsibility. One observer said, "Organization planning is what you want to call it." However certain central characteristics of organization planning units had begun to emerge by 1960. Or-

[20] Stone, "Administrative Self-Improvement," p. 456.

ganization planners do not typically engage in narrow mechanical operations. They tend to be concerned more with broad policy questions, to regard their function as one of top level coordination. This is on the assumption that the national economy, competition, and the consumer market all relate back to the internal organization of the company. Jobs and the people, particularly the executives, who fill them are responsible for what happens now and in the future. Hence an important role for organization planning is urged.

For some of the reasons noted in the previous paragraph, organization planning has been typically regarded as a general staff function. Furthermore, it could be argued that organization planning provides a rather ideal example of the general staff model. Organization planning units are typically small, are detached from day-to-day operations, concentrate on major strategy questions, and have intimate relationships with the top executives. In this context it is not surprising that the basic approach of organization planning units is in terms of programs and objectives. It has been said that "once the programs of an organization are clear and acceptable, ninety per cent of the problem of setting organization structure is over."

Commonly the organization planning unit is responsible for preparing and maintaining the basic writings relative to the organization. These fall into four general categories: (1) job descriptions for managerial positions; (2) organization manuals; (3) policy files, books, or manuals; (4) organization charts. Organization planning units have been engaged in a host of other activities, perhaps largely because they are new and still establishing their appropriate role. The oldest unit, in Standard Oil of California, has been responsible for salary administration, as an example.

Interestingly, organization planning has had a close relationship with management development programs. This has been largely because executive needs could not really be separated from the pattern of the future organization. Industry has also recognized the inter-relationship between executive capacity and organization shape. In some ways organizations take form around people; in others the nature of the organization creates a demand for certain types of executives. Organization planning has a relationship to a number of other management activities. There is a concern, for example, with manning and staffing tables, position control, and executive personnel evaluation. However organization planning units do not involve themselves directly.

In this chapter the emphasis was almost entirely on the development of organization planning in industry. This has been so because a similar trend has not occurred in government. In the public service many of the same types of staff activities take place under the general aegis of the budget.

Part Three

MODIFYING SYSTEMS

Introduction to Part Three

In preceding pages, the point has rather frequently been made that there are many ways of "seeing" the complex phenomenon of organization. Much depends on the eye of the beholder. Even where all the aspects of a scene are physically observable, we know how differing are the views of what took place. Capturing a picture of an organization is infinitely more complicated, however, because it is not physical like a building, an automobile, or a landscape. We deal here with a myriad of processes and interactions, only a part of which are concentrated in a particular locale and are visible. Thus we should expect that different people will consider different things important about the picture they think they see. It follows also that these variant perspectives will be reflected in the way in which knowledge about organization is classified. Conversely any system of classifying knowledge about organization will reflect the biases of the classifier.

Part Two of this book has employed the classic system of categorizing knowledge about organization. We use the word "classic" as an adjective to describe a "coherent system embodying principles and methods accepted as authoritative in application to arts, science, and literature." In these terms the structural classification is a basic point of departure for any student of organization. However, as we have emphasized repeatedly, it represents only one perspective. There are many "overlays" on the job-task hierarchy which provide us with different views of these complex processes in operation. Some of these were mentioned in Chapter Two, notably communication, power, decision, sociometry, and function. At that point, we were concerned only with developing a general sense of the complexity of the actual organization pattern.

Now it seems appropriate to think of the overlays as systems modifying the job-task structure. Some of these modifiers, such as the power factor, can be charted; others, such as cultural setting, cannot. Some, such as status systems, have very pronounced social aspects; others, such as functionalism, are largely work-oriented.

In the chapters of Part Three we will deal with those modifying elements which are largely social. In a later chapter the decision will be analyzed as a basis for organization building. The effect of staff functionalism, as a work-oriented modifier, was treated earlier within the conventional framework of the literature of hierarchy. In all cases, however, we should bear in mind the fundamental point that there are many elements at work amending the nature of organization behavior. They can be classified in a great many ways. Our aim is only to enable the reader to sample the full range of these factors at work, which in last analysis tend to be present in any social system.

We start by observing the obvious fact that every individual represents a system of his own with personal perceptions, goals, and needs. How he arrives at this point is, of course, a problem for the psychologists. Insofar as the student of organization is concerned, the essential thing to remember is the difference in the final product. The molding of these varied personalities into a viable whole is our basic challenge.

In the following chapter we will note that part of this task is accomplished in a self-generative way by organizations as they become social systems. They develop their traditions, taboos, and codes of behavior. This is the cultural factor, which frequently supplements and modifies the official job-task prescriptions.

In later chapters we will see that status, which seems to appear almost universally in social organisms, also specifies certain patterns of conduct and relationships. Communications are still another important influence. Power and politics prescribe still another system of conduct which may or may not accord with classic hierarchical notions. Finally, the significance of the individual to this total process is to be seen rather specifically by viewing the impact of leadership structure and behavior on the organization.

FOURTEEN

The Culture

What to Look for in This Chapter . . .

The culture places a system of constraints or limits on the individual

The culture includes knowledge, belief, art, morals, law, custom, and any other capabilities and habits man has as a member of society

Cultural awareness gives management:

- Better understanding
- Ability to predict behavior
- Vicarious experience
- Aid in facilitating change

Culture is material and nonmaterial

Institutional and professional subcultures

Studying organizations through the interaction approach

At the opposite extreme from the constraints placed on an organization by individual capacities and competences are those imposed on the individual by the organization. These latter constraints are not of course all hierarchical. We have noted elsewhere that organizations are social institutions, with a character and unique properties. As Selznick has emphasized, organizations become more than technical instruments as they are "infused with value." [1] Around each organization, then, there grow certain patterns of conduct and belief. These are considered "right" for the organization in the general consensus. They become the value system of the organization members; and it is within this context that all members are expected to operate. Thus the alternative ways in which an individual will be permitted to behave in any particular organization will be sharply conditioned by its institutional character. These restrictions apply at every level. The flexibility and discretion of the leadership is thereby limited; and every proposal for change must run the gantlet of individual perception of its conformity with the general value system.

In the last analysis there is only a certain amount of "stretch" in the individual personality and in the organization character. As Chapple and Sayles have pointed out, it is particularly important to understand the nature of these organizational prescriptions in fitting people into jobs.[2] The job, after all, is a role established formally and informally by the organization. By its very nature it is an expression of organization values. Hence the individual who finds his personality needs in conflict with these requirements should be directed elsewhere.

I • THE CONCEPT OF CULTURE

Definitions

The anthropological idea of culture provides us with perhaps the most useful conceptual tool for looking systematically at the behavior patterns which are organizationally imposed. It originated essentially as a description of the sum of human activity patterns studied by the cultural anthropologists. E. B. Tylor, writing in

---

[1] Philip Selznick, *Leadership in Administration* (Chicago: Row, Peterson, 1957), pp. 16 ff.

[2] Eliot D. Chapple and Leonard R. Sayles, "The Man, the Job, and the Organization," *Personnel* 34:8-20, March-April 1958.

1871, is often given credit for having stated the classic definition of culture. He said, "Culture . . . is that complex whole which includes knowledge, belief, art, morals, law, custom, and any other capabilities and habits acquired by man as a member of society."[3] It is important to recognize that the concept refers specifically to man, and does not concern the animal kingdom or other aspects of the natural environment. Thus we might draw a broad distinction between those things which we as humans have introduced to our environment and those things over which we have no control. One category would concern the cultural aspects of the environment, the other the natural.

This states the culture concept in very broad framework. Many anthropologists see it in more restricted terms. They are particularly anxious that the basic idea of culture as the symbolic integration of individual behaviors in a larger system not be lost. Thus we find later definitions of culture suggesting it is the "mass of behavior that human beings in any society learn from their elders and pass on to the younger generation."[4] Put another way, it is "an organized group of learned responses characteristic of a particular society."[5] An ax, for example, is man-made but it is not important as a physical artifact. It is important for the things it represents. In Australia missionaries gave steel axes to adult aborigine men and women and to young people of both sexes. Up to that time the ax had been hard to get. It was a badge of adult masculinity and a symbol of authority. The abolition of this symbolic role of the ax was ". . . probably responsible for the eventual destruction of the entire internal social structure of the group as well as of its intertribal relationships."[6]

The focus on culture, then, is an attempt to determine what the essential human-induced elements are that pattern life in a given society. Here we find no distinction between the formal and in-

---

[3] Quoted from Tylor's *Primitive Culture* in Leslie A. White, "The Concept of Culture," *American Anthropologist* 61:227, April 1959. White reports that there is great divergence of view among anthropologists as to a proper definition of culture.

[4] Ralph Linton, *The Tree of Culture* (New York: Alfred A. Knopf, Inc., 1955), p. 3.

[5] *Ibid.*, p. 29.

[6] Dorothy Lee, "The Cultural Curtain," *Annals* 323:122-123, May 1959.

formal. Indeed an endless number of factors, related in the most complex fashion, participate. The job-task hierarchy is regarded as one cultural facet, just as would be the status hierarchy. This concept has particular relevance to management because it helps to make clear that the ordering elements in any organizational situation are not the consequence of rational, hierarchical decision at any particular time. General Charles de Gaulle may have wrought a real revolution in 1958 with the establishment of the Fifth French Republic. But this will have little influence on the French predilection to cheat on taxes, to observe traditional religious practices, and in other respects to follow behavior patterns which long preceded de Gaulle's advent to power. It is undoubtedly true that de Gaulle, being a Frenchman, would not want many of these things changed. But the essential point is that changes in power and in structure do not mean that the basic values governing behavior in a given situation have changed. Generally speaking, changes in cultural habits and values come very slowly.

Applications to Management

The concept of culture can be applied to the study of organization in two ways. First, it is important to recognize that no organization can be isolated from its cultural environment. That is, organizations as social organisms must operate within the framework of the larger cultural system. As a consequence the alternatives in any given situation are greatly limited by their congruity with the values of the total culture. For example the management of an organization could not realistically consider the elimination of vacations as a means of cutting costs. Such a step would in some cases violate statutes, in many others union demands, and still others broader social expectations.

A second application of the culture concept is to consider the organization as a subculture. In such an instance the culture model is simply applied to the organization itself. As an institution, the organization is assumed to acquire its own patterns of conduct and learned behavior, developed within the context of the larger cultural pattern. We shall return to this subject.

Values to Management

By way of summarizing the significance of the culture concept to the student of administrative organization, we may note at least four ways in which this type of awareness can be useful:

Promote understanding. Many of the things that people do begin to make sense when the assumptions behind them are revealed. We are conditioned to behave, perform, and believe in certain channels because of our cultures. Thus the story is told of the Arabian sheik who, after witnessing an American motion picture entitled "The Eternal Triangle" asked why the hero did not marry *both* the women. A pathetic—and culturally out of date—individual is the foreman who still cannot believe the full employment of the last twenty years. He fails to understand why the threat to dismiss doesn't have the old "teeth."

Predict behavior. Cultural influences play an important part in determining how people will act in a certain situation. An educated European will be a better linguist than an educated American because his environment requires it. It is possible to predict with considerable accuracy that an upper-class Latin-American will speak French in addition to Spanish. A carpenter will be more likely than an accountant to join a labor union. A policeman will be more likely than a school teacher to be a day sleeper. Lawyers tend to have greater verbal facility than engineers; the law exists in an environment of words whereas engineering has a setting of mathematical symbols and graphic portrayal. Out of 100 probation workers there are certain to be many more who believe it is possible to rehabilitate criminals than there would be among 100 policemen.

Substitute for experience. In many respects, the "experienced" person is the one who has developed a sensitivity to the culture in which he operates. This is particularly true as one climbs the management ladder and therefore operates at the level where decisions tend to have a high component of value judgments. Awareness of these cultural factors, then, could possibly reduce the amount of time a person has to "live" in an organization, assimilating its value system.

Facilitating change. Traditions, customs, and patterned modes of behavior tend to stratify organization, making it difficult to change. But modern management requires flexibility; institutions should be able to adapt themselves readily to new conditions in this dynamic age. Certainly one of the prime requisites in meeting this need for change would be an understanding of the structuring influences combined with knowledge about how cultural change is accomplished.

II • COMPONENTS OF CULTURE

There are of course many ways in which cultural factors manifest themselves in organizations. Broadly speaking—and at risk of oversimplification—there are two general categories of culture, the *material* and the *nonmaterial*. The material culture includes all the physical and observable things man has created and which in turn have an effect on patterns of life and behavior. The ax is one illustration. In our day and age the automobile is perhaps the single most important physical influence on the social relations in our society. Nonmaterial culture, on the other hand, is considerably less tangible. It involves habit, belief, philosophy, and all the other conceptual inventions by which behaviors within the society and the organization come to be controlled.

Material Culture

For students of organization, the idea of material culture has special meaning. It is quite obvious that life and attitudes within organizations are greatly influenced by various aspects of physical layout and technique. Sometimes these influences are labeled the "ecology of administration." [7] We need not concern ourselves unduly with definitions here but it would seem desirable to review the way in which the anthropologist does classify the various facets of the total life setting.[8] *Environment* is "the aggregate of

---

[7] See John Gaus's pioneering essay, "The Ecology of Government," in his *Reflections on Public Administration* (University, Alabama: University of Alabama Press, 1947), p. 6.

[8] The definitions in the paragraph come from Melville J. Herskovits, *Cultural Anthropology* (New York: Alfred A. Knopf, Inc., 1955), pp. 94-95. Herskovits refers to culture as "that part of the total setting that includes the material objects of human manufacture, techniques, social orientations, points of view, and sanctioned ends, which are the immediate conditioning factors underlying behavior."

all external conditions" and is therefore composed of two parts: (1) *the habitat,* designating the natural setting of human existence; and (2) the *cultural* factors, which are obviously nonnatural. *Ecology* is a dynamic concept. It is concerned with the interaction between the habitat and the culture, with particular emphasis on the spatial distributions that result from this interaction. Thus the idea of ecology helps to emphasize for us the continual interchange between individuals as carriers of culture and their environment. The vehicle by which man adjusts to his habitat is *technology,* which includes the objects we make to secure food, shelter, clothing, and other survival necessities. Herskovits has pointed out that technology has been a significant criterion in appraising cultures because it "is the only aspect of culture susceptible to objective evaluation." [9]

Industrial organization. Among the many examples of the influence of various aspects of material culture on work ways, perhaps the most obvious is the assembly line. In the automobile industry, for example, one of the most frequent causes of quickie and sit-down strikes has been management's alleged attempt to make the line go faster than the men want to work. By and large, the jobs are unskilled and repetitive; they leave little or no room for even a very low order of decision-making by the worker. While men work together ritually, they do not develop social group relationships because the attention demanded by the job prevents social interaction.[10]

Brick factory. In a brick factory Despres has pointed out that the spatial organization of work operations, that is, ecology, has great significance to communication, authority, and decision-making. The distribution of work processes over a rather large area creates particularly serious problems of supervision. Despres studied a rather small organization, employing 40 to 50 persons. Even so, he found that spatial problems required seven or eight supervisors if traditional patterns of control were to be followed.

---

[9] *Ibid.,* p. 119.

[10] Irving Howe and B. J. Widick, *The UAW and Walter Reuther* (New York: Random House, 1949), pp. 19-25; Charles R. Walker and Robert H. Guest, *The Man on the Assembly Line* (Cambridge: Harvard University Press, 1952), pp. 65-70.

This small organization was able to meet the need by supplanting hierarchical controls with kinship controls.[11]

Clerical unit. In one company a small clerical unit was physically removed from the rest of the division by a series of barriers that provided a high degree of isolation. As a consequence the nine members of the unit had developed a much stronger sense of group loyalty, were largely removed from observation and command by anyone other than their immediate supervisor, were not greatly affected by general company policy, and enjoyed such perquisites as irregular breaks for snacks. A simple change in physical arrangements, which made these employees visible to higher officers, transformed almost entirely the character of the unit. The employees were now regarded as part of a larger labor pool, were restrained from talking, and most of all lost status as a specially treated unit. Efficiency in the section dropped and stress grew. Richards and Dobyns suggest that there existed in this company two separable culture systems when the small group was isolated from the larger. This was possible only so long as physical barriers were maintained that excluded "a more powerful social system." When the boundaries were removed, the unique culture pattern of the small group was also lost.[12]

The aircraft carrier. The extent to which naval architecture affects the pattern of culture on board ship is quite striking. The aircraft carrier in particular has worked some significant changes in the system of life which developed earlier on more conventional vessels. Largely this is due to the superimposition of the flight deck. The main deck has now become the hangar deck. Although many of the activities around which ship traditions have been built occur on the hangar deck, the architecture of the carriers has required that the ship's leadership be exercised from the flight deck. This has had a marked effect on the communications of the ship. Downs notes that problems of organizing the liberty party on one aircraft carrier were rather quickly solved because the officer of the deck could directly see that the sailors were assembling in a most disorderly manner on the flight deck. On the other

---

[11] Leo A. Despres, "A Function of Bilateral Kinship Patterns in a New England Industry," *Human Organization* 17:16, Summer 1958.

[12] Cara B. Richards and Henry F. Dobyns, "Topography and Culture: The Case of the Changing Cage," *Human Organization* 16:16-20, Spring 1957.

hand, problems with the chow line continued unresolved partially because none of the officers actually witnessed these difficulties. The chow line was on the hangar deck.[13]

The railroader. Railroading provides special ecological problems. The spanning of great distances has affected the life pattern of those who work on the trains and also those who maintain its facilities. There was a time, for example, when steam locomotives required servicing stations every one hundred miles. This meant a host of small, one-industry towns strung across the country. With dieselization this has all changed. The great majority of these service centers have been closed and thus the nature of railroad organization has been revised appreciably.[14] The railroad trainman has obviously had to be a highly mobile person; and because of this, one of the most prized goals in these organizations has been locational stability. A man in the train service may have expected at the time when the passenger fleet was in full operation at least a dozen changes in location of his home terminal. The number sometimes reached fifty during times such as those occasioned by war, depression, geographical shifts of industry, and technological upsets.[15] It is not surprising, then, that a principal trait of railroad life has been "bumping," based on seniority. The younger men had to do the moving. As they grew older and achieved status, their preference of assignment was given priority . . . a rather understandable pattern of conduct in terms of the ecology of the work.

The same kinds of problems—but involving even greater cultural complexities—have arisen in the industrialization of the lesser developed countries. One study involving the introduction of automatic looms in an Indian textile factory particularly emphasizes the relationship between technology on the one hand and social and psychological needs on the other. The new work processes had resulted in such a high degree of specialization that nearly every individual was "on his own." There were resulting production prob-

---

13 James F. Downs, "Environment, Communication and Status Change Aboard an Aircraft Carrier," *Human Organization* 17:14-19, Fall 1958.

14 W. F. Cottrell, "Death by Dieselization: Reaction to Technological Change," *American Sociological Review* 16:358-365, June 1951.

15 W. F. Cottrell, *The Railroader* (Stanford: Stanford University Press, 1940), pp. 43-44.

lems. They did not begin to reach solution until work processes were developed that provided for some degree of group interaction.[16]

Significance of the Material Culture to Organization

The brief case examples in the preceding paragraphs serve to indicate the diverse ways in which the material culture affects the nature of organization and its processes. Generally speaking, there appear to be two aspects of the material culture which are of particular consequence: (1) the *ecological* factor, which involves the manner in which the material culture requires the distribution of people in space; and (2) the *technological* factor, which clearly has an impact on ecology but is concerned more with the demands made on organization by the types of equipment and techniques used.

Effect on ecology. The constraints placed on organization by the necessity of distributing work over a large spatial area was particularly clear in the case of the brick factory. Obviously space has important implications for the system of control in any organization. It is one thing to supervise 40 men, all of whom are in visual proximity. It is quite another to supervise even half that number when they are scattered over a large geographic area. Obviously, too, ecological factors affect communication, a most simple illustration being provided by the aircraft carrier. These problems of communication and control are ultimately reflected in the centralization-decentralization pattern of the organization.

The assembly line presents a particularly intriguing aspect of ecology. The line itself is of course a technological facet of the culture. Yet its character forces a distribution of people thinly spread along its axis. The employees resemble the crowds that line the streets for a parade. Jasinski has pointed out that this ecological factor has important implications for traditional methods of organizing. Our modern production processes tend to flow

---

[16] A. K. Rice, *Productivity and Social Organization: the Ahmedabad Experiment* (London: Tavistock Publications, Ltd., 1958). This is a fascinating tale, with detective-like suspense, of the search for productivity in a society which is only beginning to discover the machine.

horizontally across acres of ground and yet we seek to maintain a vertical structuring of authority.[17]

The degree to which physical barriers of various types condition organization behavior was seen particularly in the example of the small clerical unit. This unique spatial situation resulted in differential behavior in terms of supervision, group interaction, and motivation in the group of nine people.

It is quite probable that we shall hear more in the future about these types of relationships. For example there is a developing area of study known as psychological ecology. Here the basic concern is with the way in which the individual perceives his habitat and is shaped by it. A major empirical research effort following this approach was concerned with the children of a small midwestern town (population 707). Analysis revealed that in this type of community very considerable pressure was placed on citizens to participate in a great variety of ways. Though there were not as many roles to be played as in a larger community, there still remained a great number for such a small group of people. No one could become highly specialized because he had to do so many things. The community could not afford to be selective because it had such limited talent. Children were important because of the need for their participation; and considerable skills were developed in fitting diverse personalities into the working whole. Thus the town of Midwest provided quite a different type of psychological ecology for its people than might be expected in a larger city.[18] Might the same not be true in various sizes of industrial and governmental organizations?

These types of studies do not permit us to draw any conclusions about such relationships. They do, however, suggest some intriguing possibilities. Among them are these four hypotheses which concern the effect of ecological factors on organization form and style.

- The larger the space required to perform the work of an organization, the greater will be its problems of supervision,

---

[17] Frank J. Jasinski, "Adapting Organization to New Technology," *Harvard Business Review* 37:79-86, January-February 1959.

[18] Roger G. Barker and Herbert F. Wright, *Midwest and Its Children* (Evanston, Ill.: Row, Peterson and Company, 1954).

control, and communication, and the greater its need for decentralization.

- The more horizontal the distribution of work in space, as on an assembly line, the greater will be the problems of imposing traditional patterns of hierarchical supervision and control.
- The greater the physical boundaries between units of an organization, the greater will be the difficulty of imposing a single policy standard throughout the organization and the greater the likelihood that each sub group will develop its own pattern of conduct.
- The more roles an individual is required to play in an organization, the less specialization there will be, despite the demands of the work process. This should result in more constructive social interaction and more effective skills in dealing with individual personalities.

Effect of technology. Thompson and Bates have suggested some significant ways in which technological factors affect the character of organization.[19] Among their conclusions are these:

- As a technology becomes more specialized, it appears that the organization's flexibility in shifting from one goal to another is curtailed.
- As a technology becomes more complicated, entry of a new organization into a field becomes more difficult.
- As a technology becomes elongated, any particular organization will tend to have less control over the total technological process, to be more dependent on other organizations for prior or subsequent operations in the total process (for resources and so on).
- Technological development, by requiring more specialization of personnel and equipment, adds to the heterogeneity of an organization.
- Increasing technological complication is accompanied by the proliferation of professional and technical societies and associations, each with its unique values and code of ethics.

---

[19] James D. Thompson and Frederick L. Bates, "Technology, Organization, and Administration," *Administrative Science Quarterly* 2:326-343, December 1957. The conclusions quoted are at pages 342-343.

Finally, the proliferation of specialization provides additional bases for organizational members to differentiate among themselves and hence for cleavage to develop.

Nonmaterial Culture

Herskovits has pointed out that "Culture is the man-made part of the environment."[20] As we have already seen, many of the means by which we wrest a living from the natural world in turn affect our total behavior pattern. But of course not all the factors of culture are overt and physical. Social organization is itself a part of culture, as are beliefs, systems of communication, and modes of conduct. These, then, may be considered elements of nonmaterial culture. These nonmaterial factors tend most to attract the attention of cultural anthropologists. Indeed, as we have noted earlier, most anthropologists consider the material culture only important as it reflects itself in beliefs and patterns of social behavior.

Linton has suggested that societies typically exhibit at least four common dimensions in social organization. These are:

1. Group members are classified according to age and sex and on this basis are assigned certain patterns of behavior.
2. The total membership is divided into smaller units, most particularly the family.
3. All societies recognize the existence of formal, culturally patterned relationships which individuals enter voluntarily. The functional significance of these associations will differ from society to society.
4. In every society both individuals and categories of individuals will be rated in a prestige series. In almost all societies, for example, men will rank women socially, and adults will rank children.[21]

It is particularly noteworthy that these structuring factors appear to occur in almost any social system larger than the small, face-to-face group. In the average organization in the United States, we can observe the classification of roles according to age and sex, the existence of informal groups, various types of union and professional associations which structure relationships of organization members, and various patterns of prestige grading. The com-

[20] Herskovits, *Cultural Anthropology*, p. 305.
[21] Linton, *The Tree of Culture*, pp. 31-32.

ponents of nonmaterial culture are obviously too numerous even to pretend to examine in this book. Only to suggest the importance of this perspective to a broader understanding of organization, we have selected three traits as illustrative. These are: (1) the ritual, (2) the taboo, and (3) jargon. Let it be emphasized again that this is no comprehensive look.

Ritual. The term "ritual" has traditionally been associated with religious ceremony and tribal observances requiring a number of persons to act in unison according to a prescribed formula. The purpose of the ritual is to express and enforce group solidarity. In the organization we find a number of ways—both formal and informal—in which ritual is observed. At the informal level, industrial sociologists have observed the existence of (1) rites of initiation, such as sending the greenhorn for a left-handed monkey wrench; (2) rites of passage, such as a farewell banquet; and (3) rites of intensification, such as the Christmas office party (which now appears to be passing from our cultural scene).[22]

Rituals of a more formal nature frequently have a relationship to the work process itself. In other words, the ritual has a functional purpose in line with the production goal. A familiar example is military drill, which is intended to condition people to react automatically and in unison not only to drill-field commands but to emergency battle conditions. The severe discipline of military ritual not only increases combat effectiveness but is in the long run humane because it serves to minimize casualties and save lives.

Such rituals are characteristic of organizations where human beings work under stress. For instance, some prisons count the inmates regularly, as often as every hour, and go through quite a ceremony in reporting the results of the count from the cell blocks or work stations to a central control point. Policemen approaching danger are conditioned to react automatically to different types of hazards, such as approaching a parked vehicle from the rear rather than front.

Taboos. Every society has a system of taboos. Those found within organizations often originate in the larger culture. In the motion picture industry, for example, taboos are mainly imposed

---

[22] Delbert C. Miller and William H. Form, *Industrial Sociology* (New York: Harper and Brothers, 1951), p. 292.

through censorship.[23] These taboos apply generally to areas of human conduct affecting morality. Thus a picture must avoid portrayal of sexual intimacy and take great care in depicting relations between sexes. Sin or crime cannot go unpunished. Prostitutes must not be depicted as such. Care must be taken not to offend ethnic minorities such as Negroes or Jews. Patriotic groups will protest at presentation of realism which they believe detracts from national honor and dignity.

Jargon. Many occupations have a peculiar jargon or argot. This special language is not only more efficient, direct and cryptic, it also serves as a symbol of the in-group, promoting social solidarity and adding to the sense of belonging. Railroaders are an outstanding example of an occupation group having its own special language.[24] Some groups, such as jazz musicians, have special words for the ordinary things and deeds of daily living. Because the jazz musician's professional life is relatively short and the average age very young, the turnover brings with it a new generation of terminology as well as people.

The Relationship Between the Material and Nonmaterial Cultures

Belief systems and role prescriptions tend to be a *stabilizing* factor in the organization and in society. Yet culture is at the same time extremely *dynamic.* This is particularly to be seen at the material level where advances in technology are occurring at an unbelievable rate. Few would have conceived ten years ago that there would be jet passenger planes flying at 600 miles per hour by 1960. In another decade, by 1970, there is every possibility that this speed will be up to at least 2000 miles. Every change in the material culture is bound to have its effect on the nonmaterial. Unfortunately, however, we find it much more difficult to change attitudes and value systems than to institute technological innovations. As Stuart Chase has put it, ". . . Americans are particularly spry at moving over and making room for new material inventions. Then, considerably later on, people change their insti-

---

[23] Hortense Powdermaker, *Hollywood, The Dream Factory* (Boston: Little, Brown and Company, 1950), pp. 54 ff.

[24] Cottrell, *The Railroader,* pp. 100-111.

tutions and belief systems to allow for the invention. . . ."[25] This discrepancy between (1) the material invention and (2) the beliefs and patterning of human behavior resulting from the inventions is known as the *cultural lag*. A management which permits the lag to become too great between the technical tools and the theory of their use may very well jeopardize the organization itself. In the United States cultural lag lies behind much of the problem of organizing our defense forces most effectively. The pilotless aircraft and other airborne missiles have completely changed the character of any future war. In this instance no one is able to say with any assurance what missions will be required in the future because we have had no real experience with the new technologies. On the other hand, many resist any change in the structure of our armed forces because they are continuing to make their judgments on the basis of performance in World War II and in some cases even earlier struggles. Thus the most effective organization of our armed forces has not been achieved because of inability and in some cases unwillingness to conceptualize roles and missions dictated by new technologies. The same could be said for many other organizations, both public and private.

III • SUBCULTURES

It has been said that culture is universal in man's experience, but each local manifestation of it is unique. There is, then, no particular level—governmental or otherwise—at which belief systems commonly occur. Within the larger society a considerable variation in behavior patterns and beliefs actually exists. The suggestion has been made, for example, that there are four categories of behavior within a social system. These are:

1. The *universals*, to which there is general conformity. This would include language, type of clothing and housing, and the way a group orders its social relations.

2. The *specialties*, which permit commitments to the values of subsystems that are not incompatible with those of the whole.

---

[25] Stuart Chase, *The Proper Study of Mankind*, revised edition (New York: Harper and Brothers, 1956), p. 132.

3. The *alternatives,* where the requirements of the universals and the specialties are flexible enough to provide for more than one mode of behavior.

4. The *individual peculiarities,* which involve experimental forms of behavior and actually represent the source of innovation in the culture.

The existence of *specialties,* or subsystems of values, within the total culture has particular significance to the study of organization. Two perspectives may be suggested. First, it can be argued that the organization as a social institution is itself a microcosmic culture within the larger setting, as we have already noted. This permits us to use many of the insights described earlier in this chapter in studying a particular organization. Second, the concept of specialties suggests other cultural subsystems which cut across the single organization and are based on race, ethnic origins, religion, age, and other factors. Perhaps most significant to the study of organization, however, are the belief systems which form around professional and vocational identifications. Thus it is possible to view the *specialties* aspect of the total culture pattern along two different planes. One is *vertical* and *internal,* concerning the single organization from top to bottom. The other is *horizontal* and *external,* cutting across many organizations. For purposes of convenience we can label both types *subcultures,* although the term is frowned upon by some anthropologists. The vertical type can be described as the *institutional subculture* and the horizontal type as the *professional subculture.*

The Institutional Subculture

Since organizations are social entities, it is inevitable that there will develop within each a cultural system with some unique properties. How unique these modes of behavior and beliefs are will vary a great deal according to the total environment of the organization. In general it would seem that ecological factors and the nature of the work are most significant determinants of character and commitment by individual participants. Isolation is particularly important as a conditioning factor because it implies a lessened opportunity for cross-fertilization with other systems. The ship is a good example of natural isolation. Social, as well as physical, isolation is to be found in the prison. But isolation does not determine the type of culture pattern which will emerge. It simply provides the setting in which it can flourish. The aircraft carrier, for example, is begetting quite a different culture from that of the battleship because of the difference in the architecture of the two vessels.

The nature of the work helps to erect an institutional subculture. This is especially true where the organization is relatively homogeneous and where there is relatively little opportunity for employment mobility. The police department of a city is a good example of an institutional subculture largely arising from the nature of the work. Police have highly irregular hours, reducing the possibility of normal social intercourse; furthermore the demands of their work have caused many police officers to develop a perception of incompatibility with other segments of the society. Finally, it should be noted that there is very little movement from one police department to another. Jobs are filled on a "closed promotion" basis.

A variety of environmental factors thus operates to specify the traits in a particular institutional subculture. And these are not generally subject to hierarchical amendment. As Nelson has pointed out, control in a prison is a life-and-death matter. It is ". . . a matter of survival, with the hazards involved in loss of control nakedly present at all times to color the atmosphere and the human relations of the situation."[26] It is quite obvious that the kind of organization and management required for this institutional subculture must differ markedly from that required in a newspaper office, where individual initiative and creativity remain important. Hence the model of an institutional subculture provides us with still another way of identifying the forces that actually structure an organization.

---

[26] E. K. Nelson, Jr., *Study of the Role and Function of the Prison Officer* (Unpublished doctoral dissertation, presented to the Faculty of the School of Public Administration, University of Southern California, June 1959), spirit process, p. 14. In private conversations Nelson has indicated other important determinants of the prison subculture: (a) more rigid separation of roles between keeper and kept, (b) nature of people being punished, (c) a totally male society, and (d) the essentially small prison world of isolation.

The Professional Subculture

Professionalization is the consequence of a highly skilled and specialized society. The twentieth century in the United States has seen the rise of hosts of new professions and expansion of others. As a means of upgrading performance in these various efforts, much emphasis has been placed on standards of conduct that relate to the profession and not to the institution. What is a profession? York Willbern has said, "It would be a brave soul indeed who would try to compile a list of professions, or to designate any exact criteria for exclusion or inclusion." [27] Suffice it to say, those who are engaged in vocations which are commonly recognized as requiring special learning and knowledge tend to be members of professional subcultures. The most common of these professional subcultures are law, medicine, the clergy, engineering, and accounting.

The development of these and many other professions, though perhaps desirable for the society as a whole, have had an important consequence for organizations.[28] This is to be seen in the conflict between the institutional subculture with one set of values and the management subculture with another. Thompson and Bates have emphasized this point, saying that with increasing technology, ". . . there is more likelihood for organizational members to owe loyalty or allegiance to a profession as well as to the organization, greater opportunity for the demands of the organization to conflict with those of the profession, and at the same time a greater opportunity for the individual employees to enforce demands on the organization by invoking sanctions from the profession." [29] Willbern has said essentially the same thing in

---

[27] York Willbern, "Professionalization in the Public Service: Too Little or Too Much?" *Public Administration Review* 14:14, Winter 1954.

[28] Willbern lists eight rather major social problems that have arisen as a consequence of professionalization; *ibid.*, pp. 18-19. James Burnham has seen in the trend toward professional management a great threat to traditional bases of power in the society. See *The Managerial Revolution* (New York: John Day, 1941).

[29] Thompson and Bates, "Technology, Organization, and Administration," p. 343.

indicating that professionalization ". . . increases the difficulty of coordination of governmental functions." [30]

There has been some research—not enough—which suggests the nature of the conflict between these two subcultures. The professionals have been described as the "cosmopolitans" and the institutionalists as the "locals." [31] In general the cosmopolitans have the greater mobility, see their future less in the organization, and obviously place the values of the professional subculture above the institutional subculture.[32] One concrete result of this situation is that members of the institutional subculture, by virtue of their immobility, tend to have a long record of service in an organization; the professionals tend to stay in any single organization a short time.[33] Exceptions to this general pattern are those who have a professional identification but whose skills are not easily transferable to another organization. The police, as noted earlier, are one example.

Our purpose in this section has been to emphasize the importance of looking at organizations through the eyes of the anthropologists and to think of organizations as embracing many of the attributes of a larger social system and a culture. We see, too, that cultural conflict is almost inevitable in organizations because of the existence of two differing types of value systems—one built on loyalty and belief in the institution and the other on a commitment to one's profession. It is also important to emphasize again that these configurations of culture occur at no particular hierarchical level, nor do they follow any particular organization axis. They arise as people feel the necessity to identify with a particular social system.

---

[30] Willbern, *op. cit.*, p. 19.

[31] Alvin W. Gouldner, "Cosmopolitans and Locals: Toward an Analysis of Latent Social Roles–I," *Administrative Science Quarterly* 2:281-306, December 1957. Gouldner notes that the categories originated with Robert Merton.

[32] For an early and interesting study of a state government bureaucracy see Leonard Reissman, "A Study of Role Conceptions in Bureaucracy," *Social Forces* 27:305-310, March 1949.

[33] In research on administrative distance in a government research laboratory, Edward Jones has made this general finding in comparing engineers and scientists on the one hand and administrators on the other. The study is as yet incomplete and unpublished.

IV • INTERACTION THEORY

The applied anthropologists have taken a particular interest in the problems of organization. A result of this interest has been the development of a somewhat different focus on organization processes. Chapple, one of the best known of the applied anthropologists, suggests that the following assumptions have guided this approach:

1. Organization is a system of relations between people.
2. The culture of the organization—techniques, processes, spatial layout, paper systems, and so forth—determines the pattern of individual conduct within the organization. "The technology and the systems and procedures of operation and control inextricably bind people together in a web of routine which in turn is given structural form by the division of the labor and responsibility." [34]
3. The real question is how we observe this phenomenon.
4. The way to look at organizations is to observe how people behave with one another on the job. We must determine "where individuals come into contact, in what order, how often, and for how long . . ." [35] In short we study *interactions.*

Miller has pointed out that four types of interaction sets are most frequently analyzed: (a) those between the superiors and subordinates in the hierarchy's "supervision" set, (b) those between line and staff specialists, (c) those between workmates on work-related matters, and (d) those between workers on personal and nonwork-related matters.[36] Each of these contacts is then analyzed in terms of its origination, the nature of the response, the duration, and the frequency of the contact. Miller has noted that William F. Whyte, one of the foremost advocates of the interaction approach, has particularly emphasized the importance of origination. The question simply is whether A or B originates the action. Whyte has concluded that this is particularly important

---

[34] Chapple and Sayles, "The Man, the Job, and the Organization," p. 9.

[35] Eliot D. Chapple, "Contributions of Anthropology to Institutional Psychiatry," *Human Organization* 13:11-15, Summer 1954.

[36] Frank B. Miller, "'Situational' Interactions—A Worthwhile Concept?" *Human Organization* 17:37-47, Winter 1958-59.

in the hierarchical situation. He believes that any flow of work which consistently has subordinates originating more to superiors than they respond is intolerable and "leads to disequilibrium."[37]

Chapple has sought to carry the analysis further to include such aspects of interaction as tempo, adjustment, synchronization, and dominance. With such data Chapple feels that a much more effective job can be done of fitting the right person to the right job. He points out that the interactional approach not only tells a great deal about the nature of a single job but also sets it in a total environment of individuals and processes. Jobs ". . . also differ according to the personalities who fill the surrounding organizational positions."[38] Chapple has developed methods of testing individuals for their ability to "live" in a particular organizational situation.[39]

V • SUMMARY

Culture is a conceptual means of looking at a total social organization and has been the primary focus of the cultural anthropologists. Culture is classically defined as ". . . that complex whole which includes knowledge, belief, art, morals, law, custom, and any other capabilities and habits acquired by man as a member of society." In essence culture is composed of all the things we humans have created. It is therefore changeable, in contrast to that which is natural and over which we have no control.

The concept of culture provides us with an important way of looking at organizations. In the general sense it helps us to recognize that the individual is not a free agent in any social system. Within that system there develop beliefs and habits of conduct which are in turn regulators and controllers. More specifically, the idea of culture provides us with important insights because (1) it emphasizes the importance of seeing organizations as part of a

[37] *Ibid.*, p. 44. See William F. Whyte, *Human Relations in the Restaurant Industry* (New York: McGraw-Hill Book Company, Inc., 1948), for an example of this approach.

[38] Chapple and Sayles, *op. cit.*, p. 11.

[39] Eliot D. Chapple, "The Standard Experimental (Stress) Interview as Used in Interaction Chronograph Investigations," *Human Organization* 12:23-32, Summer 1953.

larger social system and therefore subservient to those larger values; and (2) it suggests some perspectives on organizations themselves as social systems.

Culture may be divided into broad categories: that which is (1) material and (2) nonmaterial. With regard to the material aspects of culture, two terms are particularly significant. One is *ecology,* which deals with the relationships of people distributed in space. It helps to emphasize for us the continual interchange between individuals as carriers of culture and their environment. The other term which is important is *technology,* which essentially encompasses the tools and techniques by which man creates a living situation for himself. These material aspects of culture have great relevance to the way in which organizations are created and made operative. A number of illustrations were provided in the chapter. Perhaps the most striking is the aircraft carrier, where we see that introduction of a flight deck—a technological change—has had important ecological consequences.

Nonmaterial aspects of culture also affect the nature of organizations greatly. The ritual, the taboo, and jargon were discussed as three examples of this significance. One of the greatest problems is that we have difficulty in adjusting our belief systems and patterns of conduct, that is, our nonmaterial culture, to changes occurring in the material world. This is known as *cultural lag.* As a consequence organizations sometimes respond quite inappropriately to certain situations because the nonmaterial value system has not yet caught up with the material realities. This seems to be an important consideration in the current debates over U. S. defense organization. No one is quite sure whether arguments are being made in terms of what the various services did in World War II or in terms of what present weapons technology requires.

An organization may be considered a subculture. This does not mean it is any the less a part of, or subordinate to, the demands of the larger culture. It simply suggests that within the larger context there is a place for subsystems which are elaborations of the basic value pattern of the society. We may note that these subcultures are organized along two planes: (1) the *vertical,* which concerns a single organization and tends to embrace the total hierarchy from top to bottom, and (2) the *horizontal,* which cuts across many organizations and develops its system out of the kind of work being performed. In this chapter we have called the vertical configuration an *institutional* subculture and the horizontal a *professional* subculture. The rise of the professional subculture—another consequence of specialization—is most to be seen in such activities as dentistry, engineering, accounting, and education. It has caused a rather serious division in many organizations between those who are members of the institutional subculture, the "locals," and the members of the professional subculture, the "cosmopolitans."

The applied anthropologists have taken a special interest in problems of organization. Their unique methodological approach is the study of interactions, which they consider the key to an understanding of the dynamic behavior patterns in an organization. Essentially the study of interactions concerns who originates contact with whom, with what response, for what period of time, and how often. It is particularly helpful in identifying the real dimensions of a particular job.

FIFTEEN

Status

What to Look for in This Chapter . . .

Status: the grading of positions in the social structure
Social stratification in the United States society as a whole
Effect of stratification on occupational mobility
Factors upon which status is based in organizations
Symbols of status
- Title and pay
- Ceremonies of induction and appointment
- Perquisites
- Physical arrangements

Functions of status systems
Sociometric study of status systems and social structure

The job-task hierarchy is based on positions that people fill. Hence the shape of its structure is determined by the arrangement of positions. This same general approach is taken by sociologists in looking at societies as social systems. Societies are viewed as complex organizations of positions which people fill. A study of these positions and their inter-relationships therefore provides us with a picture of the social structure. Placed in the context of administrative organization, this primarily suggests that we should expand our frame of reference beyond the formal hierarchical position to include the other positions that people fill in social systems affecting the organization.

We must realize that the positions people occupy, and the symbols surrounding them, do much to shape the nature of organizations. Again it must be emphasized that these positions do not exist in a single social system. As we saw in the previous chapter, there may be professional subcultures involved; and of course the many smaller groups within an organization all have positions to be filled. Furthermore positions in outside systems may be very significant. The shop steward, for example, plays a unique role in the organization because of a position accorded him by the union, an outside system.

The position is the beginning point. But more important is the dynamic process by which these positions are arranged in a social system. Anthropologist Linton emphasized that every culture engages in some type of prestige grading. As in the formal job-task hierarchy, then, we find that positions in all social systems tend to be rated and arranged according to certain standards that have been established by the culture. The title of this chapter thus arises out of the concept that best describes this general process, *status.* We use it broadly here to describe the comparative esteem which members of the various social systems accord to the positions in them. Dubin suggests that status can be thought of as "the rank occupied by a work organization member on some scale of value." And status relations in an organization concern "interactions between two or more members determined by their respective ranking on a value scale." [1]

Note that status is largely a matter of perception. People grade positions primarily in terms of their understanding of a social system and acceptance of its norms. Typically, therefore, the president of a company has greater status in the formal hierarchy because acceptance of this situation is essentially a condition of membership in the system. It will be noted that status does not

---

[1] Robert Dubin, *The World of Work* (Englewood Cliffs, N.J.: Prentice-Hall, Inc., 1958), p. 36.

necessarily involve individual behavior. Status is accorded on the basis of the potentialities of a position in the organization, not what is actually observable of that work by members. Barnard has said, "It is the presumption of capacities and limitations without necessary regard to the immediate concrete activities of the individual that is the essential feature of systematic status."[2]

The net effect of status is *stratification*, separation between the various grade levels in that system. This is most to be seen in the formal organization, where the various levels of the hierarchy clearly connote the idea of stratification. Essentially there are only two possible kinds of status relations: (1) those between equals in status, and (2) those between superiors and subordinates. The relationship among equals tends to take place at the informal group level, where there are few barriers to communication and interaction. The superior-subordinate relationship is most pronounced in the formal organization, with the consequence that blocks to communication and understanding also tend to concentrate at this point.

Status levels may not be restricted to a particular social system. Indeed we often find that systems themselves are graded, which obviously has important societal consequences. The predisposition in the Union of South Africa, for example, to think of the white culture as superior to the black has ramified into every facet of life in that country. In other cases the grading of systems does not occur but status is recognized in one system because it is known to exist in another. Thus Americans have been particularly respectful of the various kings and queens visiting the United States because of their status in their own countries. Finally, status itself may invoke greater loyalty than the more typical cultural and institutional commitments. This is particularly true of socio-economic status, which may bind people more tightly than their ethnic and racial involvements. For example Simmons found in studying the implications of social class for the administration of public health that upper strata Mexican-Americans were more at

---

[2] Chester I. Barnard, "The Functions of Status Systems," in Robert Merton *et al.*, *Reader in Bureaucracy* (Glencoe, Ill.: Free Press, 1952), p. 243. Reprinted from "Functions and Pathology of Status Systems in Formal Organizations," in William F. Whyte, editor, *Industry and Society* (New York: McGraw-Hill Book Company, Inc., 1946), pp. 207-243.

ease with similar class Anglo-Americans than with lower class Mexican-Americans. Ethnic and cultural ties were less significant in this instance than the social stratification in the society as a whole.[3]

I • STRATIFICATION AND MOBILITY IN THE AMERICAN SOCIETY

The factors which operate to create status and structure social relationships exist to a large extent outside the organization. This is of course what we might expect, for organizations are shaped basically by the culture of which they are a part. Indeed so close is this relationship that in general we may expect that the low-status person in the society as a whole (based on such indices as race, nationality, sex, age, education, and so forth) will also be low-status in the formal organization. By the same token the high-status person in the formal organization will also have generally higher status in the society. Thus the status situation in organizations is affected by conditions in the larger society in two important ways: (1) the degree of stratification within the organization will generally reflect the extent of stratification in the society as a whole, and (2) status levels in the society as a whole will markedly affect individual opportunity to move into varying positions in a particular organization.

Community Stratification

Some indication of the stratifying influences at work in the American society, and hence on our organizations, is to be obtained from several well-known community studies.

Yankee City. Warner discovered a social hierarchy of six categories in "Yankee City," reduced to five in later studies.[4] In Yankee

---

[3] Ozzie G. Simmons, "Implications of Social Class for Public Health," *Human Organization* 16:8, Fall 1957.

[4] W. Lloyd Warner and Paul S. Lunt, *The Social Life of a Modern Community* (New Haven: Yale University Press, 1941); W. Lloyd Warner and Associates, *Democracy in Jonesville* (New York: Harper and Brothers, 1949). The Warner studies have stimulated considerable criticism by other social scientists. See Seymour M. Lipset and Reinhard Bendix, "Social Status and

City there was both an "upper upper" and a "lower upper" class, although in later studies these were combined into a single upper stratum because there were so few at that level. Yankee City proved to be Newburyport, Masschusetts, a seaport near Boston which had been prosperous in the days of the clipper ships. Personal data were obtained on approximately 17,000 inhabitants. The method of gathering information included interview, observation, and the gathering of such written materials as diaries, scrapbooks, genealogies, directories and institutional records.

Whereas any brief outline of the Yankee City studies must necessarily be an oversimplification, its essential finding was the following six way class structure:

Class	*Percentage of Population*
Upper upper	1.44
Lower upper	1.56
Upper middle	10.22
Lower middle	28.12
Upper lower	32.60
Lower lower	25.22
Unknown	0.84

The study was undertaken during the early days of the depression of the 1930's. During that time the first strike, with resultant unionization, took place in the shoe industry which occupied a large place in the local economy. The research staff made a special study of the strike and of the social organization of the shoe business.[5] The manufacture of shoes had in a century been transformed from a locally-owned industry based upon manual skills to machine fabrication in factories owned and controlled from New York. The local managers were outsiders, a native having relatively little chance to rise in a hierarchy with few managerial posts. Old manual skills had disappeared and local operators were at the most merely semiskilled. Warner and Low make much of the deterioration in the status of shoemakers, brought about by the breakdown of the

---

Social Structure: A Re-examination of Data and 'Interpretations,'" *The British Journal of Sociology* 2:150, June 1951; Harold F. Kaufman, "An Approach to the Study of Urban Stratification," *American Sociological Review* 17:430, August 1952; Otis Dudley Duncan and Jay W. Artis, "Some Problems of Stratification Research," *Rural Sociology* 16:17-29, March 1951.

[5] W. Lloyd Warner and J. O. Low, *The Social System of the Modern Factory* (New Haven: Yale University Press, 1947).

skill hierarchy.[6] They were impoverished by comparative loss of income and their pride in occupation was broken by loss of skill. They had become unskilled laborers performing one small operation on an assembly line basis.

Jonesville. Jonesville is a midwestern town presumably in upper Illinois, with an agricultural economic base modified by some local industry. Studies showed it had a stratified social class system which compared with that of Yankee City as follows: [7]

Class	*Percentage of Population in:* *Yankee City*	*Jonesville*
Upper	3	3
Upper middle	10.22	11
Lower middle	28.12	31
Upper lower	32.60	41
Lower lower	25.22	14

One third of Jonesville's employed population worked for a local industry identified as "The Mill." The company was owned by Chicago capital and most of its top management lived outside of Jonesville. The social hierarchy at the mill was quite stratified, as was the job ladder.

At least four influences could be identified which led to such stratification. *First,* the children of managers were preferred for the better jobs. *Second,* the technical jobs required training which could not be secured by experience in the mill. *Third,* management claimed that union emphasis on seniority prevented selection of gifted persons for the first rungs of promotion. *Fourth,* the dead-end nature of the job hierarchy resulted in a lack of enthusiasm and low prestige for mill employment.[8]

Social Mobility

Warner points out that there is considerable social mobility in America in spite of its stratified social hierarchy. Ours is a class system as distinguished from a caste system in which one is bound for life to the status in which he is born. Our egalitarian beliefs are not a sham, because our class system is open.[9] Our social and

---

[6] *Ibid.,* p. 66.

[7] Warner and Associates, *Democracy in Jonesville,* p. 24. The population of Jonesville was about 6,000.

[8] *Ibid.,* pp. 112-113.

[9] *Ibid.,* pp. 297-298.

political philosophies furnish effective and useful counterbalances against establishment of a caste system.

Mobility factors. While one means of upward mobility is the accumulation of wealth, it will not in itself automatically put one into the upper class. To do so, money must be translated into the symbols and behavior of that class. In other words it must be spent for the purposes of maintaining one's position rather than hoarded. There is a status value attaching to types of income from high to low as follows: (1) inherited income, (2) investment income, (3) profits and fees, (4) salaries, (5) wages, (6) charity or relief. To progress from (5) to (2) might be accomplished in one lifetime, but from (5) to (1) would require longer.

Other means of moving upward are by acquiring education, developing special talents, and marriage. Physical attraction and sex may help a woman to transcend class. Warner also mentions "the acquisition of moral and ethical social codes of superior groups, the acquisition of secular rituals at superior levels, learning the social skills (speech, etc.) of those in higher groups, and participation in cliques, associations and churches that are frequented by the higher groups."[10] One may move down in the social hierarchy by losing money, marrying a person of lower class, behaving like a lower class person, and moving around in lower class circles. However, loss of money does not immediately push one downward.

Mobility in the business world. A study of 8,000 top executives[11] in the 1950's was designed so that it could be compared with a smilar study conducted in 1928.[12] The original study had predicted that mobility would decrease and that by mid-century occupational advancement from the lower levels to the business elite would largely disappear. However this has not come to pass. While the change between the 1920's and the 1950's was not great, it was decidedly in the direction of greater mobility. The single highly significant causative factor lies in the area of education.

---

[10] *Ibid.*, p. 296.

[11] W. Lloyd Warner and James C. Abegglen, *Occupational Mobility in American Business and Industry* (Minneapolis: University of Minnesota Press, 1955); Warner and Abegglen, *Big Business Leaders in America* (New York: Harper and Brothers, 1955).

[12] F. W. Taussig and C. S. Joslyn, *American Business Leaders* (New York: The Macmillan Company, 1932).

The acquisition of a college education is the most certain means for a laborer's son to become a member of the top management team. Moreover, those managers whose fathers were also executives have considerably more education than their forebears. Hence the conclusion would seem to be that while status may help one to enter an American management hierarchy, there is also very considerable occupational mobility. Education is apparently a tremendous factor in overcoming the handicap of low birth.

II • STRATIFYING INFLUENCES IN THE ORGANIZATION

Management institutions tend to stratify, even in democratic America. They acquire set ways of doing things which people are reluctant to change. Incumbents acquire status and perquisites which they defend against onslaught, erecting bastions of security against change.[13] While societies need a stability which gives them continuity, there is nevertheless the danger that excessive stratification will weaken them by creating inflexibility. Undue resistance to change can make an institution unfit to meet new conditions and may even cause its downfall when confronted with crises. What are some of these stratifying influences?

Ascribed Status

Ascribed status is that which accrues from position in the social hierarchy. It is a position which an individual possesses independently of the job hierarchy. Thus Warner found in Jonesville that the children of management had preference for the better jobs at the mill. It need not be entirely a matter of kinship, but may accrue from club membership, one's former association, professional reputation, the "old school tie," or eminence in competitive sports. Ascribed status facilitates movement into the higher rungs of the scalar ladder without working up through the job hierarchy.

---

[13] At least one applied anthropologist explains this phenomenon in terms of social equilibrium. Institutions strive toward equilibrium. The problem of the administrator is to bring about desired changes with a minimum disturbance of equilibrium. Eliot D. Chapple, "Anthropological Engineering: Its Use to Administrators," in Schuyler D. Hoslett, *Human Factors in Management* (New York: Harper and Brothers, 1946), pp. 267, 274.

Examples are the retired admirals and generals who became corporation executives after World War II, the professional athlete whose associations have given him entree which his business attainments would otherwise not have provided, the fraternity brother who is introduced as the "right kind of person," and the sons of top management.

The influence of ascribed status is not necessarily bad, but it could provide that inflexibility which constitutes an invisible flaw. The essence of it is that one secures hierarchical position on the basis of some consideration of status outside normal job placement practices. It could be stratifying to the extent that it stifles normal competition for promotion and recognition and defers to status achieved outside the job hierarchy. Moreover, cronyism, kinship, and long association often create social ties which make it difficult to achieve normal turnover. People stay on after their usefulness has ended, or when their lack of personal growth has prevented the organization from adapting to new competitive situations.

Education

The production processes are becoming so technical that an irreducible minimum of formal education is required even for lower supervisors. It is becoming increasingly difficult for the person who left school early to rise in management hierarchies. Even the journeymen in such new areas as electronics must know a certain amount of background theory. It has been observed that, "In some companies today, it is practically impossible for the non-college man to move up even as far as foreman." [14] The effect of this may not be so stratifying in America, where practically everyone who is so motivated can obtain an education, as in parts of the world where such opportunities do not prevail. It may result in the situation where a father is doing a semiskilled task while his engineer son in the same hierarchy is several steps above him. It is stratifying in the sense that opportunities to rise beyond a certain restricted level are denied to the rank and file. Mobility is limited.

---

[14] William Foote Whyte, "Organization and Motivation of Management," in L. Reed Tripp, editor, *Industrial Productivity* (Madison, Wisconsin: Industrial Relations Research Association, 1951), p. 107.

Another stratifying influence is that of the scientific and intellectual process itself. The brains behind the productive processes of our technological civilization are not to be found in the shop but in the laboratory. The shop does what the laboratory tells it to do. To be sure, the production engineers have contributed immensely to increased productivity, but they are also doing what the laboratory tells them. This has tended to accord the research scientists special preferred status often approaching that of an elite. One lay hospital administrator even claimed that the deference and obeisance accorded medical doctors made them into a sort of priesthood. Being above ordinary mortals in the sense that their professional opinions cannot be controverted by laymen, they can with considerable impunity resist those aspects of administrative coordination which are distasteful to them.

Type of Work

Closely related to education and specialization in its effect on stratification in the organization is the type of work performed.[15] This is most to be seen in the professions where rather rigid status lines have been drawn. One study showed quite clearly that the status of psychiatrists is superior to that of psychologists and psychiatric social workers. This difference in status was recognized by all three groups and as a consequence the influence of the psychiatrists in any interpersonal situation was considerably greater.[16]

Promotion from Within

Institutions stratify because of promotion from within and failure to introduce outside blood. A study made in a typical American state university showed that 42 per cent of appointments to professorships were alumni.[17] The investigator hypothesized at least

---

[15] This is called *functional* status by Barnard and is unique because it depends, not upon authority and jurisdiction, but upon work for its significance. Barnard, "The Functions of Status Systems," p. 242.

[16] Alvin Zander, Arthur R. Cohen, and Ezra Stotland, "Power and the Relations among Professions," in Dorwin Cartwright, editor, *Studies in Social Power* (Ann Arbor, Mich.: Institute for Social Research, 1959), pp. 15-34.

[17] A. B. Hollingshead, "In-Group Members and Academic Selection," *American Sociological Review* 3:826-833, December 1938.

three reasons for this: (1) egocentric administrators who prize their own viewpoints above others, hence (2) they appoint people whom they believe will be sympathetic to the administrative viewpoint and docile; (3) it is easier and more economical to appoint someone close at hand. While even the most eminent universities tend to be inbred, this affliction is not absent in some of our most successful industrial corporations. It is not easy to bring in outsiders at the middle and upper hierarchical levels if there are insiders who feel entitled to the appointments. The social sentiments of the people who make up the organization favor selection from within, with the result that administrators hesitate to go counter to this opinion. In civil service jurisdictions the law often requires that positions must be filled by promotion from within.

Promotion from within tends to stifle venturesomeness, initiative, and desirable heresy. The colloquialism describing this is "sticking one's neck out." It has been said that progressing up the ladder in the lower military grades depends partly on keeping out of trouble. In such an organization one can never tell when a colleague today may be on the promotion review board of tomorrow. Hence, the normal pressures are in favor of conformity, meticulous obedience to rules, and sycophantic behavior in general.

Age, Tradition, and Seniority

Institutions tend to stratify with age.[18] It becomes difficult for people to believe that methods which were once successful can become obsolete. Furthermore, they are apprehensive of threats to their personal security. Younger persons educated in the new approaches may make them look like old fogies. So the natural thing is to seek security by exalting the old ways.

III • SYMBOLS OF STATUS SYSTEMS

If there is any doubt about the existence of status systems within organizations, one easy way of checking is to look for the presence of symbols of status. We would predict that any such

---

[18] See Hypothesis No. 9 in Carroll L. Shartle, "Leadership and Executive Performance," *Personnel* 25:379, March 1949.

research-minded reader would find few situations where a good share of the symbols cited below are not present. The symbols of course play an important role in systematizing status. They help the various members of the institution to understand better the role and the position of themselves and each of their fellow members. The most common of these indicators of status are:

- Title and pay of a position in the formal organization.
- Ceremonies surrounding induction and appointment to the position.
- Rights and privileges attaching to the position.
- Physical attributes of the position, such as workplace and furnishings.

Position Title and Compensation

The name attaching to a position is undoubtedly the single most significant indicator of status in the formal organization. This is particularly true in organizations where the job scheme is based on rank, as in the military and in the foreign service. In the military, particularly, one is constantly reminded of status by means of address—"Private Jones," "General Allen." There is also supposed to be a direct relationship between status in the organization and pay; and frequently employees will complain bitterly if their pay level is beneath their perceived status. A salary plan is considered definitely askew if the assistant is making more than the chief. The basis of pay—hourly wages or salary—also connotes status. The hourly workers are generally low status.

Ceremonies of Induction and Appointment

The manner in which appointments are made and officers installed is another important means of clarifying status. For example the Queen of England, as ruling monarch, is installed at Westminster Abbey with great ceremony. It is a ritual that would not be appropriate for the installation of the president of the Ladies' Aid. Thus the way in which we handle appointment and installation in an office suggests a great deal about its importance in the organization.

Rights and Privileges

Clothing and insignia. One of the most visible ways of indicating status is by clothing and other insignia. Again the military provides us with our best example, both uniforms and insignia explicitly showing rank. We have, however, other examples. There is the time-worn "blue collar—white collar" distinction. The laborers who work for wages are generally regarded as "blue collar." The administrative and clerical people—those on salary who do not work with their hands—are typically "white collar." It has become fairly general practice for shop supervisors to wear smocks over business suits to separate themselves from the overalled rank and file.

Perquisites surrounding the job. One of the evidences of top status in an organization is visible disregard for the rules that apply to most other employees. Freedom from the time clock, the right to take a long lunch hour, flexibility on coffee break schedule, and many similar behaviors tend to become more common as one moves up the status hierarchy. Another set of perquisites stems from the assumption that the higher one goes in the organization, the more valuable he becomes. Therefore extra efforts need to be made to keep him happy and productive. This may result in a regularly assigned company car or perhaps even a chauffeur, plenty of secretarial help, and other similar privileges. Finally there are the perquisites that seem designed only to emphasize status differentials within the organization. The executive dining room and reserved parking spaces are common examples.

Physical Attributes

The workplace and its surroundings is another extremely visible symbol of status. This begins with its general location. Arrival at the executive level in an organization is frequently signalled by the assignment to an office on a particular floor or section of a building. Size of office, its layout, the degree of privacy, and furnishings are important. The presence of an adjacent conference room bespeaks high status, as does a private entrance which permits one to avoid persons waiting. Does the secretary sit in the same room with her boss? Not if he is high-status. Size of desk, presence or absence of carpeting, color of carpeting, conference table, easy chairs and couch, and even a lowly water bottle all are frequently parts of a visual language by which the participants of a social system are alerted as to respective roles.

IV • FUNCTIONS AND PROBLEMS OF STATUS SYSTEMS

While stratification leads to many problems within an organization, it is also well to realize how status and its symbolism serves an important function in the promotion of organization purposes. Downs' study of an aircraft carrier revealed, for example, how status could be used to insure orderly conduct in the assembly of liberty parties. The ship had been operating on an egalitarian basis, with constant confusion as to who was first. The solution adopted was simply to put liberty parties back on a rank basis, with the highest status man having priority. Order was restored and even the low status people got off faster. No one seemed to have any complaints. Thus status provided a basic coordinating mechanism that required little personal intervention by officers of the ship.[19]

The Functions

There are three basic functions of the status system in an organization. These are:

- To maintain effective and authoritative communications within the organization.
- To provide organizational incentives.
- To develop a greater sense of personal responsibility.[20]

Communications. Status is the primary means by which the authoritativeness of communications in an organization is estab-

[19] James F. Downs, "Environment, Communication, and Status Change Aboard an American Aircraft Carrier," *Human Organization* 17:14-19, Fall 1958.

[20] The general outline of this section comes from Barnard, "The Functions of Status Systems," pp. 246 ff.

lished. Title particularly is used to identify the organization role of the order giver, the order receiver, or the informer. On a battlefield, the insignia often play this role. Status symbols help to clarify the nature of the structure and thus to suggest appropriate communication channels.

Incentives. From what was said earlier about the nature of status symbols, it is not surprising that many persons are motivated to seek high status positions. They may simply want the perquisites and other attributes of status to satisfy their own personality needs. In some cases the incentive is a less personal one. It is probable that at least some men who have served in high public office have done so to achieve other social goals. There can be no doubt that status is an important motivator, whatever its basic cause. Observe how many people will throw themselves into some activity when they have been accorded a position of status in the program, whether it be the community chest drive, beautification of the downtown area, or the school PTA carnival.

Responsibility. While people strive to achieve status, it may very well be true that they struggle harder to keep from losing it. In all countries of the world—although perhaps a little less so in the United States—people fear "losing face." Face in this context generally means status. This is a severe psychological wrench to the individual. Consequently both the apprehensive person and the ambitious one are driven by status needs to discharge their tasks with somewhat greater responsibility.

Problems of Status

As we have already observed, the primary effect of status is to establish two kinds of relationships: (1) one of equals, and (2) one of superiors and subordinates. In formal organizations, it is quite obvious that the entire pattern of symbols is designed to signal the precise nature of these subordinate-superior relationships to all members. The effect of this emphasis on status is to ease some of the difficulties of coordination and communication in the organization. As long as status is regarded only as a means of accomplishing these purposes, it is extremely useful. Status becomes a pathological facet of organization when it is regarded as an end in itself. We are all familiar with the individual who spends all his time making sure that others know he is the superior officer.

Thus there is a very great danger in emphasizing inequality of status. The gulf may become so great as to preclude any kind of joint action or real agreement on goals. The term social distance is often used to characterize the size of this gulf. Various studies have shown that it is desirable to keep the social distance between top and bottom from becoming too great. Obviously the erection of barriers has its impact particularly on communication, a point which Downs emphasized in his study of the aircraft carrier. Organizations are held together by communications; yet the social distance between officers and men in the Navy has been so great, in Downs' opinion, as to endanger the whole cooperative system. The captain lives alone, eats alone or with relatively few people, and never really gets down with the men. Indeed other officers on a carrier have only the most formal contact and visit enlisted quarters only for inspection.[21]

The emphasis that a status system must necessarily place on the position, rather than the man and his immediate acts, is another major area of danger. It is inevitable that some positions will fall to inferior people. Yet the status system demands that these differences not be recognized. There is always the assumption that individuals can handle the job assigned. Not only is there the obvious problem which develops where a man is not up to his job, there is also a question of morale and motivation. The status system requires that the individual retain his perquisites, compensation, and other symbols of office so long as he continues in his position. This is regardless of his conduct of the office or arrangements made with others to do the work. It frequently occurs, then, that the status system is not in accord with a general perception of the way in which rewards and perquisites within the organization should be fairly distributed.

The status system helps to routinize organization, primarily through its contribution to the formal communication system. But routinization can quite easily become stratified inflexibility. Promotion from within is one example. Barnard has pointed out that

---

[21] Downs, *op. cit.*, pp. 14-19.

the "circulation of the elite" also becomes more difficult.[22] The more formal the organization and the more the emphasis on status, the less is the opportunity of movement within the organization. Consequently there are definite barriers to making greatest use of the most able people in the organization.

Finally, it is quite apparent that the incentives provided by the status system can have pathological consequences. The official who takes his year's equipment budget to buy himself a new desk and handsome leather furniture is all too common in our organization life. We are constantly beset with the problem of providing enough perquisites and symbols to make the status system workable and not so many as to handicap the real functioning of the organization.

V • THE STUDY OF SOCIAL STRUCTURE

Social structure consists of the set of relationships among those who are members of a society or institution.[23] For rather obvious reasons it is desirable to know what the shape of that structure is. If the formal command hierarchy were the only consideration, this would be a relatively easy task. But this of course is not the case. The concept of status plays an important part in such an analysis, for it is in the grading and classification of positions that structuring basically occurs.

Researchers on social structure in organizations have followed an approach which does not differ in great degree from that of the applied anthropologists. Here again we find the social structure is largely postulated in terms of the nature and type of contacts of organization members. As a consequence some writers have referred to organization structure as a "fabric of roles" and a "stable system of coordinative relationships."[24]

---

[22] Barnard, *"The Function of Status Systems,"* p. 252.

[23] A. R. Radcliffe-Brown, *Structure and Function in Primitive Societies* (London: Cohen and West, Ltd., 1952), pp. 178-187.

[24] Robert S. Weiss and Eugene Jacobson, "Method for the Analysis of the Structure of Complex Organizations," *American Sociological Review,* 20:551, December 1955; also Robert S. Weiss, *Processes of Organization* (Ann Arbor, Mich.: Institute for Social Research, 1956), p. 3.

A basic method of analysis used is *sociometric*, which has been defined as a "method for discovering, describing, and evaluating social status, structure, and development through measuring the extent of acceptance or rejection between individuals in groups." [25] One study dealing with a government agency engaged in conducting and supervising research provides an illustration of this method. People in the organization were asked to designate their patterns of contact with others. In this case particular attention was directed toward 196 members of the professional and administrative staff. During the course of an interview, each respondent was asked to fill out a "Personal Contact Check List." [26] on which he designated the persons with whom he worked most closely. Then he was requested to "indicate the frequency of his contacts with them, reasons for the contact, subject matter discussed and the relative importance of the contact, each on a four or five point scale." [27] The organization was found to consist of 22 primary work groups which made up 82 per cent of the personnel; the other 18 per cent was comprised of liaison persons who held the groups together.

Between the two major units of the organization, the Administrative Division was found to be more "hierarchic" than the Operating Division, which laid less stress on status difference, was characterized by intimate person-to-person contacts, and was therefore more flexible.

Shartle and Stogdill used the same general technique to study the pattern of relationships in naval organizations.[28] Another example, based on studies at the University of Southern California of three city governments, indicates the reason formal hierarchical position plays a major role in determining status in the total social system. In Chart 15-1 it will be noted that the City Manager is the center of contacts. Reference to the position of the engineer suggests, however, that hierarchical status is not the only factor

---

[25] U. Bronfenbrenner, "A Constant Frame of Reference for Sociometric Research," *Sociometry* 6:363-372, November 1943.

[26] Reproduced in Eugene Jacobson and Stanley Seashore, "Communication Practices in Complex Organizations," *Journal of Social Issues* 7:28-40, 1951.

[27] Weiss and Jacobson, *op. cit.*, p. 663.

[28] Carroll L. Shartle and Ralph M. Stogdill, *Studies in Naval Leadership: Final Technical Report* (Columbus: Ohio State University Research Foundation, 1953, mimeo), pp. 56 ff.

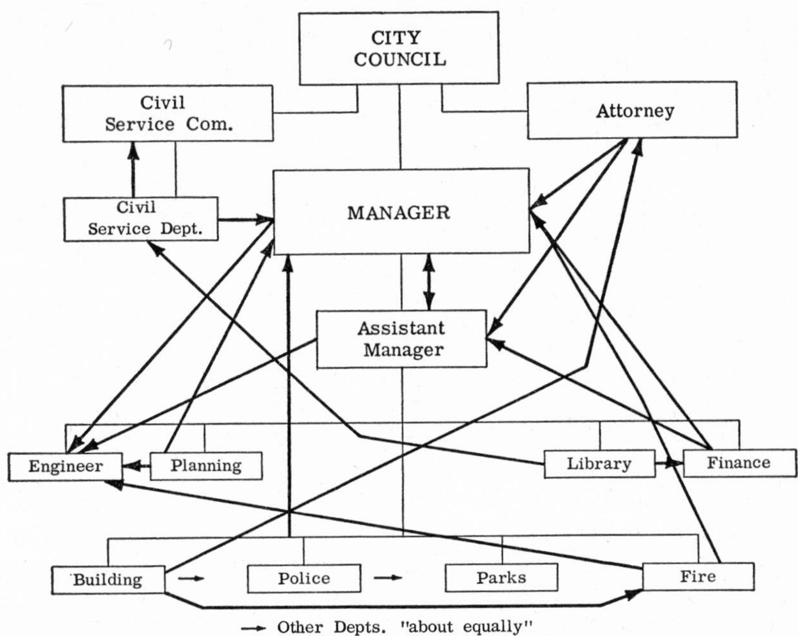

CHART 15-1. *Sociometric view of two "most frequent" contacts of manager, his assistant, and department heads.*

of significance. The engineer is regarded as a high-status person in city governments principally because of his professional identifications, his membership in a professional subculture. But this study would indicate that his high status also comes from the centrality of his functional role to the work of many other departments.[29]

Thus it does appear that the sociometric approach provides a somewhat different—and valuable—perspective on social structure in an organization. It tells much about the status relationships in the organization; the centrality and the peripherality of various

[29] Unpublished research by Frank P. Sherwood.

positions; the functional nature of the position—whether liaison, coordinative, or isolate; and something of its significance to other positions in the organization. There are other uses of the sociometric technique which dwell more on the behavior of the individual in the organization. The human relations group at the University of California, Los Angeles, has developed a "Multi-Relational Sociometric Survey" scale designed to provide information on the extent to which people understand the nature of their role in an organization, behave in terms of their understanding of that role, and are satisfied with it. Its developers also say that such a technique can yield data on the extent of centralization in the organization by identifying the number of interpersonal relationships in which the various individuals participate.[30]

The sociometric technique therefore has a number of applications to research in organization. Among other things it may serve as a method of:

- Testing morale.
- Recording how individuals are socially adjusting to their jobs.
- Determining the intangible factors of cooperation.
- Locating informal groups.
- Selecting leaders, supervisors, foremen, and managers.
- Locating social factors which affect production.[31]

VI • SUMMARY

Organizations are of course social structures. Hence many of the dynamic forces which we have more commonly thought of as operating at the larger social level are also present in the job-task hierarchy. One rather universal feature of social systems, as Linton has pointed out, is that there is some arrangement for prestige grading. Thus all the positions in the social system are not regarded as equal and the identification of superior-subordinate relation-

---

[30] Irving R. Wechsler, Robert Tannenbaum, and Eugene Talbot, "A New Management Tool: the Multi-Relational Sociometric Survey," *Personnel* 29: 85-94, July 1952; also published as University of California Institute of Industrial Relations Reprint No. 25 (Los Angeles, 1952).

[31] J. H. Jacobs, "The Application of Sociometry in Industry," *Sociometry* 8: 181-198, May 1945.

ships does much to shape the social structure. The term which best describes this pattern of grading is *status.* Status is used to characterize the comparative importance given to the various positions in the organization by its members. Status relations, as Dubin has described the term, concern the "interactions between two or more members determined by their respective ranking on a value scale." It is particularly important to note that status tends generally to attach to a position, rather than to any individual or his acts.

Stratification is another significant concept which relates closely to status. The creation of levels between groups of positions is a consequence of prestige grading; and this is stratification. The term is useful because it suggests the existence of barriers, or demarcation lines, between positions in the organization.

The nature of stratification in the larger society affects greatly the character and functioning of status systems within organizations. In general the degree of stratification within the organization reflects the society as a whole and the mobility of individuals within the organization will depend in part on status relations outside the organization. Thus studies of community stratification and social class have important implications for the understanding of administrative organization. They are an important modifying element of the job-task hierarchy.

Within organizations there are a number of stratifying influences. Among the most important are (1) ascribed status, which involves one's position in social systems existing outside the job-task hierarchy, (2) education, (3) type of work, which Barnard has identified as functional status, (4) promotion from within, and (5) age, tradition, and seniority.

Since the status system is designed in considerable degree to clarify respective roles in an organization, it follows that a rather elaborate pattern of symbols should also have developed. Four categories of these may be identified: (1) title given to position and its pay, (2) ceremonies surrounding induction and appointment to a position, (3) rights and privileges attaching to the position, and (4) physical attributes of the position, such as workplace and furnishings.

It is quite clear that the status system plays an important organizational role. It provides a kind of automatic coordination that reduces the need for personal intervention at many points in organization work. This is perhaps best to be seen in the use of status to establish the authoritativeness of communication. Status systems also provide important incentives in organizations. On the other hand, we must realize that there are basic dangers in the use of status systems. In the formal organization particularly, the emphasis is almost entirely on relationships of inequality. If these are overstressed, there may be created such a gulf between the various levels as to foreclose effective communication and prosecution of organization goals. The "circulation of the elite" may also be inhibited in a highly stratified organization where emphasis is placed almost entirely on the positions, rather than on the quality of the people who occupy them.

Since status means so much to the shaping of social structure, it is quite natural that considerable research in organization should have focused on this reference point. Such research tends to be *sociometric*. Like the work of the applied anthropologists, this approach is concerned in large part with interactions among members of the social system.

SIXTEEN

Communication

What to Look for in This Chapter . . .

Communication is important in the functioning of organizations

Communication theory derives from electronics and automation

The feedback loop and the capacity for learning, memory, will, and consciousness

New communications theory and traditional concepts of hierarchy

Continued need for structuring of communications channels

The circular relationship of information and decision-making

Communication is one of those multi-purpose words that mean many things to many people. To the semanticist it connotes the idea of words and human relations, and this is of course present in all studies of organization. The term has been borrowed in recent years to confer novelty and fresh approaches upon old activities, namely, (1) the teaching of English in college, and (2) advertising, public relations, and market research. In this chapter an attempt will be made to confine our consideration to communication as it affects organization structure. We will depend heavily upon the Wiener cybernetics model (see below for description),[1] but it should be noted that some social scientists doubt the Wiener model can be applied to social organization.[2]

I • COMMUNICATION AS STRUCTURE

The suggestion has been made that organization can be compared to anatomy and administration to physiology, but even those who draw such easy analogies would undoubtedly protest against complete compartmentalization. Just as anatomy and physiology are interrelated, so are structure and process. It is nevertheless helpful from the standpoint of organization analysis to emphasize structure at this point, and a number of authorities have referred to communication as a basis for organization structure.[3] The term structure as utilized here connotes a *stable set of relationships.*

The Theoretical Model

If the viewpoint is taken that information constitutes the lifeblood of the functioning organization, the channels and apparatus for the transmission of such information become the organization structure. Wiener's thesis is that man can control his environment only through information, which is transmitted through units called *messages.* Thus the message becomes in a sense the basic component of organization analysis, although Wiener does not say this in so many words. He compares what goes on in organizations with both the model of the automatic machine and nervous system of animals.

Much of modern communication theory is traceable to the relatively new discipline of communication engineering, which is in turn a product of the electronic age and its expansion during

---

[1] Norbert Wiener, *The Human Use of Human Beings,* revised edition (New York: Doubleday Anchor Books, 1954).

[2] Roy R. Grinker, editor, *Toward a Unified Theory of Human Behavior* (New York: Basic Books, Inc., 1956), pp. 51-52.

[3] Wiener, *op. cit.,* Chapter 5; Herbert A. Simon, *Administrative Behavior* (New York: The Macmillan Company, 1957); Chester I. Barnard, *The Functions of the Executive* (Cambridge: Harvard University Press, 1938); James G. March and Herbert A. Simon, *Organizations* (New York: John Wiley and Sons, Inc., 1958).

and after World War II. That is why much of the terminology is expressed in engineering terms. Thus "entropy" comes from the second law of thermodynamics.[4] "Feedback" is essentially an engineering concept, and such phraseology as "network," "loop," and "circuit" flows from electronic and machine applications. Indeed, modern large scale organization is being seriously affected, if not modified, by communication engineering.

Entropy. The concept of *entropy* in physics has surprising relevance to any discussion of the communications structure. It is a term which suggests the degree of ignorance, chaos, and randomness in a system. It is closely interlinked with notions of organization and information. Entropy can be resisted only by organization; and organization depends primarily on information. It is interesting that scientists were only able to develop highly complex heat machines when they turned their attention to questions of entropy and communication.

For our purposes it is important to realize that there is a strong tendency toward disequilibrium both in the physical and social world. The physicists' problem of developing informational devices that would provide proper systems of control for their heat machines is a case in point. The same kinds of problems obviously exist in human organizations. Indeed such factors may very well be critical in limiting size and specialization in our modern organizations. In the physical world, entropy is measurable. It represents the amount of "slippage" in performance that results from communications shortcomings. Thus the "information concept has made entropy, as a measure of ignorance, precise in an extended domain. . . ."[5]

In any given situation there are of course limits to the amount of entropy that can be tolerated; and the system of organization must be sufficient to secure the performance of a specified function. There is, too, a certain amount of "noise" entropy in each situation. It arises from errors and distortions in the communications system. This type of entropy is particularly a problem in human organizations.

An example well known to those familiar with production organ-

---

[4] Wiener, *op. cit.*, pp. 28-29.

[5] Jerome Rothstein, *Communication, Organization, and Science* (Indian Hills, Colorado: The Falcon's Wing Press, 1958), p. 34.

izations is the practice of filtering information as it travels through various hierarchical stages. People on the lower echelons deliberately distort messages going up in order (1) to give the boss the information that will please him, and (2) to present their own performances in the best light.[6] In the same manner, messages going down the hierarchy are often deliberately altered for various reasons. Sometimes staff people on subordinate levels "edit" the message in order to assert authority or to put it in line with their own interpretations of policy. In other cases the messages are altered by intermediate echelons because the leaders there know that such alternations will make them more acceptable to those below.

But perhaps the principal cause of "noise" entropy in large-scale organization is the sheer size and weight of hierarchy, coupled with the disposition of people to resist regimentation. In the one case the vast impersonal nature of hierarchy builds inertia. In the other instance people tend to hear what they want to hear and ignore that which they do not want to hear. They even go so far as to devise defensive "noise."

Homeostasis. Just as entropy represents a tendency toward ignorance and chaos, there are forces in nature which cause us to resist these things. Such a behavior incentive, to be found in both the plant and animal world, is sometimes called *homeostasis*.[7] It impels a striving toward equilibrium and stability while embodying that type of change which is necessary to maintain health. Homeostasis is thus dynamic and variable in nature while striving for orderliness and system.

In the world of human organization it is encouraging to know that there is strong motivation toward such self-regulation and stability. It suggests that people will respond to planning and coordination. Furthermore the idea of homeostasis helps to provide some perspective on the reasons why humans have, in a naturalistic way, moved in the direction of very complicated interpersonal organizations.

Feedback. This recognition of the need to resist entropy

---

[6] Kenneth E. Boulding, "The Jungle of Hugeness," *Saturday Review* 51:4-13, March 1958.

[7] For discussions of homeostasis as applied to social theory see Roy R. Grinker, editor, *Toward a Unified Theory of Human Behavior*, pp. 147, 264.

spawned a new discipline in the post-World War II years. It is known as *cybernetics*, a word borrowed from the Greek and meaning *governor*. Cybernetics is the study of control and communication. Its purpose, as Wiener reported, is to develop a language and techniques that will not only attack the general problem of control and communication but will also find ". . . the proper repertory of ideas and techniques to classify their particular manifestations. . . ."[8] The central idea in cybernetics is feedback. In its simplest form, feedback is the kind of communication an actor receives from a live audience. If the crowd is enthusiastic, the performer reacts with similar enthusiasm. There is in a way a closed circuit between performer and audience with continuing interchange of information. That circuit is not possible on TV. As a consequence many performers find it a frightening medium. There is no feedback, no communication, no control.

Essential to feedback is the notion that the flow of information is actually having a reciprocating effect on behavior. That is why the term *loop* is frequently associated with feedback. This circular pattern involves the flow of information to the point of action, a flow back to the point of decision with information on the action, and then a return to the point of action with new information and perhaps instructions. A primary element in this process is the sensory organ, the instrument through which information is obtained. Until recently only the animal organism, particularly the human brain and nervous system, was sufficiently developed to possess this capacity. For us humans the message comes through pretty rapidly when we put our finger on a hot stove.

The automatic machine. But we have now reached the point where we can equip our automatic machines with sensory organs; and thus the same general principles of feedback can be applied mechanically.[9] In fact, it has been said that our new highly complicated machines are an imitation of life. While it is not necessary here to discuss such interesting cliches as machines' inability to "think" for themselves—their reliance on the brain of man for succor—the fact remains that they do have the ability to combat entropy. Their sense organs detect errors and thus facilitate "nega-

---

[8] Wiener, *The Human Use of Human Beings,* p. 17.

[9] Editors of Scientific American, *Automatic Control* (New York: Simon and Schuster, 1955), p. 123.

tive feedback," by which is meant messages warning of danger or the need to take a different course. The sense organs in the earlier machines were vacuum tubes such as those in radios or television sets, but now the smaller transistors are coming into use.

The machines also have "memory" in the sense that they can store up information for future use. This memory may be of a rather simple nature as when in preparing a payroll a series of holes on a punch card recall the alphabetical spelling out of a payee's name on a check and cause the machine to print it, as well as the amount due. But they can also store much more complex information such as directions for a lathe to mold a particular piece of metal into the desired shape. Visitors to the Brussels Fair of 1958 will remember that one of the American exhibits was a computer which could be manipulated to deliver answers to a variety of questions, even the recounting of events in history. Some of these machines have gone beyond the punch card stage and now use either punched or magnetic tape.

The Organization Analogy

Having granted that automatic machines resemble biological organisms and that communication is an important factor in the physiology of organization, the skeptical observer might still question the analogy between animals, machines, and production organizations. The crux of the problem would seem to be the importance one places upon the feedback apparatus as an element in organization. And it may very well loom larger in some enterprises than in others, but one is hard put to think of any where it is not essential. Organizations, in common with human beings and machines, seem to have such attributes as ability to learn, memory, will, and consciousness.[10] All of these are related to messages and the communication process.

Organization learning. One of the chief processes by means of which machines and organizations learn is through feedback, combined with memory. The original "teaching" perhaps comes from goal-centered messages which issue from the decision centers to the performers who have sensory organs which react to such

[10] Karl W. Deutsch, "Mechanism, Teleology and Mind," *Philosophy and Phenomenological Research* 12:185-222, December 1951.

messages. In the animal organism these are nerve centers, in the machine they are vacuum tubes or transistors, and in the organization, communication centers. Learning through feedback is a dynamic and continuous process wherein there is mutual and reciprocating accommodation.

The sensory organ communicates error. In the machine it may take the form of a message signalling danger that tolerance is being exceeded. In the human organism the nerve cells in the housewife's finger tell the brain that the iron is hot. In the organization the signal of error will refer to production goals. These compensating messages may go on *ad infinitum* and in their totality they constitute the outward manifestation of the learning process because each message modifies the other and governs ensuing behavior.

Organization memory. Memory in the automatic machine is manifested by either the form, die, or cams which guide the cutting or shaping of parts, or the data on the punched cards or tape. These memory data are "stored" so that they can be called up in case of need. The same is true of the organization where the memory is contained in all of the enduring records such as accounting ledgers, correspondence files, statistical tabulations, or production reports. The organization manual and job descriptions, as well as standard practice writings constitute parts of the organization's memory. Thus communication centers are located near to memory storage points, convenient to the sources of information. Messages are effective in resisting entropy and promoting homeostasis to the extent that they reflect reality. Hence facts must be stored so that they will be available when needed.

Organization consciousness. Several years ago when electronic data-processing was beginning to force itself on the attention of management a worried questioner asked a speaker at a management conference how a decision-maker was to defend himself against being swamped by the torrent of data which the machines were about to gush forth. The answer is, of course, that the machines furnish that defense through the concept of consciousness, another analogy with the animal organism. It also has its counterpart in traditional management ideology, just as feedback was foreshadowed by Fayol and others. Consciousness is little if any different from the "exception principle" so familiar to orthodox management ideology. The manager who is a delegator and who practices the "clean desk" maxim gives his attention only to the exceptional situations which are called to his attention by various types of reports signalling danger points.

The same is true of a mechanized data-processing network; the great mass of material goes through and is stored in the memory cells without being noticed. Certain tolerances are established and when the sensory organs detect that those tolerances are being approached, signals are sent out.[11] They call the dangerous situation to the attention of the decision-makers, who formulate and transmit corrective messages. When the emergency is past, the great mass of data continues to go into memory storage without notice until another emergency is signalled.

The problem of consciousness is related to the existence of policy because decision and action tend to become routine where policy is established and well known. Communications flow, decisions are made, and actions are taken automatically without requiring conscious attention. Thus policy is a product of role expectations. People in an organization will behave in accordance with a pattern expected by others; and this pattern becomes policy when it is stabilized in types of situations which recur frequently or repetitively.[12] The messages and signals become routine except when decision or action out of the ordinary occurs, in which case danger signals arouse consciousness on the part of those whose role it is to attend to the problem at hand.

Organization will. An organization is said to have a "will," composed of the "the set of internally labeled decisions and anticipated results, proposed by the application of the system's past and by blocking of incomparable impulses or data from the system's present or future."[13] Examples of "will" in familiar settings are: (1) the United States Forest Service's long-standing preference for selective cutting of timber as against clean-cutting; (2) the pacifism of the Quakers; and (3) a department store's refusal to open its display windows on Sunday. The latter is a perfect example of organization memory sending a message from

---

11 Deutsch, *op. cit.*, p. 205.

12 John T. Dorsey, Jr., "A Communication Model for Administration," *Administrative Science Quarterly* 2:307,310, December 1957.

13 Deutsch, "Mechanism, Teleology, and Mind," p. 209.

the past which reflected the religious scruples of the long dead founder.

II • INFORMATION CHANNELS AND HIERARCHY

It is quite apparent that information is a principal basis for decision. The information needed in making a decision is likely to exist in many places with the result that facilities must be provided for transmitting that information to the decision centers. The conduits for such transmission may or may not follow hierarchical channels. One writer distinguishes between structure and dynamics, stating that dynamically, "administration appears as a patterned whirl and flow of communications. . . ."[14]

It is at this point, of course, that some of the new concepts come most directly into conflict with one of the dominant aspects of traditional organization theory, the requirement that communications shall flow through command channels. Today we find that such a precept is no longer as sacred as it once was. No less an administrator than Ralph J. Cordiner has insisted that communications should never bog down in channels. A person in one division is expected to seek information from another division by calling "straight across the company" on the telephone.[15]

Structuring Communication Flow

Reasons for observing channels. In general, however, it is desirable to spell out who shall communicate with whom and what matters are to be limited in circulation. There are at least three reasons for this. In the *first* place, it may be desirable to render obeisance to hierarchy in certain instances where a tense atmosphere has not yet subsided into that desired equilibrium which tolerates communication outside of channels. In other words there may be fewer ruffled feathers if the orthodoxy of "through channels" is observed. *Secondly,* organization objectives will often be better served if certain messages are kept secret—future intention

---

[14] Dorsey, *op. cit.*, p. 307, 310.

[15] Ralph J. Cordiner, *New Frontiers for Professional Managers* (New York: McGraw-Hill Book Company, 1956), pp. 65-66.

to purchase land or establish a new branch, or development of new products for a competitive market. A *third* factor is discussed at greater length below: the proposition that the structuring of communications leads to more effective results than when they are unstructured.

Need for conscious structuring. If "many alternative channels are available for few messages, the functioning of the network may be hampered by indecision; if many messages have to compete for few channels, it may be hampered by 'jamming.'"[16] The result is that the communication system needs to be based on some relatively stable operating rules; the channels should be specified, and the priorities and preferences for various types of messages indicated. From the standpoint of traditional management ideology, one of the most sensitive points involves conflict between the functional network and line of command. It may be desirable to minimize such tensions by spelling out what kinds of messages functional specialists may transmit without pre-consultation with the line of command, and *vice versa* messages from subordinates in the line of command to functional specialists on a superior echelon.

There are undoubtedly types of organizations in which channels tend to become secondary. For instance, this was found to be the case in a unit devoted wholly to scientific research.[17] Easy access and informal interchange outside of channels became the rule. One's standing in the group was enhanced by a reputation for maintaining an open door.

Research Findings

All of this talk about networks, grids, and loops should not cause one to jump to the conclusion that the hierarchical concept is to be banished from organization theory. *Far from it!* Experiments conducted by Bavelas indicated that the communicator's centrality of location facilitates his recognition as a leader by the group. Furthermore, in groups where the locations of the members favor centrality of leadership, communication is more effec-

---

[16] Deutsch, *op. cit.*, p. 202.

[17] Robert S. Weiss, *Processes of Organization* (Ann Arbor, Mich.: Survey Research Center. 1956), p. 9.

tive. In other words hierarchy facilitated communications, as against laissez-faire evolution of group relationships. However, morale was greater under laissez-faire than under hierarchy.[18]

A replication of Bavelas's experiment by Guetzkow and Simon showed that communication was more effective in groups that had centrally structured leadership. They remark, however, that "current management literature on the topic of communication leaves one with the expectation that certainly a reduction in communication restrictions should lead to a more adequately functioning organization."[19] They go on to say that their findings do not warrant any such conclusions, and warn "the practical communications expert working in industry or government" to be wary of the advice of those who advocate less structure in communications.

III • INFORMATION AND DECISION-MAKING

There are those who see the communication and decision-making processes as, if not identical, at least so interdependent that they become inseparable in practice. Dorsey says that a decision occurs on "the receipt of some kind of communication, it consists of a complicated process of combining communications from various sources and it results in the transmission of further communication."[20] Decision centers must of necessity either coincide with or be in conjunction with communication centers.[21]

A preliminary analysis of a number of actual decisions pointed up quite vividly the interrelationship between decision, communication, policy, and authority.[22] Those who attempted a con-

---

[18] Alex Bavelas, "Communication Patterns in Task-Oriented Groups," in Dorwin Cartwright and Alvin Zander, *Group Dynamics Research and Theory* (Evanston, Ill.: Row, Peterson, 1953), p. 505. (Reprinted from the *Journal of the Acoustical Society of America* 22:725-730, 1950).

[19] Harold Guetzkow and Herbert A. Simon, "The Impact of Communication Nets upon Organization and Performance in Task-Oriented Groups," *Management Science* 1:233, 250, July 1955.

[20] Dorsey, "A Communication Model for Administration," p. 309.

[21] Herbert A. Simon, *Administrative Behavior* (New York: The Macmillan Company, 1957), pp. 155-156.

[22] These decisions were collected by a graduate seminar composed of very mature persons, some of them administrators.

tent analysis of these decisions were in the beginning influenced by: (1) Mary Follett's concept of circular response and integration, and (2) a social science value system which regarded group processes as a profound modifier of hierarchy. Hence there was at least some expectation that the decision process would be revealed as circular in general conformation. As was the case with the studies of communication by Bavelas, Simon, Guetzkow and others, reported above, hierarchy cannot be minimized as a leavening force in the decision-communication process.

A more correct characterization of the decision-communication process would be to refer to "decision chains," or a system of "sequential decisions." While information may sometimes follow a circular path the chain of decision centers takes on hierarchical conformation. The circular element is nevertheless present in the necessity for reciprocation, which is the very essence of feedback in modern communications systems. Thus there was the case of the captain of an infantry company who, after the Remagen bridge break-through, received a written order from his battalion commander to undertake a frontal assault on a hill position. The company commander conducted a reconnaissance which indicated that a frontal assault would court disaster whereas a flank attack had chances of success. He communicated this information to the battalion commander who somewhat reluctantly modified the order. The hill was taken by roundabout means with minimal cost. The reporter of the case, a veteran infantry officer, claimed that military concepts of hierarchical relationships would have inhibited this type of reciprocal communication in former days. The more likely procedure would have been to start the attack as per orders and change plans to meet the situations encountered.

Sometimes a breakdown in communication requires an on-the-spot decision to be made by the most likely person in the scalar chain. The foreman of a subcontractor requisitioned construction materials according to the plans in his possession, but someone at the yard pointed out that the job did not call for that type of material. This was communicated to the superintendent who immediately consulted the estimator. His notes showed that the material in present plans was not that used in figuring the estimates. Somewhere between the original and final plans a more costly item was included. The subcontractor's superintendent decided to authorize construction according to revised plans, even though it might entail loss, rather than hold up construction. Did this constitute circular decision-making?

Another decision actually took on aspects which were definitely circular in structure because the organization was more circular than hierarchical. This was a weak mayor-council city with a chief administrative officer reporting to both the mayor and the council. The question was whether to buy a machine that would save $6,000 a year in clerical expense. The department had the money and requisitioned the item, but an analyst under the administrative officer vetoed it under a mayor's directive to suspend capital expenditures. The city council was approached and it asked the administrative officer to reconsider but he backed up his aide. Council members appealed informally to the mayor's office, where it was suggested that the work could be processed by machines existing in the elective controller's office. This proved feasible and that was the solution.

IV • SUMMARY

There can be little doubt that communication is central to the life of organizations. Some even say it is at the base of organization structure. Indeed the traditional theory of organization places great emphasis on "going through channels" as the basic means of preserving unity of command within the pyramid.

In more recent years communications theory has become the central concept in developments in electronics and automation. It is postulated that man can only control his environment through information. Yet there are continuous forces at work which tend to distort communication and to promote disorganization. These forces are sometimes called *entropy*, from the concept so called in mathematical physics. They are counterbalanced by a seemingly natural tendency toward stability and equilibrium, which in itself is dynamic. This is sometimes known as homeostasis.

In the drive to resist entropy and induce homeostasis, the effectiveness of the communication process is central. If an appropriate feedback loop has been created which provides a reciprocal and compensating pattern of messages, the organization should function in a stable fashion. Both the animal organism and the automatic machines provide the model for this system of control through communication.

The effect of these new theoretical constructs has been to place great emphasis on opening any communications blocks within the organization. And unfortunately the traditional pattern of "going through channels" has in many circumstances been cumbersome, occasionally contributed to distortion, and been time-consuming. In a sense it is the concept of hierarchy which has been on trial; for the burden of much of the recent theory is to permit no tampering with the communication channels for the sake of the command channels. In other words, if the hierarchy cannot accommodate itself to the new significance of communications, it is the traditional notion of hierarchy which must be amended. Ralph Cordiner, for example, has insisted that communication should never bog down in channels. The communications must get through, even if the niceties of hierarchy must be forsaken.

In actual practice, some communications have gone through channels and some have not. This has led to a rather popular notion that fewer hierarchical restrictions on communication—that is, less structuring—would improve organization performance. Research evidence, however, does not necessarily support this view. Bavelas found, for example, that the hierarchical principle provides for a more *efficient* system of communication, though it may be harder on the morale of the participants. Guetzkow and Simon also found that communication was more effective in groups which had centrally structured leadership. Thus it would seem that the consequence of developments in communication theory has been to place greater emphasis on communications as an organizational factor and as a means of creating structure. It does not necessarily mean that traditional notions of hierarchy should be completely sacked.

The relationship between the communications system and decision-making is extremely important. If decision-making and communication processes are not identical, they are so interdependent they become inseparable in practice. As a result all studies of communication inevitably involve decision-making.

SEVENTEEN

Power and Politics

What to Look for in This Chapter . . .

Organization politics is the network of interaction by which power is acquired, transferred, and exercised

Policy is distinct from politics

Politics in an industrial organization—the Dalton study

Typical arenas for political tension:

- long run *vs.* short run (production *vs.* maintenance)
- line *vs.* staff
- labor *vs.* management
- struggles for promotion
- distribution of rewards
- interpretation of organization doctrine

Politics in a governmental organization—the State Department

Power and politics are terms that have not traditionally been a part of management literature. Indeed they have been popularly limited to those activities which surround campaigns for elected public office and those which have to do with governmental policy-making. This orientation has led to the assumption that business organizations do not possess within themselves a political structure. Even in government one of the central purposes of reform groups has been to rid the organization of "politics," this to be done by placing the administrative apparatus under civil service. Thus in both business and government there has been an implicit expectation that the internal structure of the organization may be free of politics while the organization as a whole reacts to its external environment on a political basis.

Is such a simplified view of the way in which power is acquired and exercised really tenable? Bear in mind that in an earlier chapter, we pointed out that authority and power are not the same thing. Hierarchical status suggests official legitimacy, the right to make decisions and supervise others. It does not necessarily mean that individual occupants of such status positions possess the *capacity* to see that their will dominates. Nor does the concept of the formal authority pyramid really tell us anything about the interpersonal systems of influence that prevail over decision-making in the official hierarchy. Those in high level positions have to depend on someone to provide information and advice; and in some cases there is such a regularized pattern of assistance that real power shifts to the adviser. The official structure remains the same. Finally, the concept of the authority pyramid tells us nothing about how particular individuals advance to positions of status in the hierarchy. Are we to assume that all promotions and appointments are highly routinized and according to merit? We of course know this is not the case; and hence there is discretion exercised by someone in deciding who is to receive a certain post. As a consequence there is just as much jockeying, just as much contest, for many hierarchical posts where the succession is not as clear as in a public election.

It seems fairly apparent, then, that the forces which dominate and control the internal organization cannot be explained entirely in terms of traditional managerial concepts of hierarchy and authority.

At this point we may refer briefly to definitions of the two basic terms in this chapter. *Power* was earlier defined as "the capacity to secure the dominance of one's values or goals."[1] For

[1] Cf. p. 77.

our purposes influence may be roughly regarded as synonymous with power. Thus power and influence are in a sense static. They reside in someone or some office. Therefore we need to have another term to describe the network of interactions by which power is acquired, transferred, and exercised upon others. We call this process *politics.* Many years ago Lasswell put it simply and most meaningfully when he titled a book, *Politics–Who Gets What, When, How.* He went on to say that in politics the "unifying frame of reference . . . is the rich and variable meaning of 'influence and the influential,' 'power and the powerful.'"[2]

The basic proposition of this chapter is that the "who gets what" dynamic is endemic to every organization, regardless of size, function, or character of ownership. Furthermore it is to be found at every level of the hierarchy; and it intensifies as the stakes become more important and the area of decision possibilities greater. Although it is common to think of policy and politics as synonymous because we are most aware of the exercise of power on the big decisions, it is nevertheless important to recognize that they are not the same. Policy suggests broadly the setting or articulating of goals. Politics concerns what is frequently a raw contest for power without any particular reference to the directions or goals of the organization.

It might be said for example that authoritarian leaders gather up much of the policy setting in their own hands. They seem formally to make all the big decisions, leaving the impression that the arena of political activity has been thereby lessened. But this does not necessarily occur. Indeed, there is some evidence that the struggle for influence and influential alignments within a dictatorship becomes more frantic than ever. To summarize, politics is the *process* by which power and influence are acquired and exercised. The particular goals sought may fall in the "policy" category or may concern a relatively low level contest for promotion.

Organizational politics is a subject that seems destined to command increasing interest in the years ahead. In this sense it is a part of the more general concern with the social processes which lie at the heart of organization behavior. Noteworthy, too, is the

---

[2] Harold Lasswell, *Politics–Who Gets What, When, How* (New York: Whittlesey House, 1936), p. 19.

fact that this more intensive look at the totality of organization life, not just its formal mechanisms, has served to spotlight the realities of political life in such units. Miller and Form have reported that ". . . political processes run through the social structure of industry." Those who participate in such hierarchies "must learn to play the appropriate roles. Such roles require adaptability to the techniques of conflict, accomodation, and cooperation. If they are successful, they may gain power and status. If they fail, others rise to take their places." [3] Three articles appearing in the *Harvard Business Review* in the late fifties also emphasize this trend toward political realism. One, by Martin and Sims, returned to Machiavelli and his somewhat stark and naked theory of power.[4]

In the field of public administration a similar note of political realism has been injected by Albert Somit in his plea for "realpolitik" in the teaching of administration. Somit says that from the administrator's point of view, "the administrative structure is also the scene of an unending and desperate battle for personal survival, power and prestige. In large part, his career depends upon his skill at the game of bureaucratic realpolitik, i.e. his mastery of the administrative verson of 'who gets what, when, and how.' " [5]

I • THE MILO STUDY

It may now prove profitable to take a look at power and politics as they actually operated within one organization. Fortunately the writing of this section has been made easier by the published research of sociologist Melville Dalton.[6] Dalton's thesis was much the same as that of this book. He recognized that organizations

[3] Delbert C. Miller and William H. Form, *Industrial Sociology* (New York: Harper and Brothers, 1951), p. 339.

[4] See N. H. Martin and J. H. Sims, "Thinking Ahead: Power Tactics," *Harvard Business Review* 34:25-36 ff; November-December 1956; Malcolm McNair, "What Price Human Relations?" *Harvard Business Review* 35:15-39, March-April 1957; Robert N. McMurry, "The Case for Benevolent Autocracy," *Harvard Business Review* 36:82-90, January-February 1958.

[5] Albert Somit, "Bureaucratic Realpolitik and the Teaching of Administration," *Public Administration Review* 16:292-295, Autumn 1956.

[6] Melville Dalton, *Men Who Manage* (New York: John F. Wiley and Sons, Inc., 1959).

did not function strictly according to the official prescriptions; and he therefore wanted to discover the ways in which the official was modified by the unofficial.

In order to pursue this objective Dalton literally lived in an organization. He was officially a member of the staff of an industrial firm of 8,000 employees, to which he gave the fictional name of Milo Fractionating Center. The locale was the area of Mobile Acres, a heavily industrialized region of the central United States. In addition, two other manufacturing firms and one department store came under his surveillance. But it is particularly the story of Milo that provides a rich insight into the actual workings of a large private organization. Before proceeding further in a description of this research, however, we must insert one caution. This was the kind of study of human behavior that dug very deeply and probed a veritable hornet's nest of interests and involvements. It could be done only by promising anonymity. Thus there is no possibility of another researcher validating the Dalton findings. And we have had enough experience with the studies of anthropologists to know that no human is free of error and bias. Even with this reservation, the Dalton research made a real contribution because it dug so deeply. Dalton revealed himself as a perceptive and resourceful observer. In very few places in the management literature can the reader obtain such a sense of the fullness of organization life as here.

Dalton discovered that there were six problem areas which seemed continually to recur. These were: (1) pressures for economy; (2) "cooperation" of officially powerless experts with their administrative superiors, involving the relationship of the line and the staff; (3) the conflict between unions and management in interpreting at the plant level labor agreements made at the corporate level; (4) uncertainty about standards and strategies of promotion, particularly at the middle and top management levels; (5) the difficulty of identifying and rewarding employees who were making different degrees of contributions to the organization; and (6) the dilemma of the individual executive in seeking to resolve the official doctrines of the firm with the reality-oriented claims of subordinates and associates.[7]

---

[7] *Ibid.*, p. 4.

The significance of this list lies in the fact that without exception Dalton found politics—that is, influence maneuvering—a central feature. In each case it will be noted that there was a wide latitude of behavior possibilities; and this of course meant that decisions were inevitably made in terms of the power resources available to any individual or group at a particular time. The pressure for economy may not at first seem to fit into this category, but deep in this pressure lies a conflict of great potential political consequence—that between production and maintenance. As will be seen later in this section, this conflict had much to do with the nature of political activity, in respect to the plant and corporate headquarters, among the production executives and between production and maintenance officials.

Did these problem areas develop because the four firms studied by Dalton were atypical? Would other organizations reduce the arena of political activity by invoking more prescriptions and rules from the top? Dalton produced rather voluminous evidence that answers to these kinds of problems are not easily or routinely come by. The answers arise from the situation; and any attempt to prescribe in advance may very well result in strangulation of the organization through bureaucratic red tape. In the end, then, such decisions inevitably attract struggles for power and influence because they involve choice between alternatives. It is no answer to say that decisions should not be made or that choice should somehow be removed from the decision-making process. On balance there is every reason to believe that the firms studied by Dalton were rather typical.

Power Structure at Milo

One of the most interesting aspects of Dalton's work is his attempt to put on paper the working power structure in the Milo plant. In Chart 17-1 there is a simplified version of the "official map" of Milo. Contrast this assignment of formal authority with what Dalton considered to be the actual distribution of power in Chart 17-2. The differences are quite striking. Dalton arrived at his appraisal by asking fifteen Milo participants to rank the various officers in terms of the "relative deference of associates, superiors, and subordinates to his known attitudes, wishes, and informally expressed opinions, and the concern to respect, prefer, or act on

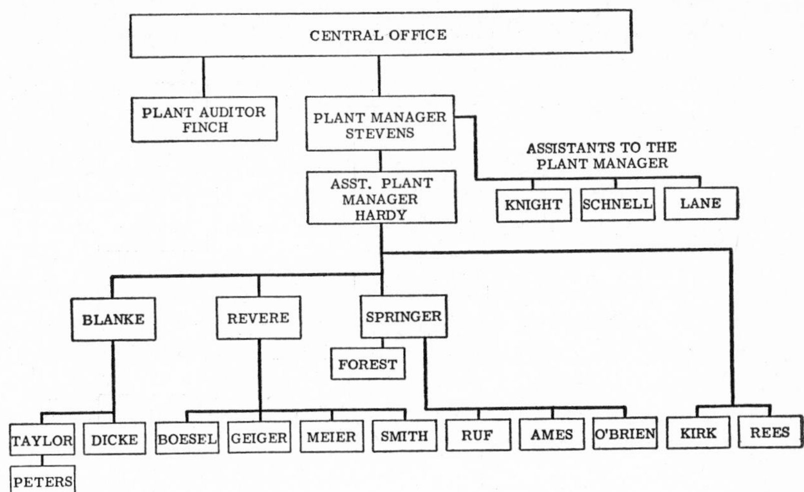

CHART 17-1. *Milo formal chart simplified* (SOURCE: Dalton, *Men Who Manage*, p. 21).

them."[8] The assumption that such power structures can be identified and that they do have operational significance has been accepted increasingly in recent years. Hunter's research suggests its operation at the community level; Mills in particular has written persuasively of its existence on the national plane.[9]

Although Dalton's unofficial power structure showed a substantial number of discrepancies from the official authority chart, three are particularly worthy of note:

(a) The assistant plant manager, Hardy, was accorded equal status with the manager, Stevens.

(b) The third most powerful man in the organization was a staff person, Rees, who was superintendent of industrial relations. Note, too, that those particularly responsible to him were Finch, the plant auditor who was supposed to report to corporate headquarters, and Kirk, the head of production planning.

(c) The superintendents of the three manufacturing units in the plant, Divisions A, B, and C, did not enjoy the same actual

[8] Dalton, *Men Who Manage*, p. 20.

[9] Hunter used a roughly similar technique to that of Dalton in identifying

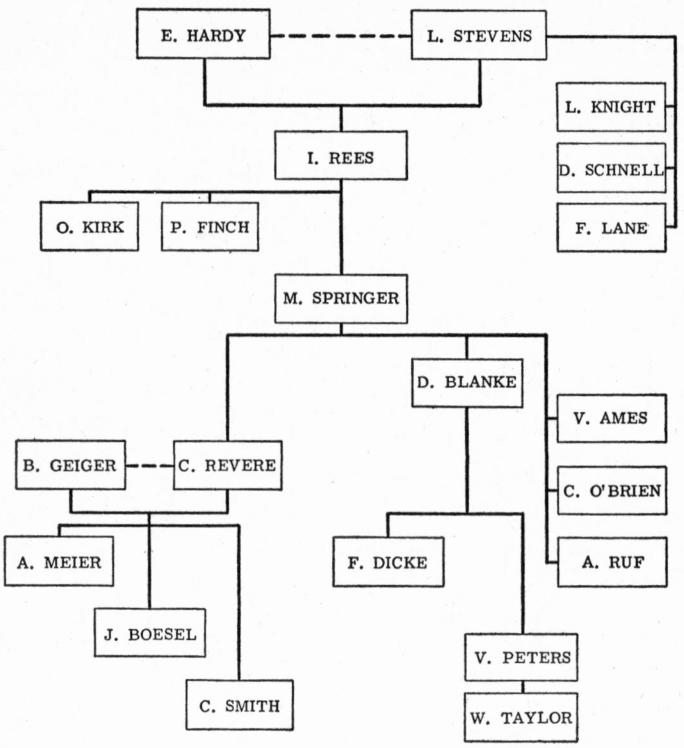

CHART 17-2. *Milo chart of unofficial influence* (SOURCE: Dalton, *Men Who Manage,* p. 22).

power status in the organization; and in one case the relationship between the division superintendent himself and his assistant was the same as between Stevens and Hardy.

---

the power structure in Atlanta, Georgia. See Floyd Hunter, *Community Power Structures* (Chapel Hill: University of North Carolina Press, 1953).

Mills' work is based on a wide examination of studies in the field, yet it is highly controversial because of its interpretations and basic propositions. He identifies five power eras. The first, from the revolution through the administration of John Adams, exemplified power in the hands of many-sided, gifted individuals who were equally at home in the social, economic, political, and military realms. The period from Jefferson to Lincoln was characterized by a loose coalition of power in the hands of economic interests, with a rather dis-

Hardy and Stevens. The placement of Hardy on the same status level as the plant superintendent was based on a number of considerations. It was observed for example that while Stevens usually opened staff meetings, he quickly gave way to Hardy who dominated thereafter. Hardy's approval was deemed indispensable in the more important promotions; during breakdowns and emergency stops, it was fear of Hardy, rather than Stevens, that caused alarm among the supervisors; and in many significant cases staff officers saw Hardy as the principal man to convince concerning the value of a project.

Dalton also pointed out that Hardy's social activities, his occupation experience, and perhaps even his physical appearance were important to him in achieving his power status. Hardy was under forty, athletic, and "very handsome." He was active socially; Stevens was withdrawn.

The position of Rees. The role of Rees, the superintendent of industrial relations, is of particular importance because the staff unit he headed had not typically been a significant one at Milo. His "weak" predecessor had been promoted out of the position to an ambiguous and unimportant status as "assistant to" Stevens. Rees, who was also under forty, apparently acquired his power through his close associations with corporate headquarters. Indeed he was presumably sent out from the "office" to strengthen the department. Because of this he had power alignments outside the plant itself and thus he was in a different relationship to Stevens and particularly to Hardy. It is a situation quite familiar to those in government service where not infrequently some of the key administrative officials are elective and therefore freed from the usual command restraints.

---

persed pluralism tempered strongly by Jacksonian concepts of status. The third period, beginning in the fourth quarter of the nineteenth century, saw the rise of corporate industrial interests as masters of the power structure, an era which continued, with a brief fourth interlude of the New Deal, until it merged into a contemporary fifth phase. This was characterized by a coalition between corporate ownership, corporate management, and the military. "The seemingly permanent military threat places a premium on the military and upon their control of men, material, money and power; virtually all political and economic actions are now judged in terms of military definitions of reality; the higher warlords have ascended to a firm position within the power elite of the fifth epoch." See C. Wright Mills, *The Power Elite* (New York: Oxford University Press, 1956), p. 275; also available in the paper Galaxy Books series.

In this instance Rees was the only one who really challenged Hardy. On one issue he came into open conflict and he said, "The Office put that system in here and by God we're going to make it work, not just tolerate it!"[10] Dalton's general analysis was that Hardy exceeded his official authority in every field of plant activity except those Rees interpreted as lying within his industrial relations sphere, which he defined rather broadly. Thus Rees had real power in the organization because he was regarded as the unofficial spokesman for corporate headquarters.

Power of Division Superintendent Springer. Just below Rees in the power structure was Springer, superintendent of Division C, who in the formal chart ranked equally with the superintendents of Divisions A and B. In this instance Springer's influence over his two colleagues was rather clearly evidenced in that they first conferred with him before asking important favors from Hardy. How did Springer achieve this status? Largely it was a reflection of Hardy's power. Springer, who had come from corporate headquarters, worked for four years in Division B when Hardy was its chief. The two had an extremely close relationship.

One Division chief, Revere, was the lowest ranked of the three superintendents. Indeed one of his subordinates, Geiger, was considered to possess as much influence. Here Dalton noted two reciprocal factors at work. In the first place, Revere was relatively near retirement and living out his time. He was not interested in dominating plant events. On the other hand, the forty-two-year-old Geiger headed the major production unit in the division. Thus the nature of his official responsibility enhanced his power position, even in the relationship to his immediate superior.

Summary. Dalton suggests rather strongly that the nature of the power configuration in Milo developed from the personalities who occupied key positions. He finds that those who possessed power were the "promoters," those who saw the organization as dynamic, who viewed risk-taking as a way of life. Age seems to have been an important factor in the structuring of these attitudes. The most influential group, for example, had an average age of 42.2 years; the least influential averaged 55.5 years.[11] These basic tend-

[10] Dalton, *Men Who Manage,* p. 25.
[11] *Ibid.,* p. 31.

encies were then reinforced by official position, relationship to corporate headquarters, and other social attributes.

With personalities as a key variable in the struggle for power at Milo, it is not surprising that various types of alliances among these individuals would be the prime means of acquiring and expanding influence. Dalton calls such alliances *cliques* and suggests that there are three general types: vertical, horizontal, and random. The vertical cliques involve people at various levels in the hierarchy and may provide a reciprocal relationship where the higher officer protects his subordinates and they in turn tell him of threats to his position. In some cases, however, the clique is formed largely to provide protection from the top. The horizontal alliance is composed of people of the same status who combine either to combat a threat or to effect a change. The random clique follows no particular axis of the hierarchy and tends more to be based on social attractiveness than other factors.

Politics and Promotions

There were a number of ways in which Dalton found the power structure operative at Milo—in staff-line relations, in labor-management contacts, and in the system of rewards. Two particularly significant areas, however, will serve to illustrate the fundamental proposition of this chapter that power and politics are an intrinsic part of organization life. One reveals the way in which pressure for production creates political problems. The other concerns the ever present problem of promotions, the struggle upwards.

The politics of promotion is certainly not a new idea to anyone who has had even the briefest glimpse of organization life. Why should this be an area of such intense maneuver? Dalton suggests the reason is that we have so few criteria by which to judge people. The business of fitting people to jobs remains highly judgmental and personal; hence it is inevitable that there should be a struggle for the dominance of one set of values over another. At Milo, Dalton made an analysis of 190 line officers. He found that age and years of experience were not important for appointment and promotion. There was no regular progression through the hierarchical levels, as would occur where age and length of service were major criteria of promotion. Similar analyses of educational backgrounds showed some correlation between position and years of schooling. Yet very frequently the specialization in school had nothing whatsoever to do with the present job; and there were enough people without extensive schooling to suggest that education was not a controlling consideration for most managerial positions.

Thus the result at Milo was a quest for competence intermingled simultaneously with the imposition of some stringent unofficial prescriptions. These included (1) membership in the Masons and not in the Roman Catholic Church, (2) Anglo-Saxon or German ethnic background, (3) membership in a local yacht club, and (4) Republican orientation in politics. Dalton found that nearly 70 per cent of all management people were Masons and only 13 per cent were Catholics. He also discovered that over 90 per cent of all management people were from the Anglo-Saxon, German, and Scandinavian ethnic groups. The Yacht Club had 114 management people as members; and the only appropriate newspaper for a management person to carry into the plant was a famous "isolationist" journal. No executives had served the government except as Republicans.[12]

Without any well-established official standards of executive performance, Dalton believes that managers tend to place their greatest confidence in people who are generally like themselves. Thus unofficial requirements develop. They serve to solidify and perpetuate existing power patterns within the organization.

The very nature of the system suggests, too, that a process subject to so many influences outside individual and official control must be a prime focus of political activity. Its very inconsistencies as to the official route upward "naturally provoked fears, speculation, and search for unofficial routes." [13]

Politics and Production Pressure

Although production would seem to be a value upon which everyone can agree, the goal of maintenance is often in conflict with it. The supervisor on the line is judged by the amount of work he gets out, the maintenance supervisor by the consistency

---

[12] Dalton, *Men Who Manage*, pp. 178 ff.
[13] *Ibid.*, p. 167.

with which the machines operate. The maintenance man has the tendency to worry, to want production stopped at the least sign of trouble. The production man wants to take a chance, or at least hopes the breakdown will occur on the next shift. In many ways, then, the maintenance-production battle is another version of the standing debate over long-term and short-term goals.

Dalton captured some of the components of this type of struggle at the Milo plant. He noted that direct costs of labor and material were easy to control but it was in the general area of equipment upkeep that "cushions" were sought. He wrote:

> Hence this area of upkeep was used by the department chief as one means of relieving cost pressures on himself. In using the escape he of course competed obscurely with other heads groping for similar devices. Hence at times calculating alliances were formed to share an expedient. As pressures for economy increased, many operation executives placed low short-run production costs above concern for equipment. That is, they favored continuous use of the equipment with shutdowns only for breakdowns followed by minimum repair and quick resumption of production.[14]

For a decade Milo had operated a system of shops where different types of maintenance functions were performed. When the work was done, the appropriate operating unit was billed for the cost. Dissatisfaction was mounting in certain parts of the plant, however, for two reasons. Some heads of operations complained because there was a backlog of 1500 orders, which hit almost entirely at those units with the least powerful and assertive leaders. The other problem was that charges for work varied a great deal, with some departments having to pay more for the same kinds of services than others. Clearly there was a system of favoritism operating in which the less effective of the production chiefs were taking the beating.

Ultimately top plant management concerned itself with the problem. First, an incentive wage scheme was established for maintenance workers in order to beat the backlog problem. Second, a new central control unit was established to receive and route all maintenance orders to the shops. The new unit's major function was to lessen the possibility of favoritism by reducing contact between operations and maintenance units and by adhering to a

---

[14] *Ibid.*, p. 33.

fixed numerical sequence in processing orders. Furthermore, cost estimates were to be made on each job and this was to be compared with actual cost.

The new system was successful in that it did eliminate the backlog and revise charges for maintenance work. But in accomplishing these goals, it was alienating all the aggressive supervisors who had prospered under the old system. They were no longer getting the same breaks and their maintenance costs were soaring. Actually the two groups of supervisors were reversing their positions. Some members of the less aggressive group had cut their maintenance costs in half; and they were now engaging in various informal arrangements to obtain favors. This became more pronounced as the aggressive supervisors increased the vigor of their attack on the new system as one of "red tape," "slowing down production," and "no good estimates." Ultimately the new system was abolished and maintenance was almost completely decentralized to the individual departments.

In the debate that surrounded the scrapping of the system, Dalton reports that the real issues were never discussed. Although the system was created to "check 'politics' it was undone by politics because such relations were not understood and were officially rejected as improper. . . ."[15] Furthermore the political conflicts now continued *within* the departments. Assistant Manager Hardy sought to settle these problems by suggesting that responsibility for maintenance costs be placed on the maintenance men. What this did, however, was to free operations from any sense of responsibility for maintenance.

At about this time the focus of the conflict shifted. Corporate headquarters was now interesting itself in the problem. It was no longer a question of *who* in Milo was to control but *how* to combat infringements on local autonomy. The struggle thus became one between the office and the plant.

The corporate approach emphasized the purchase of replacement parts. All parts costing $500 or more were to be inventoried and a permanent system for record-keeping was to be installed. Henceforth all purchases would require corporate approval. To administer the program the office proposed that two new super-

---

[15] Dalton, *Men Who Manage*, p. 4.

visory positions be created. In filling these positions, we again see the Milo plant power structure in operation. The Hardy group selected the two men and made sure they were not able people. The purpose, of course, was to insure the two men could be controlled at the plant level even though they were officially to have free and direct contact with corporate headquarters. The situation was further complicated by the fact that the two men were relatively independent of each other. It was hoped that each man would be free of local pressures and that the new system of control would prove "simple, direct, and manageable."

The first maneuver after the appointments of the two supervisors was a request for the parts inventory. But plant officials dragged their feet. They did not supply the information. Six weeks went by; and finally the new supervisor responsible for this part of the work defied the Hardy group and reported to the office that he was receiving no cooperation. Six officials from corporate headquarters came out, praised the new supervisor, and censured plant heads for failing to cooperate. It was clear to the plant people that the supervisor had to be won over. They gave him a bigger office, flattered him, consulted him. Finally these blandishments, along with a fear of reprisals and the assurance that he would be protected by appearances, caused the difficult supervisor to go along.

Parts inventories of a type were furnished. "Surprise" inspections ordered by corporate headquarters to insure the accuracy of reports were made. There developed a system of cooperation among the various production chiefs to use each other's storage areas when the inspections came. The reports, "roughly accurate," did flow into corporate headquarters and they apparently did serve a planning purpose. Within the plant the tensions between operations and maintenance were reduced by the common threat from corporate headquarters. As Dalton summarized the results of the conflict, ". . . the Milo chiefs preserved their conception of local rights and at the same time raised morale. Conflict between principle and action in this area had not, of course, 'ended' but it was contained and existed latently."[16]

The purpose of this rather extended description of political

---

[16] *Ibid.*, p. 49.

activities at the Milo Fractionating Center is to emphasize the universality of this aspect of human behavior. Put another way, there is still the necessity of demonstrating to many readers the extent to which power and influence form a part of the sum of organization behavior. The Dalton study reveals very clearly the way in which the "official map" of the command structure is amended by individual and group abilities to acquire and exercise power, in short, to operate politically.

II • POLITICS IN THE GOVERNMENT HIERARCHY

Political life within the government bureaucracy differs perhaps most strikingly from private organizations in the relatively greater opportunity for appeal to power sources outside the immediate hierarchy. This is to be seen, for example, in the role of the police chief in the average council-manager municipality. In the formal hierarchy he is a subordinate of the city manager; actually he often possesses power which is approximately equivalent to, or greater than, that of the manager. This power lies partially in the great significance of the function for which he is responsible, partially in the status accorded him by the community as a whole, partially in the opportunities available to him to do strategic favors for influence centers in the community, and partially in the traditions of autonomy for the police department.[17]

At another level, the same type of phenomenon can be seen in the relationship of the Director of the Federal Bureau of Investigation, J. Edgar Hoover, to his top commander, the President of the United States. A study of FBI retirement legislation during the Truman administration showed rather clearly how policies were proposed and promoted by the FBI with which the President was in basic disagreement. The support of the FBI in the Congress, however, made it impossible for the President to crack down on this "out of channels" activity.[18]

Generally speaking, however, politics within government offices

---

[17] Frank P. Sherwood, "Roles of City Manager and Police," *Public Management* 41:110-113, May 1959.

[18] Harold Stein, editor, *Public Administration and Policy Development* (New York: Harcourt Brace, 1952), pp. 649-660.

conforms to the pattern Dalton describes for private industry. One brief illustration will suffice. It involves another case from those developed by the Inter-University case program, which incidentally provides a rich store of examples of the political process operating within government agencies. The history of the Foreign Service Act of 1946 shows the manner in which the informal power structure operated within the Department of State, at least on certain issues. The Secretary of State at that time was James F. Byrnes; the Undersecretary was Dean Acheson; and the Assistant Secretary responsible for the Foreign Service was Donald S. Russell, friend and former law partner of Byrnes. Though he had superior hierarchical status, Acheson's role in this case was sharply circumscribed because of the close tie between Byrnes and Russell.

It happened that Acheson did not agree entirely with the position sold to Byrnes by Russell; but he could hardly take a forthright role in the dispute which eventually involved the State Department, the Bureau of the Budget, the Congress, and the President. Acheson's reasoning was apparently based on the fact that ". . . the Secretary and Russell were intimate friends . . . Russell had dealt directly with him [Byrnes] in securing his approval of the bill; in case of disagreement, the Secretary would be predisposed to back Russell, not Acheson." [19] Thus do we see the same kind of modifications of the "official map" in the U. S. State Department that Dalton found in the Milo Fractionating organization.

III • SUMMARY

The purpose of this chapter has been to illustrate the manner in which the political process occurs in all organizations. Politics is the process by which power is acquired, transferred, and exercised upon others. Or, as Harold D. Lasswell once put it, "politics —who gets what, where, when, how." There is a tendency to treat policy and politics as synonymous. Actually they are not. Politics may operate where a major decision involving the ends of the organization is concerned, or the same process may also be observed in the contest for promotion to a relatively low level job. Policy

---

[19] *Ibid.*, p. 704.

describes decisions taken in the organization which are largely judgmental and relate rather directly to the goals of the organization. Politics is the process by which contesting forces vie for favorable outcomes on decisions. The stakes may be of major consequence or they may be relatively minor in terms of the total interests of the organization.

There appears to be a growing recognition of the political process in organizations. To some extent this appears to be a reaction against some aspects of the human relations movement. It is now being recognized that interests inevitably come into conflict in any social organism. There is no "right" answer, no syrup that can soothe over these contests. They must occur.

Much of the chapter is concerned with a description of the political process as it operates in one industrial organization, based on an extremely insightful study by Melville Dalton. The firm employed 8,000 people, was fictitiously named the Milo Fractionating Center in Dalton's book, and was located in the Middle West. This rather extended report on politics in an industrial organization has been included because it is popularly assumed that such enterprises are relatively free of the process.

Dalton found that the areas of political conflict arose around decisions for which there are no prescribed, routine answers. There was a ceaseless sparring for position among the various leaders in Milo. The combat involved the pressure for production as opposed to the longer-run need for adequate maintenance, the clash between the operating people and the staff men, the controversy between labor and management in interpreting the broad terms of a contract, uncertainty about the standards and strategies of promotion, difficulty in identifying and rewarding worthy employees, and the problem of individual executives in squaring official doctrines with the reality-oriented claims of subordinates and associates.

At Milo there was an identifiable power structure which differed appreciably from the "official map." Most significant was the status of the Assistant Manager, Hardy, who ranked equally with the Manager, Stevens. Third ranked man in the power structure was the industrial relations chief, who derived his influence from his close relationship to corporate headquarters.

The attempt to resolve problems of favoritism in maintenance service and charges provides a rather revealing picture of politics at Milo. Plant officials who were contesting among themselves quickly closed ranks when the corporate headquarters became concerned about Milo's maintenance problems. Ultimately the plant people were able successfully to thwart a reporting program demanded by corporate headquarters. This was done by collusive action at the plant. However officials at the corporate level were satisfied because they received reports which provided "roughly accurate" data for top echelon planning purposes. Dalton believed that the real conflict between maintenance and operations was never resolved because no one was willing to face it as a political issue.

In governmental organization, the same political dynamics can be observed. Cases published by the Inter-University Case Program provide particularly valuable insights into the functioning of this process within public bureaucracies. A study of the 1946 Foreign Service Act's origins and legislative history shows how the traditional hierarchical roles in the U. S. State Department were amended by certain power factors.

EIGHTEEN

The Structuring of Power

What to Look for in This Chapter . . .

- Power is: visible, related to social goals and values, and derived from a number of sources
- Work and work assignments affect the structuring of power
- How functional exclusiveness contributes to individual power
- "Iron law of oligarchy"—Michels
- Coöptation concept—Selznick
- Direction and content of communication as a determinant of power structure

In the preceding chapter our interest was largely concentrated on the way in which the political process operates within organizations. We dealt with theoretical aspects of power only to the extent necessary to indicate its relationship to the political process. Now it seems appropriate to return to a more systematic consideration of the power concept itself.

I • CONCEPTS OF POWER

Although the basic notion of power seems to be generally understood, this apparent simplicity is quite deceptive. Only in recent years have political scientists, sociologists, and social psychologists undertaken in any systematic way to investigate its dimensions. Prior to that, its presence was commonly noted; but it was almost as if power had a metaphysical quality. It could be talked about, but it could not be explained. Today the literature and research on power is growing rapidly.[1] In this section we will examine some of the dimensions of the power concept. These areas include: (1) the nature of power, (2) the visibility of power behavior, (3) the relationship of power to social goals and values, and (4) some of the common bases of power.

The Nature of Power

Concern about the nature of power expresses itself not so much in terms of abstract definitions as it does in terms of scene and character of its application. Lasswell and Kaplan, for example, limit power analysis to human beings. They note that power "involves a human relationship, not power over things."[2] They also seem to see power as an active, observable phenomenon, noting that power is "participation in the making of decisions."[3] Wolfe has a roughly similar orientation, and suggests that power ". . . is the potential ability of one person, *O*, to induce forces on another person, *P*, toward (or against) movement or change in a given direction, within a given behavior region, at a given time."[4]

Such statements probably agree with most general conceptions of the power dynamic. Furthermore they are in accord with the usual picture of government politics where complex issues are

---

[1] One important example of the expansion of the literature is Dorwin Cartwright, editor, *Studies in Social Power* (Ann Arbor, Mich.: Institute for Social Research, 1959).

[2] Harold Lasswell and Abraham Kaplan, *Power and Society* (New Haven: Yale University Press, 1950), p. 75.

[3] *Ibid.*

[4] Donald M. Wolfe, "Power and Authority in the Family," in Cartwright, *op. cit.*, p. 99.

typically simplified into struggles between individuals. We saw much of the same kind of behavior in the Milo Fractionating Company, where Assistant Manager Hardy clearly had attained his power status because of many personal leadership qualities.

However it is important to recognize that there are aspects of power which do not necessarily relate to leadership. There are forces in organizations which operate regardless of the individual actors and their leadership qualities, creating certain predispositions toward dominance within the system. As was noted earlier in this book, vocational relationships among social workers, clinical psychologists, and psychiatrists automatically accord the latter a dominant influence in their interactions. Thus it is important to view the power dynamic broadly and to recognize that more is involved than individual personality orientations and attributes.

Dubin has suggested a means of looking at these various approaches to power, placing them in three major categories:

- *Power of*—involving individuals or groups who wield power, their characteristic behaviors as power holders, and their social origins.
- *Power to*—involving the consequences of acts of power—what is done in the behavior involved in exercising power.
- *Power in*—involving the sources of power within the social system.[5]

Dubin contends that, to the present, most interest has been concentrated on the first two categories. The first of these concerns the manner in which individual leaders or groups acquire and exercise power. The second deals with the outcomes which arise from the exercise of power by these individuals and groups. This latter category is one, of course, to which political scientists have directed a very considerable amount of their attention. The third area of analysis, *power in*, is a less common point of departure but one which is relevant to the interests of this book.

Visible and Invisible Power

Many times the exercise of power is not visible. This of course complicates any attempt to ascertain the manner in which pat-

[5] Robert Dubin, "Power and Function," unpublished manuscript, p. 1

terns of influence operate to control behaviors within an organization. Yet it is quite apparent we are dealing here with a phenomenon which sometimes operates consciously and sometimes unconsciously, which sometimes appears subtly and sometimes ponderously, and which sometimes occurs directly and sometimes indirectly.

In short, influence can be exercised in a great many different ways. It has sometimes been suggested that we limit the definition of power to those situations where the exercise of influence is conscious and deliberate. In addition, of course, there are many situations where influence relationships tend to develop without intentional design. Largely this is because of ascribed status factors, which were discussed in Chapter 15. Thus we have situations (a) where people try to exercise power consciously but do not have status to support their attempts; (b) where both status and conscious exercise of power are present; and (c) where influence is exercised unconsciously because of the existence of status.

Hence it is quite apparent that the identification of the power structure within an organization is not always easily accomplished. As Dalton's study reported in the previous chapter revealed, it takes time and sophistication to arrive at an approximation of these relationships. Some administrators have the knack of divining the nature of these forces intuitively. They are lucky. For most, a seemingly invisible hand presents a frightening unknown in the administrative environment.

Power and Values

There is among many people a resistance to thinking in terms of power. Part of this resistance, at least, seems to lie in the common assumption that a power orientation requires acceptance of the power value. That is, any expression of concern about power automatically marks one a Machiavelli. Since it is socially unacceptable to admit that one aspires to power simply to secure the deference of others, there is a general reluctance to confess that power factors enter into decisions at all.

Although it is true that the acquisition of power itself is not infrequently the motivation behind many actions, it does not necessarily follow that the manipulation of power need be only for the purpose of securing power. Power may be exercised to secure other, and more paramount, goals. Lasswell and Kaplan have written on this point that "Power is itself, of course, a value, and an extremely important one; but no assumption is made here as to its being always and everywhere more important than other values."[6] In short an attempt to develop a greater awareness of an organization's power structure does not mean that the school administrator or the hospital administrator or the police chief has lost sight of his basic mission.

A concern about power and power structure may only mean that the administrator is sophisticated enough to realize that the achievement of a goal depends on acceptance and approval of that goal at certain significant decision points in the environment.

Bases of Power

Why is it that power appears at certain points in an organization and not at others? What factors are significant to the acquisition and exercise of power? These are of course critical questions to those who would understand the nature of the political process within their organization. They are also highly significant in enabling the individual actor within the organization to exploit his own attributes in a time of political combat. Lasswell and Kaplan have suggested eight forms of influence which are critical. These are physical power itself, respect, rectitude, affection, well-being, wealth, skill, and enlightenment.[7]

French and Raven point out that categorizing the bases of power is difficult because in actual instances it is "rare" that any one power element alone is at work.[8] The most common factors in power situations, they feel, fall into five primary areas: (1) reward, (2) coercion, (3) legitimacy, (4) identification with the power figure—referent power, (5) expertise. Both reward and coercion, which are types of sanctions, are in a sense derivative bases of power. The ability to reward or punish must stem from certain other favorable factors in the environment, such as wealth or

---

6 Lasswell and Kaplan, *Power and Society*, p. 77.
7 *Ibid.*, p. 87.
8 John R. P. French, Jr., and Bertram Raven, "The Bases of Social Power," in Cartwright, editor, *Studies in Social Power*, p. 155.

hierarchical status. Power based on legitimacy involves the subordinate's perception that his superior has the right to influence him and he has an obligation to accept that influence. French and Raven indicate that legitimate power is approximately the same as many concepts of authority.

Where identification with the power source is a basic element in inter-relationships, there is a "feeling of oneness" between the superior and subordinate. This desire to identify with the power source is typically the result of the attractiveness of the individual leader or the groups to which he belongs. Thus the greater the attraction, the greater is the identification and the greater is the power. In the fifth category, expertise is the significant element in acquiring power. Here the subordinate must feel that the superior knows and is not trying to deceive him.

A comparison of the Lasswell-Kaplan and French-Raven categories suggests a rather common agreement as to the general foundations of power. However the differences in the lists do suggest the difficulty of developing categories upon which there can be entire agreement. Although gaps can be found in each, it is also true that the categories could be defined broadly enough to cover most of the omissions that might be suggested. For our purposes it is perhaps only important to note that the French-Raven list seems to be oriented more towards a social process. There appears to be less inclination to fix attention on the attributes of the individual in the situation. This serves to emphasize an earlier point, that power in an organization is based not only on the attributes of the individuals involved but also on the system itself.

French and Raven take one further step. On the basis of their analysis, they speculate provocatively on the behavior of power where these various elements are at work. They suggest that:

- Power based on identification (referent power) will have the broadest range of the various types; and perhaps the range of expert power is most limited because it generally applies only to certain knowledge areas.
- Power will be reduced when its exercise is attempted outside its perceived limits.
- The stronger the power base, the greater the power.
- Coercion causes a decrease in attraction for the power center

and higher resistance; reward operates in the opposite manner.

- The more legitimate the coercion, the less likely it will be to produce resistance.[9]

It is important to note that French and Raven suggest certain strategies in the selection of power instruments: (a) check the depth of the power base, (b) seek legitimacy in the exercise of power, and (c) avoid the use of power that has its base in coercion.

II • POWER AS A PROPERTY OF ORGANIZATION

One of the essential ideas of hierarchy is that varying amounts of power shall be bestowed upon certain roles within the system. The higher the level of coordinating responsibility, presumably the greater the power. Thus, as one moves up the pyramid, he acquires an increasing amount of power. Obviously this is an over-simplified view of the influence phenomenon in a complex social structure, largely because traditionalists fail to realize there is more than one basis of power. Traditionalists—those who equate official command with power—also tend to see organizations as closed systems. They seem to assume that organizations are antiseptically clean of influences from outside. As a consequence there is relatively little attention paid to the manner in which organizations adapt internal power alignments to external influences.

In this section we will be concerned about three basic problems: (1) the ways in which organizations as formal entities do participate in the distribution of power, (2) the theory that power in organizations tends inevitably to concentrate in the hands of a few people, and (3) the manner in which organizations adapt to external power forces.

Organization Factors in the Allocation of Power

Although it is apparent that hierarchical authority does not alone add up to power in the organization, we should not leap to the opposite view that organizations have no power to bestow. There

[9] *Ibid.*, p. 165.

are some very significant ways in which the organization assigns power to various roles.

Structural power. Role in the hierarchy provides, in terms of the French and Raven analysis, some important power attributes. Perhaps most significantly it endows legitimacy. Thus deference is paid to those who we consider have the "right" to impose certain demands. It is quite likely that legitimacy is a more dominant factor in power relations than many of us would expect. An individual's acceptance of the social structure in general, which is largely a pattern of organization, implies approval of the role assignments within it. As French and Raven have pointed out, "legitimate power in a formal organization is largely a relationship between offices rather than between persons. And the acceptance of an office as *right* is a basis for legitimate power—a judge has a right to levy fines, a foreman should assign work . . ."[10]

Another aspect of structural power is the ability to invoke sanctions. In general it may be supposed that the further one moves up the hierarchy, the greater is his capacity to provide rewards and exact punishment. However, this is far from universal. Argyris found in his study of a bank, for example, that there were actually few rewards or penalties to be distributed by the hierarchical leaders.[11] Aside from this, however, it seems fairly clear from the vast amount of human relations research—dating back to Elton Mayo and the Hawthorne (Western Electric) study—that neither the "big stick" nor the "lollipop" is the best long-run means of exerting influence. Indeed there are enough constraints on the use of sanction-based power in most organizations as to make this a somewhat lesser grant of capacity from the hierarchy than would first appear.

Functional power. One of the most significant ways in which the formal organization allocates power is through specialization and division of labor. Dubin, in particular, has emphasized this view.[12] The very act of specialization creates a pattern of dependence, in which each participant in a greater or lesser degree

---

[10] *Ibid.*, p. 160.

[11] Chris Argyris, *Organization of a Bank* (New Haven: Labor and Management Center of Yale University, 1954), pp. 62 ff.

[12] Robert Dubin, *The World of Work* (Englewood Cliffs, N.J.: Prentice-Hall, Inc., 1958), pp. 47 ff.

contributes to the organization objective. Specialization, says Dubin, "creates automatic dependence. A specialized job operating in isolation produces nothing useful." Power therefore becomes "the effect that the kind of performance, or failure to perform, has on the rest of the organization."[13]

This perception of function-based power is quite different from structure-based power. Here the fundamental element is the work performed rather than the status position occupied. As a consequence this focus on function suggests a power model quite different from that of the formal organization chart.

In the *first* place, it is assumed that everyone in the organization is an agent in its work, is included in the pattern of dependence, and therefore possesses some power. This assumption suggests two important variances from the hierarchical perception, which conceives of power as absolute at the top and nonexistent at the bottom. The functional view argues that the lowliest man in the pyramid possesses some power; this being the case, there are restraints on the exercise of power throughout the organization. Perforce, the system of specialization minimizes the possibility of absolute power. Indeed this may help to explain why absolutism was a much more prevalent form of social and political structure in the days before the industrial revolution and great specialization.

Although every type of work possesses some power, the exact amount will vary from function to function. Some work is more important than other tasks in maintaining the present system and enabling the organization to perform as currently desired. For example, Dubin has shown graphically how the role of the inspector in a manufacturing unit may contain much greater capacity for influence than his position in the hierarchy would suggest.[14] In making this kind of analysis, the fundamental question asked is, "How much of a difference the operation of a function makes to a given state of a system."[15] Since inspection is so significant to the functioning of an industrial system, the role acquires power attributes beyond those possessed by the foreman on an assembly line. Hence again we see that the analysis of function in an organization may provide quite a different picture of power relation-

---

[13] *Ibid.*, p. 48.

[14] *Ibid.*, p. 54.

[15] Dubin, "Power and Function," p. 11.

ships than that prescribed in the official pyramid. Rather than follow channels, function-based power increases as the importance of the particular activity to the maintenance of the total system increases.

There is one further feature of functional power which provides insight on the nature of organization power structures. This involves the number of people who participate in a particular activity or decision. More specifically, would we expect one person occupying a particular role to have more power than several persons? Dubin argues that he would and advances the following hypothesis, "For any given level of functional importance in a system, the power residing in a functional agent (functionary) is inversely proportional to the number of other system functional agents capable of performing the function."[16] We assume that each function in an organization harbors a certain amount of power. If there are many agents participating, individual power will be less than if the power of that function were concentrated in one person. In certain respects we can say presidents of corporations are powerful because they alone are responsible for the exercise of a certain functional responsibility. Similarly, a hierarchically unimportant file clerk may have very considerable influence because she, like the president, enjoys a monopoly over a certain functional area. It is quite probable that such power drops off rather sharply as soon as there is any sharing of role. In fact, Dubin suggests that even as few as five available substitutes make the impact of functional exclusiveness on the power structure almost negligible.

This type of analysis has important implications for organization behavior and structure. If we assume that different activities possess differing amounts of influence potential, it follows that the assignment of these functions within the organization will do much to determine the structure and exercise of power. Put another way, the organization through its assignment of functions has an important vehicle for allocating its power resources. Pragmatic proof of this general proposition is to be seen in the continuing conflicts among units in all large organizations over the placement of certain functions. Yet little effort has been made to deal with the problem systematically in the literature of organization analysis.

---

16 *Ibid.*, p. 21.

Is it not possible that the analyst should first ascertain the power potential of each function as a prime basis for determining "who should do what" in the organization?

The second implication involves functional exclusiveness and its relationship to structure. If there is a fear that power may accrue to certain functionaries within the system, we have at hand a simple structural answer. We simply assign the role to several people. This of course is an old story to political scientists. The separation of powers doctrine and the proliferation of boards and commissions at the state and local level are illustrative applications of this fundamental precept. Similarly the use of committees in business. Frequently these devices have been criticized, perhaps most notably in the literature of governmental management, because they are costly in man-power and cumbersome in decision-making. Hence there is sometimes the inference that boards and committees are "irrational" organizational mechanisms. However the avoidance or elimination of functional exclusiveness may be more important to the organization than certain other costs, in which case a structure with many hydra-headed units may be much more appropriate than the usual tight pyramid.

Oligarchy in the Organization

There is another school of thought, however, which argues that none of the structural-functional adjustments noted above can prevent the accretion of power in the hands of a few within the organization. It is claimed that a basic dynamic of organization process is an inexorable passage of control into the hands of an elite, an oligarchy. The theory is certainly not a new one; indeed it is probably as old as organizations themselves. One of the most articulate advocates of the position is Roberto Michels, who, writing in 1915, advanced the "iron law of the oligarchy."[17]

Although it is true that Michels was writing about social and political organization on the grand scale, he tended to assume that the tendency toward oligarchy was inherent in all forms of social

[17] Roberto Michels, *Political Parties, A Sociological Study of the Oligarchical Tendencies of Modern Democracy*, translated from the Italian by Eden and Cedar Paul (London: Jarrold and Sons, 1915), pp. 393 ff. Others who advanced somewhat similar ideas in a rather general attack on democracy were Gaetano Mosca and Vilfredo Pareto, whom Michels quotes approvingly.

organization. Thus his "iron law" that "oligarchy is, as it were, a preordained form of the common life of great social aggregates . . ." has found its way into a variety of literature on organization.[18]

Michels bases his theory of a "universally applicable social law" on two factors: (1) the significance of organization size and (2) the clash of interests within any highly specialized organism. As to the first point, Michels contends that power inevitably falls into the hands of the few as organizations grow larger because of the impossibility of its exercise on any mass basis. Hence the tendency toward oligarchy increases as the size of the organization increases. In a small organization, he says, it is possible to keep everyone involved. This is important not only because it makes for intelligent participation but also because it equips any member of the group to assume leadership. In a sense, then, the leadership role has been divided among a number of people; and no single person possesses enough control over these vital functions to acquire a substantial power posture in the organization. Michels illustrates his point by drawing on the early union experience of Italian agricultural workers. To keep the leadership under control, management negotiations were only possible when the union representative was given written authority signed by every member of the union. For the same reasons, the books of the union were open for inspection by members at all times.

As organizations grow, however, this style of participation becomes impossible. It is at this point that power begins to pass from the mass into the hands of an oligarchic elite. The few begin to acquire an absolute control over the most vital functions of the organization and thus establish themselves in power.

Michels' second point is also strikingly related to some of the concepts of functional analysis. He believes that the division of labor—specialization—within organizations hastens the move toward oligarchy. This is true for two reasons, the first of which relates back to size. As organizations grow and become complex, the individual roles become more specialized. Fewer and fewer people have the particular competences to fill these unique niches; and

---

[18] *Ibid.*, p. 407. See John M. Pfiffner and Robert V. Presthus, *Public Administration* (New York: Ronald Press, 1953), p. 63, as one example of its currency.

thus we see "expert" power emerging. Michels feels this happened in the British trade union movement.[19] Specialization also promotes oligarchy, Michels contends, because each of these units "creates for itself, as soon as it becomes consolidated, interests peculiar to itself."[20] Then begins the power struggle in which one of these interests, or a combination, must emerge dominant. Thus the organization elite appears.

Certainly there is abundant evidence to support much of the Michels' contention. Many organizations do seem to be controlled by small elites. However, even in these cases, it is doubtful whether their power is as absolute as Michels would contend. On balance the "iron law of oligarchy" remains a provocative hypothesis, perhaps worthy of a great deal more testing than has occurred in the 45 years since Michels wrote. But it is probable that Michels himself has propagated the same kind of oversimplification which caused him to be so critical of Marx and various democratic theorists.

Adjustments to External Power Forces

Earlier we emphasized that organizations are seldom truly closed systems. Some organizations—such as a bank and a city government—have contact with the outside at every level of the structure. Others—such as an industrial plant—have significantly fewer of these contacts but they still do not exist in isolation. This being true, it follows that outside influences will have varying degrees of effect on the internal power structure. In the Milo Fractionating Center, it appeared that these outside influences were primarily those from the corporate level. On the other hand Selznick found in a study of the Tennessee Valley Authority that external forces, particularly the land grant colleges, were quite a prevalent factor in the development of the power structure in that agency.[21]

Unfortunately our knowledge in this field is very small. We have little systematic theory about the way in which internal

[19] Michels, *op. cit.*, pp. 32-33.

[20] *Ibid.*, p. 406.

[21] Philip Selznick, *TVA and the Grass Roots* (Berkeley: University of California Press, 1949).

power structures react to outside influences. Thompson and McEwen have emphasized the importance of environment to these power adjustments. Since organizations exist in an interdependent relationship to the larger society, others must inevitably influence organization behavior. They hypothesize that one way of analyzing the degree of power exercised by outside influences is to identify the time of entry of these forces into the decision-making structure. The earlier the entry, the greater the power. Thompson and McEwen establish four models of entry along a continuum: (1) *competition,* which is a condition of influence but not one in which formal entry occurs, (2) *bargaining,* where separation of power centers is retained, (3) *coöptation,* where the informal sharing of powers occurs, and (4) *coalition.*[22]

The work of Selznick deserves further mention. His concept of coöptation is rooted in the assumption that every organization must either formally or informally adapt to the power realities contained within itself and its environment. This conforms to Selznick's general view that organizations should be regarded as social communities, with a character and unique properties of their own.[23] As Selznick puts it,

> The organization imperatives which define the need for coöptation arise out of a situation in which formal authority is actually or potentially in a state of imbalance with respect to its institutional environment. . . . Failure to reflect the true balance of power will necessitate a realistic adjustment to those centers of institutional strength which are in a position to strike organized blows and thus to enforce concrete demands.[24]

Selznick defines coöptation as the process by which power, or the burdens of power, are shared. It may occur either formally or informally. If the need is primarily to endow presently established power centers with legitimacy, the coöptation will be formal. In such a case there is no actual transfer of power. It simply appears to occur in order to provide an aura of respectability for

---

[22] James D. Thompson and William J. McEwen, "Organizational Goals and Environment: Goal Setting as an Interaction Process," *American Sociological Review* 23:23-31, February 1958.

[23] Philip Selznick, *Leadership in Administration* (Evanston, Ill.: Row, Peterson, 1957).

[24] Selznick, *TVA and the Grass Roots,* p. 26.

the organization as a whole. It is a familiar device in both business and government. Businesses seek to build confidence in management, improve public relations, and benefit themselves in other ways by appointing persons of reputation to the board of directors and to honorific offices. The practice is also common in government, particularly when an agency has been receiving a bad press. Such formal coöptation is particularly a way of life for most nonprofit, charitable, and educational institutions. The fundamental problem, of course, is to be sure that the respect and legitimacy accorded such individuals does not become so great as to wrest actual power from its present holders.

When organizational imperatives require the actual sharing of power, Selznick states, such an accommodation tends to be informal. This is necessary because adjustment to such power nuclei may not accord with general perceptions of legitimacy. "It therefore becomes useful and often essential for such coöptation to remain in the shadowland of informal interaction."[25]

It is possible that coöptation may occur entirely within the organization. As we noted, however, Selznick found in the TVA that both formal and informal accomodations involved forces outside the Authority itself. Formal coöptation occurred through the official status accorded local power cooperatives, thus attesting to the "grass roots" character of the agency. Informal coöptation involved adjustment to the land grant college interests through TVA's Agricultural Relations Department.[26] In general it would appear that Selznick's theory is most useful in explaining the manner in which internal power structures are amended by external influence centers.

III • COMMUNICATIONS AND POWER

In Chapter 16 we considered the manner in which communications influence the nature of organization. A further indication of

[25] *Ibid.*, p. 261.

[26] It should be noted that Selznick's specifics on the TVA experience have been subjected to some criticism. However the model presented by Selznick, accurate or inaccurate as to illustrative details, deserves to be reported as a substantial contribution to the theory of organization and power.

the importance of this is the role of communication in the power struggle. Since communication is a basis for many of our formal organization arrangements, it is inevitably a participant in the organizational allocation of power. Communication is also at the core of interpersonal, human relationships. It is a central part of the leadership pattern, which involves other bases of power within an organization.[27] Thus communication serves as a bridge between those aspects of power provided by organization form and environment and those which are a function of individual capacity and interaction.

Cartwright suggests that power lies behind the interest communication presently receives in social psychological theory. He points out that "Communication is the mechanism by which interpersonal influence is exerted. Without communication there would be no group norms, group goals, or organized group action."[28] All communications, it is argued, carry some influence; but some have greater influence than others. Thus the problem is to discover what it is about a person, a role, or a group, which causes one communication to acquire more power than another. Rumor is an important aspect of these considerations. Cartwright tells of an action-research project at the University of Michigan, in which things seemed to be progressing quite nicely. Several new community activities had been initiated, but in the process new leaders began to emerge to replace the old ones. Quickly these new programs came to a halt. The rumor had been spread that the project leaders and the new local leaders "were taking orders from Moscow."[29]

The effect on power of the direction and content of communication is of particular consequence to the subject matter of this book. It is in this area particularly that we see the communication dynamic in an organizational context. Obviously the idea of com-

---

[27] Chapter 21 contains a detailed explanation of the manner in which Herbert Simon would use communications analysis in the building of a formal organization pattern. The significance of communication to leadership is argued by Robert Tannenbaum and Fred Massarik, "Leadership: A Frame of Reference," *Management Science* 4:1-19, October 1957, also available as Reprint No. 68 (Los Angeles: Institute of Industrial Relations, University of California, 1958).

[28] Dorwin Cartwright, "Power, A Neglected Variable in Social Psychology," in Cartwright, editor, *Studies in Social Power*, p. 7.

[29] *Ibid.*, p. 8.

municating "through channels" has its origins in a concern about power. Communication out of channels reduces the power of the immediate supervisor and increases that of his subordinate and superior. Thus the direction of communications, their frequency, and their content tell us much about the power relationships within the organization.

March and Simon have been particularly aware of this communication potential. In highly specialized organizations, they contend, information enters the organization at certain specified points. Here the communications are screened and categorized in terms of a conceptual scheme which has been approved by the organization. Thus there is only one place of entry for most communications and only one real way of looking at them. All other parts of the organization are dependent on these gatekeepers for the degree to which the data reflect reality. The "person who summarizes and assesses his own direct perceptions and transmits them to the rest of the organization becomes an important source of information premises for action . . . by the very nature and limits of the communication system, a great deal of discretion and influence is exercised by those persons who are in direct contact with some part of the 'reality' that is of concern to the organization." [30]

March and Simon label the communication of judgments rather than facts "uncertainty absorption." It is used "consciously and unconsciously, as a technique for acquiring and exercising power." [31] Hence another way of gaining insight into a power structure is to ascertain points at which "uncertainty absorption" occurs and in what degree. This system of analysis seems to have particular relevance for much of decentralization theory, which tends commonly to assume that subordinate levels *want* to communicate upward. Much of performance budgeting philosophy in the government, for example, has been based on this premise. It has been argued, therefore, that the big task is developing the mechanical procedures by which this may be made possible.

Actually some of the most bitter political conflicts occur between the various echelons of an organization, as the Milo Frac-

---

[30] James G. March and Herbert A. Simon, *Organizations* (New York: John Wylie and Sons, Inc., 1958), p. 165.

[31] *Ibid.*, p. 166.

tionating study revealed. And typically communication has been a most important power weapon available to the lower echelons. Indeed, in terms of raw power considerations, it is doubtful if any lower level person would ever consciously desire to reduce the amount of uncertainty absorption in higher echelons. His power interests, in short, lie in communicating upward as many judgments and as few facts as possible. In retrospect it is possible that this rather simple power consideration has been instrumental in thwarting many decentralization moves, including performance budgeting and other types of reporting efforts.

V • SUMMARY

In Chapter 17 we took the position that the political process is a part of life in all organizations. We then attempted to show how politics permeates the organization fabric, particularly that of a large industrial firm. In this chapter we have been concerned with some of the theoretical aspects which surround the central ingredient of politics—power. It is a subject which is particularly relevant to this book because there has been little recognition of the ways in which an organization may, through its structure, allocate power resources.

The power concept should not be viewed narrowly. It pervades much of social and organizational behavior, sometimes overtly and sometimes covertly. Neither should we be unwilling to face its existence, as seems to be the disposition of many administrators. Concern about power does not automatically render one a Machiavelli. Actually power may be exercised to secure other, and more paramount, goals. A school administrator is not necessarily oblivious to his educational commitments because he thinks in power terms. He may simply be sophisticated enough to realize that the achievement of a goal depends on its acceptance and approval at certain significant decision points in the environment.

The foundations of power are diverse. French and Raven suggest that power based on the identification of the influenced with the influencer provides perhaps the greatest range of opportunity. Power based on expertise has perhaps the most limited range of usefulness. It is also significant that legitimacy appears to be consequential in reducing resistance to the exercise of power, thus again suggesting the close tie between formal and informal aspects of organization.

A little recognized aspect of the structuring of power is the extent to which the work of an organization and its distribution is influential. Dubin has particularly emphasized this point. He has argued that specialization itself creates a pattern of dependence of each participant on the others. Thus no one in the organization is without some power and no one has absolute power. All functions of course do not have the same importance, and hence we may assume that those functions which are least dispensable enjoy the greatest power potential. The question to ask in assessing this power potential is how much of a difference the operation of a function makes to a given state of a system. Thus the assignment of functions within an organization will determine in considerable degree its power structure.

Not only do the functions themselves possess inherent power, the number of people involved in their performance is another significant variable. The president of an organization is typically powerful because of the functions over which he has control and also because he alone has that control. A lowly bookeeper, though dealing with a relatively unimportant function, may acquire considerable power because control is concentrated. The sharing of functional responsibility rapidly dissipates this power. Dubin suggests that when more than five participate, this factor becomes negligible in power considerations. Thus we may say that the amount of individual power increases as the number of fellow participants in the activity decreases. Dubin labels this concept "functional exclusiveness."

One persistent theory of the behavior of power in organizations is that control ultimately passes to a small elite. Michels has called it "the iron law of oligarchy." He contends that the scale of organizations and the clash of specialized interests within them prevents any mass participation in organization affairs. This concept has had a great deal of currency in the literature of organization. However it still remains untested.

How do power structures, elite or otherwise, change? How do organizations create necessary systems of adjustment to changing power alignments within themselves and in the institutional environment? Selznick's concept of coöptation postulates two different patterns of accomodation, the formal and the informal. Formal coöptation is primarily an attempt to secure legitimacy without actual change in the power structure. Informal coöptation involves a real shift in power alignments but without the necessity or desirability of attaching legitimacy to the change. Selznick based his model on research in the Tennessee Valley Authority.

Cartwright points out that power lies behind much of the interest of social psychology in communications. The basic reason for communications is to exert influence. Thus it is not surprising that communication should be an important consideration in the structuring of power in an organization. March and Simon have suggested that one way of gaining insight into an organization's power relationships is to ascertain the points at which "uncertainty absorption" occurs and in what degree. Uncertainty absorption takes place when the recipient of a communication receives judgments about facts, rather than the facts themselves. Thus the people who decide what information to transmit, and with what interpretation, have considerable power potential.

NINETEEN

Leadership

What to Look for in This Chapter . . .

Leadership and power:
- the influencers
- the commanders

Basic functions of the leader:
- maintains membership of group
- gets group objectives attained
- facilitates interactions among members

Situational factors that are as critical to a leadership function as personal factors

Leadership style—for example, authoritarian or democratic—and its relations to the formal and informal organization structure

---

Leadership is often regarded as *the* important modifier of organization behavior. Impatience with the mechanics of organization is one consequence: "Get the right man in the leadership job, and all your problems will be solved."

No one will deny that such counsel can pay dividends. We have all observed occasions where a change in the leadership has had a pronounced effect on the organization. There is, as one illustration, General Omar Bradley's story of the problem of command in the 90th Infantry Division during World War II. The 90th was brought to Europe by a new division commander who had had no chance to train with it. It was thrown into the Normandy bridgehead and performed miserably. After four days, the division commander was relieved. But a new general and a thorough shakeup of the staff made little difference. The division was floundering so badly that Bradley's subordinates wanted to break it up, sending the men to other units.

However Bradley rejected the idea. His refusal was at least in part based on his own philosophy of command in the military: ". . . man for man one division is just as good as another—they vary only in the skill and leadership of their commanders."[1] Thus the answer to the 90th's problem was not to destroy the division but to find the right man for command. Bradley's next choice turned out to be such a person. The new commander made exactly 16 changes in the 16,000 man organization. When he left the division a few months later to assume command of a corps, "his successor inherited one of the finest divisions in combat on the allied front."[2]

Bradley's strong conviction that the men at the top make the difference—and his vindication by the performance of the 90th—is rather dramatic testimony that leadership can be an important modifier of organizational behavior. Unfortunately, however, the relationship is not as simple as this one example might make it appear. Research on leadership in the last decade reveals how complex it is. Bradley himself showed his awareness of the other leadership dimensions in the painstaking care with which he went about finding the right man to meet the peculiar needs of the First Division at a tense time in Sicily. He noted that the First was "the equal of several inexperienced divisions."[3] Yet he sacrificed the division commander and his assistant because of a failure to observe regulations and senior commands. The successor, chosen

---

[1] Omar N. Bradley, *A Soldier's Story* (New York: Henry Holt and Company, 1951), p. 297.

[2] *Ibid.*

[3] *Ibid.*, p. 154.

because he was a totally different type, was equally successful with the division in France.

As with the other modifying elements described in previous chapters of Part Three, the subject of leadership is a very big one. It is a time-honored topic of discussion. Our review of it in this chapter will therefore be restricted to an examination of the relationship betweeen leader and organization and the way the one works on the other in a reciprocal fashion.

I • THE IDEA OF LEADERSHIP

The concepts of power and leadership have much in common. In the last analysis certain people are leaders because they exercise power. Indeed it is unthinkable that a leader should not have power. Consequently the exercise of influence is a central part of most definitions of leadership. That does not mean that leadership and power are the same thing. A leadership act represents a choice of power instruments. It is in a sense the point at which power is activated. Thus we find "Leadership always involves attempts on the part of a *leader* (influencer) to affect (influence) the behavior of a *follower* (influencee) or followers in *situation.*"[4]

This relationship to power suggests that leadership, like power, cannot be equated with position in the official hierarchy. Leadership basically involves the capacity to influence; and this cannot necessarily be endowed by position in the formal structure. Sometimes this is referred to as the difference between *headship* and *leadership.*[5] This distinction seems important because of its relevance to (a) democratic values and (b) processes of control in the organization.

Democratic values. Positions of power in an organization can be secured in a variety of ways. Some writers restrict the use of the term *leader* to those people who obtain the role of influencer

---

[4] Robert Tannebaum and Fred Massarik, "Leadership: A Frame of Reference," *Management Science* 4:3, October 1957. Also available as Reprint No. 68 (Los Angeles: Institute of Industrial Relations, University of California, 1958).

[5] Cecil A. Gibb, "Leadership," in Gardner Lindzey, editor, *Handbook of Social Psychology,* Vol. II (Cambridge, Mass.: Addison-Wesley Publishing Co., 1954), p. 882.

as a consequence of group decision or endorsement. The essential difference is in respect to the *source* of the power which is being exercised. Gibb has noted that there is "almost general agreement in the literature of the last few years that leadership is to be distinguished, by definition, from domination or headship." [6] The master and the slave, the teacher and the pupil, the military officer and his men, and even the business executive and his employees are given as examples of the headship relation.

A distinction on these grounds, however, appears to have dubious merit; and this may be another instance where social scientists are letting a value prejudice interfere with logic. It is questionable whether the sources of power in any situation can be precisely divided and identified, as we noted in the previous chapter. It is also quite obvious that position in the hierarchy is an important element of influence. The distinction based on this reasoning would seem to make little sense in terms of the problems General Bradley was facing with his commanding officers. It is perhaps better to recognize that headship and leadership are not the same things and that the real difference is power. A person who has no influence may be a head of an organization; he becomes a leader as he gains influence.

Control processes. The other facet of the distinction concerns official *command* and *leadership*. In these terms command is seen as the exercise of power granted by the formal hierarchy. It generally operates in routine situations. It is continuous and regular. It is usually sufficient to insure adequate performance because participants expect and accept such behavior. Most workers simply do not care to challenge such commands.[7] In contrast leadership is concerned with the nonroutine. Essentially it occurs when participants care enough to challenge the official command. Leadership is perhaps most required when issues of morale and change arise.

Such a distinction seems particularly important in helping an executive to conceptualize the full scale of his role. In short he

---

6 *Ibid.*

7 Robert Dubin, "Industrial Workers' Worlds: A Study of the 'Central Life Interests' of Industrial Workers," *Social Problems* 3:131-42, January 1956. In this empirical study Dubin found that work is not as important to most people as is generally thought from the nonmaterial standpoint.

should not waste himself trying to lead in matters where followers are quite willing to accept routine orders. It has been suggested that this is simply another version of the notion that the best executive is the one with the clear desk.[8]

In summary we have to remember that positions of hierarchical importance are inextricably bound to leadership but they are not the same. The executive who understands the distinction will see his own role more clearly. He will know that position is not enough. He will understand that much in any organization must be routine and is acceptable to the participants. He will reserve his leadership resources for those occasions when something more is at stake. This is very close to Shartle's view that a leadership act "is one which results in others acting or responding in a shared direction. Leadership is therefore judged in terms of what *others* do."[9]

Functions of Leadership

There are as many views of the functions of leadership as there are writers and researchers. It is obvious, too, that the detailing of functions will depend on one's general concept of leadership. However, some feel that the identification of leadership acts should precede the development of any generalized concept of leadership. One view, for example, is that the essential function of the leader is to work toward unity and cohesiveness in the organization and to see that membership in it is a pleasant, satisfying experience.[10] Gordon has said about the same in observing that "a potential 'leader' of a group somehow must perceive what it is the group wants, he must contribute something that will move the group closer to that goal, and finally his contribution must be 'accepted' before he can be said to have patterned the group's behavior."[11]

---

[8] Robert Dubin, *The World of Work* (Englewood Cliffs, N.J.: Prentice-Hall, Inc., 1958), p. 392.

[9] Carroll L. Shartle, *Executive Performance and Leadership* (Englewood Cliffs, N.J.: Prentice-Hall, Inc., 1956), p. 106.

[10] John K. Hemphill, *Situational Factors in Leadership,* Bureau of Educational Research, The Ohio State University, Research Monograph No. 32 (1949), p. 79.

[11] Thomas Gordon, *Group-Centered Leadership* (Boston: Houghton Mifflin Company, 1955), p. 51.

The studies of leadership at Ohio State University in the beginning of the 'fifties provide us with perhaps the best information as to what the functions of leadership are. These are particularly interesting because the Ohio State work was largely concerned with leadership in formal organizations, most particularly the U.S. Navy. Parenthetically, the Ohio State studies represent perhaps the most exhaustive effort in American research to get at the leadership question *as such.* They represent seven years of work, dating from 1946 to 1953. Publications emanating from this research were issued, however, as late as 1957.

The Ohio State group established nine dimensions which were considered descriptive of the leadership function. As a result of research and statistical analysis, however, it was decided that three basic functions are unique to the leadership role.[12] These are:

- *Maintenance of membership.* This involves the closeness of the leader to the group, the frequency of his interactions, and his acceptability to the group.
- *Objective attainment.* The leader has a basic responsibility for seeing that work patterns are stable and understandable. He must also see that the group achieves its goals.[13]
- *Group interaction facilitation.* The leader works to facilitate effective interaction among organization members. Communication is a particularly important feature of this dimension.

II • DIMENSIONS OF THE LEADERSHIP ROLE

So far we have been discussing the concept and functions of leadership. Observe, however, that nothing has really been said as to whether this is the activity of an individual or a group. The question is of particular significance in large organizations because

---

[12] Shartle, *op. cit.*, p. 117.

[13] Carl J. Lange, Vincent Campbell, Robert V. Katter, and Fred J. Shanley, *A Study of Leadership in Army Infantry Platoons* (Washington: George Washington University, Human Resources Research Office, 1958). Performance-orientation showed significantly on studies of effective and ineffective leadership performance in infantry platoons.

of the tremendous demands placed on those in top executive positions. To what extent do they as individuals represent the leadership of the organization?

Individual Leadership

There is an understandable inclination to think of leadership in a group or an organization as residing in one person. Perhaps the most extreme example of this is the tendency among many people to see the President as *the* U.S. Government, despite the fact that there are millions of civilian and military people who are direct participants in such a large undertaking. Belief in the idea of an individual leader has certain authoritarian overtones. It conveys the notion of an order-giver, a dominant individual, one who is playing all the important roles in the organization. It also has a relationship to the formal organization pyramid because almost inevitably the man in the highest status position is assumed to be the leader.

This line of thinking has resulted in many attempts to ascertain what qualities make one man a better leader than another. Tests in particular have been developed to probe for these significant traits. They have involved such possibilities as (1) physical and constitutional factors (height, weight, physique, energy, health, appearance; (2) intelligence; (3) self-confidence; (4) sociability; (5) will (initiative, persistence, ambition); (6) dominance; and (7) surgency (i.e., talkativeness, cheerfulness, geniality, enthusiasm, expressiveness, alertness, and originality).[14]

While various of these individual dimensions have appeared in leadership studies, the assumption of a leadership syndrome or leader type has been called "futile."[15] No consistent pattern of traits has emerged. We still cannot say there is an elite group of men destined for leadership regardless of the organizational circumstances in which they find themselves.

---

[14] Ralph M. Stogdill, "Personal Factors Associated with Leadership: A Survey of the Literature," *Journal of Psychology* 25:35-71, January 1948.

[15] J. P. Guilford, *Personality* (New York: McGraw-Hill Book Company, 1959), p. 470.

Leadership Structure

The idea of leadership structure is essentially a counter-view to the personal trait approach we have been discussing. In both instances, of course, people are involved. The essential difference is that leadership structure is predicated on the idea that *no one* person has all the leadership functions.[16] They may—and probably will—be dispersed among a number of different people with different kinds of competences. Thus the principal question is whether leadership is a "one-man show" in an organization or whether many get into the act.

As we might expect, the idea of leadership structure is closely associated with the proposition of the previous chapter that every member of an organization has some power. This accrues to him simply because he is a member of the organization and therefore must be considered important to it. Here much the same thought is being expressed. There are many different acts which go to make up the leadership process. These require the participation of a considerable number of people who exercise influence in varying amounts to provide the cohesiveness, the atmosphere, and the progress toward organizational goals required. In short, if it is true that power is dispersed throughout the organization, then it follows that leadership must be also.

The idea of leadership structure is undoubtedly a more balanced view of the way things have to be in any complex organization. Only in a small, face-to-face group could one man possibly dominate the leadership process. It is well, then, to recognize that there are limitations to the "great man" or "father" image of leadership. On the other hand it is also important to realize that the need for the *top* leader role still remains. He is the symbolic spokesman, the coordinator supreme, the important participant in decisions as to goals, the primary change agent, and the example to the organization. Even cut down this much, the man at the top

---

[16] Ralph M. Stogdill and Kathleen Koehler Haase, "Structures of Working Relationships," in Stogdill, editor, *Leadership and Structures of Personal Interaction,* Bureau of Business Research, The Ohio State University, Research Monograph No. 84 (1957), p. 3.

still has a monstrous responsibility. It is only fair that our researchers and theorists should help to take some of the burden from his shoulders.

III • SITUATIONAL FACTORS IN LEADERSHIP

Who does the leading is of course important. But *where* and *under what* circumstances is at least an equally important consideration. Since 1945 much of the emphasis in leadership research has been placed on probing the situational aspects that surround the exercise of leadership. This concern about the situation also represents a rejection of the concept of an individual leadership elite. The basic assumption is that the situational variables rank with those applying to the individual or individuals who happen to be playing the roles, in the leadership process. In the field of city management, for example, the relationship of the individual leader personality to his community is a matter of great importance. The aggressive, self-starting leader may do very well in one community and find himself in considerable trouble in another.

Jobs and Organization

Much of the Ohio State leadership research was directed toward these kinds of questions. It was assumed that differences in leader performance could be analyzed in terms of four variables:

- The cultural environment
- Differences between individuals
- Differences between jobs
- Differences between organizations [17]

Influence of jobs. The particular interest of the Ohio State people was in ascertaining the extent to which jobs and organizations condition leadership behavior. Their general finding: a great deal. One study, which unfortunately was based on a very small sample, is particularly suggestive of the nature of this relation-

[17] Ralph M. Stogdill, Robert J. Wherry, and William E. Jaynes, "A Factorial Study of Administrative Performance," in Stogdill, Carroll L. Shartle, and Associates, *Patterns of Administrative Performance,* Bureau of Business Research, The Ohio State University, Research Monograph No. 81 (1956), p. 42.

ship. It was an attempt to predict how naval officers would behave in new jobs on the basis of (1) their performance on the previous job and (2) performance by their predecessor in the new job. The significant general finding was that the future behavior of a man in a leadership job can be predicted almost as well on the basis of a study of its present occupant's behavior as of the new leader's past performance.[18] This led Shartle to the conclusion that "less than half" of leadership performance "could be ascribed to the man and a little over half to the demands of the particular job." [19] If other studies support these findings, the result should be a substantial redirection in much of our thinking about executive performance. Our search for greater proficiency will force us to probe more deeply those facets in the hierarchical environment which are critical to individual leadership behavior.

It is doubtful that we are going to find any easy or universal answers to these questions. Indeed the idea of situational analysis assumes a certain uniqueness. The Ohio State studies showed, for example, that there were many variations in the broader pattern: (1) when a person changes from one position to another of a similar nature, he tends to perform as before; (2) when the job is different, he tends to follow the previous occupant; (3) a man's leadership pattern is less likely to change when he is transferred to a position of the same status, more likely to change if it is higher status; (4) people who have had executive experience tend to perpetuate previous patterns and those who have not tend to follow their predecessors; [20] and (5) there is a tendency to act as before in interpersonal relations and to adopt the patterns of previous occupants in those forms of work which involve individual effort.[21]

Which is more important in prescribing these leadership patterns: the job or the total organization?

The Ohio State studies provide evidence that the job is probably the more significant of the two. This is occasioned by the fact

---

[18] Ralph M. Stogdill, *et al. A Predictive Study of Administrative Work Patterns*, Bureau of Business Research, The Ohio State University, Research Monograph No. 85 (1956), p. 68.

[19] Shartle, *Executive Performance and Leadership*, p. 94.

[20] *Ibid.*

[21] *Stogdill, et al., op. cit.*, p. 62.

that demands of a job almost inevitably force a leader into certain kinds of activities. It was found, for example, that the nature of his position forces a commanding officer to spend a major share of his time on decision-making and coordination. Such requirements do much to set the framework within which the leader must operate. It means, too, that the number of leadership options available to the individual is thereby reduced.

Influence of organizations. The impact of the organization on leadership behavior is a little more difficult to ascertain. At this level we are dealing with a large social system which has its effects in a number of different ways. Many of these may be considered cultural. The Ohio State studies cast doubt, however, on the degree of significance of these factors. Fleishman examined the differences between military and industrial organizations and came to the conclusion that there were more differences in leadership patterns *within* these types of organizations than *between* them.[22] Jaynes, who found "very few" significant differences among leadership types in various organizations, seemed to sum up the Ohio State view. He said, "These results of this study suggest that variance in performance in the sample studied is more closely related to the type of position which an officer occupies than to the type of organization in which his position is located." [23]

These analyses should be interpreted with some caution. The Ohio State people studied a rather small number of organizations. And there is abundant other evidence, perhaps not as rigorous in its research design, which suggests substantial differences between types of organizations. A study of the Federal Government executive showed that he, in contrast to the business official, "tends to work with a less homogeneous group of executives, administers programs that are generally larger in scope and public significance, lacks privacy in his unofficial as well as official life, and periodically undergoes trial by public debate." [24] A study by

---

[22] Edwin A. Fleishman, "Differences between Military and Industrial Organizations," in Stogdill, Shartle, and Associates, *op. cit.*, pp. 31-38.

[23] William E. Jaynes, "Differences between Jobs and between Organizations," *op. cit.*, p. 30.

[24] Marver H. Bernstein, *The Job of the Federal Executive* (Washington: Brookings Institution, 1958), p. 37.

Fortune of 1700 top executives shows that even within the major categories of business enterprises the lot of the leader is quite different in terms of his background, tenure, work week, and basic decision problems.[25]

Leader-Follower Relationships

While the Ohio State group has concentrated on jobs and organizations as variables which condition the leadership process, other researchers have tended to look particularly at the effect which individual differences may have. Within this framework it is common to establish two broad categories of individuals, (1) leaders and (2) followers. It is pointed out that, in the last analysis, the follower is the one who either accepts or rejects leadership. "The follower's persistent motivations, points of view, frames of reference or attitudes will have a hand in determining what he perceives and how he reacts to it. These psychological factors in the individual follower cannot be ignored in our search for a science of leadership." [26]

In this distinction between leaders and followers, we again see the close relationship between power and leadership. Note that concern about the attitudes and perceptions of followers only becomes important if it is assumed they have the capacity to accept or reject leadership acts. It is apparent, then, that the rationale for this type of research rests in the assumption that power is distributed throughout the organization.

Follower perceptions of the leader. This orientation to the phenomenon of leadership has produced some interesting findings. One is that followers themselves have conflicting notions of what they want in a leader. Most seem to expect the leader to exercise influence and yet are not happy in submitting to it.[27] This problem may differ, however, in terms of the personality orientation of the followers. Sanford found that followers with an authori-

---

[25] "1,700 Top Executives," *Fortune* 60:138 ff., November 1959.

[26] Fillmore H. Sanford, "Leadership Identification and Acceptance," in Harold Guetzkow, editor, *Groups, Leadership, and Men* (Pittsburgh: Carnegie Press, 1951), p. 156.

[27] Shartle, *Executive Performance and Leadership*, p. 119.

tarian personality tend generally to be more comfortable where influence is being exercised. They see leadership in personal, rather than process, terms.[28]

Significance of hierarchical status. One aspect of followership which has appeared in other contexts in this book concerns the effect of hierarchical status on follower acceptance of the leader. We noted earlier that status systems help to signal prescribed relationships in the formal organization. Status must also be regarded as one form of legitimacy which conveys power. The research evidence indicates that people do want roles charted in an organization. That is, they want formalization, a point which has been made previously. A laboratory study at the University of Michigan revealed that subordinates tend to be threatened more by the leader's use of power where the structure offers few guide lines and cues for action. When the leader exercises power in a well-defined situation, the individual is less likely to see the situation as threatening.[29]

But whether hierarchical status is a guidepost which the follower is inclined to accept remains a question. Research at Ohio State seems to indicate that organization morale is highest when the organization structure (which would certainly seem to involve hierarchical status) is perceived most accurately. Shartle and Stogdill write that their research suggests "the desirability, not only of informing members regarding the duties they are expected to carry out, but also regarding the identity of the persons whom they are to regard as junior and senior to themselves."[30] On the other hand, a laboratory study at the University of Michi-

---

[28] Sanford, *op. cit.*, pp. 162 ff.

[29] Arthur R. Cohen, "Situational Structure, Self Esteem, and Threat-Oriented Reactions to Power," in Dorwin Cartwright, editor, *Studies in Social Power* (Ann Arbor: The University of Michigan, 1959), pp. 35-52. Other studies in organization behavior support these findings; see A. L. Comrey, J. M. Pfiffner, and W. S. High, *Factors Influencing Organization Effectiveness: A Final Report* (Los Angeles: University of Southern California Bookstore, 1954, mimeographed).

[30] Carroll L. Shartle and Ralph M. Stogdill, *Studies in Naval Leadership: Methods, Results, and Applications: Final Technical Report* (Columbus: Ohio State University Research Foundation, 1953, mimeographed), p. 31. See also Ellis L. Scott, *Leadership and Perceptions of Organization,* Bureau of Business Research, The Ohio State University, Research Monograph No. 82 (1956). Scott notes that the breaking of the chain of command may often be the beginning step in the development of informal organization (p. 110).

gan did not show hierarchical status to be a significant factor in inducing acceptance of the leader on the part of the subordinates.[31]

Functional experts and followership. Studies in followership also tend to throw some light on another perennial problem of organization, the functional expert. Our pragmatic experience tells us that the technical people have great influence because of their knowledge. Guilford has noted that information, particularly that which is specialized and technical, may be about as close as we can get to a universal trait of leadership. He says the leader "can lead at least as long as his superior knowledge is of use to the group." [32] The research in followership tends to support this view.[33] These findings add further support to the idea of a leadership structure. They also suggest that the emergence of staff people into positions of dominance in many organizations may have a more deep-rooted foundation than many had supposed. Further, it is possible that the exercise of this technical influence may operate in our increasingly complex organizations to curtail drastically the power available to the top leader.

Summary of Situational Forces

Tannenbaum and Schmidt have summarized much of this situational philosophy in explaining how to choose a leadership pattern. They suggest that there are three types of forces which are significant to the executive in making his choice.[34] These are:

- Forces in the manager himself
- Forces in the subordinates
- Forces in the situation

The *forces in the manager* involve his (1) value system, that is, the extent to which he thinks individuals should have a share in

[31] John R. P. French, Jr., and Richard Snyder, "Leadership and Interpersonal Power," in Cartwright, *op. cit.,* pp. 118-149.

[32] Guilford, *Personality,* p. 471.

[33] A rather elaborate field study at the University of Michigan confirmed the hypothesis that "The effectiveness of an influence attempt by the leader (or member) increases with increasing perception that he is an expert in the area of the influence attempt." French and Snyder, *op. cit.,* p. 148.

[34] Robert Tannenbaum and Warren H. Schmidt, "How to Choose a Leadership Pattern," *Harvard Business Review* 36:98 ff., March-April 1958.

the decisions which affect them; (2) confidence in his subordinates; (3) own leadership inclinations, that is, under what circumstances he feels most comfortable; and (4) feelings of security in uncertain situations.

The *forces in the subordinates* include (1) strength of needs for independence; (2) readiness to assume responsibility for decision-making; (3) tolerance for ambiguity; (4) interest in a problem and feeling of its importance; (5) degree of identification with the goals of an organization; (6) knowledge and experience; and (7) expectations that they should share in decision-making.

The *forces in the situation* include (1) type of organization, which involves cultural facets, size of working units, geographical distribution, and the degree of inter- and intra-organizational security required to attain goals; (2) group effectiveness; (3) problem itself, particularly the extent of its complexity; and (4) amount of time available to make a decision.

IV · LEADERSHIP STYLES AND ORGANIZATION

Leadership style has also been the object of much interest during the "situational" studies of the period since World War II. Efforts have been made to determine the extent to which the *way* a person leads affects the performance of the organization or group. As we might expect, the assumption of researchers has been that people perform best when they consider themselves full participants. This assumption, of course, has deep roots in social psychology. As one writer has put it, "The behavior of all persons seems to be influenced by an all-pervasive desire for ego-recognition, that is, for a sense of personal worth—a sense of importance. . . . This results in a powerful drive to be regarded as important, that *my* being here now and doing what *I* am doing makes a significant difference which others important to me clearly recognize and communicate to me. Fundamentally, each of us wants strongly to feel that we count." [35]

[35] Rensis Likert, "Motivational Dimensions of Administration," in Robert Walker, editor, *America's Manpower Crisis* (Chicago: Public Administration Service, 1952), pp. 110-11.

Authoritarian-Democratic Leadership Styles

Pioneering work at Iowa. Doubtless the Hawthorne studies and the writings of the Mayo group did much to build support for the managerial significance of this theory. However it was a series of laboratory studies at the University of Iowa in the late 'thirties that provided a dramatic and comprehensible way of thinking about leadership style. Three leadership types were experimentally created: (1) authoritarian; (2) democratic; and (3) laissez-faire. Main emphasis, however, has been placed on the two "opposites," the authoritarian and the democratic. The authoritarian leader has been variously described as directive, production-centered, nomothetic. The democratic leader has also been called participatory, employee-centered, and idiographic.

In the Iowa studies, which involved the observation of a small group of children, traditional notions about the leadership pattern were shaken rather violently. It was found that (1) democracy can be efficient, especially in terms of promoting originality and motivation; (2) autocracy can create much hostility and aggression, especially toward scapegoat members; (3) autocracy can create discontent that does not appear on the surface; (4) there is more dependence and less individuality in autocracy; and (5) there is more group-mindedness and more friendliness in a democracy.[36] It is curious that this research, in addition to triggering many other studies based on the same general model, was also picked up by the managerial practitioners. It became a central theme of the "human relations" movement which flourished in the decade after World War II. This application to the leadership processes of large organization was made in spite of the fact that the evidence

[36] These studies are classics in the literature of social psychology and education. They are summarized in a number of books. The summary above is from Ralph White and Ronald Lippitt, "Leader Behavior and Member Reaction in Three 'Social Climates'" in Dorwin Cartwright and Alvin Zander, *Group Dynamics Research and Theory* (Evanston, Ill.: Row, Peterson and Company, 1953), pp. 585-611. Another good source is Ronald Lippitt and Ralph White, "An Experimental Study of Leadership and Group Life," in T. M. Newcomb and E. L. Hartley, editors, *Readings in Social Psychology* (New York: Henry Holt and Company, 1947). Any text in social psychology will also provide a description.

came from the observation of a few children in a laboratory situation in a midwestern college town.

Michigan studies. In general the research done since that time has tended to support the basic findings of the Iowa group. This is particularly to be noted in the work of the Institute of Social Research at the University of Michigan, which undoubtedly did more research on organization and group behavior in the decade of the 'fifties than any other institution. A major attempt was made, through survey research, to discover whether the observations of the small group applied also in the large organizational situation.

What has emerged is a picture not greatly different from the authoritarian-democratic model. Analysis of a number of large organizations, including an insurance company, a railroad, and a utility, revealed that the "best" pattern of supervisory leadership is employee-centered and general in nature.[37] The leader is concerned with employee welfare first and production second. He engages in a general rather than a close surveillance of his subordinates. There are many other studies which might be reported; but most of these validate the work already noted or examine nuances within these broader categories. The basic point is that in research and in practice, we now talk of two leadership styles: the democratic and the authoritarian. And most of the research has seemed to support the desirability of moving toward the democratic type.

Relationship of Leader Style to Hierarchy

How does this choice of patterns bear upon the more general problem of organization?

Basic conflict. We must remember that the job-task hierarchy

[37] As with the Iowa studies, the Michigan work has been reported in a great many places. A good summary is Robert L. Kahn and Daniel Katz, "Leadership Practices in Relation to Productivity and Morale," in Cartwright and Zander, *op. cit.*, pp. 61-628. See also Likert, *op. cit.*, 89-117. A recent Michigan study based on three leader styles as models is reported in Howard Baumgartel, "Leadership Style as a Variable in Research Administration," *Administrative Science Quarterly* 2:334-60, December 1957. Baumgartel found that democratic leadership was associated with the highest scores on a number of different measures of the motivations and attitudes of the scientists in eighteen laboratories.

is essentially a command concept. Its pyramidal form rests heavily on legality and formal authority. And though we may recognize that this pattern is amended in many ways, it is far from abrogated. The question, then, is whether a democratic, individual-centered leadership pattern can be integrated into organization forms which are basically authoritarian. The influence exercised in many management hierarchies does not derive necessarily from its participants. They represent only one interest group. Property owners, consumers, government, and perhaps even the public at large are others. Whether it be called leadership or headship, the fact is that the sources of control do not rest primarily with the employees. In such cases the executive's primary task may be to serve as intermediary *between* groups, rather than recognizing the employees as the sovereign body.

Thus leadership style does have a great deal to do with organization form. Democratic leadership seems to make a great deal of sense where ultimate power rests with the participants, as is the case in our political jurisdictions, in labor unions, and in many smaller voluntary groups. The possibilities of its application are considerably lessened as we move into situations where power is not so neatly lodged in the participant group, as is the case with employees of a business or of a government agency. It also seems apparent that traditional elements of hierarchy, such as unity of command, collide rather markedly with the group-centered philosophy.[38]

Return to middle ground. There is evidence that we are returning to some kind of middle ground on these matters. Apparently no one has the intention of reverting to the pre-Hawthorne "mechanical man." On the other hand, the wholesale commitment to the democratic, employee-centered leadership philosophy has lessened. This new ground has been termed "reality-oriented" leadership.[39] The emphasis on power is one aspect of this new direction. The findings on formalization are another.

---

[38] Chris Argyris, *Personality and Organization* (New York: Harper and Brothers, 1957); see particularly Chapter VII, in which Argyris emphasizes the conflict between the participatory leadership pattern and the traditional doctrines of hierarchy.

[39] *Ibid.*, pp. 205 ff.

In addition some research did emerge during the decade of the 'fifties which contradicted the generalizations of the Iowa group. Fleishman, Harris, and Burtt found evidence that directive foremen were more proficient than the considerate ones and that grievances were not appreciably higher.[40] In addition, later studies at Michigan did not prove that employee-centered behavior necessarily increases productivity. It was found that "if a leader abdicates his interest in and responsibility for production it has an adverse effect on both productivity and morale. 'Soft' leadership, over-emphasis upon consideration, is not conducive to high morale. A moderate amount of emphasis on production is required to avoid both low production and low morale. . . ."[41]

Finally, we should not forget that leaders in a hierarchy are typically confronted with several sets of demands and expectations from a number of different directions. There is a conflict within the role itself. The kind of leadership which can initiate ideas and move a group toward its goals may not be the kind which is well liked and holds a group together. The leader is the morale builder on the one hand and the policy mover on the other. It has even been suggested that groups need two leaders, in part because it is hard to find such a combination in one person and in part because leaders tend to do those things which are popular and morale builders in preference to those which may offend in moving the group toward its goal.

Not only are there built-in conflicts in the leadership role, the expectations of a leader's superior tend to be quite different from those of the subordinate and of the peer. As a result the leader who is considered highly effective by his superior may receive little support or affection from his subordinate.[42] In the production units of one factory, it was found that the subordinates liked supervisors who were considerate; superiors liked supervisors who

---

[40] E. A. Fleishman, Edwin F. Harris, and Harold E. Burtt, *Leadership and Supervision in Industry,* Bureau of Educational Research, The Ohio State University, Research Monograph No. 33 (1955).

[41] Stanley E. Seashore, "Administrative Leadership and Organizational Effectiveness," in Rensis Likert and Samuel P. Hayes, Jr., editors, *Some Applications of Behavioural Research* (Paris: United Nations Educational, Scientific and Cultural Organization, 1957), p. 59.

[42] Scott, *Leadership and Perceptions of Organization,* p. 65.

emphasized formal responsibilities in the organization.[43] Thus leadership style and behavior are closely tied to the goals of the organization and the people within it. In later chapters, we shall see how this problem of the individual and the organization conditions leadership and many other aspects of organization life.

V • SUMMARY

We inevitably come back to the basic point that the essential ingredient in the organization is the individual. This is most strikingly seen in the effect which the individual leader may have on an organization. The significance of individual leaders was particularly emphasized by our military commanders during World War II. A change in the commanding general and 16 other officers in a 16,000-man division completely transformed the organization into a highly effective fighting unit.

Though we can find many dramatic instances where the one leader has made the difference, we still know very little about the conditions of such occurrences. For example, rather exhaustive studies have not revealed a set of leadership traits which are broadly applicable. In one instance, the successful leader may be tall, in the next short. One leader may have a tremendous command of language, as Churchill did; another may be incapable of writing.

Research so far has demonstrated that the leadership phenomenon is a great deal more complex than simply looking at the individual personality at the top of a hierarchy. In the first place, it may be that the person in the top position is not actually the leader. Leadership conveys the idea of ability to influence others; and this ability may exist elsewhere in the organization than at the very top. More probably leadership is diffused, with many persons contributing to the total leadership of the organization. This emphasis on leadership structure is far removed from more traditional notions of the "great man" as leader.

Secondly, we must realize that the personality systems of the

---

[43] Fleishman, Harris, and Burtt, *op. cit.*, pp. 95 ff.

followers are also involved. Their motivations and expectations affect greatly the way in which a leader may be permitted to lead. As Shartle emphasized, a leadership act "is one which results in others acting or responding in a shared direction. Leadership is therefore judged in terms of what *others* do."

Finally, there is the situation, which is a general concept encompassing all other factors in the total setting. It most certainly involves the leadership job, the organization in which the job is located, and the problem calling for leadership action. The Ohio State studies reveal that the demands of the job are particularly important in specifying leadership behavior. Indeed it has been hypothesized that the requirements of a particular leadership job may be the most important determinant of such behavior.

The influence of the organization as a whole on leadership is not so clear. Some studies reveal that differences in leadership *within* organizations are greater than *between* them. On the other hand it does seem apparent that leaders perform very much in terms of the climate in which they find themselves. One study showed that supervisors tend to be considerate when their superiors are considerate with them. A study of federal executives suggested marked differences between their behavior patterns and those of business managers.

Leadership style has been another focus of research interest in the last two decades. Here two basic models have emerged: the authoritarian and the democratic. Much of the research has tended to support the democratic leader pattern, which is obviously in accord with our basic value system. However, in more recent years we have become increasingly uneasy with the sharp separation of these two styles. It is questionable, for example, whether the totally democratic approach can be made to fit our well-established hierarchical form of organization. It also seems apparent from later research that too much employee-centeredness can result in low production *and* low morale. We are therefore moving toward a middle ground, sometimes called "reality-oriented" leadership.

Part Four

TWO MODERN MODELS OF ORGANIZATION

TWENTY

The Fusion Process

What to Look for in This Chapter . . .

Fusion Process theory recognizes the existence of separate goal needs of individuals and of the organization

Fusion Process theory recognizes that organization
- —is a dynamic activity
- —includes formal and informal behavior
- —is an open system

Three processes are described:
- socializing: activities contributing to organization goals
- personalizing: activities contributing to individual actualization
- fusion: simultaneous operation of personalizing and socializing

Fusion Process exemplified by Argyris' study of a bank

In the forefront of the effort to develop a new theoretical framework of organization based upon empirical research and logical analysis have been two individuals: (1) E. Wight Bakke, who has been joined at the Yale University Labor and Management Center by Chris Argyris; and (2) Herbert Simon, who for the past several years has been directing research efforts from his position as professor at the Graduate School of Industrial Administration at Carnegie Institute of Technology.

Although Bakke and Simon are not the only ones who have made significant contributions to the metamorphosis in organization theory, they deserve our particular attention because of rather distinctive efforts to engage in organization model-building. In other words, they have moved beyond the destructive phase of tearing down many of our older and dearly held dogmas; they have ventured forth in a positive attempt to build a new base for organization theory. From their work, therefore, we can develop a more concrete picture of the changes that are taking place in this field. Fortunately both Bakke, aided notably by Argyris, and Simon, aided by Guetzkow and March, have undertaken enough research oriented to their theoretical framework to provide this opportunity.

The approaches of the Yale and Carnegie Tech groups are somewhat different, though they are both solidly planted in the behavioral sciences.

(1) The *Yale* group appears to have a strong social-psychological orientation. The concern is primarily with the processes by which the individual and the organization *adapt* to the needs of each other.

(2) The *Carnegie Tech* group has seemed to concentrate on those intellective processes which tend particularly to lie at the heart of large-scale organizations: decision, power, and communication. As a matter of fact, Simon has rather clearly indicated that he considers this level of analysis to require significantly different conceptual properties than primary group theory, upon which the social psychologist has tended to concentrate.[1]

---

[1] ". . . the level of primary group theory must pay much more attention to the personal values that are emergent from the process of group interaction itself, the acculturalization of individuals to the group, and the particular forms of cohesion that rise out of face-to-face interaction and individual sensitivity to group approach." Herbert Simon, "Comments on the Theory of Organization," *American Political Science Review* 46:1139, December 1952.

I • BASIC IDEAS

The *Fusion Process* with which the Yale group has become identified has been developed over a period of more than 20 years of study in many types of organizations, such as a department of a hardware factory, a business machines factory, a telephone company, a steel mill, two local unions, a commercial bank, an educational institution, a research organization, a bank, and a hospital. The primary goal has been the creation of an integrated theory of human behavior that would cut widely across all forms of social organization and would provide a framework for "interpreting, understanding, predicting, and regulating behavior." [2]

In the Yale approach the two essential orienting points are:

- The *Organization,* and particularly the Social Organization;
- The *Individual.*

> The first problem in all organizational life is how to take an aggregate of varied individual people, with varied capacities and predispositions and get them involved in cooperative activity which adds up to success for the organization and satisfaction for the individuals concerned. In short, the problem is to integrate the individual participants with the organization.
>
> Our first job is to get clearly in mind the essential characteristics of the "things" we are trying to integrate. These things are basically (a) the organization, and (b) the individual. . . .[3]

The Organization

The principal features of the social organization are:

(1) An aggregate of people,

[2] E. Wight Bakke and Chris Argyris, *Organization Structure and Dynamics* (New Haven: Labor and Management Center, Yale University, 1954), p. 1. There are a number of statements on the Fusion Process, the more recent being E. Wight Bakke, *Bonds of Organization* (New York: Harper and Brothers, 1950); E. Wight Bakke, *Organization and the Individual* (New Haven: Labor and Management Center, Yale University, 1952); and E. Wight Bakke, *The Fusion Process* (New Haven: Labor and Management Center, Yale University, 1953). The latter publication contains a chapter on research design for field studies of the fusion process. The cited document actually is a separate print of the Yale statement of program objectives and activity in Chris Argyris, *The Present State of Research in Human Relations in Industry* (New Haven: Labor and Management Center, Yale University, 1954).

[3] Bakke and Argyris, *op. cit.*, p. 4.

(2) Associating and solving problems together over time in a state of interdependency,
(3) utilizing particular basic human, material, identical, and natural resources,
(4) for the achievement of both individual and collective consequences (definable by reference to the characteristic dynamic tendencies toward personal, group, and organizational survival and actualization),
(5) through patterned behavior which may be defined as:
   (a) a system of interdependent essential processes supported by specifications, codes, and other reinforcements (labeled bonds of organization), or
   (b) a system of reciprocal roles, supported by specifications, codes, and other reinforcements,
(6) in ways possessing an individuality as revealed and supported by an organization charter,
(7) within a natural and social environment presenting them both with opportunities for, and with obstacles to, the maintenance of the organization and the achievement of its intended consequence and those of its participants.

Such a statement of properties clearly seeks to comprehend *all types* of organizations—economic, political, social, military, and so forth. Other features to be noted in this conceptualization of organization are: (1) the substance of organization is dynamic activity or behavior; (2) both formal and informal behavior are involved; and (3) the organization system is seen as *open,* rather than closed, with stimuli coming from without as well as within.

> Organization is a very human activity; it consists of people interacting with each other, but as modified and influenced by nature, material things, and, almost all ideas. The people in an organization have needs to fulfill and goals to achieve which are to a considerable extent personal in nature, and sometimes in conflict with organizational goals. Yet to achieve many, perhaps most, of these personal goals they must collaborate with other people, and the moment they do so a first step has been taken toward the creation of an organization.[4]

[4] *Ibid.,* p. 9.

The Individual

Certain propositions have also been developed about the nature of the individual, who, like the organization, is seen as an aggregate of parts. It has been reported that this conceptualization of the individual has been developed from a survey of theoretical and empirical research in personality theory, clinical psychology, and psychiatry by Argyris, and from Bakke's interviews since 1931 with around 10,000 persons as to their standards of successful living.

1. The *individual has parts,* which may be classified as:
   (a) Biological equipment with its inherent capacities,
   (b) Impulses to activation.
   (c) Abilities of a physiological, psychological, and social sort.
   (d) Predispositions, such as reflexes, habits, attitudes, prejudices, convictions, sentiments, intentions.
2. The basic action tendency of this total personality system is *self-actualization* (self-maintenance, development, expression, and realization).
3. The more specific manifestations of this self-actualization process develop *within a particular culture.*
4. Self-actualization is obtained through *goal-directed* behavior.

The Fusion Process

These statements of the properties of (1) the organization and (2) the individual now lead to the basic idea of the *fusion model.* Note first, however, that the organization is made up of individuals, and both of these elements are viewed in highly dynamic terms. They are both seeking to express themselves, to accomplish certain goals. There must, then, be *two* behavior processes operative in the situation:

- That which is contributing toward the organization's accomplishment of its goals, the *socializing* process, and
- that which is allowing the individual to actualize himself through the agency of the organization, the *personalizing* process.

> The socializing process is defined as that by which individuals are made into agents of the formal organization and/or the informal group. The process by which the individual is made into an agent of the formal organization is called the *formal* socializing process; that by which he is made into an agent of the informal group is called the *informal* socializing process.
>
> The *personalizing* process is defined as that by which the individual actualizes himself and by which aspects of the organization *and* informal group are made into agencies for the individual.[5]

With both the socializing and personalizing processes operating *simultaneously* in the organization, and both equally important, it follows that much depends on the extent to which these processes are congruent and compatible. They fuse in the *role* of the individual who must be the agent through which organization objectives are accomplished and by which his own needs are met, both formally and informally. If an individual gains satisfaction from work but gives nothing to the organization, the *socializing* requirements are not being met. If the organization demands are being met but there is no satisfaction for the worker, the *personalizing* dimension is being sacrificed. Only when personalizing *and* socializing demands are simultaneously being actualized, can we say that *fusion* is really occurring. Then the *Fusion Process* is operative.

The fusion process therefore consists of the simultaneous operation of the socializing and personalizing processes. (Chart 20-1.) It is composed of individuals, formal organizations, and informal groups engaged in their customary and characteristic activities interacting to achieve a balance or equilibrium, which Bakke and Argyris have chosen to call *fusion.* This simultaneous operation develops for the individual a *role* which constitutes a fusion of his formal and informal functions and conduct. A role in turn can be broken down into units of behavior called *activities,* which make up fusions of formal and informal tasks or acts. The positional term applied to these formal and informal fusions and the standing is *status.*

The following statement summarizes the results of the fusion process:

---

[5] Bakke and Argyris, *Organization Structure and Dynamics,* pp. 17 ff.

- The fusion of *Formal Tasks, Informal Tasks,* and *Acts* = Activities.
- The fusion of *Formal Function, Informal Function,* and *Conduct* = Role.
- The fusion of *Formal Position, Informal Position* and *Standing* = Status.

Reference to Chapter 3, particularly the section on groups, suggests the extent to which the Yale group has developed the fusion model from the conceptual statements of the social psychologists. The work of Kurt Lewin, cited in that chapter, seems particularly related to the fusion model.

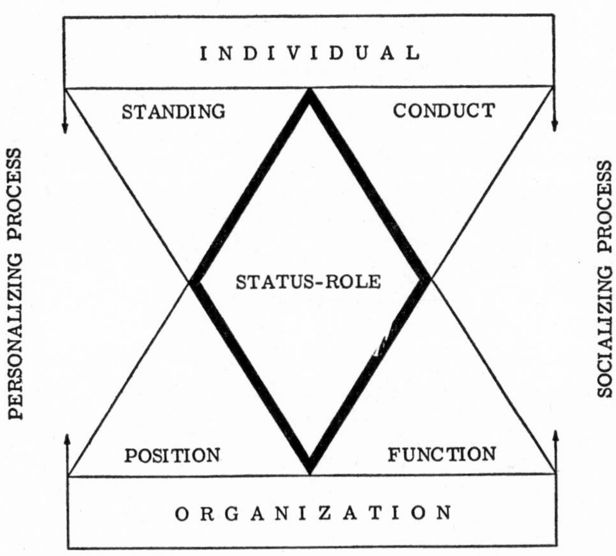

CHART 20-1. *The fusion process* (SOURCE: Bakke, *The Fusion Process,* Yale Labor and Management Center, 1953, p. 20).

II • AN EMPIRICAL USE OF THE FUSION MODEL

After approximately a decade of developing a conceptual model of the organization and the individual out of a great variety of research projects, the Yale Labor Management Center in 1953 published its effort to test its theory of the fusion process. Undertaken by Professor Argyris, the study concerned the operation of a bank and has been termed by Director Bakke "a landmark in the program of studies at the Yale Center."[6] Perhaps its greatest significance from our point of view is its contribution as a systematic way of looking at an organization. Obviously it is much too early to make any estimate of the validity or lack of validity of the propositions which accompany the fusion model.

The bank concerned was one of the oldest and largest in the city and had a total employment of about 200 in its main office. In the course of his research Argyris concentrated primarily on the trust department, the tellers, the auditors, and the bookkeepers. He interviewed approximately 80 per cent of all those working in the main office, and in some of the smaller departments he quizzed 100 per cent of the employees. From each of the interviews Argyris sought (1) to get a picture of the organization's "steady state," that is the processes by which effort was coordinated and work accomplished; and (2) to compute a fusion score for each of the employees.

From what was said previously, this attempt to compute a fusion score depends on an analysis of the personalizing and socializing processes. Argyris summarizes the approach in this fashion:

1. Personality and organization are discrete organized systems.
2. Each desires to actualize itself.
3. The activities by which the personality attempts to actualize itself through its individual agents are brought together for study and labeled the *personalizing process*.
4. The activities by which the organization attempts to actualize itself through its individual agents are brought together for study and labeled the *socializing process*.
5. Two general hypotheses were defined regarding these two processes:
   (a) The greater the expression of the personalizing process, the the greater the fusion of the individual with the organization.
   (b) The greater the expression of the socializing process, the greater the fusion of the organization with the individual.
6. The "thing" being expressed is:
   (a) In the case of the personalizing process, a set of pre-dispositions (Personality Factors) towards a certain type of individual behavior.

[6] Chris Argyris, *Organization of a Bank* (New Haven: Labor and Management Center, Yale University, 1954). The quotation above is from the Foreword by E. Wight Bakke, p. ii.

(b) In the case of the socializing process, a set of activities (Organizational Factors) considered essential to the operation of the organization.

7. A scale with ordinal properties is postulated to describe the degree of expression of the personalizing and socializing process. The scale has four "units." They are:
   0. No expression whatsoever.
   1. Minimal expression
   2. Adequate expression
   3. Maximum expression
8. The measurement of the degree of expression is judged:
   (a) In the case of personality factors from the point of view of the individual.
   (b) In the case of organizational factors from the point of view of the organization (formal and informal).[7]

Thus two scales are established, one measuring the extent to which the personality is expressed through the organization and the other the degree to which the organization fulfills its needs through the behavior of its employees. It is to be noted, too, that the personalizing score must be obtained from the individual, the socializing score from the point of view of the organization.

What is to be gained from a computation of fusion scores? Such a question can obviously best be answered after a report of Argyris' findings. Here it may simply be observed that its dominant contribution seems to be in the area of personnel selection and placement. It suggests a rather specific means of getting beyond the formal task statements and thus seeing the demands of the organization in broader compass. It then places these requirements against the stated personality needs of the individuals in the organization. If the individual is asked to perform in a role in which he is insecure and dissatisfied, it is quite apparent that he will do a minimal job and will leave as quickly as possible. The study of the bank emphasizes the need for such congruency and that the natural process of selection facilitates this adjustment.

Personality Factors

The personality factors upon which the personalizing process score was based were:

---

[7] *Ibid.*, pp. 189-90.

Passive. The predisposition to have others initiate action and not to initiate action for others.

Recluse. The predisposition to avoid having others initiate action as well as to avoid initiating action for others. The person desires to do his work and be left alone.

Self-Responsible. The predisposition to be his own boss, that is, to substitute his own authority, reward and penalty, and perpetuation acts for similar formal tasks.

Variety-Seeking. The predisposition to experience many and different work activities.

Mathematically minded. The predisposition continually to work with mathematical details.

Community Wage Conscious. The predisposition to accept as just, only wage rewards that are comparable to, or better than, those given in the community for similar work.

Security Conscious. The predisposition to seek the experience of stability, predictability and surety in one's life.

Directive. The predisposition to initiate action for others.

Sociable. The predisposition to interact and communicate with others in such a way as to minimize overt hostility and maximize overt friendliness.

Upward Mobile. The predisposition to advance in the hierarchy of the organization.

Challenge Rejecting. The predisposition to reject any work which requires anything but a minimal amount of physical and psychical energy.

Challenge Accepting. The predisposition to accept work which represents a challenge to the person's abilities.

Industrious. The predisposition to work hard, to keep busy during the work day.

Short Hour-Minded. The predisposition to work less hours than is the case at the present.

Reconciled. The predisposition to remain at the present job with no aspiration for advancement in terms of new jobs.

Mechanical-Minded. The predisposition to work with machines.

Detail-Minded. The predisposition to work with minute, microscopic items.[8]

Organizational Factors

The organizational factors upon which the socializing process score was based were:

Passive Work. Participants are required primarily to receive initia-

[8] Argyris, *Organization of a Bank,* pp. 198-201.

tion of action from others rather than initiate action for others.

Isolated Work. Participants are required to have minimal (or almost) no interaction with others.

Self-Guided Work. Participants are required to be their own bosses, that is, to substitute their own authority, reward and penalty, and perpetuation acts for any missing or non-operative comparable tasks.

Varied Work. Participants are required to work primarily with mathematical details.

Low-Wage Work. Participants are required to work for wages that are less than those given in the community for similar work.

Security. Participants are required to experience stability, and surety in their work, rather than wages that are equal to or better than those paid for similar work in the community.

Directive Work. Participants are required to direct the activities of other participants.

Diplomatic Employee Work. Participants are required to interact and communicate with other participants in such a way as to minimize overt hostility and maximize overt friendliness.

Increasingly Responsible Work. Participants are required to better themselves and to advance in the hierarchy of the organization.

Continuous Work. Participants are required to keep busy during the work day.

Free Time Advantage Work. Participants are required to experience the numerous holidays and the short hours (compared to industry) rather than wages that are equal or better than those paid for similar work in the community.

Blind Alley Work. Participants are required to remain at their present jobs and not to aspire for advancement.

Multi-Detailed Work. Participants are required to work primarily with minute, microscopic items.

Diplomatic Customer Work. Participants are required to be friendly and tactful with customer contacts.

Accurate Work. Participants are required to perform work with minimal inaccuracy. Accuracy of work, in this case, is valued over quality of work.

Hostility Accepting Work. Participants are required to do work in which it is necessary to accept the hostility of other participants.[9]

Findings

Perhaps the most striking fact about the Argyris research is the extent to which variations in personal needs and organization demands existed among the departments of the bank. In marked

---

[9] *Ibid.*

degree these divergencies were to be seen both in Argyris' observations and interviews and in his computation of fusion scores. Surprising, too, is the extent to which individuals with certain predispositions seemed to move into organizational situations providing opportunities for their expression.

Two of the departments, trust and tellers, seemed most to personify the bank "type." They had close ties to the customer, were generally "followers" in their attitudes, had high socializing scores and reasonably high personalizing scores. They tended to remain in the bank for a long period. Yet there were some important differences even between these two groups. The nature of the trust function requires a considerable amount of self-guided effort and at the same time a considerable exercise of authority by the officers. The same contradiction is to be seen in the personalizing scores. Individuals were attracted to the work by the desire to participate in self-responsible activities; but they were offended by the exercise of authority. Hence the personalizing scores tended to be low for newer employees particularly.

In contrast the tellers were not subject to the same kind of supervision; neither did they have as strong a desire for self-responsibility. Thus they tended to feel less the conflict between organization and individual that characterized the trust department. In general the tellers most completely fitted into the usual stereotype of the bank . . . passive, stable people who placed a high premium on employment security. It is not surprising, therefore, that the tellers tallied the highest fusion scores.

The other two departments, auditing and bookkeeping, were much less typical of our common conception of the bank operation. The auditors, who were in the unenviable position of checking on others, differed less from the "ideal type" than did the bookkeepers. Like the tellers and the trust people, the auditors were in the bank in part because of its security and because they liked a certain amount of isolation in the work situation. The most essential difference was that the organization demanded the auditors to be directive, rather than passive in their work approach. They also had to be able to accept tensions that were not present in the other work situations.

Since there were only three persons in the auditing department, the distribution of fusion scores reveals very little. This fragmentary evidence does suggest, however, that the bank has had somewhat greater difficulty fusing the individual with the organization in this department than in the other two. Socializing scores were high, indicating that the bank's purposes were being served; but two out of the three personalizing scores were relatively low.

It was in the fourth department, bookkeeping, that the contrast with the other units was very sharp. Here the workflow was machine-oriented, a "right type" of bank employee was absent, and security as a basic personal aspiration did not appear. In short the bookkeeping department comprised a group of girls who had very little interest in their work, had been attracted to it by the short hours, and did not expect to stay long. There was about a 50 per cent turnover each year. Here, too, organizational objectives came most into conflict with personal ones. The girls wanted to be self-responsible and they wanted freedom to sing, whistle, visit, and so forth. The demands of bookkeeping operation, however, are highly formal. They do not permit this opportunity for individual discretion. As might be expected under these conditions, the fusion scores in the bookkeeping department were lower than in any of the others. This was true, in terms both of achieving organizational and personal goals.

Thus we see that, through the fusion model, the bank has been revealed to us in considerably different terms than a more casual observation might have suggested. It is seen as a community of highly diverse groups, involving formal and informal interactions, and achieving in varying degrees organizational and personal goals.

III • SUMMARY

Two elements of the fusion model are particularly noteworthy: its emphasis on (a) the *totality* of the organization process and (b) the identification of individual aspirations and goals separable from those of the organization.

As indicated earlier, much of our traditional organization theory and model-building has concentrated only on formal statements of relationships. In the fusion model there is a clear attempt to get beyond this level of analysis, to deal also with the informal. The desirability of such a widening of our perspective was quite plainly seen in the study of the bank. There evidence was presented to indicate (1) that the number of personality factors wanting expression is to some extent a function of formal organization demands, (2) that informal group needs tend to develop most where it is difficult for employees to obtain satisfaction from the formal workflow, and (3) formal organization demands arise in circular fashion from informal activities which are themselves the outgrowth of earlier formal requirements.

A recurring theme of this book has been that the individual does not become less of an individual because he joins an organization. The fusion model attempts to build this premise into its structure. Thus it is assumed that the successful organization is one which meets its own needs and those of the individual. Although this clearly places tremendous demands on the organization, Argyris' study indicates that the problem is eased considerably by the fact that personality types tend to seek the situation automatically which permits expression of their unique needs. Thus the directive types moved into auditing. Further, where people do feel themselves in the right niche, it appears that their service as agents of the organization is improved. The bookkeepers, clearly at odds with organization demands, also tallied the lowest socializing scores. One final point: the organization, composed as it is of subsidiary constellations with differing requirements, has need for as many different personality types. In the bank it appeared the attempt to get the "right type" into the bookkeeping department, where quite a different personality was required, represented a failure to understand the true organization.

If a model can be regarded as mirror of the reality, it can be seen from the foregoing that the fusion model has provided a means of looking at organization quite different from that which has dominated traditional, more formal thinking.

TWENTY-ONE

The Decision

What to Look for in This Chapter . . .

Man as a choosing organism—but not necessarily a rational one

Organization structure as comprised of patterns of behavior which are relatively stable and change slowly

Keys to the decision approach:

- Identification of decision centers
- Identification of channels by which communications are carried

Controllership study—its recommendations disagree with traditional unity of command precept

The significance of the decision as a primary orienting point in organization theory has long been central to the approach and philosophy of Herbert Simon. Like Bakke at Yale, Simon for more than two decades has been pondering these questions and evolving his own formulations. His first important work in this field was undertaken in association with Clarence Ridley, then Executive Director of the International City Managers' Association. These two refined and expanded an earlier effort by Ridley to provide a basis for decision-making in the municipality. Published in 1937, the monograph was entitled *Measuring Municipal Activities*.[1] It was in 1945, however, that Simon's pioneering and perhaps most significant work, *Administrative Behavior,* was published. With the decision as his basic frame of reference, he took to task most of the earlier propositions on organization, labeling them ambiguous and useless. Since *Administrative Behavior,* Simon has concentrated with his colleagues on the sharpening of his basic theory. This has involved considerable research at Carnegie Institute of Technology and has resulted in such publications as *Centralization versus Decentralization* (1954), *Models of Man* (1957), and *Organizations* (1958).

I • SIMON'S BASIC IDEAS

While it is perhaps possible to construe the decision concept in rather narrow, mechanistic terms, this has not at all been the Simon approach. Like the group at Yale, Simon has seen the organization problem in its total social and psychological context. His basic assumption has been that the features of organization structure and function derive from the characteristics of human problem-solving processes and rational human choice.[2] Thus the members of an organization are not to be viewed as mere mechanical instrumentalities. They must be regarded as individuals who have wants, motives, and drives, and are limited in their knowledge and in their capacities to learn and to solve problems. The organization is, in these terms, an extension of individuals making choices and behaving on the basis of their understanding of their environment and their needs.

---

[1] Clarence Ridley and Herbert Simon, *Measuring Municipal Activities* (Chicago: International City Managers' Association, 1937). Many writers have since joined Simon in placing emphasis on the decision. Harold J. Leavitt has recently suggested that this will be the predominant orientation of organization theory in the future: *Managerial Psychology* (Chicago: University of Chicago Press, 1958), p. 301.

[2] James G. March and Herbert A. Simon, *Organizations* (New York: John Wiley and Sons, 1959), p. 169.

The Organization

Human organizations are regarded by Simon as systems of interdependent activity, encompassing at least several primary groups. There are three *levels* of multi-person units: (1) the *smallest* is the primary group; (2) the *largest* is the institution, such as the state, economic system, etc.; and (3) systems *in between* are organizations. In such a definition there is a great deal of ambiguity, as Simon has pointed out. Organizations may exist *within* organizations—"a whole agency, a bureau, or even a section of a large department may be regarded as *an* organization." [3]

In later writings Simon has placed increased emphasis on the human organism. Adaptive behavior, largely in terms of "one thing at a time," is basic to the existence of organization structure. Such structure exists only as patterns of behavior which are relatively stable and change slowly. People do not want to tackle too many problems at once. By necessity they must settle on some habits of conduct. These, then, constitute organization *structure;* and it is in the development of these patterns, which obviously involve decision-making, that attention can be concentrated profitably.

The Decision

In the very first paragraph of *Administrative Behavior,* Simon has indicated how significant the decision is to his system of thinking. He has written that traditional discussions of administration emphasize the action process, getting things done; and so-called principles are laid down to aid in achieving such action. In all such discussion scant attention has been paid to the choice which prefaces all action, to decide what is to be done rather than how to do it.[4]

The first step in building an adequate theory of organization (and hence a model) is the development of an appropriate unit

---

[3] Herbert A. Simon, "Comments on the Theory of Organization," *American Political Science Review* 46:1130, December 1952.

[4] Herbert A. Simon, *Administrative Behavior,* second edition, (New York: The Macmillan Company, 1957), p. 1.

of analysis. That is why Simon has placed so much emphasis on the decision. He has concluded that the analysis of the *role* played by individuals in an organization is not precise enough; similarly a study of acts or actions remains too general. He regards the decision *premise* as a much smaller unit of analysis and therefore more appropriate. Many premises are involved in any specific decision or action and are incorporated in the definition of a single role. "The central notion," he has written, "is that a decision can be regarded as a conclusion drawn (though not in any strict logical sense) from premises; and that influence is exercised by transmitting decisions, which are then taken as premises for subsequent decision."[5]

In this view there is not an expectation that decision-making is necessarily rational. As a matter of fact Simon has appeared to become less sure over the years that even the rationality he assumed in *Administrative Behavior* was appropriate.[6]

The really critical factors in the decision process, then, are (1) the availability of information and (2) the computational capacities available to deal with the information. Man should not be regarded as even "intendedly" rational, as the models of economic man and administrative man suggest. We should substitute the concept of a "choosing" organism of "limited knowledge and ability."[7]

The point of reference that Simon uses to analyze organization behavior is, then, a human organism capable of choosing, problem-solving, and decision-making. But it does not possess infinite powers, it is limited to doing a few things at a time and can deal with only a small part of the information stored in its memory or existing in its environment.[8]

General Comments

How can such an emphasis on decision be applied to a more general model of organization? Note that decision premises arise largely out of information and the ability of the individual to

---

5 Simon, "Comments on the Theory of Organization," p. 1132.

6 "I now feel that . . . I yielded too much ground to the omniscient rationality of economic man." Simon, *Administrative Behavior,* p. xxxv.

7 Herbert A. Simon, "A Behavioral Model of Rational Choice," *Models of Man* (New York: John Wiley and Sons, Inc., 1957), p. 241.

8 March and Simon, *Organizations,* p. 11.

handle that information. Thus the key to this approach to organization is identification (1) of the decision centers, and (2) of the channels by which communications are carried. Put in the words of March and Simon,

> 1. Communication traverses definite channels, either by formal plan or by the gradual development of informal programs.
> 2. Information and stimuli move from sources to points of decision; instructions move from points of decision to points of action; information of results moves from points of decision and control.
> 3. Rational organization design would call for the arrangement of these channels so as to minimize the communication burden.[9]

The manner in which this type of analysis can provide a foundation for the structuring of organization may be seen in the following hypotheses suggested by March and Simon:

- As one moves toward the top of a hierarchy, the possibilities of rationality decline. He must deal with phenomena in grosser and more aggregative form.
- The division of work according to purpose (or subgoals) tends to foster insularity by building in a subgoal bias. Other subgoals and other aspects of the goals of the larger organization tend to be ignored in the decisions of the subunit, even though conflicts may exist.
- Division of work on the basis of process (subprograms rather than subgoals) will be carried furthest in stable environments. It is likely, too, that organizations, in order to permit a greater degree of process specialization, will devise means for increasing stability and predictability of the environment.
- Specialization is most apt to be found when the organization has stability and is not continually adapting to a rapidly changing environment.
- The degree of local autonomy may reflect the precision of coordination. When communication is poorly developed and control from the center made difficult, there is very apt to be a considerable degree of local discretion for the reason that little else is possible.
- The influence structure in an organization is set in large part by its communication system. More precisely, it is suggested

---

[9] Quoted from March and Simon, *Organizations,* pp. 166-67; *numbering added.*

that the "locus of uncertainty absorption" is extremely significant. Thus persons closest to the reality communicate their "facts," which cannot be checked, as a conscious or unconscious means of acquiring and exercising power.

- The greater the communication efficiency of a channel, the greater its usage. Further, channel usage tends to be self-reinforcing. Once the channels have been well established, their pattern will have an important influence on decision-making processes and particularly upon nonprogrammed activity.

It is apparent from these hypotheses that there has been identified in the decision premise a basic unit of analysis which appears applicable to the major questions of organization model-building. We may now turn to an instance where this approach was actually used in the creation of an organization structure.

II • A PRAGMATIC USE OF THE DECISION MODEL

In any large organization the accounting department is a unit having a rather peculiar relationship to the whole. Its function cuts both horizontally and vertically, reaching down to the lowest echelon and yet affecting the most senior of men in the organization. The proper role of this unit in the total structure therefore provides a most interesting test of the decision approach.

Under the sponsorship of the Controllership Foundation, a team led by Simon studied seven large companies with geographically dispersed operations. They did not necessarily represent a cross-section of American business, but they had all approached the problem of organizing the controllership function in different ways. The question which the Carnegie Tech group sought to answer by creating an appropriate model was:

How should a company's accounting department be organized in order that the data it assembles will be of greatest usefulness to the operating executives of the *business* in making decisions and solving problems? [10]

---

[10] The report of this study is found in Herbert A. Simon, Harold Guetzkow, George Kozmetsky, and Gordon Tyndall, *Centralization vs. Decentralization in Organizing the Controller's Department* (New York: Controllership Foundation, Inc., 1954).

In contrast to the more traditional approach of analyzing authority relationships, the Carnegie Tech group took these steps:

- Studies were made of the most important types of decisions taken in the organization; how accounting data might be useful in making these decisions; and at what point in the decision process accounting information could be most usefully injected.

> . . . By observation of the actual decision-making process, specific types of data needs were identified at particular organizational levels —the vice presidential level, the level of the factory manager, and the level of the factory head, for example—each involving quite distinct problems of communication for the accounting department.[11]

- Recommendations were made in terms of the accounting department's responsibility for providing information and exerting influence on these operating decisions.

> . . . Recommendations for organizational change were to be implemented by bringing about changes in the communication patterns—in the patterns of who-talks-to-whom-how-often-about-what, rather than by formal changes in the organization charts.[12]

Types of Information Required by Management

Thus the departure for this study—as might be expected—was the decision which found its premise in greater or lesser degree in accounting information. Several key points in the decision-making hierarchy were identified:

1. The Chief Executive
2. The Company Vice-Presidents for Sales and for Production
3. Division Executives
4. Factory Managers and Regional Sales Managers

The identification of these decision centers led to the further question: what *types* of accounting information are required at these points? Predictably, it was found that the executives at these various levels did *not* require the same types of information. Furthermore, it was discovered that the extent to which the information was used depended in considerable part on the closeness of

---

[11] Simon, *Administrative Behavior,* p. xx.
[12] *Ibid.*

the relationship between the accounting people as information sources and the operating people as consumers. What might be a good organization pattern for the use of certain types of accounting data, then, might be quite inappropriate for other types. *Three* categories of information, each serving a different purpose at a different point in the decision hierarchy, were identified:

- *Communication to provide information on the results of activities: Score-Card.* Here the fundamental question is, "How well am I (*or* is he) doing?" Such a question becomes very important to the factory supervisor who has the basic responsibility for getting the work out.
- *Communication to evoke programs: Attention-Directing.* Here the fundamental question is, "What problems shall I look into?" Data which serve as a score card for a lower level supervisor may very conceivably operate in an attention-directing role for a higher level official. The latter must look for the trouble spots, and be concerned about variations from the norm.
- *Communication to provide data for application of strategies.* Here the fundamental question is, "Which course of action is better?"

This analysis of information categories presents important insights into the organizing process as it affects the accounting function. It makes quite clear that the communications channels which operate *horizontally* must be given as much weight as those which operate vertically. Thus, in terms of "score card" analysis, the important relationship is between the cost analyst and the department head (see Chart 21-1) and is occasioned by the importance of standards at this level. Operating supervisors need to have confidence that standards established are realistic and that environmental factors are considered in their establishment. The same general situation applies with "attention-directing" information, with the basic horizontal contact between the factory manager and the factory accountant (Chart 21-1). As a consequence, the Carnegie Tech group concluded, ". . . for effective attention-directing service, it is essential for the controller's department to develop direct and active channels of communication with

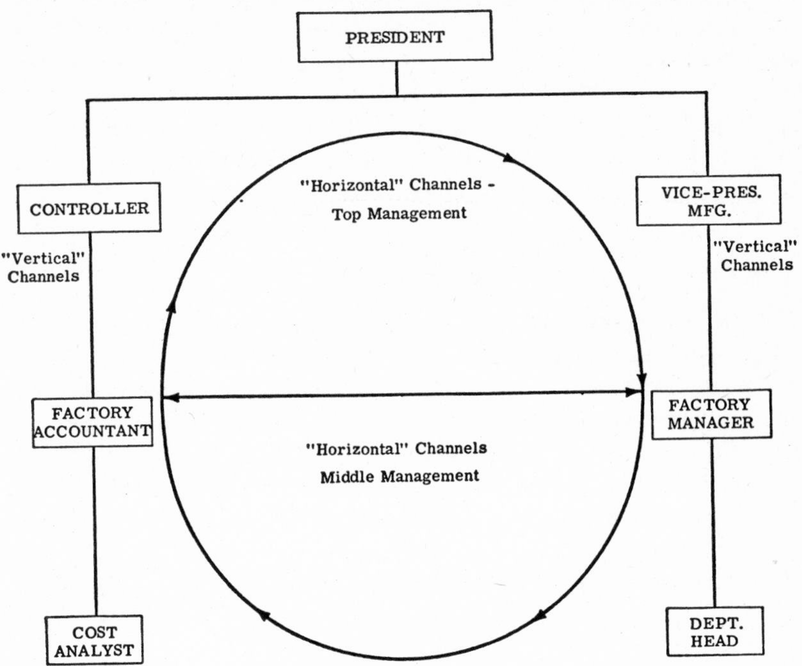

CHART 21-1. *"Horizontal" and "vertical" channels of communication* (SOURCE: Simon *et al., Centralization vs. Decentralization in Organizing the Controller's Department,* p. 48).

the operating executives at those points in the organization where operations are being measured."[13]

While the same horizontal pattern obtained in the case of problem-solving questions, i.e., factory manager to factory accountant and chief executive to company controller, a fundamental difference lies in the fact that not only are regular reports provided but also special studies are made. As a consequence there seems less need to create the same kind of close-working relationship necessary in the score-card and attention-directing areas.

To summarize, the most essential point to note is that there is no such gross product as accounting information. For purposes of

[13] Simon *et al., Centralization vs. Decentralization in Organizing the Controller's Department,* p. 3.

organizational analysis, we must think of a number of categories of data; further, the channels through which such information should appropriately flow depend on its nature and usefulness to the various members of the organization. Put another way, there is no single "right" channel of accounting communication; and hence, a good way of organizing the accounting function involves using different channels for different purposes.

The Functions of the Controller

As a consequence of this analysis of communications, the Carnegie Tech group concluded that there are three major areas of the accounting function, each of which can be separated from the other. These are:

1. *Record-keeping,* which involves bookkeeping and preparation and distribution of periodic accounting reports. In making judgments as to where this mechanical aspect of the accounting function might most appropriately be located, such factors as cost, access to information, promptness in reporting, uniformity of reports, and control from an auditing viewpoint are all considered significant. It is to be noted that no special problems of communication are involved in the record-keeping function; hence it can be approached in rather conventional organization terms.

2. *Current Analysis,* which involves assistance to the operating departments in providing meaningful score-card and attention-directing information. Here proximity to the operating units is the most important locational consideration. Not only must there be be promptness of presentation but also confidence in the reliability and integrity of the data. Easy horizontal communication is therefore essential.

3. *Special Studies for Problem-Solving Purposes,* which involves participation in the use of accounting information to satisfy unique management requirements and to suggest strategies. Again the factor of horizontal communication is a most significant element. These special studies cut across departments and have to be attacked at the company-wide, or at least factory-wide, level.

Juxtaposing communications and functions, a rough model for accounting organization now begins to emerge. It can be based on the following assumptions:

- Communications and decision premises are largely irrelevant to organization arrangements for the *record-keeping* function.
- Closeness to operating units is a basic requirement in organizing for the *current analysis* function; thus decentralization would normally be indicated.
- An opportunity to interrelate with other major segments of the organization on a company-wide or factory-wide basis is primary in organizing for the *problem-solving, special study* function; thus centralization would normally be indicated.

The Company-Wide Controller's Organization

In these few pages, it is obviously impossible to describe in detail all the steps through which the Carnegie Tech group went in arriving at certain conclusions about the most appropriate organization of a controller's department. Therefore we will look only at two structural models which have arisen from this analysis, one at the company-wide level and the other at the factory level.

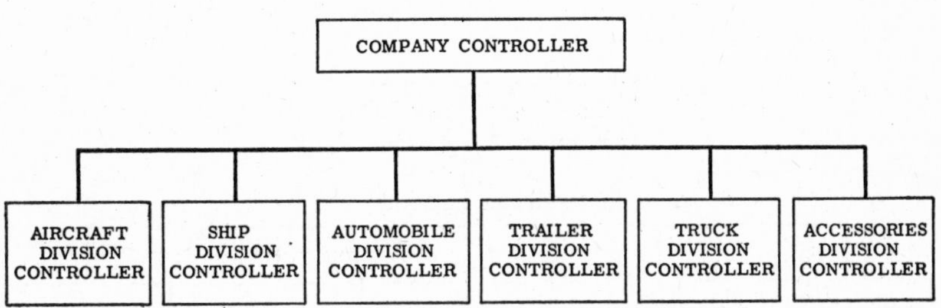

CHART 21-2. *Company-wide accounting organized on "divisional" basis.*

At the company level two main alternatives for organizing the controllership functions are (a) "divisional" and (b) "functional." Under a *divisional* plan, the principal subordinates of the company controller are divisional controllers, each responsible for a complete system of sales, manufacturing, and general accounting for some one division of the operations (Chart 21-2). Obviously, if such divisions or bureaus do not exist or if the accounting function

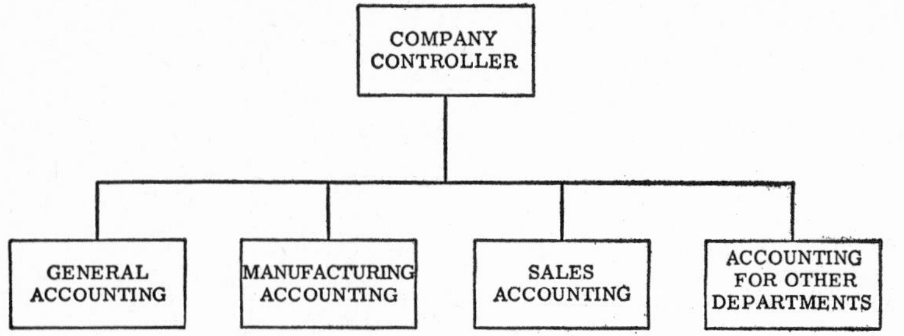

CHART 21-3. *Company-wide accounting organized on "functional" basis—paralleling as close as possible operating departments.*

has not been decentralized to that level, such an approach would not be possible.

The *functional* basis of organization presents two alternatives:

(a) A classification of functions that parallels, as far as possible, the operating departments (see Chart 21-3).

(b) A classification of functions which would be based on the Carnegie Tech group's communication analysis, separating record-keeping, attention-directing services and problem-solving services (see Chart 21-4).

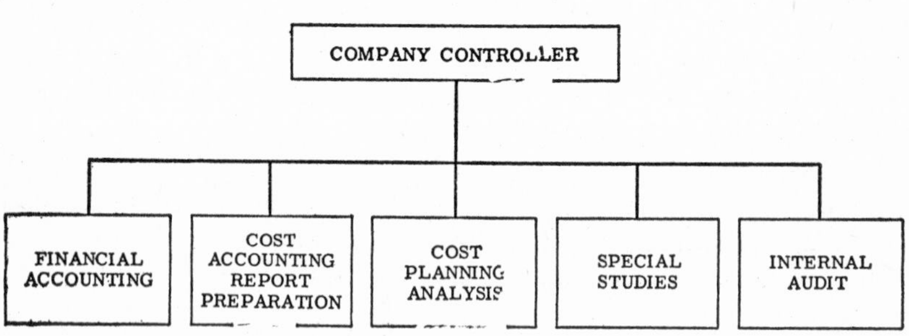

CHART 21-4. *Company-wide accounting organized on "functional" basis—using communications analysis.*

The organization model which came out of a weighing of these alternatives was "not particularly revolutionary," but it does reveal quite clearly the effects of the analysis of communications (see Chart 21-5). It is really an amalgamation of both functional ap-

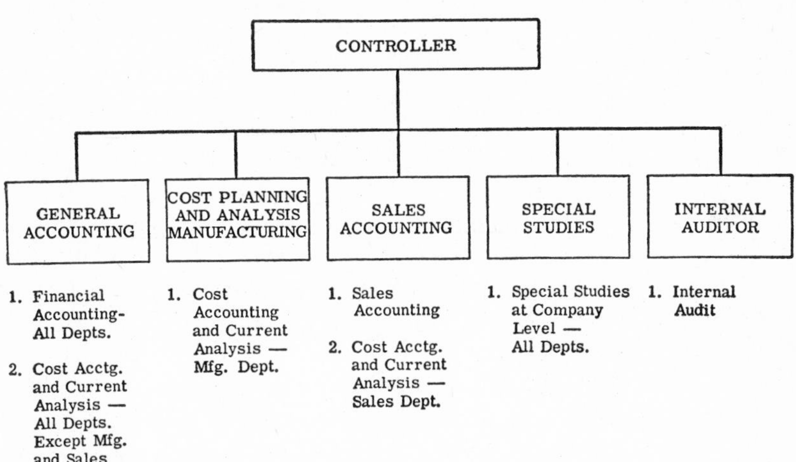

CHART 21-5. *Company-wide accounting organization proposed by Carnegie Tech Group* (SOURCE: Simon *et al., Centralization vs. Decentralization in Organizing the Controller's Department,* p. 71).

proaches, in which perhaps the most noteworthy element is the special studies unit. The creation of this latter section at the top-management level is clearly a consequence of the communications analysis. It may be noted, too, that the Carnegie Tech group's approach tells us as much about what *not* to fight for in an organization as what we should. In this instance top-level organization for current analysis is not of great importance because the crucial horizontal communication must occur at lower echelons with operating people. Thus the development of the organization partially along manufacturing and sales function lines does not represent any significant compromise.

Relationships Between Factory and Company Headquarters

Although the significance of communications to organization is not a new finding, practitioners have typically been unwilling to face up to its implications because of its incompatibility with one of the most time-tested of hierarchical credos, unity of command. In the relationship of the factory accounting program to the company level, however, the unity of command precept has been able to contribute little in a real sense to some difficult questions. Traditionally, there have been two authority patterns suggested for the relationship of the factory accountant to the factory manager and to the home office—both designed to avoid conflict and presumably preserve unity of command. In Chart 21-6 (a) we see the first alternative, which is to place the factory manager so that he has all units under his direct control. The Company Controller has no formal power over the person on whom he must depend at the lower level, the factory accountant. From the Controller's perspective, then, the situation is complicated by a series of relationships which in most cases can only be made to work by informal arrangements.

The second alternative, shown on Chart 21-6 (b), suggests a different orientation. Here unity of command is preserved in the relationship between the Company Controller and the Factory Accountant. It is the factory manager who suffers under this arrangement, since he has now lost control over one of his important staff people.

The problem involved here is a major one in many organizations. Since the communications pattern of Chart 21-1 must exist under any circumstances, the various structural approaches serve only to hamper or inhibit communications. They do not stop it. Despite this, managers as a whole have found it emotionally impossible to abandon the familiar "unity of command" principle. In most cases they prefer to live with a formal chart which they know does not represent a true picture of authority relationships.

The Simon group's conclusions on this point are therefore of consequence. The recommendation: *Forget the unity of command idea. If it is discovered that the administrative situation requires communication to flow both vertically and horizontally, formalize this pattern in the structure.* Specifically, in the case of the factory accountant, there is much to be said for recognizing organizationally his twofold responsibility to the factory manager and to the company controller. It was found, furthermore, that some companies have created such a formal arrangement without disastrous results. On this point the Simon group has written:

> The survey team's thinking . . . has been set forth at length because there has been much disagreement among writers on administration and among practicing managers on the essentiality of unity

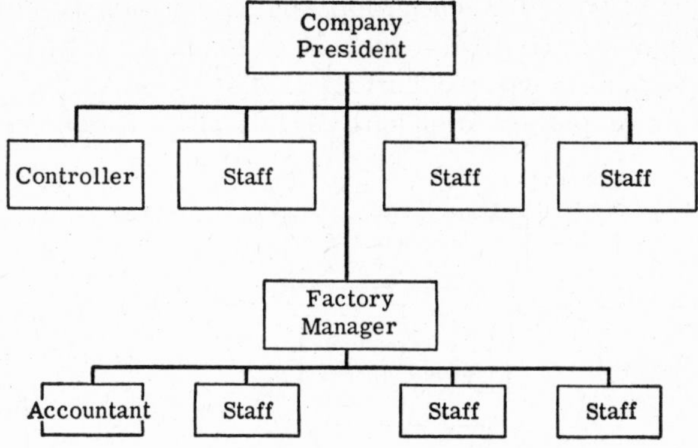

CHART 21-6a. *A "unitary" field organization.*

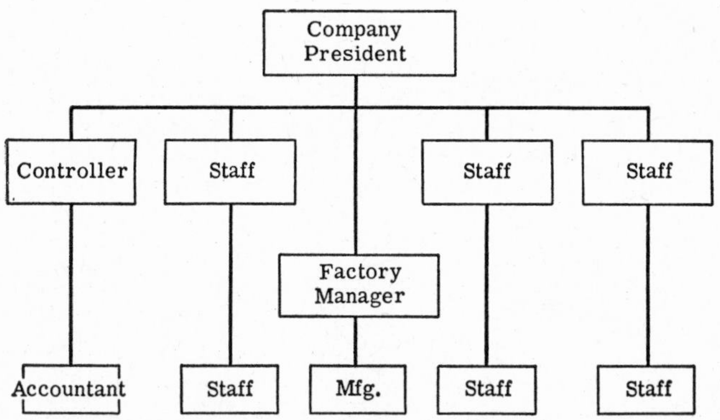

CHART 21-6b. *A "functional" field organization.*
(Note that in both these alternative field organizations, the principle of "unity of command" is observed. The "functional" pattern, however, has no integrating mechanism at the field level.)

of command. Until further studies can be made on this point, the evidence cited here indicates that a division of formal authority over the factory accountant is entirely workable, provided that the controller's department has acceptance and support of company manufacturing executives. A man *can* serve two masters provided that the two masters are not working at cross purposes.[14]

---

[14] Simon *et al., Centralization vs. Decentralization,* p. 83.

Thus the Carnegie Tech group suggests the feasibility of an organizational arrangement which is in striking contrast to traditional theory, as shown in Chart 21-7. Its close relationship to the communications pattern of Chart 21-1 is also of significance.

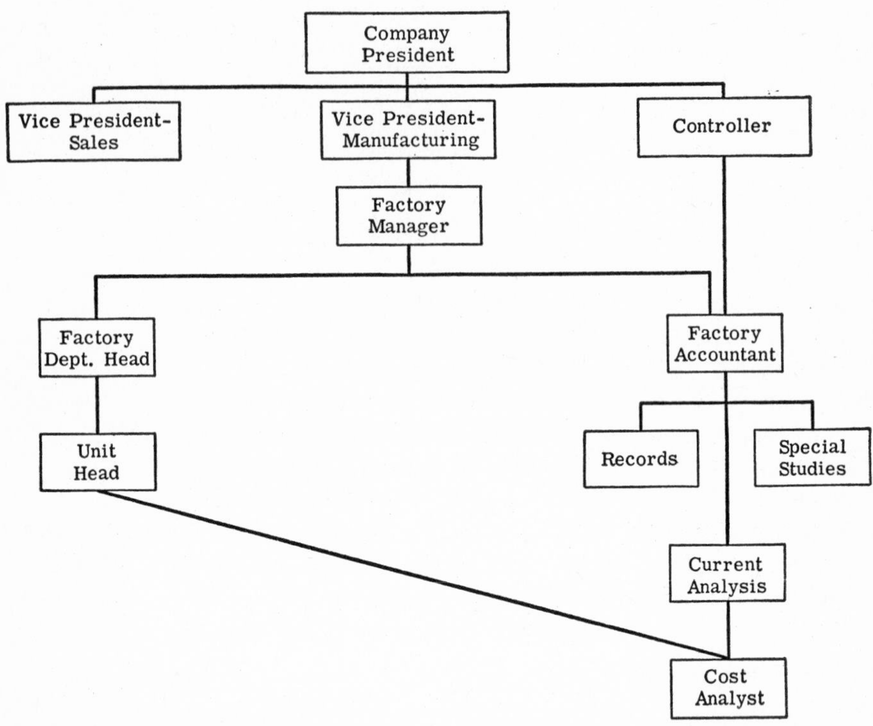

CHART 21-7. *A simplified view of proposals for organizing accounting function at company-wide and factory levels (note absence of unity of command).*

Organization Within the Factory

As a final example of the way in which the Carnegie Tech group made its analysis (1) by looking at the points at which decisions were made and (2) by noting the manner in which decision premises were developed out of information, the model suggested for the internal structure of accounting in a large factory is instructive.

Here again we find the three major functions of accounting, each of which is considered separable: current analysis, record-keeping, and special studies. As might be expected, too, from a review of the points of decision and communications pattern in Chart 21-7, the need for horizontal communications is recognized. Hence current analysis functions are decentralized so that Department heads and cost analysts will have close contact; special studies are centralized at the factory level to afford close cooperation with other staff departments; and record-keeping is centralized for cost and other reasons.

III • SUMMARY

The decision model is based on the idea that human beings, with all their failings, are continually being cast into problem-solving situations where choices are made. Thus we need to know who makes decisions and the base of information from which decision premises are drawn.

In the study of controllership in several large factories, we find that this method of analysis was followed. The points of decision were identified, as were the kind of decisions to be made. Since information served as the initial stimulus for the decision, as the means of guiding action, and as the vehicle for reporting action results preparatory to taking new decisions, it was obvious also that the analysis of communications content and flow was a necessary step.

On the basis of these data, the Simon group came to certain conclusions about the nature of the accounting function in a large company. In many respects these findings were not particularly dramatic or striking, but they do suggest some rather sharp departures from classic organization. Further, it would appear that the decision, with its companion study of information flows, has proved itself to be a practicable means of organization analysis.

Part Five

PERSPECTIVES

TWENTY-TWO

What Do We Want in the Modern Organization?

What to Look for in This Chapter . . .

Multiple goals in organizations

Significance of the multiple goals concept to organization research

Relationship of individual need satisfaction to achievement of over-all organization goals

Likert's proposal for measurement of organization well-being

What is a good organization?

In the last analysis this is the fundamental question, the payoff, so to speak. But how do we know when an organization is good or bad? Against what benchmarks can the executive evaluate his organization and its performance? The significance of the problem is quite apparent. In the management situation judgments are constantly being made as to how well things are going, when changes are to be made, and what types of reforms are to be instituted. The man who sits on top of an organization and is blissfully unaware of a cauldron of problems is headed for trouble.

The chief who doesn't know what to expect, who institutes change for the sake of change alone, also would appear to be asking for difficulties. And the manager who wants change but has no means of evaluating the kinds of changes necessary faces problems. In short the executive is always appraising his organization and its performance either explicitly or implicitly. Despite this, there is an appalling lack of attention given to this important problem. Frequently, too, the results of organization research studies are grossly misused by practitioners because no attention is paid to the standards by which the reported success was measured.

One writer who has recently pointed to the significance of this problem of organizational evaluation is Chris Argyris. As a result of his research and consulting, he has reported that traditional ideas of organizational health are "over-simplified and at times misleading." [1] He has written that it is not correct to assume that such "products" of the organization as low absenteeism, low turnover, low grievance rates, and high production are always valid indicators of organizational health.[2] Indeed such outward symbols of successful operation may give quite an erroneous picture of the real situation; and a failure to face up to this problem could involve grave national risks.

The basic dilemma occurs when we ask ourselves what standards we should use in judging the functioning of an organization; and, in turn, these judgments of course affect executive decision-making. In essence, the organization's (and the executive's) goals assume paramount importance. Goals are really the benchmarks, the standards, against which performance is compared. Put another way, we must first have a direction for our efforts; then a judgment can be made as to what progress has been made along that path.

A very brief example of the way in which the identification of goals affects directly the character of organization behavior is to be seen in a study of the role of the prison officer. E. K. Nelson, Jr. found that a fundamental conflict in goal philosophy in modern

---

[1] "In This Issue," *Harvard Business Review* 36:10, November-December 1958.

[2] Chris Argyris, "The Organization: What Makes It Healthy?" *Harvard Business Review* 36:107-116, November-December 1958.

correctional administration between social treatment of offenders as the paramount value (Goal 1) and custody as the important consideration (Goal 2) ramified through every administrative tendon of the prison. It was difficult to judge the performance of the individual officer or of a group because no one was quite sure which of the two contradictory goals was the more important. As a result, Nelson (himself a former warden) concluded that real advances in prison organization "must await the solution of dilemmas in conceptions of the cause and treatment of criminal behavior, particularly in regard to present efforts to combine treatment with punishment in the institutional milieu." [3]

I • THE CONCEPT OF MULTIPLE GOALS

While an important first step is to recognize the primacy of goals as a basis for evaluating the status of an organization, this does not carry the analysis far enough. It will be recalled from an earlier chapter that organizations are interacting entities in which the desires of the individual, the group, and the organization are in a continued state of adaptation. Indeed one of the problems of the executive is to weigh the organization's needs and wants against those of the individual and the group, a point to which we shall return. But what are the organization's needs? Can they be so neatly packaged? In most cases the expression of the organization's goals is not simple, but represents the full complexity of any large social phenomenon. There are difficulties of separating the long and the short run goals, the human from the material needs, the individual interest from the organization as a whole, the means from the ends. In short, there is *no one* goal by which an organization can be judged. The bases upon which decisions and appraisals of performances are made involve a host of uneasy compromises of conflicting value demands.

---

[3] E. K. Nelson, Jr., *A Study of the Role and Function of the Prison Officer* (Los Angeles: Unpublished Doctoral Dissertation presented to the School of Public Administration, University of Southern California, 1959). Quotation is from dissertation abstract published in the *Final Oral Examination Program*, May 18, 1959. See also Richard H. McCleery, *Policy Change in Prison Management* (East Lansing, Mich.: Michigan State University, 1957).

Ways in Which Organization Goals Multiply

In previous chapters we saw that organizations are a part of a total society. They do not exist in isolation. Therefore *how* they pursue their goals has a great deal to do with individual and group well-being. This is particularly true in an industrial society such as the United States where immense cooperative systems engulf everyone; hence these larger social values must be reflected in organization behavior, public or private. Minimum wage laws, the workers' right to organize, provisions against the exploitation of children, and fair employment practice requirements are examples of social values which importantly condition the means a U. S. executive may use to achieve certain organizational goals. Hitler's forced labor battalions are said to have achieved their work goals rather spectacularly but the humans involved were regarded as machines which were expendable and inexpensive. Obviously the price for these accomplishments was more than most people are willing to pay. Thus are social limits set in a good part of the world on the extent to which the individual's interest can be sacrificed to those of the organization.

In government. In the field of government affairs, the problem of multiple goals is clearly to be seen. First an agency must be concerned about the accomplishment of its stated purposes, such as protection of forests, construction and maintenance of roads, provision of welfare services, and so forth. But this is only the beginning of the process. Seldom is a government given sufficient monies to accomplish these purposes in any absolute sense. Citizens, and particularly taxpayer groups, therefore tend to transfer their concern from accomplishment of the stated goals to the efficiency with which the job is being done. Thus an organization may be considered "good" because it is making 100 per cent use of its available resources even though it may be providing only about 15 per cent of the necessary police protection in a community. A third goal, economy, also frequently intervenes. Some people, both inside and outside governments, do not really care what missions are accomplished and with what degree of efficiency. They are interested only in keeping costs, and hence taxes, low. Thus stated, mission, efficiency, and economy are a triumvirate of goal orientations which frequently form the basis for evaluating the quality of government.

In business. In private business it has long been argued that the profit and loss statement provides a very tangible evidence or organizational health. Admittedly, private business does function in a different environment from that of government and the voluntary associations. Instead of looking at the stated mission of a business, we may assume that its economic status provides some measure of its social utility. But for the individual business the problem is not that simple. Particularly is a conflict to be seen in terms of long- and short-run goals. There are many occasions when an immediate profit might be obtained to the long-run detriment of the organization.[4] Can it be said, for example, that American Motors was a less effective organization in the hard years of 1955–57 when President George Romney sought to sell the idea of a compact car? The losses of the company were staggering in those years; but by 1959 the company was making substantial profits on the basis of design and industrial developments of the money-losing period.

Multiple Goals and Administration

The experience of the Soviet industrial system has caused Frank to raise some provocative questions about the function of multiple goals in an organization.[5] He has found that in the Soviet Union factory managers are judged by a wide gamut of standards, some imposed by the bureaucracy, some by the party, and some by the community and other forces. It has been literally impossible for any manager to live up to all these demands; and no one really expects him to. As a result there is a policy of selective enforcement of the various prescribed standards. At times the tolerated violations are flagrant; at others the slightest violation may be enough to destroy a person.

---

[4] The conflict between production and maintenance people in the Milo Fractionating Center reported by Melville Dalton, *Men Who Manage* (New York: John Wiley and Sons, Inc., 1959), is a particularly good illustration. See Chapter 17, above.

[5] Andrew Gunder Frank, "Goal Ambiguity and Conflicting Standards: An Approach to the Study of Organization," *Human Organization* 17:8-13, Winter 1958-59.

Though possibly Frank uses the Soviet Union as an extreme case, he suggests that the conflict of goals is not unique—is, in fact, a rather widespread phenomenon. Yet most of our ideas about rational organization rest on the assumption of a single goal, or at least compatible ones. Thus ". . . The more traditional approach is implicitly to begin with a single system goal, or a set of somehow commensurable ones and, assuming perfect knowledge, to derive nonconflicting standards. This procedure then leads to the familiar analyses of organization." [6]

However, it may be more logical, Frank argues, to begin any organization analysis with the assumption that goals and standards of behavior are in conflict. With "conflicting standards analysis" we treat the entire managerial situation as an ambiguous one in which goal choices are constantly being changed and new assignments of priorities made. Perhaps the most interesting aspect of the Frank thesis comes in his claim that this is really quite a desirable state of affairs. Ambiguity, he points out, really amounts to discretion. As a consequence, organization flexibility is promoted. Administrators are prevented from handling matters by "rules alone"; indeed, "subordinates, as well as superiors, [become] policy-makers." [7] Decentralization is also fostered as each man exercises his initiative. Control, on the other hand, does not suffer because superiors have broad discretion to select from a number of possible standards in judging and imposing sanctions on those who work for them. Subordinates are therefore more apt to remain sensitive to their superiors and to understand their "real" objectives. Frank thus raises some interesting questions which deserve further research. At the very least, he provides a useful perspective on the concept of multiple goals and its relationship to administrative process.

Leadership and Multiple Goals

It is through executive decision-making and action that organization goals are articulated; and the leader holds responsibility for accomplishment. Obviously, then, the measures of success for

---

[6] *Ibid.*, p. 11.
[7] *Ibid.*

leadership are inextricably tied to measures of success for the organization.[8] As a result researchers in leadership encounter essentially the same problems as students of organization. The significance of goals to leadership analysis has been emphasized by Tannenbaum and Massarik, who have written that "No leadership act is inherently effective or ineffective; it might be either, depending upon the goals with reference to which it is assessed."[9]

Tannenbaum and Massarik also point to the complexity of goal structure in organizations, noting that "the very multiplicity of co-existing goals encountered in most real-life situations makes clear-cut measurement [of leadership] difficult. Further the usual goal clusters contain elements that have differential weight in the attainment of still 'higher' goals in a hierarchy."[10]

Multiple Goals and the Problems of Research

Organization researchers have been plagued by the kinds of problems mentioned in the preceding paragraphs. This has been true because the researchers have sought to advance our knowledge of organizations by studying what the good ones do and the bad ones do not, and vice-versa. As Likert has explained it, this approach seeks to "measure and examine the kinds of leadership and related variables being used by the best units in the organization in contrast to those being used by the poorest. In essence these studies are providing management with a mirror by measuring and reporting what is working best in industry today."[11]

But again the fundamental question arises: On what basis do you separate the good from the bad? In some cases researchers have simply asked executives to judge their subordinate units as to effectiveness without providing any more detailed instructions. The other typical criterion has been the productivity of the organization, that is, the amount of work produced compared with the

---

[8] The significance of organizational performance to personal future is particularly to be seen in the case of Soviet industry. *Ibid.,* p. 9.

[9] Robert Tannenbaum and Fred Massarik, "Leadership: a Frame of Reference," *Management Science* 4:8, October, 1957; also available as Reprint No. 68 (Los Angeles: Institute of Industrial Relations, University of California, 1958).

[10] *Ibid.*

[11] Rensis Likert, "Developing Patterns in Management: I," American Management Association, General Management Series No. 178, 1956, p. 35.

amount of resources expended. Obviously each of these approaches has its shortcomings. In one case reliance is placed on the subjective judgment of individual executives, which may or may not reflect the goal orientation of the organization. In the other only one of several organizational goals is used to separate goodness from badness.[12]

It is interesting that there has been virtually no attempt by researchers to separate good and bad organizations on the basis of their stated program accomplishment. Apparently there are two reasons why so little use has been made of his criterion. *First,* there are many instances where the accomplishments of stated programs cannot easily be reduced to objective measurements . . . a problem particularly in government. *Second,* there is no way of estimating the degree to which a great number of variables other than the organization element may have contributed to the achievement of certain objectives. Profits may be a stated goal; but, as we have noted, there are few who would have much faith in a division of good and bad organizations on the basis of earning records alone.

Research findings on organization effectiveness are therefore based primarily on judgments as to which of the multiple goals in an organization are most important. There is no way to make this part of the study scientific; for no one can prove that productivity is more or less important than worker satisfaction. These depend importantly on how we view life. It is the reason why the basis upon which good and bad organizations are separated becomes so important in analyzing any report utilizing this type of research approach. Furthermore it must be remembered that there may have been unanticipated results which were not controlled or measured at the time the one index of goodness was under the microscope.

---

[12] The Institute of Social Research, University of Michigan, has particularly centered its interests on the study of large-scale organization and used the research designs mentioned. Two widely quoted studies are examples: One in an insurance company used the efficiency measure; the other, of a railroad, used leadership evaluations. See Daniel Katz, *et al., Productivity, Supervision and Morale in an Office Situation* (Ann Arbor, Mich.: Survey Research Center, 1950) and, Daniel Katz *et al., Productivity, Supervision and Morale among Railroad Workers* (Ann Arbor, Mich.: Survey Research Center, 1951). Since that time the Institute has made studies based on other criteria of goodness.

Conclusions

To summarize:

- Organizations have more than a single goal, some of which may have been provided from outside the organization.
- The interaction of goals will produce a different value framework in different organizations.
- Goals cannot really be separated from the means of their accomplishment.
- The decision on best organizational arrangements in any particular situation must ultimately be shaped by the set of goals which are sought.
- It therefore follows that there is no one group of organizing prescriptions that will be universally applicable.

Sophistication in these matters thus requires a quality of philosophy, a tolerance of ambiguity, and a recognition that the very nature of the organization phenomenon is such as to render quick and easy answers impossible. There is much in the literature—in this book—that is useful. But such good can be destroyed by slavish committment to abstract principles applied regardless of the organizational setting. In short, the administrator must have a firm understanding of what he and his organization are seeking, and under what general conditions, before he begins worrying about the style and tactics of organizing.

II • THE HUMAN EQUATION IN MEASURING ORGANIZATIONAL PERFORMANCE

Two Categories

While the human being's interests and needs certainly are an element in nearly every organization's goal constellation, a growing dissatisfaction with management's present tendency to think of effectiveness in largely mechanical and production terms requires further discussion of this problem.[13]

---

[13] As an illustration of preoccupation with non-employee measures of organizational effectiveness a general session of the 41st Annual City Managers'

Ethical issue. There is first the *ethical* question. To what extent should organizations provide participants with an opportunity for growth and maturation? To what extent is the organization responsible for seeing that people enjoy their work experience? And how should this social obligation be weighed against the requirements of productivity? Since these are questions of great social significance, we shall return to them for detailed consideration in the following chapter.

Here we will refer only to the argument of Fred H. Blum for a "social audit." The basic purpose of such an audit (which was carried out by Blum in Robert E. Lamb, Inc., a medium-size industrial engineering and construction firm) is to find out how well—or how poorly—the organization is satisfying the basic human needs of its employees. It is pointed out that the audit differs from the morale survey because it is concerned "with the workers as people in their own right rather than as functional parts of the organization." [14] Blum justifies the importance of such an estimate of organization well-being on the grounds that human values must be restored "to that key position lost during the nineteenth century." He continues: "It is because efficiency has become industry's principal concern that the social audit has its essential contribution to make. It challenges the effectiveness of the prevailing concept in such a way as to make human values *central* and to relegate technical-mechanical considerations to a *secondary* role." [15]

Self-interest. There is, second, the *self-interest* question. To what extent should the organization concern itself with the interests of the workers in order to accomplish its organization goals?

With regard to this issue two extremes of approach may be found in American management. One has been that of Taylorism, in which individuals have been viewed as being very much like machines which possess enough brain power to pursue their economic self-interest in a rational manner. Thus, if the right wage

---

Association Conference on "Measuring Organizational Effectiveness and Performance" developed eight criteria, none of which dealt with human resources. (From the mimeographed report of the session held October 21, 1958).

[14] Fred H. Blum, "Social Audit of the Enterprise," *Harvard Business Review* 36:77, March-April 1958.

[15] *Ibid.*, p. 84.

incentives are provided and the correct physical arrangements are made, little attention need be paid to other aspects of employee well-being. The opposite view may be attributed to the more avid of the so-called "human relations" advocates who have claimed that the happy worker is the good worker; to them, "employee-centeredness" is the surest way to achieve organizational goals.

Research has rather clearly demonstrated that neither of these extremes is the answer to the self-interest question. The famous Hawthorne experiments approximately 30 years ago rather effectively demolished the proposition that humans are very much alike, resemble machines, and mechanically pursue economic ends.[16] On the other hand studies also reveal that complete abdication to individual wants and needs by the organization is no answer either. Likert wrote that on the basis of a study he made in 1937, he believed that morale and productivity were positively related: that the higher morale, the higher the production. But "substantial" research findings since then have shown that this relationship is much too simple.[17] All kinds of combinations may occur—high morale and low production, low morale and low production, high morale and high production—which indicates the lack of any fixed and clear-cut relationship.

Likert's Modified Theory

Despite the fact that the relationship between production and morale is not as neat as was once supposed, Likert has argued that the maintenance of human resources must be considered a vital element in gauging organizational effectiveness. Scientific management has demonstrated its capacity to obtain high productivity; but its "critical weakness," according to Likert, has been the evoking of resentments, hostilities, and adverse motivation and attitudinal reactions. Such negative attitudes are not in the long

---

[16] For a general perspective on this research see Elton Mayo, *Social Problems of an Industrial Civilization* (Boston: Harvard Business School, 1945). For more detail, F. J. Roethlisberger and William J. Dickson, *Management and the Worker* (Cambridge: Harvard University Press, 1939).

[17] Likert, "Developing Patterns of Management: I," pp. 37 ff. See also Likert's earlier "Motivational Dimensions of Administration," in Robert Walker, editor, *America's Manpower Crisis* (Chicago: Public Administration Service, 1952), pp. 105-106.

run interest of any organization and they manifest themselves in communications blocks and restrictions, high scrap loss, lowered safety, higher absence and turnover, increased grievances, and work stoppages. In the future Likert believes emphasis on short-term production goals will cause even greater hostility because the trend generally is toward giving the individual greater freedom and initiative. Today, ". . . people are less willing to accept pressure and close supervision than was the case a decade or two ago." [18]

Overemphasis on production measurements. In the face of this trend, however, the present practice involves a tendency to evaluate managerial and organization performance almost entirely in terms of production-oriented measurements. The failure to consider the human assets of the organization in appraising performance is now regarded by Likert as a "serious vulnerability" in present theory and practice. "As a consequence," he writes, "many companies today are encouraging managers of departments and divisions to dissipate valuable human assets of the organization. In fact, they are rewarding these managers well for doing so!" [19]

Such an approach to appraisal possesses all the weaknesses of the scientific management movement, Likert believes. It pays too little attention to the significance of motivation and goes back to the old premise that humans are simple economic men. He has suggested a "modified theory" of organization and management which takes advantage of the "great power" of human relations research findings by recognizing:

1. The character and magnitude of the powerful motivational forces which control human behavior in working situations; and
2. The manner in which these forces can be used so that they reinforce rather than conflict with one another.[20]

Two central concepts. This analysis has led Likert to propose two central concepts in the "modified theory." The *first* is that the pattern of interaction between the superior and his subordinates

---

[18] Likert, "Developing Patterns of Management: I," p. 44.

[19] Rensis Likert, "Measuring Organization Performance," *Harvard Business Review* 36:41, March-April 1958.

[20] Rensis Likert, "Developing Patterns in Management: II," American Management Association General Management Series, No. 182 (New York: 1956, pp. 3-29.

should be supportive rather than threatening; and the *second* is that management can make full use of its human resources only when each employee is a "member of a well-knit and effectively functioning work group with high interaction skills and performance goals."[21]

A year-long study of four divisions in a large organization tends to give support to the Likert thesis. Two of the divisions operated along "modified theory" participative lines; the other two were hierarchically-controlled and exposed to extensive scientific management analysis. On the basis of time studies in the hierarchically-controlled two divisions, orders were given to cut staff by 25 per cent.

At the end of the year the hierarchically-controlled divisions had increased productivity by the 25 per cent required by the personnel cut. In the case of the "participative" divisions, one also increased by about 25 per cent and the other by 15 per cent. It was in other respects than productivity, however, that *the results* of the experimental study appeared significant.

1. *Turnover* in the hierarchically-controlled units rose because of the employee's feeling of excessive pressure for production.
2. There was an *increase* in the employees' sense of responsibility to get work done in the participative divisions; a *decrease* in the hierarchically-controlled divisions.
3. There was an *increase* in favorable attitudes toward high-producing individuals in the participative division; a *decrease* in the hierarchically-controlled divisions.
4. There was an *increase* in employees' satisfaction with their superiors as their representatives at high levels in the participative divisions; a *decrease* in the hierarchically-controlled divisions.

In reviewing the results of this experiment, Likert has concluded that the productivity increase in the hierarchically-controlled units was obtained at a cost of liquidating part of the investment the company had made in its human organization. The quality of the human organization deteriorated as a functioning social system and this was manifest in increased hostilities, greater reliance upon authority, a decline in loyalty, and less interest in increasing

[21] Likert, "Measuring Organizational Performance," p. 43.

production and more in restricting it. If this experiment had been continued over another year or two, Likert believes that productivity and quality of work would have actually declined in the hierarchically-controlled units.[22]

Thus the "modified theory" suggests the great significance of individual morale and satisfaction to the *long-term* interests of the organization. Furthermore Likert believes that approximate measurement of the status of these human resources is now possible, though obviously this would not be as precise as in the case of plant and equipment. Present methods can "enable management to size up present trends, analyze their relationships, and guide company operations accordingly."[23]

Variables to be measured. The variables which Likert suggests for measurement of a "corporation as a whole, a division, or a smaller group" include:

1. Extent of loyalty to the institution and identification with it and its objectives.
2. Extent to which the goals of units and individuals facilitate the achievement of the organization's objectives.
3. Level of motivation among members of the organization with regard to such variables as:
   (a) Performance, including both quality and quantity of work done:
   (b) Concern for elimination of waste and reduction of costs;
   (c) Concern for improving the product;
   (d) Concern for improving processes.
4. Degree of confidence and trust among members of the organization in each other and in the different hierarchical levels.
5. Amount and quality of the teamwork in units and between units of the organization.
6. Extent to which people feel that delegation is effective.
7. Extent to which the members feel that their ideas, information, knowledge of processes, and experiences are being used in the decision-making processes of the organization.
8. Upward, downward, and sideward efficiency and adequacy of the communication process.
9. Leadership skills and abilities of supervisors and managers, including their basic philosophies of management and orientation toward leadership processes.[24]

---

[22] *Ibid.*, pp. 43-49.

[23] *Ibid.*, p. 49.

[24] Rensis Likert, "Motivational Approach to Management Development," *Harvard Business Review* 37-77, July-August 1959.

Problems of Measurement

Although he would not disagree with Likert on the importance of human resources to the organization's long-term interests, Argyris does not feel we have reached a point at which measurement of these human factors is possible. As noted earlier in this chapter, his research makes him very skeptical of such typical indicators of organizational health as low absenteeism, low turnover, low grievance rates, and high production.

In part Argyris' incredulity derives from his strong opinion that the present hierarchical form of organization is essentially incompatible with the development of healthy, mature individuals.[25] What may really be happening, he argues, is that employees have simply become apathetic, indifferent, and alienated. They have lost their need for maturity, as have the managers who must deal with them. The manager therefore uses "immature leadership patterns (i.e., those that emphasize money and de-emphasize human values). It is not long before the organization loses its basis for vitality and health." [26] In the process, people have become vegetative; their aspiration levels are so low that they are satisfied with such a leadership pattern and environment.

A study of a "healthy" manufacturing organization of 500 people has also contributed to Argyris' skepticism. The company was known for its "good" human relations, with the supportive and friendly leader a keystone of the organization's philosophy. A survey of attitudes revealed that employees (92 per cent) thought the organization was a good place in which to work; that they (75 per cent) did not feel they were constantly being pressured to produce; that they (74 per cent) felt management was good, interested in employees' welfare, and never treated workers like machines; they (90 per cent) were satisfied with wages; and they unanimously (100 per cent) felt management had a right to expect the employees to work hard.[27]

---

[25] Chris Argyris, *Personality and Organization* (New York: Harper, 1957). See Chapter III, pp. 54 ff.

[26] Argyris, "The Organization: What Makes It Healthy?" p. 107.

[27] These findings and subsequent references, *ibid.*, 107-116.

Seeking to look behind these attitudes, however, Argyris received other responses which raised his suspicions.

1. Even though most found the plant a good place to work, few (less than 25 per cent) made any close friends there.
2. The reason management was considered "good," was because it paid good wages, provided secure jobs and hardly ever bothered the employees. Nearly everyone (99 per cent) said they did not know how management felt about them and did not care.
3. Though there was great satisfaction with wages, 65 per cent said they got no personal satisfactions from their jobs otherwise. Less than 25 per cent aspired to any positions of responsibility.
4. Practically none (4 per cent) of the employees had any suggestions for improving their job performance; and 85 per cent added that such changes would be management's responsibility.

What causes the apparent contradiction? Argyris, of course, explains it by his proposition that organizations and society in general are forcing individuals into immature personality patterns. The individual places emphasis on wage satisfaction because he has really abdicated any hope that he can "truly realize his potentials" or express his total personality.

Under our present system of appraising and evaluating human resources, Argyris feels that we are simply rewarding apathy, indifference, alienation, and non-involvement. Everyone will suffer: *management* because few will aspire to positions of responsibility; *employees* because they will become "simplified" human beings; and *organization* because alienated, apathetic participants will tend to make it rigid, defensive, and highly resistant to change. Thus "management is faced with one of the most difficult *human* problems ever to challenge man." [28]

III • SUMMARY

Any serious consideration of the organization process must inevitably turn to the question of goals. Why is cooperative action

[28] *Ibid.*, p. 116.

necessary? What does it seek? Only when we have some clue as to objectives can we make any judgments as to the effectiveness of performance by any organization. Unfortunately this fundamental issue has either been overlooked or consciously avoided in much management practice and research. As a consequence judgments have been made concerning the validity of certain prescriptions without any real statement of the values the organization seeks to advance.

But the problem is not simply that of identifying the one goal or set of compatible goals of an organization. The fact is that organizations—and individuals too, as a matter of fact—have multiple goals. And these goals are as often conflicting as compatible. Frank has particularly advanced this thesis, noting that a conspicuous shortcoming of much of the traditional literature is the assumption of a single value.

He has also pointed out that the presence of conflicting goals is not as disconcerting a situation as it may seem. The existence of such ambiguity actually fosters greater discretion all along the line and it may also have salutary effects on the process of control.

The following five points present the logic of the "multiple goals" argument and its relevance to organization:

1. Organizations have more than a single goal, some of which may have been provided from outside the organization.
2. The interaction of goals will produce a different value framework in different organizations.
3. Goals cannot really be separated from the means of their accomplishment.
4. The decision on best organization arrangements in any particular situation must ultimately be shaped by the set of goals which are sought.
5. It therefore follows that there is no one group of organizing prescriptions that will be universally applicable.

The problem of goals is particularly to be observed in seeking to establish the appropriate relationship between the attainment of organizational ends and individual objectives. Partly this is a social question which we shall examine in detail in the next chapter. Partly, however, it is self-interest question. In this latter context we ask in what degree, if any, the achievement of individual needs promotes the aims of the total organization.

It seems apparent that organizations must be concerned with the preservation and maximization of their human resources. This does *not* mean, however, that attention to individual needs will necessarily feed into the traditional criteria of organization effectiveness, such as increased profits, higher production, and so forth, in any *short-run* way. As Likert's experiment so well reveals, the manager who puts his faith in these mechanical indices may be short-changing the *long-run* interests of his organization. Yet these long-run needs, which cannot be equated in any clear-cut way with immediate production interests, are presently ignored in evaluating organizational performance. Profits, production, and efficiency so completely dominate evaluation standards that the executive ignores their short-run maximization at very considerable peril.

Not only do present habits of thought militate against giving full weight to the development of human resources in organization, there is also the serious question whether we as yet know the real dimensions of this problem. Argyris would apparently disagree with Likert that social science instruments for measuring the status of these resources presently exist. Indeed, his research suggests that the executive who relies on the traditional indices of morale and satisfaction may be as far from meeting the long-term human resource needs of his organization as the production-oriented one.

From the foregoing it follows that no one can say with any degree of certainty by what standards an executive ought to appraise the performance of his organization. And it is questionable whether the time will ever arrive when there will be any pattern answers to such a question—so much does the setting of an organization and its own goal orientation affect the whole process of appraisal. Indeed the ability to perceive these various goal aspirations and to set them in some kind of workable relationship—to "satisfice," in Simon's terms—may very well be the most critical of qualities a successful leader must possess.

TWENTY-THREE

Organization as a Social Issue

What to Look for in This Chapter . . .

The issue: to what extent should the individual be controlled and governed in his behavior by the group or organization?

William H. Whyte's *Organization Man*

Bureaucratic stresses on the individual

Conflict or cooperation?

Factors intensifying the problem in the United States

One approach: emphasis on systematic processes for accommodation to various interests and needs

The concurrent existence in the organization of at least three basic levels of needs and goals—the individual, the group, and the organization itself—suggests the nature of a problem which has come in recent years to concern a growing number of people. That question is: *To what extent should the individual be controlled and governed in his behavior by the group or organization?*

Should such dominance be carried far enough, the social effects are quite apparent; and here it must be borne in mind that the large private organization is just as important a part of this total picture as any public agency. The development of a habit of submissiveness and conformity on the job could easily carry over into other social and political behavior. A pair of famous novels suggest two possibilities of life under such circumstances, neither of which is appealing.

In *Brave New World,* Aldous Huxley wrote more than twenty-five years ago about a life of somnolence and uniformity. Everyone, except for a few odd ones, had been lulled into a life of happiness. There was no hardship, no irritation with things, no lack of material satisfactions.[1]

In George Orwell's *Nineteen Eighty-Four* an even more frightening prospect of society was suggested. Here, fear was substituted for salubrious satisfaction as the governing force. Obviously Orwell took the model of twentieth century dictatorship and then proceeded to show how modern technological advances, plus some old-fashioned devices of torture, could be used to destroy any possibility of individual or group resistance.

Obviously Huxley and Orwell were addressing themselves to questions which extend, in terms of their significance, far beyond the scope of this book. However it is important to recognize that organizations, by their very nature, play a highly important part in the social processes involved. These questions demand the reflection and consideration of every thoughtful student of organization theory.

I • CAUSES OF CONCERN

There are some major reasons, too, why the issue has assumed increased significance in the United States at this particular time.

Ubiquity of Large Organization

First, the proliferation and development of large scale organization is a primary factor. It is said that the 200 largest industrial

---

[1] It may be noted that Huxley published in 1958 another book, *Brave New World Revisited* (New York: Harper and Brothers), in which he finds little reason to change his original prognostications.

corporations of the United States own about half of the industrial wealth; and C. Wright Mills has pointed out that *eighty* per cent of the people who work for a living "do so by working for 2 or 3 per cent of the population who now own 40 to 50 per cent of the private property in the United States."[2] This is a complete reversal from the situation in the early nineteenth century when it has been estimated that eighty per cent of the workers were self-employed enterprisers. Hence it may be seen that the individual's role in organization life is a central one precisely because so many of us are involved in the problem.

The Garrison State

Second, the demands of the "garrison state" have unquestionably permeated every facet of today's life. It is now more than twenty years since the United States began to prepare in earnest for World War II. Many thought that victory over Germany would allow a return to a relatively uncomplicated life where the government and total social organization requirements would not be great. Instead we find that the two decades have presented consistent threats to our survival. The spending of our government has increased to $120 billions. We have had trouble adjusting ourselves to this new milieu; and the era of McCarthyism (1950-54) mounted such a sizable attack on individual freedom and prerogative that it became clear Orwell's *Nineteen Eighty-Four* was not at all beyond the realm of possibility. In short, it now becomes apparent that the demands of the atom age have been such as to require a complete reorientation of the individual's relationship to the society.

Attack on Behavioral Scientists

Third, the period after World War II has witnessed the flowering of the behavioral sciences. Students of these subjects have multiplied, funds for research have increased many-fold, and the books on the subject have proliferated. However these develop-

---

[2] C. Wright Mills, *White Collar* (New York: Oxford University Press, 1953), p. 63. Also available as a Galaxy Book paperback.

ments have not been greeted with unanimous enthusiasm. The editors of *Fortune* magazine have particularly led an assault on the assumptions they consider to underlie this work of the social scientists. William H. Whyte has undoubtedly been the most prolific in this respect. He has charged that the "social engineers" are interested only in a "stable equilibrium," a condition which he feels to be quite in contradiction to the motive forces that built American society. With regard to these charges, Whyte has written:

> . . . to become a social engineer only two basic premises need be learned. The first is the primacy of the group. Its harmony is the important goal, and the individual has meaning chiefly as he contributes to that goal. This premise digested, you are now one step from being a social engineer. For the second premise flows from the first. To achieve this "integration" we must turn to the "scientific" techniques. By measurement and codification you enable people to find how everyone else is thinking and unthinking and adjust accordingly. In a word, groupthink.[3]

Daniel Bell, another editor of *Fortune,* has also attacked social science research, noting particularly that there has been a "curious discounting" of the "economic man." He has written, "To say, in fact, that the American worker is not really or primarily interested in money contradicts, in a deep sense, the very motive power of the economic system. Why else would people submit themselves to such a work environment?" [4]

Although it may be noted here that social scientists do have answers to the charges leveled by such critics as the *Fortune* editors, these quotations are reproduced only to indicate some of the thinking that lies behind the present concern about the individual's relationship to the organization. Essentially what the *Fortune* editors are charging is that the social scientists have a bias against the individual and against his traditional ways of thinking and behaving. By their attack, people like Whyte and Bell are seeking to redress the balance.

---

[3] William H. Whyte, Jr., *Is Anybody Listening?* (New York: Simon and Schuster, 1952), p. 208.

[4] Daniel Bell, *Work and Its Discontents* (Boston: Beacon Press, 1956), p. 29.

II • THE ORGANIZATION MAN

For the reasons cited, and undoubtedly others as well, the concern with the individual role in the organization has struck a popular chord. Clearly many people have come to feel an artificiality and a facelessness in their organizational life; and more and more find themselves in the regularized and deadening uniformity of suburbia, the 9 to 5 beat, of "the man in the gray flannel suit." [5] As a consequence Whyte's 1956 book, *The Organization Man,* became a non-fiction best-seller.[6] This status was achieved despite the fact that the book is partly a rather uneven collection of *Fortune* articles which were clearly "loaded" toward the author's point of view. Nevertheless, the book is a provocative one; and it is now the accepted statement of the pressures being brought by modern organizations against the individual.

Whyte's Argument

Whyte's argument runs along the following lines:

- *The social scientists are trying to replace the "Protestant Ethic," which emphasizes the individual, with the "Social Ethic."*

> By social ethic I mean that contemporary body of thought which makes morally legitimate the pressures of society against the individual. Its major propositions are three: a belief in the group as the source of creativity; a belief in "belongingness" as the ultimate need of the individual; and a belief in the application of science to achieve the belongingness (p. 7).[7]

- *The organization has no properties of its own; and creativity must come from the individuals in the organization.*

> Organization of itself has no dynamic. The dynamic is in the individual and thus he must not only question how The Organi-

[5] Sloan Wilson, *Man in the Gray Flannel Suit* (New York: Pocket Books, Inc.).

[6] William H. Whyte, Jr. *The Organization Man* (New York: Simon and Shuster, 1956), later republished as a Doubleday Anchor book in paperback form.

[7] Citations *ibid.,* Doubleday Anchor edition.

zation interprets his interests, he must question how it interprets its own (p. 440).

- *People do not cooperate just to cooperate.*

> . . . they cooperate for substantive reasons, to achieve certain goals, and unless these are comprehended the little manipulations for morale, team spirit, and such are fruitless (p. 440).

- *The conflict between the individual and the organization has always existed and always will.*

> To say that we must recognize the dilemmas of organization society is not to be inconsistent with the hopeful premise that organization society can be as compatible for the individual as any previous society . . .
>
> The fault is not in organization, in short; it is our worship of it. It is in our vain quest for a utopian equilibrium, which would be horrible if it ever did come to pass; it is in the soft-minded denial that there is a conflict between the individual and society. There must always be, and it is the price of being an individual that he must face these conflicts (p. 14).

- *The individual must fight the organization.*

> . . . Not stupidly, or selfishly, for the defects of individual self-regard are no more to be venerated than the defects of co-operation. But fight he must, for the demands for his surrender are constant and powerful, and the more he has come to like the life of organization the more difficult does he find it to resist these demands, or even to recognize them (p. 448).

There can be little doubt that *Fortune* editor Whyte raises some provocative questions. To a considerable extent, however, his apprehensions seem to develop from very questionable premises. For example, Riesman's point that the U.S. culture is moving toward "other-directedness" would seem to invalidate Whyte's charge that social scientists by design are installing their own "ethic." It hardly seems likely that a plot of such gargantuan proportions could be carried off by a relatively few social scientists.

In some respects the Whyte analysis is oversimplified. There is no recognition of the difference between natural social groups and the larger, more artificial organization. Both, says Whyte, are equally authoritarian and dangerous. Certainly, too, Whyte is at issue with anthropologists and sociologists like Malinowski and Selznick who have identified unique properties in the organization itself. Indeed, others have argued that the issue of the individual relationship is all the more pressing because organizations *do* seem to generate a behavior pattern which is separate from that of the individual. C. Northcote Parkinson's now-famous "law" of bureaucratic multiplication would seem to be of such a character.[8]

The *most fundamental,* and in some ways the most questionable, assumption made by Whyte involves man's natural predisposition toward cooperation. It is an issue to which we shall return, but note that there is no more important point at which to begin to think about organization theory than whether man is basically inclined to cooperate with the group. If Whyte is correct and man is always in conflict, then it could certainly be argued that the reduction of conflict as an organizational goal is quite unnatural and possibly undesirable. In any event, it is to be observed that much of Whyte's argument is rooted in the assumption that there are *no* natural pulls which cause men to get along with their fellows in a group situation.

Other Voices

Others have raised questions recently in a vein which is not altogether different from the Whyte thesis.

Educators. A professor in one of the United States' most highly organized universities has observed that the individual is weak against the organization which by its very nature dominates him.

> Leaders know well that an emotional outlet is served by organization and use its total strength as a tool. Scholars, even the meek ones, show their special brand of independence because they have specialties, ideas and opinions. Nevertheless, organizations multiply without provocation, one breeding another. While they serve necessary ends, they can also be used to manipulate people and obtain unethical objectives. In organization the individual sells a portion of his soul regardless of the merit of the organization, for he puts himself in a position to be used or manipulated.[9]

---

[8] The law is that "work expands so as to fill the time available for its completion." From this it is claimed that the size of an organization has nothing to do with the amount of work to be done. Other factors, inherent in the organization, are determining. C. Northcote Parkinson, *Parkinson's Law* (Boston: Houghton Mifflin Company, 1957), p. 2.

[9] Max S. Marshall, "What Price Organization?" *School and Society,* 79:17-22, January 23, 1954.

The professor goes on to say that universities are *over-organized* in at least three different ways. First there is the proliferation of administration itself.

> Second, the committee system leads to so much ineffective ritual that worthy members of the Faculty become either discouraged or subservient to the committee on committees. And third, an inexhaustible supply of leaders is dividing the field of knowledge to establish new departments which they can head.[10]

Economists. The economists, too, have had a concern with the problem. Embracing the "central tradition" (as John Galbraith has called it) of Ricardo, Malthus, and Adam Smith, economists tend to think of man as a rational being capable of making his own enlightened decisions.[11] One of the most penetrating of recent social science volumes treats of the price system as in many respects opposed to hierarchical organization, which is assumed to be tantamount to government regulation. Thus to most economists and businessmen today the price system is synonymous with freedom; it is the symbol of the individual entrepreneur exercising his ingenuity unfettered by the restrictions of a regulative hierarchy.[12]

The President of the University of California, Economist Clark Kerr, has pressed this point of view. He has argued particularly against Elton Mayo's proposition that modern organizations must recapture some of the friendliness and warmth, "togetherness," of medieval work groups.[13] Such an approach, it is claimed, causes the individual to submerge his own individuality in that of the group. Kerr says:

> The liberal economists . . . have an almost opposite view of heaven on earth. Man, they believe, is a reasoning being and is primarily motivated by a desire to maximize his individual welfare.

---

[10] *Loc. cit.*

[11] John K. Galbraith, *The Affluent Society* (Boston: Houghton Mifflin Company, 1958), p. 24.

[12] R. A. Dahl, and C. E. Lindblom, *Politics, Economics, and Welfare* (New York: Harper and Brothers, 1953), pp. 173 ff.

[13] Elton Mayo, *Social Problems in an Industrial Civilization* (Boston: Graduate School of Business Administration, Harvard University, 1945). Mayo writes, for example (p. 76), ". . . For all of us the feeling of security and certainty derives always from assured membership of a group. If this is lost, no monetary gain, no job guarantee, can be sufficient compensation."

> Competitive markets are used to spur managers on to greater efficiency. Reliance is placed primarily on regulated self-interest, and a freedom of choice (as consumer, worker, and voter) is considered essential. By the nature of things, loyalties are divided—to self, to family, to state, to employer, to union—and in this division is seen the guarantee of freedom.[14]

Sociologists. In the Kerr statement the emphasis on individual rationality is to be seen; and from this point of view it contrasts sharply with the comments of sociologist C. Wright Mills, who is equally concerned about the individual's role in the new organization society. However, Mills observes a fundamental difference. Rational behavior currently is to be ascribed to the organization, not to the individual. He observes:

> In the eighteenth and nineteenth centuries, rationality was identified with freedom. The ideas of Freud about the individual, and of Marx about society, were strengthened by the assumption of the coincidence of freedom and rationality. Now rationality seems to have taken on a new form, to have its seat not in individual men, but in social institutions which by their bureaucratic planning and mathematical foresight usurp both freedom and rationality from the little individual men caught in them. . . .[15]

Bureaucratic Stresses

Mills' claim that the organization has assumed the role of rationality from the individual lends further point to the assumption that the emergence of large-scale operations has indeed provided a new dimension to the age-old problem of man's relationship to his society.

Incompatibility of goals. Karl Marx, who must be considered a philosopher of the Industrial Revolution, dealt with an apparent incompatibility of goals between the workers and the owners of the means of production. He believed this conflict could be resolved only by a change in the system of ownership which would in fact make the society the proprietor. Was this a reasonable assumption? Can societal and individual interests be brought into complete harmony by the adoption of certain legal and economic

---

[14] Clark Kerr, "What Became of the Independent Spirit?" *Fortune* 48:110, July 1953.

[15] Mills, *White Collar*, p. xvii.

measures? The record would seem to indicate not. It is very doubtful that any type of collectivization can be of great significance in resolving such a basic problem. Even when the workers own the means of production themselves, they as a group join with their managers in imposing restraints, which may be socially desirable, but which impose great personal hardship. This was the lesson the British coal miners learned. After the mines were brought under public ownership, it was found that the coal still had to be gotten out of the ground as economically as possible. The workers' lot changed very little. The society's drive for economic production just did not square with the individual's concern about his own interests.

The failure of collectivization, Marxist or otherwise, to bring about a resolution of these conflicts again emphasizes the deep-seated *social* character of the issues with which we are dealing. There are no quick and simple answers to such multifaceted questions.

Procedural demands. In a now-famous essay, the sociologist Robert Merton pointed to another type of dilemma that pervades the organization-individual relationship.[16] Large-scale operations, by their very lack of face-to-face contact, he points out, must rely on impersonal means of coordination and control. This means that great emphasis must be given to rules and procedures; and a member of the organization departs from them only at extreme personal peril. Thus the rules and procedures become an end in themselves because they are so significant to the "rational," predictive functioning of the organization. Any personal tampering with the prescriptions to fit an individual case, and thus perhaps better to meet the announced goals of the organization, becomes a very hazardous undertaking. It is far better and safer to avoid such risks. As a consequence, "instrumental" values become more important than "terminal" values; and all the manifestations of bureaucratic red tape become apparent. In short, there emerges the "bureaucratic personality," without individuality, creativity, or originality.

---

[16] Robert K. Merton, "Bureaucratic Structure and Personality," first published in *Social Forces* 17:560-68, 1940; reprinted "with minor modifications" in Merton *et al., Reader in Bureaucracy* (Glencoe, Ill.: The Free Press, 1952), pp. 361-71.

The discouraging part of Merton's analysis, which incidentally has been reprinted in countless publications, is that he sees the conflict as inherent in the system. Like Mills, he is inclined to think organizations do have the capacity for rational behavior; and further, this is promoted by well-established formalization. Hence the individual, being less predictable and rational, is bound to find himself at odds with the system. This is a condition to be accepted and understood. Its eradication does not seem possible.

III • THE NATURE OF CONFLICT

Does the imposition of restraints, either by group or organization, automatically produce a set of *conflict* reactions in the individual? If such is the case, is the resulting conflict necessarily bad? Depending on how we may answer these questions, it appears that two broad approaches to organization-building are possible:

- If we assume that conflict must inevitably be present, there are two possibilities of behavior:
  - (a) We can do our best to erase conflict on the supposition that it is bad for the organization.
  - (b) We can simply accept conflict as a fact of organization life, on the supposition that we have no other alternative.
- If we assume that conflict is not endemic in the situation, we can then eliminate it as a primary focus of our attention. We can concentrate on cooperation because we assume it is just as natural as competition.

All three alternatives are clearly rooted in assumptions which seek to place man in his most natural state. It is a question about which political philosophers have argued for the centuries; and in many respects forms the basis for rationalizing the role of our largest organization unit, government. Thomas Hobbes, for example, claimed that life was naturally mean and competitive. Governments rose as a device for preventing anarchistic self-destruction. On the other hand, John Locke, seeking to arrive at the same conclusion, saw man as natively cooperative. He argued that people got together on a rational basis, decided that there were some types of protective services they could not adequately perform themselves, and thus governmental organizations were created.

The Locke position is quite in contrast to Whyte's, which follows the Hobbesian analysis much more closely. In the social sciences themselves, the basic model of the individual in conflict with the group is strong. This approach is suggested in Kurt Lewin's statement that the basic question for the individual is how to "satisfy one's own individual needs without losing membership and status within the group." [17] It might also be said that the methodological orientation of social psychology, the relation of the individual to the society, suggests differences, or conflict.

After a most thorough canvass of all the pertinent social science literature, Argyris has appeared to conclude that the imperatives of large organization are such as to require a fairly high degree of formalization. Yet these necessities do not accord with the maturation needs of the individual, as described earlier. What results is a series of adaptations, involving "many definable subsystems of different complexities and makeup. Some are composed of individuals; others of group and individuals, and still others of individuals, group and organizational (formal and informal) components." [18] Essentially Argyris returns to the idea of *fusion,* in which all goals are recognized and then compromised in the process of interaction. The book has been criticized by some social scientists, however, for its basic assumption that man must be in conflict with the organization.

The criticism of Argyris' belief in the existence of conflict now directs us to the work of the anthropologists, who have made it their business to study the behaviors of societies all over the world. One of the purposes of such research has been to discover what human nature really is. We do many things that we consider deeply ingrained, that we see done by many others around us, and that we assume to be beyond our capacity to control. Yet such behavior traits are frequently *socially*-induced. That is, they may be

---

[17] Kurt Lewin, *Resolving Social Conflicts* (New York: Harper and Brothers, 1948), p. 87.

[18] Chris Argyris, *Personality and Organization* (New York: Harper and Brothers, 1957), p. 249.

common among most of us in the United States and not exist at all in Nigeria. Thus the anthropologists have something to tell us about the nature and limits of human conflict and cooperation.

The anthropologists have found that the amount of competition, and thus in a sense the amount of internal conflict, varies appreciably from society to society. This is to be seen in Ruth Benedict's *Patterns of Culture,*[19] which has in more recent years been criticized in terms of specifics but not so much in terms of basic findings.

Anthropologist Ashley Montagu has taken an extremely affirmative position that human beings are essentially cooperative. He blames Sigmund Freud in large part for the present common assumption that "men are not gentle, friendly creatures wishing for love," but that they have a "constitutional tendency to aggression against one another. The question we have to ask is: What is the evidence for these statements?"[20] Montagu thinks there is little. On the contrary, he argues:

> Man is not born with a built-in-system of responses to the environment, as are most other creatures. On the other hand, man is born with a built-in system of plastic potentialities which under environmental stimulation are capable of being caused to respond in a large variety of different ways (p. 37).[21]
>
> Indeed, it may be unequivocally stated that every human being is born *good,* good in the sense that every infant is born with all its energies oriented in the direction of conferring and receiving, of exchanging creatively enlarging benefits. The purposes of the infant are constructive—not destructive. He desires to live as if to live and love were one (p. 40).
>
> It is not human nature but human nurture that is the cause of human aggression. Human nature is good, and treated as such leads to goodness. It is for us to realize, in the light of the accumulated evidence, that being born into the human species means that the individual so born is capable of becoming whatever it is within the capacity of that individual to become (p. 41).

As a consequence, serious questions can be raised as to the fundamental assumption of Whyte and Argyris that man is in-

---

[19] Ruth Benedict, *Patterns of Culture* (New York: Mentor Books, 1946).

[20] M. F. Ashley Montagu, *Anthropology and Human Nature* (Boston: Porter Sargent, 1957), p. 36.

[21] Page citations, *Ibid.*

nately in conflict with the organization. It may be more correct to say that certain attitudes and beliefs in the society tend to sharpen conflicts and competition. As to whether such conflicts would exist in an absolute state of nature, we cannot say; for the very existence of relationships between men sets in motion cooperation or conflict. From this point of view, Whyte's imperative to *fight* the organization hardly seems to face up to the real issue.

IV • FOUR FACTS FOR CONSIDERATION

That we are dealing here with a serious matter hardly need be emphasized at this point in the chapter. It is worth reiterating, however, that the problem is one which concerns far more than those involved in organization theory. Indeed there is no facet of the society which does not in one way or another have an involvement. Thus to draw any conclusive generalizations with regard to these issues would certainly be presumptuous. At this point it is only possible to suggest certain dimensions which indicate their complexity and general significance.

- *The retention of individuality in the U.S. society may be more difficult than in many others.*
- *The problem is not simply one of consciously-identified goal conflicts between the individual, the group, the organization. It involves also the means of decision-making.*
- *Basic needs of various types of institutions vary and this affects the total system of behavior.*
- *How individuals and groups adapt to other needs and perceptions would appear to be a more appropriate focus for the analysis of the problem than conflict.*

U. S. Cultural Aspects of the Problem

The culture of the United States is a contradictory one. It is highly competitive in many respects; but in other ways it is not highly individualistic. Systems of cooperation, developed particularly through a broad range of voluntary organizations, are quite a striking trait of the culture.

Another contradiction is to be seen in behaviors with regard to personal freedom. In many respects, a distinguishing feature of the American administrative environment is the extent to which the worker is recognized as an individual with dignity. No matter what our job or our status in the organization, we have come to have certain expectations about the way in which we are to be treated. On the other hand, the American executive particularly seems to feel greater pressure than ever to conform to business and community value systems. Even his personal and family life is not his own; and one's wife is not infrequently the difference between appointment to a high-level job and relegation to the lower echelons.[22]

These contradictions are thus set in perspective by Riesman's argument that the system of control in the U. S. society is shifting away from the family, as the basic orienting unit, toward one's friends and associates. This is a consequence, he feels, of our highly mobile urban culture. Yet *inner-directed* people, Calvinist in their approach and hewing close to family-established values, continue to abound in the society. Furthermore there is no one who can say which pattern is more appropriate.

Robert Merton's explanation of the way in which the demands of predictability in the large-scale organization affect individual behavior gives particular emphasis to this aspect of the problem. Will it be possible to create, in our ever-growing businesses and governments, counterattacks on the basic tendency toward impersonality, as identified by Merton? It is doubtful whether modern management, even with its emphasis on human relations and participation, has really come up with solid responses to this need.[23]

Goals and Other Elements of Conflict

Much stress has been given in this and the preceding chapter to the point that varying goal levels exist *within* the organization. The individual does not cease to exist simply because he joins a

---

[22] Note the substantial amount of literature in recent years having to do with executive wives.

[23] In many respects the weakest part of Chris Argyris' excellent book, *Personality and Organization,* is its failure to provide any substantial answer to the conflict between the individual and the organization in the American society.

CHART 23-1. *The pulls on an individual within an organization.*

group or an organization. Hence the opportunities for divergence in needs and aspirations, and as a consequence goals, are almost infinite. However, as March and Simon have pointed out, it it not enough to think of conflict in the organization as simply a matter of strife over consciously considered goals. It is suggested that at least two other factors have great importance: (1) differences in perceptions of reality; and (2) the degree of felt need for joint decision making.

Plurality of the U. S. Society

To those who have traveled widely abroad, one of the most striking aspects of the United States society is its plurality of institutions. In most cases we as individuals divide our loyalties and our participation among many organizations. The national government is powerful, yes; but it has its competitors from the state and local level. And the strong business elements in the society, often through varying types of associations, serve to slice up power and thus to create a system of multiple loyalties for the individual. The significance of this situation is apparent: it would be very difficult for basic changes to occur in our society *by design*. They would have to arise from our total cultural system.

Even then, such changes may not spread universally among organizations. As Selznick and other sociologists have pointed out, the basic needs of institutions differ appreciably. The research laboratory, the television studio, and a magazine like *Fortune* are institutions where individual freedom of expression is much more important than in a cleaning establishment, a candy factory, or an automobile showroom. As basic institutional needs vary, so do adaptive mechanisms. Indeed, in certain types of management institutions such as a large ship or a hospital, various traits and beliefs are so well systematized and so identifiable that we may say there exists a *subculture.*

The spectacularly successful novel of American management, *Executive Suite,* is actually built around the theme of change in the basic needs of an institution, a furniture company.[24] In the early, post-Civil War days of industrialization in the United States, the emphasis in management had to be on mechanical know-how. The engineer who could design the machines and keep them running was kingpin. Rather early in the twentieth century the salesman began to take over. Production was no longer the real problem; moving the goods in a competitive situation was the prime requirement. In mid-twentieth century the need had again changed. It was the designer, the original and creative person, who succeeded the super-salesman to the presidency. Such a cycle

---

[24] Cameron Hawley, *Executive Suite* (Boston: Ballantine Books, Inc., paperback edition, 1952), p. 346.

might, it seems, be well applied to the automobile industry, where the shape of a tail fin has sometimes meant the difference between profit and loss.

In the last analysis it is important to remember that basic needs will vary from one institution to another at various points in time and space. Precisely because there are so many organizations, adapting to their needs in such a variety of ways, it is doubtful that we can generalize about relationships between the individual and the organization. Furthermore, because of the pluralistic nature of the U.S. society, it is questionable that any systematic attempt to change behavior across the board would be very successful.

Adaptive Behavior

From the philosophical point of view, the relationship of the individual and organization has much interest. However, the positing of an ideal situation must remain an academic issue. We do not know whether such a relationship should contain some elements of conflict, as Whyte seems to suggest, or whether it should be based on cooperation, as Montague argues. Without this basic agreement, it is obvious that further elaborations must be theoretical and subjective.

At the practical level, it would appear that awareness of the excessive number of interactions within a complex organization involving different goals and perceptions of reality is a prime requisite. In this sense the *processes* by which adaptation is made to these various demands of the individual, of the groups, and of the organization itself are probably a more rewarding focus than conflict. In a sense the adaptations that must take place suggest that we think of politics in a more inclusive sense than has been customary. We cannot expect everyone or every group to have the same needs and goals; it would be a sad world if they did. Yet these divergences of interests, so common among the members of family, do not necessarily suggest conflict. It is as easy to assume that what men want are the devices by which all the contrasting demands can be exposed and by which decisions reflecting all the interests at play can be taken.

V • SUMMARY

In recent years there has been a growing concern with organization as a major new dimension of society. This in a sense is another facet of our shifting systems of living which find their roots in the industrial revolution and the movement away from an individualistic, family existence on the farm. In the early nineteenth century, for example, it has been estimated that eighty per cent of the workers were self-employed enterprisers. Today it is calculated that 200 corporations own over half the industrial wealth of the nation. In short most of us are employees and we can expect to spend our working lives as members of large organizations. What does this mean to us as individuals? What does it mean to the society as a whole?

First of all, it must be noted that these significant social questions extend beyond the frame of reference of this book. Organizations are artifacts of more basic trends in the society; and any real answer to some of the questions raised lies more deeply in the social fabric than the systems of cooperative endeavor we evolve. At the same time it is quite obvious this problem must be of deep concern to the student of organization, as well as others.

A book by William H. Whyte, published in 1956, seemed to capture much of the popular disenchantment with large-scale organization. It was as a consequence a non-fiction best-seller. Whyte charged that the social scientists were trying to create a new social philosophy of "belongingness." He said that the conflict between the individual and the organization had always existed and always would. If the individual, who possessed all the resources of creativity, were silenced, there would be nothing to replace him. Therefore, the individual must "fight" the organization.

Perhaps the most basic assumption of Whyte was that of conflict between the individual and the organization. It is an assumption which has also governed much of the writing of Chris Argyris. However this is not a scientifically verifiable fact. Anthropologists, Ashley Montagu in particular, are not at all sure that conflict represents man's natural state. They argue that there are cultures which do not evidence such aspects of conflict as competition, frustration and aggression, and so forth. Thus cooperation may be the natural tendency of man.

Four factors seem particularly worthy of consideration in respect to this problem.

1. The retention of individuality in the U.S. society may be more difficult than in many others because of our great urban development, our security commitments, and the general trend of our culture toward "other-directedness."
2. The problem is not simply one of consciously-identified goal conflicts between the individual, the group, the organization. It involves also the means of decision-making.
3. It is important to remember that in an extremely pluralistic society, such as the U. S., no particular group or organization —least of all the social scientists—can secure control over mores and habits. With our many institutions having varying needs, it is probable that much of the stress we might otherwise feel will be counterbalanced by a diversity of organization demands.
4. It would seem that the most worthwhile approach to the kinds of problems raised by this chapter lies in the improvement of the *processes* by which accommodation of the various interests is achieved. In a very real sense this returns us to the concept of politics. We must expect that there will be areas of dispute, whether the organization is directly involved or not. Hence a most basic need is to perfect devices that permit the exposure and consideration of contrasting demands in the decision-making process.

TWENTY-FOUR

The Organization of the Future

What to Look for in This Chapter . . .

- Future size of organizations
- Cultural environment of the future organization
- Continuing changes in the nature of the work force
- Effects of the developing revolution in information technologies on the future organization
- The top executive in the future
- The structural shape of the future organization
- What lies ahead for decentralization

What will the future organization be like? The question has particular pertinence for young people who are moving out of the colleges and have a lifetime of contact with organizations ahead of them. Obviously no one can say with any certainty what lies ahead. If the protracted controversies between the Soviet Union and the United States end in war, it may very well be that the most significant question will involve interaction and communication for the last two people on the globe.

Nevertheless the process of prediction does serve a useful purpose.[1] It should help to summarize some of the principal points we have been seeking to make in the preceding 23 chapters. It should serve to identify some of the trends which have sunk deep enough to continue on into the future. Finally, thinking about the future might help to foster a more philosophical view of the total organization problem. There may result a slightly lessened inclination to expect that "answers" will be found today or next week to the many curious paradoxes and contradictions which must abound in any complex social organism.

Trends which today appear vital enough to project into the indefinite future are:

- The size of corporate organizations will continue to increase.
- The cultural environment in which organizations operate will lay increasing stress on the needs of the individual.
- Automation and other technological improvements will continue to change the basic composition of the work force, with more emphasis on staff specialization and less on middle management.
- Many factors will operate to make the image of a top executive as decision-maker and coordinator increasingly untenable. The executive in fact will be a group and will encompass many forces within the organization.
- Instead of looking like a pyramid, the organization of the future will look more like a rectangle. It will have more people at the top, fewer at the bottom, and fewer intervening layers.
- Decentralization, based largely on the model of federalism, will increasingly become the means of coping with the problem of size in organizations.

---

[1] There are certain pretensions inevitably associated with the process of prediction. We would not claim absolute humility; but we would hope that the reader will understand we claim no divine infallibility. In fact this kind of chapter, more than any other, makes an author wonder how he ever had the temerity to write a book.

I • THE FUTURE SIZE OF ORGANIZATIONS

While it is quite apparent from what has been said earlier in this book that there are many dimensions which make the study of organization intellectually significant, the question of size continues to occupy a central position. All around us the trend toward bigness continues in the United States society. Some of it is program-oriented; some is not. That is, some growth represents expansion in the present area of programs and activities through more outlets and more factories. Other growth represents "diversification" where the corporate organization draws under its wing a greater variety of programs and activities.

It has sometimes been argued that program-oriented growth is desirable but diversification is not. In these terms the tremendous change which has occurred in food distribution in the major urban centers with the move away from "Mom and Pop" stores to units of at least 20,000 square feet and acres of parking is good. The purchase of a pen company by a razor company several years ago —a diversification move—was apparently bad. The central argument here seems to be that organizations operate best when they concentrate on a few activities; they become more artificial and less effective as they add functions.

Is There an Optimum Size?

However the big question of size still remains size itself. When is big too big? Here we need not concern ourselves with the larger social and political question suggested by the anti-trust laws. In respect to the needs of the organization itself, is there a point of diminishing returns? In much of the literature there seems to be a general assumption that there is such a limitation. Kenneth Boulding, an economist, for example has argued that there is an "iron law of size."[2] This so-called law would apply differently in various settings but Boulding insists it is nevertheless present. Thus

[2] Kenneth Boulding, *The Organizational Revolution* (New York: Harper and Brothers, 1953): "A third iron law is that organizations of all kinds have an optimum size . . . ," (p. 78).

each organization contains within it a point beyond which an increase in size alone will render it less effective than previously. Other writers seem to have arrived at their concern about size at least partially because of their commitment to the idea of the organization as a pyramid. A central interest therefore is the ability of the individual at the top to provide the necessary integrative leadership. Marshall Dimock has written, for example, that optimum size is reached when "the chief executive can no longer synthesize the work of his program and deal with his subordinates *personally.*"[3]

In actuality the optimum size of an organization is not as simply ascertained as Dimock suggests, nor is it as ironclad a matter as Boulding argues. Dimock himself writes approvingly of the American Telephone and Telegraph Company and yet it has hundreds of thousands of employees, only a few of whom the president can deal with personally. Certainly, too, American Telephone and Telegraph has a reputation for being one of our most effective management institutions.

As of the present time, then, we are still groping with the question. We worry that size may have important consequences to an organization but we have no absolute evidence that it does. Only one thing seems to be clear at this point. We are in the midst of an unprecedented trend toward corporate bigness. Note the emphasis on *corporate* bigness. In industry this has not meant that factories themselves have gotten bigger. It is not being suggested that prisons, hospitals, or institutions as individual operating units have necessarily participated in this growth pattern. As a matter of fact, the reverse has frequently been true. Indeed the Gillette Company has 15 factories and 24 sales companies with a total of 10,000 employees; the plants typically have a labor force of between 150 and 600 people.[4]

Reasons for Bigness in Future

Importance of resources. At the corporate level, however, the

[3] Marshall E. Dimock, *Administrative Vitality: The Conflict with Bureaucracy* (New York: Harper and Brothers, 1959), p. 259; italics added.

[4] Howard Gambrill, Jr., "The Multiple Factory System," in *Toward The Factory of the Future,* American Management Association, Special Report No. 82, 1957, p. 71.

trend is undeniable. It is occurring largely because new technologies require more resources. Machines themselves cost more. Resources are needed too, to provide increased specialization, more know-how, and necessary research. It has been said that more money was spent on research in 1955 alone than in the twenty-year period before 1940. The research and development resources of the large organization are in themselves a tremendous competitive asset; and these resources apply not only to product improvement but to production processes, marketing, advertising, management, and many other aspects of the total organization activity. Koppers Company found, through its research and development unit, that moving goods twenty-four hours faster to its customers enabled it to reduce operating capital by $1.1 millions.

Emphasis on stability. In the last analysis the trend toward bigness will probably continue because it is only the large organization which has convenient access to financing opportunities. Here we may assume that stability has become a more important factor than innovation. The impact of the financial houses on organization size can be revealed in several different ways. The most obvious is that the smaller independent is simply not regarded by lenders as having sufficient know-how and capacity to carry on an expanded activity. For example the largest department store in a city of 500,000—an independent—found it impossible to finance a large shopping center. The ownership and management of the center was taken over by an organization operating many other similar facilities and the department store which had exercised the original initiative became a tenant. In the same metropolitan area an individual who owned a department store doing a volume of more than $1,000,000 a year required more than two years to secure the necessary financing for expansion into a new building and other facilities. He was convinced that a chain operation would have found many eager lenders for the same risk.

It is also important to note that bigness creates its own snowball effect. In 1959 the largest lumber transaction in history took place when the Booth-Kelly mills and lands in Oregon were sold to the Georgia-Pacific Company for approximately $93 millions *in cash.* There was only one other bid, of something over $85 millions, by U.S. Plywood. Only organizations of similar scale could have commanded the finances and the know-how to acquire another organization of such size. In future it seems almost inevitable that such acquisitions or mergers will occur because no other alternative purchaser exists.

Risks of Bigness

Loss of individual initiative. What risks do we run in this seemingly inevitable move toward bigness? We have indicated that many argue size alone can destroy the effectiveness of an organization. Within this general context the most frequently expressed fear is that size is harmful to individual initiative and creativity. Here it is assumed that the processes of bureaucracy tend to discourage these qualities more in the large organization than in the small. However, there is not a great deal of research which either supports or denies the point. Dimock cites reports of the Acton Trust in Great Britain which claim a positive relationship between increasing size and problems of morale.[5] Thomas found that workers in the smaller units of the Michigan State Department of Social Welfare had a better understanding of their role and a higher ethical commitment than those in the larger units. However he concluded that the setting of the small community was probably more influential in creating these attitudes and understandings than organizational size.[6]

Inflexibility. Aside from the question of the individual's initiative and morale, the other dominant fear of size is inflexibility. It is argued that size reduces adaptability and the large organization is incapable of seizing on opportunities as quickly as the small. As we have noted above, however, the large organization seems quite able to counter this liability with the superior resources it ultimately throws into the fray. It is also questionable whether such a "great man" theory of opportunity exploration exists in any sizeable amount at the present time and whether it will be significant in the future. Technological improvements today are so complex, involving so many skills, that, it can be argued, only the large research and development operation provides the real base

---

[5] Dimock, *Administrative Vitality: The Conflict with Bureaucracy,* p. 257.

[6] Edwin J. Thomas, "Role Conceptions and Organizational Size," *American Sociological Review* 24:30-37, February 1959.

for innovation and invention in our increasingly complicated society.

Conclusion

On balance there seems to be little point in fighting the inevitable. There are too many advantages to large scale organization. All the forces in our social system seem to be moving in this direction. The concept of culture as a body of knowledge and technique expanding at least in geometric proportions supports this view. That is, the more we know, the faster we learn new things and the less possible it is for any one person to command all knowledge. Specialization, then, is inevitable and group research mandatory. Edison might have discovered electricity alone but neither the atomic bomb nor space missiles have been such a product of individual research. Teller is sometimes called the father of the hydrogen bomb, not because he actually created it, but because he led the team which did.

We should not underestimate the dangers in size. They are real. The opportunity for individual expression of initiative probably does not occur as automatically and as easily.[7] Policy changes inevitably require much greater consideration because they involve so many forces and have such impact. Our real concern should be in developing means of minimizing these shortcomings and maximizing the advantages. Basically this has been the focus of our effort in this book.

II • THE CULTURAL ENVIRONMENT OF THE FUTURE ORGANIZATION

One of the central points of this book has been that organizations do not exist apart from their cultural context. They are social organisms. They are not artificial mechanical entities. Therefore

---

[7] Henry A. Kissinger, a political scientist and foreign policy expert, has written a very stimulating essay on some of the problems of securing creativity in an administrative organization. See "The Policy Maker and the Intellectual," *The Reporter* 20:30-35, March 5, 1959. This also is the theme of Dimock's *Administrative Vitality*.

we cannot expect an organization to be anything more than a reflection of the social values which exist at any particular time. We may *want* to get back to a Victorian era, or in Riesman's terms to "inner directedness," [8] but if we attempt to *do* so in a particular organization over which we have influence, the results may very well be disastrous.

Emphasis on the Individual

We live in an era of mounting emphasis on the dignity of the individual. This is not just a facet of the culture of the United States. Throughout the world in varying degrees, human beings are discovering themselves as individuals and demanding from their governments and other organizations greater respect for their needs and interests. In the United States, as we indicated in the first chapter, this emphasis on the individual has been part of our national history. Recent decades have witnessed a further liberation of the individual. He is more mobile than ever. He expects and receives more of his total product. He is literate and in general better informed, though it might be debated whether he is better educated. Rensis Likert has been particularly vocal in emphasizing the nature of this change, as we have pointed out earlier.[9] This shift in individual expectations is having and will continue to have its effect on basic organization relationships, Likert believes. Much of the present and most of the past have been characterized by "man-to-man" contacts in which the element of status was very strongly present. In keeping with the general cultural climate, one man was supposed to have authority over another. It was in the nature of things. In the future organizations will tend increasingly to be composed of peers, people who are parts of teams and who do not recognize such marked status differentials. This of course represents a marked shift in our hierarchical orientations and more generally in the decision process.[10]

---

[8] See Chapter 3.

[9] See Chapter 23.

[10] Rensis Likert, "Motivational Dimensions of Administration," in Robert A. Walker, editor, *America's Manpower Crisis* (Chicago: Public Administration Service, 1952), pp. 113-117.

Relationship Between Individualism and Nonconformity

It would be inappropriate to leave this brief reconsideration of the cultural context in which our organizations operate without referring once again to the thorny question of the organization and the individual. As we have noted at previous points in the book, there is not common agreement that our culture system really provides for a liberation of the individual. Blum argues, for instance, that we lost a sense of individualism in the nineteenth century and have never regained it. Whyte is concerned about the loss of the Protestant Ethic. What Whyte and Blum really are aroused about is the nonconformist in the organization. What Likert is talking about is the perception by the average individual of his relationships to organization and the society. It is quite possible that society's value system may provide for an expanded role for the individual who *accepts* the group value system. The person who refuses to accept these values may literally be forced out of the organization. Thus we can at the same time place great emphasis on the individual and also make life unbearable for those who deviate from the norm. Certainly the latter problem must be regarded as a real one. On the other hand, it is also important to realize that the great majority of people do conform and the administrator must deal with their value systems as he finds them.

There seems little doubt that the administrator will face this curious paradox in the future. He will have to be very much concerned with the conforming individual's demands for expression and satisfaction; and this will have its implications for organizing. But it is also quite probable that social pressures will make it increasingly difficult to deal with the nonconforming person. In fact the building of iconoclastic vitality into the organization of the future may be one of the administrator's number-one problems. As we indicated earlier in the book, it will most certainly occur with regard to the administration of research and development programs.

III • CHANGES IN THE NATURE OF THE WORK FORCE

Since organizations must be influenced by the people who inhabit them, it follows that changes in methods of work and the human requirements involved will importantly influence their shape and character. Automation has of course been the predominant factor in the changes that have been occurring and will undoubtedly continue. Its story is too familiar to require repetition. The most obvious consequence of automation is that it has freed a great many people from routine production tasks; hence fewer of our population are direct producers and more are facilitators. The figures on this change are very striking. We noted in an earlier chapter that in the decade 1947-57 such nonproductive job areas as professional, clerical, sales, and administrative had a rate of growth *fifteen* times that of the production jobs.[11]

There are several other ways in which this machine-induced change in our work force can be illustrated. In approximately three short decades such a change in productive technique has been wrought that at 1929 levels of productivity the Gillette Company would require 100,000 people to do the work that 10,000 do today.[12]

Increase in Nonproduction Workers

How does this affect the over-all composition of an organization's labor force? The experience of one small plant is perhaps illustrative. At the end of the decade of the 'forties, the company had 100 employees, 80 of whom were in the plant and 20 in the sales and office organizations. There were five graduate engineers. Ten years later there were 350 employed, but the percentage directly in the plant had dropped from 80 per cent to 65 per cent. Twelve per cent of the labor force was engineers, 40 out of the 350, and they covered five specialties within the engineering

[11] See p. 126. Studies by Professor Frederick H. Harbison also suggest the tremendous change in the labor force and more particularly the greatly increased proportion of highly trained people. He suggests this may well have an effect on the number of union members. Reported in *AMA Management News*, August 1959, p. 5.

[12] Gambrill, "The Multiple Factory System," p. 71.

field. Even so, the president of the company reported that "we can't afford the degree of specialization that we need." [13]

Implications

More specialization. The implications of these trends seem quite clear. Our productive institutions—and to a lesser extent other organizations—will be concerned more in the future with managing *things* than people. The undifferentiated mass of people at the bottom is being quickly whittled down. On the other hand the operation of very complex things demands a high level of technical skill. This is to be seen particularly in the maintenance function. Once this was the task of the grease monkey; but this is no longer true. The doubling of plant investment per employee in the decade of the fifties provides the basic reason for this change. Thus, "Today, the more complex maintenance operations require not only a plant engineer but a staff of qualified engineers and specialists to cope with the rapid advances being made in automation." [14]

What will the maintenance operation be like in the future? George Martin hazards this prediction:

> The maintenance operations of the plant of the future may be directed by a "director of maintenance." For larger or multi-plant operations a vice president in charge of maintenance will not be unusual, with qualified engineers to supervise various phases of maintenance operations; each of these engineers will in turn have staffs of area supervisors, maintenance foremen, specialists, and mechanics. Since the equipment will be very critical and production maintained at very high speeds, the electronic relays used to check, measure, guide and perform other various functions must themselves be constantly checked and tested with sensitive maintenance equipment.[15]

Not only have changes in technologies themselves brought about an increase in specialization but it also seems clear that they have contributed indirectly to further increases in specialization. For the nature of coordination in a highly specialized organization

---

[13] Earl F. Harris, "Where the Factory of the Future Begins," *Toward the Factory of the Future,* p. 7.

[14] George J. Martin, "Maintenance Operations in the Plant of the Future," *Toward the Factory of the Future,* p. 30.

[15] *Ibid.*

must be quite different from that in an undifferentiated one. As we learned earlier in the book, a person might successfully supervise the work of a large number of people if it is routine, relatively simple, and geographically close. As specialization occurs, this is less and less the case. Thus specialists are needed to coordinate the work of the machine and more specialists are required to coordinate the work of the specialists. While this raises the haunting spectre of Parkinson's law, it should be clear by now that the forces producing this change are much more complex than the law would suggest. And there can be little doubt that these same forces will continue to operate on the organizational environment of the future.

Changes ahead in public organizations. What will be the fate of government and educational administration in the period ahead? Certainly the experience of the past has been that the public service in general has been less directly affected by technological change because it is not essentially a production operation. This will undoubtedly continue to be true. However productivity pressures will probably mount; and this will mean more emphasis by staff people on opportunity exploration. Indeed it will become quite a task just to keep up with the fast moving technological world. Consider what is happening to the purchasing function. Some large purchasing offices have automated to the extent that all routine items are processed by machine, including the final order-writing. Does this reduce the number of purchasing people? Not at all. The purchaser now becomes more than a "pencil pusher." He is "using machines to free himself for the really creative aspects of purchasing, intelligent negotiation, value analysis, long-range research, judgment of suppliers' capabilities, and the overall administration of the function." [16]

As another perspective on the changing nature of the purchasing function, the transition in warehousing is to be noted. First there is the reduction in warehouse labor due to new techniques. Recent designs have more than halved the number of people required in such facilities. But more importantly there is a totally new concept which considers the maintenance of goods on shelves as costly

---

[16] Paul V. Farrell, "The Purchasing Agent of the Future," *Toward the Factory of the Future,* p. 46.

and uneconomic. The ideal is to have a continuous flow from production to consumer with goods stored as little "as possible—and preferably not at all." [17] It has been reported that systems have been designed, engineered, and installed in which goods from some 5,000 suppliers flow through what used to be called a warehouse and on their way within 45 minutes. Thus the warehouse becomes a distribution center in which scheduling of transportation and products becomes all important. The human work involved is certainly of a specialized staff type. Here again we see the proliferation of adjective or indirect labor. Yet the net effect is a savings; and it is the type of opportunity exploration which will be about as important in public agencies as in private business.

Basically, then, we will see the same trend toward staff specialization in public agencies as in private organizations, largely because of the need for opportunity exploration. Also it may be noted that some government operations will be affected directly by automation and in at least limited degree the model of industry will affect organization thinking in the public sphere.

IV • EFFECTS OF THE INFORMATION REVOLUTION

Though it is basically a part of technological change, the development in communication deserves a special place in this chapter. Its significance to organization has been emphasized at other points in the book, most notably in Chapter 17. An excellent essay in the *Harvard Business Review* on "Management in the 1980's" identified the revolution in information technology as the most significant new variable in organization and management.[18] Such importance is ascribed to these communication developments for two basic reasons:

(1) There is the sheer efficiency with which data can be stored and transmitted to decision centers. This has meant that organizations have been able to grow in every direction without sacrificing that control which must be based on information. Put another

---

[17] Allan Harvey, "The Warehouse of the Future," *Toward the Factory of the Future,* pp. 64 ff.

[18] Harold J. Leavitt and Thomas L. Whisler, "Management in the 1980's," *Harvard Business Review* 36:41-48, November-December 1958.

way, the information revolution has quite apparently expanded the optimum control limits in organizations.

(2) Developments in data processing have begun to work major changes in the decision-making structure of organizations; and this undoubtedly will be a major trend of the future. The ability of these machines to store information, to assemble relevant facts, to interpret them in terms of established criteria, and to make decisions is undoubtedly the principal feature of these developments. The introduction of the "mechanical brain" to organization life means that decisions, particularly at the middle management level, can be transferred from the human being. And in most cases the "brain" will make a better decision.

Such decisions might include the number of turnstiles to open during the rush hour at a toll bridge, involving such variables as weather, the day's traffic experience, and other factors which might influence peak volume. Another example might concern the decision as to whether to call for standby power in an electric plant. Under such circumstances the decisions are made at the central communications center, flashed to the operating unit, and implemented in terms of prescribed routines. In such a circumstance there is no place for the superintendent who once achieved his status because he had the experience, intuition, and knack to come up with rather good daily decisions on these matters. It has been suggested by Leavitt and Whisler—and there is mounting evidence to support the contention—that the mechanical "brain" is hitting hardest at the middle management level. The line supervisors still have to deal with their subordinates, though there may be fewer of them. The top managers still have basic policy decisions. But it is in terms of the operating decisions formerly made by middle management that the impact of electronic mechanization is most being felt.

V • THE TOP EXECUTIVE IN THE FUTURE

As we have noted at many points throughout this book, traditional theories of organization have been pyramid-oriented and thus placed great emphasis on the individual at the top as the central coordinating figure. It is a notion very firmly planted in most managerial minds.

Changes in the Top Staff

Yet the implications of the trends discussed earlier in this chapter would argue that the dominant leader figure of the past will become even more anachronistic in the future. Size, cultural factors, and information technologies all will have their influence. But most importantly, the decisions to be taken are simply too complex for any one man, or even a small group of generalists, to think they have all the answers within themselves. One of the most candid admissions comes from the president of a small firm in discussing the processing technologies used by his organization. Obviously these are matters of major policy import since they involve the long-run survival of the company. Yet the president reported basic decisions were made outside the organization. Mathematical consultants were hired who had never been in the laboratory. Nevertheless the president said they arrived at a "better understanding" of chemical processing than his own staff had in two or three years in the laboratory. The mathematicians' reports included "formulas so long and complex that we don't understand them." Management had to take the decisions on faith and was fortunate enough to find them "valid and practical." [19]

Thus we again see that the geometric expansion of knowledge is having its real impact on the managerial process. The executive who sees himself in an omniscient role will do so at great personal and organization peril. This circumstance has prompted Leavitt and Whisler to suggest that the top of the organization will become even more thickly populated.[20] The presence of specialists at the top with important competences and perspectives is bound to be felt in the influence pattern of the organization. Though we may continue to perpetuate the myth of the leader at the top, decisions will necessarily be a group product. It is probable, there-

---

[19] Harris, "Where the Factory of the Future Begins," p. 14. As a consequence of these developments, it is not at all unlikely that decision-making will be the central focus of organization theory. See Harold J. Leavitt, *Managerial Psychology* (Chicago: University of Chicago Press, 1958), p. 301.

[20] Leavitt and Whisler, *op. cit.* p. 47.

fore, that the familiar superior-subordinate pattern will disappear first around the top. Here each individual will have to be recognized for his own unique contributions and any attempt to establish status levels within this constellation would border on the ludricrous. The college environment suggests the possible model. Here we find the traditional hierarchy but it is amended both formally and informally by the presence of a very large number of highly educated and professionally recognized persons in all fields of knowledge. As a consequence, particularly in the older institutions, the president has been less the order-giver, and more the collaborator and facilitator.

Gulf Between Top and Bottom

An outgrowth of this trend toward more people and more participation at the top may be the widening of the status chasm between top and bottom. We have noted that the bridge provided by middle management is being seriously weakened by electronics. And certainly there is already a record of tension and hostility between line and staff people. In Dalton's research there is the implication that staff people tend to force this differentiation in order to build status and thus presumably secure greater acceptance of their ideas in the line.[21]

VI • THE SHAPE OF THE ORGANIZATION OF THE FUTURE

The Football and the Bell

From the discussion thus far, it is now possible to draw some inferences about the shape of the organization of the future. Leavitt and Whisler suggest a particularly intriguing prospect. They are inclined to believe that the gulf between top and bottom will become so pronounced as to be reflected in the structure. The top is likely to be "drifting" and "somewhat amorphous," the bottom "more clearly pyramidal" than ever. Leavitt and Whisler believe

---

[21] Melville Dalton, *Men Who Manage* (New York: John Wiley and Sons, 1959), pp. 71-109.

that the organization chart of the future may look something like a "football balanced upon the point of a church bell." The football, of course, is top management and here is where "individual autonomy, group decision-making, and so on should arise more intensely than ever. We expect they will be dealt with quite independently of the bell portion of the company, with distinctly different methods of remuneration, control and communication."[22]

The most significant aspect of this projection is the very clear attempt to separate the organization into two parts. In fact the separation is so marked in the football-bell picture that Leavitt and Whisler are really telling us two quite distinct organizations will be operating under one label. They will differ in status, methods of operation, value systems, and perceptions of themselves. As we indicated in the previous section, it may be that this growing chasm can be bridged only by commitment to the symbol of a leader at the top.

An aspect of organization shape which is unchanged by the football-bell prediction is its depth. The typical pyramid and the bell seem about the same distance from top to bottom, thus suggesting little change in the number of layers in organizations. This seems to conform to the general expectations of Leavitt and Whisler. They believe that the information revolution may very well result in centralization, rather than decentralization, of organizations.

The Rectangle

We have pointed out, however, that the decade of the 'fifties was characterized by a move in many organizations toward *fewer levels* in the hierarchy and toward an expansion in the *span of control* of executives. In most cases this flattening occurred because of a conscious effort to delegate authority within the organization. Yet it is important to note that the number of levels in an organization does not *automatically* reveal the extent of delegation or decentralization. Conceivably there could be a rather high degree of central control over important decision areas within the flat hierarchy. It could be argued that modern devices and the

---

[22] Leavitt and Whisler, "Management in the 1980's," p. 47.

increased use of staff leave the executive better equipped to deal with more subordinates than previously. Thus the flattening puts the executive in closer touch with his organization and hence in a position of more effective control.

It seems highly probable that flattening will continue in future organization patterns, particularly as the dogma of the small span of control recedes as an important structuring criterion. There will be less and less reason in the future why the executive should limit his contacts to a relative few in the organization because, as we have indicated, his role as the individualistic decision-maker is changing rapidly. It is therefore perhaps more appropriate to think of the organization pyramid as undergoing a "squeeze" which will make it in future more like a rectangle. This accords with the Leavitt and Whisler idea that the population at the top management level will expand greatly. But it also suggests another dimension, the flattening of the hierarchy. There will be fewer levels in part because the middle management function will continue to be superseded by automatic data processing. It is also probable that the span of executive control will widen and that this will have the effect of flattening the hierarchy.

VII • DECENTRALIZATION IN THE FUTURE

There can be little doubt that the question of decentralization will continue to be a dominant theme in the future, as it has been for approximately the past twenty years. It is particularly interesting to note that the post-war period has been labeled as one of decentralization and some people are suggesting that the decade of the 'sixties is to be recorded as one of recentralization.[23]

From all that has gone before in this book, it is quite obvious that this is not the future we see. It is undoubtedly true that some organizations have decentralized because they were incapable of controlling from the top. There is merit to Likert's point that the use of only the profit criterion in judging subsidiary unit performance risks long-run survival. On the other hand the consequences

---

[23] Edward McCreary, "Countertrend to Decentralization: Top Management Tightens Controls," *Dun's Review and Modern Industry* 74:32-34, July 1959.

of monolithic centralization are apparent all over the world. Stultifying inflexibility, red tape, poor and costly service, a distorted "civil service" mentality and other manifestations of organizational dry rot have all forced urgent attention to decentralization efforts. The experience of the U.S. Post Office Department is a good illustration of what is happening. For years it was notorious for its unimaginativeness and inefficiency. Overcentralization was given as the reason for these problems. Yet the post office had operated so long in this fashion that there was a real question whether it had personnel really capable of taking on decision responsibilities. Slowly these conditions have been changing. The Post Office is decentralizing and its managerial operations are improving.

It is not likely that anyone is suggesting recentralization on the lines of the old Post Office pattern. What is really being discussed are new definitions of the relationships between top management and its operating units. Indeed the "wing clipping" seems to be occurring in over-all strategy areas, such as long-term planning, product development, and research . . . quite appropriate activities for a headquarters unit. At the beginning of the sixties, it is possible we were just emerging from the first phase of the decentralization movement. It structured decentralization by separating corporate headquarters from operating units. In the next phase, the identification of appropriate areas of authority (as in our proposed decentralization pattern) may emerge. Here it seems quite possible that long-range planning and research will become the particular bailiwick of top management.

In many respects it would appear that the model of "home rule" in local-central relationships in government may serve as an appropriate model for industry. We start with a basic structure which calls for the municipality to provide local services and for the state level to engage in those activities which are region-wide. But the relationships arising out of this basic structure differ from state to state. This is a matter partly of culture, traditions, the nature of politics and interests, and of the financial structure. Nevertheless home rule as a philosophy and as a basic structure exists in most of our states, as it does in the relationships between the fifty states and the national government. Few agree as to the exact distribution of authority and responsibility at any given time; but almost all agree as to the desirability of the general organization pattern and the institutions which have resulted. If a similar pattern should develop in industry, a substantial change in the orientation of many executives will be required. As we have emphasized, it means that particular attention will have to be paid to articulation of roles at the various levels, most notably at the corporate and operating echelons.

We do not see that information technologies in themselves will play *the* influential role in these developments. While they have actually made it possible for controls to be exercised over a larger area than heretofore, it can also be argued that the same technologies could be used to foster decentralization. The fact that top executives are getting operating results faster than ever before means that corrective action for poor lower level decisions can be taken rapidly. In general the availability of information up and down the line is thought to make decentralized decision-making more realistic. This has certainly been an important argument in the performance budgeting movement in government. Information technologies, then, seem to occupy a neutral role in structuring the decentralization-centralization pattern. They can provide important support in either direction.

VIII · THE FOCUS OF FUTURE ORGANIZATION THEORY

With so many imponderables ahead in the entire social scene, it would be rash indeed to make any estimate as to which of the many different perspectives on organization will have the most durability in creating new theory. One thing of course seems clear. The classic approach to organization structure will decline in significance. By 1960 we had reached a point where very little of the research of reputable scholars depended for its theoretical design on the traditional dogma. At the practicing and the teaching levels, however, the classic dicta were still strong. They still formed the basis for most applied management research and consulting. The most popular textbooks were firmly rooted in these approaches.

Change will undoubtedly come slowly. The bridge between practice and research—the teacher—is caught by two opposing demands. One is to prepare young people for their roles in the future. The other is to help them operate effectively here and now. Presently the conflict between these two demands is perhaps nowhere clearer than in organization theory. We cannot easily cast aside our classic categories until we have a new theory which satisfies at least three criteria: (1) is easily communicated and therefore is amenable to considerable oversimplification without disastrous distortion; (2) has greater *proven* validity than the categories we now utilize; and (3) perhaps most importantly, gains relatively universal acceptance. The teaching job is well nigh insurmountable when every researcher and theorist has his own set of categories. Despite all these handicaps, it seems inevitable that there can be only one direction of change—toward the researcher. The real issue is the speed with which the obstacles mentioned can be surmounted and much that is known about the organization world, presently in the most fragmentary way, can find its way into usefulness.

On balance it is likely that the teacher and practitioner will have to be prepared for a more complicated view of organization, which again emphasizes the difficulty of developing a new body of acceptable doctrine. For example, different people argue the primacy of such factors as role, structure and function, interaction, decision, fusion, communication, power and influence, individual motivation and satisfaction, leadership, and bureaucracy. The list is not comprehensive but it does reveal the complexities which beset us. Each of these categories involves the others; and the real argument is over which deserves the greatest emphasis. Thus the best we may be able to do is come up with a number of different snapshots of the organization phenomenon without assuming that they add up to a single synthesis.

It does appear that theory in the future will fall into two major categories: (1) that which is process and system; and (2) that which is human. This does not suggest any fundamental shifting of present interests and directions, but we may expect that the distinction will be more sharply drawn in the future, with man's control over events the chief point of demarcation.

In recent years there has been a considerable volume of research conducted on the premise that the forces in the organizational situation are largely emotional and unpredictable. Partly this is regarded as a result of irrationalities in the culture of the organization. Individual actors are buffeted about by the situation in which they find themselves. Such seems particularly to be the implication of role and interaction theory. To a lesser extent studies of leadership and bureaucracy have been similarly oriented. Further unpredictability is introduced by the personality organizations of the individuals themselves, each of whom is working from his own perceptions of unique goals. Much of the work on motivation and satisfaction would seem to fall into such a category.

Although no one is prepared to admit that man is eminently rational, there is a considerable body of research which seems to assume that man has something to say about the social forces at work in his environment. They are not entirely beyond his control. This being the case, he acts consciously to choose among alternatives in making the best accomodation of all the forces operating in any given situation. He is not, in short, a chip on the sea. This would seem to be the view of much of the work on decision-theory, on power, and to a lesser degree in the field of communications.

Another way of putting these concepts is that one broad area of research is concerned with the individual in the organization as the key analytical unit; the other is focused on the organization itself. One is human, emotional. The other is contrived, "intendedly rational."A straw in the wind as to the irreconciliability of these two approaches is the recurring emphasis on the conflict between the organization interest and the individual interest, with which we have dealt in earlier chapters. On the basis of present writing, it seems evident that increasingly we will admit the existence of the conflict. We will not attempt to put together something that now appears incompatible. If this should come to pass, it may then be that we will witness the development of a meaningful body of theory built around two quite separate categories centered (1) on the individual and (2) on the organization.

IX • SUMMARY

The purpose of this chapter has been to identify those trends which seem most likely to affect the nature of organization life in the years ahead. Such predictions, of course, do not have any "crystal ball" quality. They are more appropriately regarded as those elements of the present environment which appear to have enough staying power to affect organizations in the future. From this point of view, they become a rather useful means of summarizing some of the major themes of this book.

To "summarize the summary," then, we would suggest that the following have been some of the main ideas which have occupied us in the preceding pages.

1. However strongly some people may resist the idea, we have assumed that large-scale organization is a fact of present and future life. Indeed the involvement of nearly all our people in such organizations makes this one of our most significant social problems. Our focus—and one which we hope many others will follow in the future—has been the development of understanding about these organizations in order that they may more fully serve their many purposes.

2. We have emphasized that these large-scale organizations must be regarded as cross-sections of the total society. The values and the assumptions that prevail in any of these organizations will not differ appreciably from those in the larger society. One cultural value which has already influenced the nature of organizations greatly and will continue to do so in the future puts great stress on the dignity of the individual. This does not involve the nonconforming person so much as it does the mass of people who are essentially conformers and still want to be recognized as individuals. Riesman's concept of "other directedness" for example suggests that equality of treatment throughout the organization may grow in importance. There are many other points, such as goals, style of organization, decision-making patterns, and leadership, where this cultural value will continue to manifest itself.

3. We have been much impressed with the significance of our tremendously expanding knowledge (the cultural "snowball") on organization patterns. This knowledge is reflecting itself in an ever-faster outpouring of technological advancements, each of which requires more specialization within the society. One small company reported that the number of its engineers rose from five per cent of its total employees to twelve per cent, in only ten years. In universities it has not been uncommon for one engineering

course in electronics to blossom out almost overnight as seven. All this must have its impact on organization. It affects many of our traditional ideas of hierarchy, our notions about workers on the production line, raises questions as to the limits of specialization, and many others.

4. Developments in the field of information technology have been very important. They have suggested a vital new way of looking at organization, in which communication becomes the central means of combating disorganization and lack of coordination. Furthermore the tremendous advances in data processing have provided the means by which information could begin to play such a role.

5. We have felt that many of the things that are happening in the U.S. culture make the idea of the top executive as the real coordinator of the organization less and less realistic. It is probable that we shall continue to need individuals who will symbolize the total organization, as we do in government. But insofar as the coordinative requirements of the organization are concerned, it seems fairly clear that the executive must be a group—and a large one at that. The tremendous expansion in the office of the U.S. Presidency in the last forty years is particularly instructive. This has been done, it may be noted, without destroying the image of the President as the individual leader of the nation. It is likely that other organizations, as they grow larger, will find themselves operating on a somewhat similar pattern. This means that much of organization theory, which concentrates on the role of the person at the top of the pyramid, is due for substantial amendment.

6. It has been our expectation that the growth in size of organizations in territory, personnel, functions, finances, and so forth, will continue to make decentralization a matter of real importance. The experience of the aircraft industry, which has had a spectacular development by any criterion, lends emphasis to this assumption. The aircraft companies typically have plants operating in various geographic areas, are engaged in a considerable variety of research efforts, and are increasingly involved in enterprises far removed from manned aircraft. Such diversity has demanded decentralization of one style or another; and the real problem has been to develop behavior patterns which fit these needs. The emergence

of the corporate headquarters level as a unit with separate functions seems a particularly important step in institutionalizing these decentralization needs; and it is the reason why this development has commanded our attention so considerably in this book.

Index